69-10569 (8.12.69)

PRAEGER HISTORY OF CIVILIZATION

The Golden Century

PRAEGER HISTORY OF CIVILIZATION

SABATINO MOSCATI *The World of the Phoenicians*

NICHOLAS MANSERGH *The Commonwealth Experience:
A Critical History of the British
Commonwealth*

The
Golden Century

EUROPE 1598–1715

MAURICE ASHLEY

'Know, Sancho, I was born in this iron
age to restore the age of gold'
– *Don Quixote*

FREDERICK A. PRAEGER, *Publishers*

New York · Washington

BOOKS THAT MATTER

Published in the United States of America in 1969
by Frederick A. Praeger, Inc., Publishers
111 Fourth Avenue, New York, N.Y. 10003

© 1968 in London, England, by Maurice Ashley

Library of Congress Catalog Card Number: 69-10569

Printed in Great Britain

CONTENTS

Preface   xv
1   Towards a Golden Century   1
2   From Feudalism to Absolutism   14
3   Twenty Years of Comparative Peace   29
4   The Age of Baroque   43
5   Social Structure and Economic Life   57
6   Science and Religion   73
7   'The Thirty Years War'   84
8   The Mid-century Revolutions   102
9   The Revolution in Men's Minds   120
10 Scientific Advances and Philosophic Doubt   132
11 France and Europe   146
12 A Crisis for Germany   160
13 The Classical Moment   175
14 The Economy and War   187
15 'I have been too fond of war'   198
16 What Europe was   215
17 The Unending Quest   226
    Bibliography   237
    Index   245

LIST OF ILLUSTRATIONS

(*Between pages 128 and 129*)

1 Felipe II of Spain by Titian (Cincinatti Museum of Art, photo Mansell Collection)
2 The Escurial Palace (photo Alinari)
3 Louis XIV, painting by Largillière (the Wallace Collection)
4 Versailles, garden façade (Mansell Collection, photo Bulloz)
5 Gustav II Adolf of Sweden (photo John Freeman)
6 Felipe IV, painting by Velazquez (National Gallery, London)
7 Charles I of England, portrait by Van Dijk (National Gallery, London)
8 Peter the Great, portrait by Kneller (reproduced by Gracious Permission of Her Majesty the Queen)
9 Count Axel Ostenstierna, by David Beck (National Museum, Stockholm)
10 Cardinal Richelieu, triple portrait by De Champaigne (National Gallery, London)
11 Mazarin opening the Temple of Peace (Paris, Bibliothèque National, photo Giraudon)
12 The building of Versailles, by Van der Meulen (reproduced by Gracious Permission of Her Majesty the Queen)
13 Johann de Witt, painting by Jan de Baer (Rijksmuseum, Amsterdam)
14 A ball at the court of Don Juan, by Jansens (Musée de Lille, photo Giraudon)
15 A Spanish boar-hunt, by Velazquez (National Gallery)
16 The Tichbourne Dole (Royal Academy of Arts)
17 Dutch merchant and wife watching the return of an East India Company ship, painting by Albert Cuyp (Rijksmuseum, Amsterdam)
18 The Syndics of the Cloth Drapers Guild, by Rembrandt (Rijksmuseum, Amsterdam)
19 The marriage contract, engraving by Abraham Bossé (Paris, Bibliothèque National, photo Giraudon)
20 Family group, by Franz Hals (National Gallery, London)
21 St Joseph the carpenter, by De la Tour (Musée de Besancon, photo Giraudon)
22 Sketch of a ferryman by Lambert Doomer (photo John Freeman)
23 Painting of Fishermen by Carrache (Paris, Louvre, photo Giraudon)
24 *Repas des Paysans* by Louis Nain (Paris, Louvre, photo Mansell Collection)
25 An old woman saying grace, by Nicolas Maes (Rijksmuseum, Amsterdam)
26 Village Fair by Jan Breughel (Reproduced by Gracious Permission of Her Majesty the Queen)
27 Peasants outside an inn, by Adriaen van Ostade (photo John Freeman)
28 Scene inside an inn, by Jan Miense Molenaer (Osterreicher National bibliothek)
29 Queen Kristina of Sweden, painting by Beck (National Museum, Stockholm)

30 Madame de la Fayette (photo Giraudon)
31 Scene in a Dutch courtyard, by De Hooch (National Gallery, London)
32 Vermeer's painting of a kitchen maid (Rijksmuseum, Amsterdam)
33 The Spinner, by De Maes (Rijksmuseum, Amsterdam)
34 The Baptism of Christ, by El Greco (Palazzo Corsini, Rome, photo Anderson)
35 Christ and his Disciples at Emmaus, by Caravaggio (National Gallery, London)
36 Fresco in the Palazzo Farnese, by Carracci (Mansell Collection, photo Alinari)
37 Guido Reni's fresco of Aurora, Palazzo Pallavicini, Rome (Mansell Collection, photo Alinari)
38 Monument to Urban VIII, by Bernini, Basilica of S. Pietro (photo Alinari)
39 Innocent X by Velazquez, Palazzo Doria, Rome (Gabinetto Fotographico Nazionale)
40 The ecstasy of St Teresa, by Bernini (photo Alinari)
41 Marie de Medicis disembarking at Marseilles, by Rubens (Paris, Louvre, photo Giraudon)
42 El Primo by Velazquez (Prado Museum, Madrid)
43 The Night Watch, by Rembrandt (Rijksmuseum, Amsterdam)
44 Self-portrait by Rembrandt (National Gallery, London)
45 Self-portrait by Rembrandt (c. 1640), Kassel, Staatliche Gemäldegalerie)
46 Self-portrait (c. 1659) by Rembrandt (Andrew Mellon Collection, National Gallery of Art, Washington DC)
47 Self-portrait (c. 1663) by Rembrandt (Iveagh Bequest, Kenwood)
48 Franz Hals' painting of a toper (Collection Bonnat, Bayonne, photo Giraudon)
49 Man and woman drinking, by Vermeer (Berlin, Staatliche Museen)
50 Il Gesù, Rome (photo Anderson, Mansell Collection)
51 Le Noviciat des Jesuistes at St Germain des Près, engraving by Jean Marot (photo R. B. Fleming)
52 The interior of S. Ignazio, Rome (photo Anderson, Mansell Collection)
53 St Peter's, Rome (photo J. Allan Cash)
54 Aerial view of St Peter's, Rome (photo Anderson, Mansell Collection)
55 Dome of S. Carlo alle Quatro Fontane, Rome, by Borromini (photo Alinari, Mansell Collection)
56 Façade of S. Carlo alle Quattro Fontane (photo Alinari, Mansell Collection)
57 The Queen's House, Greenwich (photo J. Allan Cash)
58 The Town Hall, Amsterdam, from a painting by Berckheijde (Rijksmuseum, Amsterdam)
59 The Arcadian Shepherds, by Poussin (Paris, Louvre, photo Giraudon)
60 Sassoferrato's painting of the Madonna in Prayer (National Gallery, London)
61 Classical Landscape, by Claude (Barber Institute of Fine Arts, University of Birmingham)
62 The Vision of St Romuald, by Sacchi (Vatican Museum, photo Anderson, Mansell Collection)
63 Bust of Louis XIV by Bernini (photo Giraudon)
64 Bust of Louis XIV by Coysevox (Musée de Dijon, photo Giraudon)
65 Gobelin tapestry designed by Lebrun (photo Bulloz, Mansell Collection)
66 The ambassadors' staircase at Versailles (photo Courtauld Institute, London)
67 The gardens at Versailles, painting by J. B. Martin (Musée de Versailles, photo Giraudon)
68 Mignard's portrait of Madame de Montespan and her son (photo Mansell Collection)

69 Madame de Maintenon by Mignard (Musée de Versailles, photo Bulloz, Mansell Collection)

70 Portrait thought to be of Shakespeare. Artist unknown (National Portrait Gallery, London)

71 Scene from Cervantes, *Don Quixote* (Bodleian Library, Oxford)

72 Frontispiece to *Le Cid* by Corneille (Paris, Bibliothèque National, photo Giraudon)

73 Portrait of Racine (photo Rex)

74 Painting of a Molière farce, Comedie Française (photo Giraudon)

75 Portrait of Milton by Faithorne (National Portrait Gallery, London)

76 Scene from *La Finta Pazza*

77 Backcloth designed for the *Seige of Rhodes* (the Chatsworth Settlement, Bakewell, Derbyshire)

78 Interior of the Opera House, Vienna (Osterreichischer Nationalbibliothek)

79 Hanging of witches in England, after a seventeenth century drawing (Mansell Collection)

80 An impenitent heretic, from *Historia Inquisitionis* by Limborch (Mansell Collection)

81 Witches' Sabbath, by Teniers the Younger.

82 Refectory scene, by Zurbarán (Museo Provinciale, Seville, photo Mas)

83 Portrait of Gallileo, by Sustermans (Uffizi Gallery, photo Anderson)

84 Harvey's diagrams illustrating the circulation of the blood (by courtesy of the Wellcome Trustees, Wellcome Historical and Medical Museum, London)

85 Rembrandt's painting of the anatomy lesson of Dr Tulp (Foundation Johan Maurits van Nassau, Mauritshuis, The Hague)

86 Portrait of Descartes by Franz Hals (Louvre, photo Giraudon)

87 Diagram of a telescope from Descartes *Discours de la Méthode* (photo R. B. Fleming)

88 Diagram showing the refraction of light, in Huygens *Traité de la Lumière*

89 Bracket clock by van Ceulen, front view (Crown copyright, Science Museum, London)

90 Bracket clock by van Ceulen, back view, (Crown copyright, Science Museum, London)

91 The telescope at the Royal Observatory, Greenwich (by courtesy of the Trustees of the National Maritime Museum, Greenwich)

92 The compound microscope used by Robert Hooke (by courtesy of the Wellcome Trustees, Wellcome Historical and Medical Museum and Library, London)

93 Facsimile of Newton's reflecting telescope of 1668 (Science Museum, London)

94 Portrait of Grotius by van Miereweld (Rijksmuseum, Amsterdam)

95 Frontispiece to Hobbes' *Leviathan* (Paris, Bibliothèque National, photo Hachette)

96 Portrait of Samuel Puffendorf, frontispiece of his *De iure natura* (photo R. B. Fleming)

97 Portrait of Bossuet, by Rigaud (Louvre, photo Giraudon, Mansell Collection)

98 Portrait of Fénelon (photo Bulloz)

99 The revocation of the edict of Nantes (photo Giraudon)

100 Ambrogio de Spinola receiving the keys of Breda, by Velazquez (Prado Museum, Madrid)

101 The murder of Wallenstein (Germanisches Nationalmuseen, Nuremberg)

102 Engraving of Oliver Cromwell (photo John Freeman)

103   Portrait of Turenne, by Lebrun (Musée de Versailles, photo Bulloz, Mansell Collection)

104   The Duc de Villars, portrait at Versailles (photo Giraudon)

105   Prince Eugen of Savoy, by van Schuppen (Rijksmuseum, Amsterdam)

106   John, Duke of Marlborough, by Kneller (National Portrait Gallery, London)

107   The battle of Fleurus by Carducho (Prado Museum, Madrid, photo Mas)

108   The battle of Lützen, from *Theatrum Europaeum* (photo R. B. Fleming)

109   The battle of Malplaquet, from an engraving by Huchtenberg (photo John Freeman)

110   The correct use of the musket, from Jacob de Geyn, *The Exercise of Armes*

111   The correct use of the pike, from Jacob de Geyn, *The Exercise of Armes*

112   Pike heads. The Armouries, the Tower of London (photo, Ministry of Public Buildings and Works)

113   Armoured cavalryman with arquebus, from Jacob de Geyn's *The Exercise of Armes*

114   Group of plug bayonets. The Armouries, the Tower of London (photo, Ministry of Public Buildings and Works)

115   English and Dutch sailors, by Ludolf Bakhuizen

116   The barricades erected in Paris in 1648 (Paris, Bibliothèque National, photo Giraudon)

LIST OF MAPS

Northern Europe, *c.* 1620   37

Europe in 1648: the Peace of Westphalia   98–9

French Wars, 1648–1715   154

Austrian Habsburg and Ottoman Empires, *c.* 1683   162

Central Europe, *c.* 1715, showing French expansion   164

Northern Europe, *c.* 1715   209

PREFACE

I have attempted in this book to combine narrative with a synthesis and some analysis of the history of civilisation in a golden age of European history. Looking back upon my own life time, I see as two shattering events the war of 1914–18 when I was a young schoolboy and the war of 1939–45 when I was still a young man. These two European wars, which became world wars, shaped the careers of all who survived them in civilised countries. I therefore feel that war and international politics are an essential part of the general historical story of Europe and that to write about seventeenth-century civilisation while leaving them out would be to empty out the baby with the bath water. Obviously I have picked out the big things that interest me personally in this long period. I have painted with a full brush on a wide canvas. But I have been relieved to notice that at least two books recently produced by other European historians are even broader in their scope: that by M. Mousnier and that edited by Herr Golo Mann and Herr August Nitischke.

I am grateful to Geoffrey Barraclough, Isaiah Berlin, and Hugh Trevor-Roper for suggesting reading to me; I am deeply indebted to Gerald Abraham, Harry Acton, Trewin Copplestone, and Martin Turnell for advice and for reading chapters in draft; and, above all, to Ivan Roots and Frank Figgures for reading the whole book in typescript. Alistair Duncan was good enough to read the proofs. The late John Steegman kindly lent me his lecture notes on the Mannerists and Baroque art. My book is not intended for the experts, but I have tried to give a fair representation of their conclusions without excluding a few thoughts of my own.

Maurice Ashley

CHAPTER 1

TOWARDS A GOLDEN CENTURY, 1598

> Mon Dieu que le soleil est beau!
> Que les froides nuits du tombeau
> Font d'outrages à la nature!

So wrote the French poet, Théophile de Viau, in a consolatory ode, composed about 1620, describing the most familiar of all contrasts, that between the brightness of life and the darkness of death. De Viau, who has been called a seventeenth-century Oscar Wilde, was later condemned in absence to be burnt for blasphemy, though he survived to be acquitted in person. For in Christian Europe it was then still a crime to undermine faith. Men as a whole passionately believed that beyond the grave a more rewarding world awaited them; and their belief gave them the hope of it. But for the captains and the kings the departure of earthly glory was neither easy to bear nor to witness.

In the summer of 1598 at the palace of the Escurial, high and desolate in the wild Guadarrama mountains above Madrid, King Felipe II of Spain lay slowly dying. Thirty-five years earlier he had planned this vast grey building which was to be not merely a royal residence and office but a monastery for his priests and a mausoleum for his parents. It had been built to commemorate a crushing victory over the French army won by the Spaniards on St Lawrence's day and it was designed in the form of a gridiron on which St Lawrence himself had reputedly been martyred in Rome during the third century after Christ; a line of cloisters formed the bars of the gridiron, four high towers represented the inverted legs, the palace proper was its handle. Felipe, who had been carried to the Escurial from Madrid in a litter, was placed in a small room whence he could listen to the monks at their devotions, praying for his immortal soul.

Gradually the king's legs became covered with a diabetic gangrene and for many days he endured the agony with fortitude. Then, Sir William Temple wrote, 'he began to see, in the glass of Time and Experience, the true shapes of all human Greatness and Designs'. He sent for the future Felipe III in order that his son might observe how 'God had denuded him of all the glory and majesty of a monarch in order to hand them over to you'. At dawn on 13 September, at the age of seventy-one, the mighty king died.

In the past historians used to write that Felipe II presided over the decline of Spain. That is not so. When his reign came to an end he was still ruling over the largest and richest empire that existed and one more far-reaching than the world had ever known before; in Europe the predominance of Spain was scarcely challenged. Felipe II's empire consisted not merely of modern Spain, embracing the kingdoms of Castile and Aragon (including Catalonia and the Balearic Isles) but also Portugal, which Felipe II had obtained through his mother, the seventeen provinces of the Netherlands, once known as the duchy of Burgundy, much of Italy – Sicily, Sardinia, Naples, Tuscany, and Milan – and Artois and Franche-Comté, lying on the route from Spanish Italy to the Spanish Netherlands. The majesty of Spain reached across the Atlantic to South America, Central America, Cuba, and the West Indies. In Africa it comprised Oran, Ceuta, Tangier, Mozambique, Guinea, the Canary Islands; in Asia were the Philippines; and in North America California. The wealth of Mexico and Peru had been gained for Spain by Hernando Cortes and Francisco Pizzaro and their *conquistadores*, while Brazil and the islands of the Atlantic archipelago had been acquired because of the inheritance of Portugal.

It is true that in 1588 a Spanish naval armada had been defeated by the English 'sea-dogs' and that since 1568 the Dutch 'beggars' in the Netherlands had been in revolt against their masters at Brussels and Madrid; and that war had been waged with varying fortunes for years against France. Signs of future economic decay can be detected by historians looking backwards. But no serious dent had yet been made upon the apparent solidity of the Spanish possessions. On Felipe's behalf the duque of Alba, as stern as he was able, had reconquered much of the Netherlands except for the seven provinces that bound themselves together in 1579 by the Union of Utrecht. In her war with Spain England had received a setback when Sir Francis Drake, a favourite admiral of Queen Elizabeth I, had been repulsed from an attack on Portugal. On the eve of Felipe II's death the French had reluctantly agreed to the treaty of Vervins which left the provinces of Cerdaña and Rosellón, north of the Pyrenees, still in Spanish hands, thus testifying to the continuing and menacing power of the empire governed from the Escurial.

Through the variety and richness of her possessions and because of her alliances with the dukes of Savoy-Piedmont and the Habsburg emperors in Germany Spain subjected the French monarchy to a strategic stranglehold on all sides. The Spanish army had scarcely been defeated for a century. In spite of losses from storms and cannonades, the navy was far from despicable and was capable of procuring the safe arrival at the homeland each year of the treasure fleets from the Americas. The Spanish merchant navy could still rival that of any other country. And though, like other monarchies, the Spanish empire was in constant debt and required the yield from taxes and loans both to sustain the needs of war and to buy imports, the flow of gold and silver did not begin to dry up for another thirty years and long staved off permanent bankruptcy.

Such was the empire that Felipe II had ruled for over forty years, ruled like some latter-day high-ranking permanent official, reading, writing and annotating despatches, preferring paper advice to personal counsels, sitting like a spider at the centre of long webs stretching out to his numerous dominions. Though no coward, he had never been a fighting man. He never revisited Brussels after he left there when young, but gave to his princely relatives the disagreeable task of governing the disloyal Netherlanders or the unruly Portuguese. Four times he had married from policy, not love, to a Portuguese, English, French, and lastly an Austrian wife. Fifteen years after his death, marriage alliances were to be arranged between the Spanish Habsburgs and the French Bourbons, bringing hope of stability along the Pyrenees. Thus everything that money could buy or diplomacy gain or marriage cement was done to preserve the integrity of the Spanish empire in its golden age.

Historians still dispute when exactly that age ended, but assuredly a golden era yet lay ahead for Spanish art. When Felipe II died, Rubens, a Flemish genius much to be admired at the court of Brussels and destined to be a loyal and selfless servant of Spain, had not yet returned from his apprenticeship in Italy; Velazquez was not yet born; Cervantes's brilliant *Don Quixote* which was to entertain and astonish Europe, was to be published in 1605. Felipe II's granddaughter, Ana of Austria, who was to marry King Louis XIII of France in 1612, was to confer Spanish culture on her court in Paris. Spanish dramatists were read and imitated in England as well as France where the swaggering figures of the proud Spanish Don or the Spanish army captain became familiar. Throughout the first twenty years or so of the century it was Spanish culture, dress, manners, and arts that were the rage of western Europe, just as it had been Spanish wealth and dominion that had amazed it since the time of the Emperor Karl V.

If then the golden age of Spain may reasonably be said to have extended from the reigns of Karl V and Felipe II well into the first half of the century, the glorious age of Louis XIV of France, the 'Roi Soleil', still lay ahead in its second half. The palace of Versailles, not yet built, into which the French monarch moved in 1682, was no monastery nor

3

mausoleum. Upon its doors were to be emblazoned in gold the emblems of the magnificence of the king: *Nec pluribus impar*. The palace thus reflected in a golden light the grandeur of France just as Felipe's Escurial symbolised the macabre dignity of Spain.

But in 1598 France was still demoralised, divided, and licking her wounds after nearly forty years of political and religious strife. Her monarchy, now represented by the new Bourbon dynasty, could not yet rival the Habsburgs of Spain. The prolonged civil dissensions of the late sixteenth century had culminated in the wars of the three Henris – Henri III of Anjou, who reigned from 1574 to 1589, Henri de Guise, the leader of the Holy Catholic League, and then Henri Bourbon, king of Navarre, the acknowledged head of the French Protestants or Huguenots as well as the legitimate heir to the throne of France when the homosexual Henri III died. Each of the three Henris was to perish by assassination. Henri de Guise was murdered on the orders of Henri III in 1588; in the next year Henri III himself was slain by a monk; Henri de Navarre was to survive until 1610 when he too was killed by a religious fanatic. But in the meantime he consolidated his position and brought a measure of peace to his kingdom.

Henri IV had to fight hard to win and keep his throne. First he defeated the Guises, then he struggled with the Spaniards who had backed them. Believing that Paris was worth more than a Mass, he induced Pope Clement VIII to receive him back into the Roman Catholic Church, thus identifying himself with the religion of the majority of his subjects. Crowned at Chartres in 1595, he then worked for conciliation. In April, 1598, he issued the edict of Nantes whereby the Huguenots were not only guaranteed liberty of conscience but civil equality and even political control in two hundred towns where they were the dominant party. In the following month of May the French king concluded the peace with Spain at Vervins, to the disgust of his Protestant allies in England and the United Netherlands. That same summer he completed a policy of buying off his enemies still active in the Holy League. To achieve peace and order in Brittany where one of the Guises, the duc de Mercoeur, had ruled almost in independence of the Crown he paid him four million livres. Thus he thought it cheaper to pay than to fight, but he had no intention of being any man's servant. Gradually all the classes in the realm from the proud princes of the Blood down to a restive peasantry felt the grip of Henri IV's iron hand through a velvet glove.

Political peace was therefore being attained in the France of 1598 both at home and abroad. The king, now in his middle age, ambitious and no fanatic, was ever the opportunist, flexible in his methods but determined in his aims, intelligent and charming, a man without rancour towards his fellow men, and a mighty lover of women, a trait which he bequeathed to his grandson, King Charles II of England. He had to use all his skill in confronting the future. For his kingdom was exhausted; the nobility was ruined, the bourgeoisie injured by the decline of state credit, the peasants sullen and rebellious. In the late 'nineties the country suffered from widespread plague and famine. Many were unemployed; out-of-work soldiers set up as bandits and brigands and terrified the countryside. The civil wars had left the monarchy little obeyed, respected, or admired. As an institution it was by no means considered sacrosanct. For while Henri IV was proclaiming that he enjoyed the divine right which the Lord had bestowed on all kings, the doctrine that wicked monarchs might be punished or overthrown was being assiduously preached and sometimes practised.

As the dying Felipe II of Spain was handing over his huge empire more or less intact to his son and Henri IV was attempting to restore peace and order to war-torn France, what of the Holy Roman Emperor and His Holiness the Pope, who throughout eight hundred years of Europe's history had been leading actors upon the stage, waging a dramatic and continuing duel with their earthly and spiritual swords? In 1598 the emperor was Rudolf II, a Habsburg. His grandfather had been the brother of Karl V, father of Felipe II of Spain. After Rudolf's father, Maximilian I, died in 1576 his inheritance consisted of modern Austria, Bohemia, Silesia and Moravia, and parts of Hungary. But as Holy Roman Emperor he was also the acknowledged constitutional ruler of Germany, with the right to confer titles, to summon diets, and to raise certain taxes. This somewhat shadowy empire consisted of hundreds of electorates, principalities, duchies, and cities which, forty years after the peace of Augsburg, lay still uneasy and afraid.

The peace of Augsburg (1555) had been a settlement between the Roman Catholics and Lutherans of Germany whereby each individual ruler was henceforward to decide what faith his state should follow. The uneasiness was owing partly to the resurgence of Roman Catholicism throughout Europe in the movement known as the Counter-Reformation, marked by the dedicated activity of the Council of Trent (1545–53) and the foundation of the militant Society of Jesus in 1540. The situation in Germany was complicated by the emergence of Calvinism, a much more radical and ruthless form of Protestantism than Lutheranism had ever been. But more important even than these divisions among Christians throughout the Holy Roman Empire was the perpetual threat from unchristian outsiders, that is the Turkish hordes, to the security of the Habsburg lands. Vienna was then a frontier city; it had been besieged by the Turks in 1529; Hungary had become a no-man's-land between Mohammedan and Christian; and in 1595 a Holy War had been proclaimed by the Sultan Mehmed III who described himself as 'the ruler of the whole world from the rising to the setting sun'.

To meet the renewed danger the emperor called a diet to meet at Ratisbon (or Regensburg) at the end of 1598. A Lutheran preacher had during the previous year published a leaflet urging all the German people to show their ancient valour and loyalty in order to save their fatherland from a sea of blood created by infidels. But the princes who gathered at Ratisbon, especially the Protestants whose territories did not lie in the immediate path of the Turkish advance, were far from enthusiastic to fight for Germany or to preserve Christianity. Nor, it seems, was the emperor himself. For Rudolf II was one of those human oddities so often thrown up by the Habsburg dynasty. His interests lay in alchemy and astrology rather than war: always melancholy and misanthropic, at odds with his own brothers, he was by 1598 slowly but surely going off his head; he was already refusing to sign papers; and the empire remained confused and paralytic until he died in 1612. Another seventy years was to pass before a rather different Habsburg emperor, egged on by the pope, was to organise the last crusade to keep Europe inviolate for Christianity.

But the pope who reigned in 1598 was not a crusader. Clement VIII (1592–1605) was a 'politic', more concerned with extending the papal states in Italy than with raising the Cross against the Crescent. An earlier pope, Sixtus V, had succeeded in restoring the finances of the Holy See; and spoils were there to be shared. Rome became the centre of intrigues between the families from which the popes were normally elected. With Clement VIII the practice grew up of regularly putting authority and money into the hands of the pope's nephews; and indeed the popes of the century were even more nepotist than the Medicis or Borgias. It was not until towards the end of the century that nepotism was abolished and the expansion and enrichment of their secular possessions ceased to be an absorbing pursuit of the spiritual heads of the Roman Catholic Church.

To the north and east of the kingdoms of Spain and France and away from the amorphous blocks that are now called Italy and Germany was a group of virile Protestant states. In 1598 a great queen, Elizabeth I, had governed England for forty years and had become a symbol of unity and a tradition of glory. In the United Netherlands after thirty years of incessant war against imperial Spain a nation was taking shape. Originally there had been seventeen provinces, stretching from Flanders to Groningen, which had first been ruled by the dukes of Burgundy and then by the Spanish Habsburgs. After Felipe II had tried to impose the strict religious conformity conceived by the Spanish Inquisition upon these provinces they had pleaded their ancient liberties or privileges and united in rebellion against him. First led by Prince Willem the Silent of Orange, the rebel army had established an almost impregnable base in sea-and-river girt Holland and Zealand and thence had resisted a series of highly capable Spanish commanders from the duque of Alba to Don Juan of Austria, Felipe IV's illegitimate son. But in 1579 the ten southern provinces had made their peace with Spain; in August 1585, Antwerp, the wealthiest of the southern towns, had fallen to Spanish arms, and in order to carry on the war, the Dutch in the seven northern provinces concluded a treaty with England. By then Willem the Silent himself was dead, victim of assassination, but his son Maurits soon proved himself a fine soldier. In 1588 he had become captain-general of the Dutch Union and in 1589 Stadholder or executive head of five out of the seven provinces. The ten southern provinces were now governed from Brussels by Felipe II's favourite nephew, Archduke Albrecht of Austria, youngest son of the inept Emperor Rudolf. In vain the archduke tried to come to terms with the Dutch rebels. In the same year that he was appointed governor, the Dutch entered into a triple alliance with England and France and during 1597 Prince Maurits won a series of victories over the Spaniards. Although the French made peace with Spain at Vervins in the following year, the death of Felipe II immediately afterwards shook his empire and left the Dutch confident of ultimate victory and independence.

The success of the Dutch by 1598 in their long struggle was owing largely to the wealth of their two northern provinces which ever since the sixteenth century had taken advantage of their geographical position to build up prosperity by shipping and fishing, by overseas commerce, by banking, insurance, and industry and by daring mercantile ventures all over the world from South Africa to Japan. Amsterdam, the chief city of Holland, founded, it was said, on herring bones, had grown at a fantastic rate during the last two decades of the sixteenth century. Its leading citizens had replaced those of Antwerp and of the German Hanseatic towns as the most enterprising and versatile merchants and shippers in Europe. After Antwerp fell, many of the Protestants of the southern Netherlands migrated northwards. When the rebellion first began few notable differences existed in the religious complexion of the various provinces, but after thirty years of war the Protestants had mostly moved north, the Roman Catholics had come to terms with Spain, and the Netherlands were thenceforward split not along any particular linguistic or ethnic line, but between a Roman Catholic country under the rule of Spain (roughly modern Belgium) and a recently Protestantised republic, militarily protected by the rivers Meuse, Rhine, and Ijssel and embracing a uniquely affluent society centred upon the northern seaports.

7

In 1598 England had been at war with Spain for more than ten years. The military forces of Spain had no more been able to subdue the Elizabethan sailors than they had the Dutch armies. In an attempt to crush England – partly a Catholic crusade, partly a dynastic war aimed at wresting the throne from Queen Elizabeth – Felipe II had sent an 'invincible' armada to penetrate the English Channel and link with an invasion force to be launched from the Spanish Netherlands in 1588; this operation ignited the fires of war fought out by the English and Spaniards all over the globe. In 1597 a second armada of 136 ships and 9,000 men was sent out from Ferrol to invade England again. But the second armada, like its unfortunate predecessor, was broken and scattered by storms. The second attempt to invade England was in part intended to revenge the sack of Cadiz by Queen Elizabeth's young favourite, the second earl of Essex, a year earlier. Essex was a courtier with insatiable ambitions and wild improbable dreams, 'a man of a nature not to be ruled', his friend Francis Bacon called him. He was opposed in Elizabeth's Council by her old and trusted minister, William Cecil, Lord Burghley. After France made peace with Felipe II in 1598, Burghley argued in favour of following her out of the war. But his advice was not accepted and that August he died. Essex, the Adonis of the Queen's court, appeared to be supreme; but next year he was outmanoeuvred by Burghley's son, the hunchback Robert Cecil; and in the end he perished on the scaffold for high treason.

As in the United Netherlands, the war with Spain had been sustained and supported in England by commercial and financial advance. London, like Amsterdam, had become a busy trading city with a rising population and an access of wealth based upon its activity as a port, its shipping, and a growing cloth export business. In England too the forces of the Counter-Reformation had been repelled. Queen Elizabeth had restored the supremacy of the Protestant Church after a temporary reaction under her Roman Catholic sister and predecessor, Mary I, who had been one of the four wives of Felipe II. By the end of Elizabeth's reign the Church of England was more harassed by a rising Puritan movement within it, headed by men who wanted to rid the Church of all its remaining Roman Catholic practices and ceremonies than by the intrigues of dedicated Jesuits in exile to win back the island for the papacy. The Puritan movement was fairly strongly represented in the Elizabethan parliaments. And though these parliaments were not yet prepared to push matters to extremes against their ageing and beloved queen, who had defended them so astutely against the might of Spain, it was clear that a new age was dawning and that when the queen died her successor might less easily be able to withstand criticisms from his leading subjects about the conduct of the kingdom's affairs, above all in relation to religion. Since Elizabeth was unmarried, her heir was to be the first of a new royal dynasty, the Stuarts of Scotland; and so the two kingdoms in the island of Great Britain were to be ruled by, though not united under, the same monarch.

The Scandinavian countries at the beginning of the century had reached a stage of development not dissimilar from that in England and the United Provinces. After a period of turmoil both had accepted Protestantism and cut themselves off from the pope. Both looked to mercantile advancement as a means to national prosperity, but both at the same time were governed by kings with devouring political ambitions. Kristian IV, who became king of Denmark (and also of Norway) at the age of nineteen in 1596 dreamed of reconquering Sweden, which had gained her independence only some seventy years earlier. During his reign new towns were built and the navy expanded. The capital Copenhagen was itself enlarged and it was hoped to transform it into the Amsterdam of northern Europe. King Kristian also sent missions of exploration outside Europe. Danish adventurers rounded the Cape and reached Ceylon, while others sought the elusive north-west passage to China and India.

Sweden at the end of the sixteenth century was inferior to Denmark both in resources and in reputation. Lutheran Protestantism had been accepted more slowly than in Denmark; King Johan III of Sweden fancied himself as a theologian, promulgated a prayer book, and contemplated reunion with the papacy. His son Sigismund was a convinced Roman Catholic who was elected king of Poland in 1586. But when his father died in 1592 the Swedes did not want Sigismund for their king, largely because of his religion. In fact King Johan's ecclesiastical policy was condemned by a convention of the Swedish Church which met at Uppsala in 1593 where a kind of national covenant was signed. Johan's Protestant brother, Karl was invited to become lord protector by a *riksdag* or national assembly which reaffirmed the decisions taken at Uppsala. Sigismund III tried to obtain the throne by force and thus bring Sweden back into the Roman Catholic fold. A battle fought at Stangebrö in 1598, though not conclusive, in fact proved a turning point in Swedish history. Karl's authority was established (he was crowned king in 1607 as Karl IX) and though Sigismund never abandoned his aims in Sweden, he never came near to achieving them. Like the Danes, the Swedes (and the Finns who were ruled by them) had growing maritime and commercial ambitions. But they were shut out from the open seas by Denmark and constricted from expanding eastward by the power of Poland and Russia. Thus the history of Sweden throughout the century is mainly that of war: Russia had to be pushed back into Asia, Denmark compelled to open the way out of the Baltic Sea.

Russia itself was yet hardly a European power. In his 'grand design' for a peaceable Europe, written in the first half of the century, the French duc de Sully had excluded Muscovy as being Asiatic and dangerous. It is true that the lord of Muscovy and first claimant to the title of tsar, Ivan the Terrible, had sought contacts with the west. But after he died 'in a sudden access of passion' in May 1584, anarchy supervened. His son, the weak, melancholy and monkish Fedor expired childless in January 1598 and this was the end of the House of Rurik. Who was to succeed him – Nikita Romanov, his uncle by marriage, or Boris Godunov, his own brother-in-law? Boris Godunov prevailed. The title was offered to him by the recently appointed patriarch of Moscow, the supreme representative of the Orthodox Christian Church, and was confirmed by a national assembly known as the zemsky sobor. Thus in 1598 the rulers both of Sweden and of Russia were chosen by national assemblies. Boris Godunov, who had acted as regent for Fedor, wanted to secure peace at home and avoid major wars abroad. But his short reign was to be followed by a time of troubles.

Russia's western neighbour, Poland, was also in 1598 the home of confusion and anarchy. When the king of Sweden's son had been elected monarch by the Polish diet it had been thought that he might bring territorial gains with him after he received his Crown. All in fact he brought was a perpetual war with Sweden. Poland was not the only European country with an elective monarchy in 1598. Bohemia, Hungary, and Denmark were all in theory elective monarchies too. In the United Netherlands the stadholder was elected and in Venice the doge. But in Poland the king could not be elected or even considered until after his predecessor was dead. Thus Poland remained the most anarchic state in Europe: for the aim of the aristocracy was to have a feeble ruler and go on oppressing the peasantry.

Such, broadly, were the political constituents of Europe in 1598. The Spanish empire was still the most impressive and most feared of all powers; France was emerging slowly from an era of eight civil wars; the Protestant countries – England, the United Netherlands, Sweden, and Denmark – were seeking or finding prosperity through commercial and naval expansion. Germany and Italy were but names. Germany, theoretically ruled by the Habsburgs as Holy Roman emperors, was divided by three sorts of Christianity, while Austria was menaced by the Mohammedan Turks. Italy was dominated by Spain, though the papal territories and the Venetian republic constituted large independent states. Russia was entering into a period of utter confusion that was not to be resolved until the end of the century.

Politically the century was to be one of constant wars and revolutions. Yet it is not wrong to describe it as a golden century in the history of

European civilisation. The historian today, looking back and knowing much, has to make up his mind what he thinks was important. Some world historians (Oswald Spengler, for example) regarded the sixteenth century as the apogee of European civilisation, as the truly golden age. In any case a century is at best an arbitrary historical division. Clearly, for instance, the golden age of Spain continued long after the death of Felipe II as the age of Lope de Vega, Cervantes, Calderon, Velazquez, Zurbarán, and Murillo. About the United Netherlands there can be no question: the majority of Dutch historians contrast the 'golden century' of the republic with the 'periwig period' that followed in the eighteenth century. In England it was a magnificent age of poetry, the supreme English art. All William Shakespeare's tragedies were written and performed in the reign of King James I. The names of Shakespeare, Ben Jonson, John Donne, Robert Herrick, John Milton, John Dryden, and Alexander Pope alone make up the noblest catalogue of poetry in English history. Europe too saw the rise of natural philosophy or science, a more significant and constructive advance by the human mind than the revival of classical learning at the Renaissance. In England the story of science reaches out from the teachings of Francis Bacon and the discoveries of William Harvey to the theoretical physics of Isaac Newton and the chemical experiments of Robert Boyle. It was the age too of modern philosophers who acquired an international status: Descartes, Spinoza, Leibniz, Locke. Sweden's heroic age stretched from the reign of Gustav Adolf to that of Karl XII. France attained the height of her cultural influence in the reign of Louis XIV – Voltaire described it as a golden age – when the French academicians virtually dictated the taste of Europe and French was becoming an international language.

The cultural and scientific achievements of the century are what give a historian the right to entitle it golden. When the ineptitudes of rulers like Felipe III of Spain or Charles I of England have passed into the limbo of forgotten things, the names of the geniuses of this century can still be recalled and admired without qualification, for their masterpieces are the essence of the European heritage. And it is not merely a question of picking out the exploits of one or two countries. In spite of the persistence of wars and the difficulties of travel, art, literature, and science were becoming cosmopolitan. Rubens, a Fleming, one of the most versatile creative artists of the first half of the century, learned much of his craft in Italy where for a time he was engaged as court painter to the duke of Mantua. At Brussels he was patronised by the Archduke Albrecht, a German and by his Spanish wife, Princess Isabella. Queen Marie de Médicis, mother of Louis XIII, invited him to Paris, where he helped to decorate the Luxembourg, and Felipe IV of Spain summoned him to Madrid. In London he was commissioned to paint the ceiling of the Whitehall banqueting house. Velazquez too visited Italy twice and received the praise of Rubens when he was in Madrid. The French painters Nicolas Poussin and Claude Lorraine spent most of their working lives in Rome. Van Dijk, another Flemish painter, came, like Rubens, to England where he received many commissions and a knighthood from Charles I. Dutch artists were also welcomed in England as well as the Bohemian engraver, Wenceslaus Hollar, to whom Englishmen owe a clear idea of what London looked like before the great fire of 1666.

To give two examples of cosmopolitanism in literature: Cervantes was admired and imitated by the Italian Tassoni, and *Don Quixote* was avidly read by the Dutch. Joseph Addison, the English essayist, was impressed by a performance of Corneille's *Le Cid* when he saw it given in Venice.

The century opened with the burning to death of the Italian astronomer, Giordano Bruno as a pantheist, though he had done little more than draw daring deductions from Copernicus; his execution took place in Rome during the papacy of Clement VIII. In 1618 another Italian, Vanini, was burnt at the stake in Toulouse for teaching that God and nature were identical. In the middle of the century Cardinal Bellarmine, who had been mainly responsible for Bruno's fate, pressed for the punishment of the greatest scientist of the time, Galileo Galilei, also for blasphemy, but he escaped death. By the end of the century science was everywhere becoming respectable; scientists were no longer subject to disapproval or persecution. Men like Huygens and Newton had acquired distinguished international reputations. At the beginning of the century the mad Emperor Rudolf lived in Prague where he patronised two astronomers, Tycho Brahé, a Dane, and Johann Kepler, a German. In the mid-century René Descartes, an unorthodox philosopher, settled in Amsterdam where, to his surprise, everybody left him alone. Grotius, a versatile genius, when earlier persecuted by the Dutch, found a refuge first in France and then in Sweden. John Locke, the English philosopher, did much of his best work while he was in exile in Holland. Pierre Bayle, a French Protestant, settled permanently in Amsterdam to compile his famous encyclopedia, while the Jewish philosopher Spinoza spent his last fruitful year at The Hague. Gottfried Wilhelm Leibniz, Christian Huygens, Anthony van Leeuwenhoek are other celebrated names in the history of science. Pure science and individualist philosophy were satisfactory contributions to the history of European civilisation: indeed Bertrand Russell wrote that 'until the seventeenth century there was nothing of importance in philosophy'.

About the achievement of painting and architecture there can be no argument: the palace of Versailles, the town hall of Amsterdam, the

London churches of Christopher Wren, Bernini's St Peter's Piazza are enduring monuments. The great ages of music and technology were foreshadowed. Without going into every name – for they are legion from, say, the Dutch poet Vondel to the mystic Pascal or from the Flemish Jan Bruegel to the Italian Salvator Rosa – none will deny the magnitude of the literary and artistic creativeness of the century. Today as tourists swarm over Europe from America or Asia, what do they learn? That Antwerp was the city of Rubens, Madrid of Velazquez, Amsterdam of Rembrandt, London of Shakespeare.

But the century was also, one may argue, a golden age because it witnessed the emergence of the practice of toleration, especially in the Protestant countries. When it opened, the majesty of the Roman Church, armed by the weapons of the Inquisition and sustained by the missionary zeal of the Jesuits and Dominicans, still impressed and even frightened Europe. Nor were John Calvin and his followers exactly famous for their broadness of mind. One of the most fascinating aspects of the century was the way in which Europe broke through the thought barrier erected by those two highly disciplined religions to a freedom of approach in science, philosophy, and politics hitherto almost undreamt of. By the end of the century the spirit of international science was everywhere rampant and led to rationalism, naturalism and pantheism. The wide exploration of the globe and knowledge of its peoples and cultures cast doubt on the uniqueness of the Christian religion, just as the astronomers, aided by their new telescopes, could show that the Earth was not a unique phenomenon in the firmament. Everywhere academies of science and universities were being set up. Religious bigotry, if not dead, was undermined. A libertine like Viau might have found himself uncomfortable in the court of Louis XIII but would hardly have felt so in the court of his son. Vainly the Spaniards drove away their Jews and their Moors; hopelessly the French autocrat Louis XIV tried forcibly to convert his Protestant subjects to his version of the Catholic religion. The Jews and the Huguenots found homes in England, Holland, Switzerland, or Germany and stimulated and extended the cosmopolitan character of science and the industrial arts. Witch-burning was nearing its end. If purely material progress was still slow – in the realm of public administration and public finance, for example, or of medicine and agriculture – the close of the century was a peak in European civilisation, scaled in a golden era.

CHAPTER 2

FROM FEUDALISM TO ABSOLUTISM

It has been estimated that in the first decade of the century Europe covered 3,750,000 square miles of territory and contained a population of over one hundred million people. The size is based on the assumption that neither the whole of Russia nor of Turkey formed part of Europe, that its main boundaries were the Atlantic, the Baltic, the Mediterranean and the river Don. As to population, all estimates are subject to debate. Some French historians assign to their country a population of twenty million at the outset of the century, others only fifteen million. Spain (excluding Portugal) had a population of about eight million, perhaps more, concentrated mainly in Castile, England about four million, Scotland one million, Ireland another million, and the United Netherlands two or three million. The amorphous populations of Germany and Austria probably exceeded that of France, aggregating some twenty-one million, while Italy contained about twelve million. Muscovy was remarkably sparsely populated, possibly having no more than eight million. It is generally accepted that France possessed throughout the century the largest population of any kingdom under the rule of one effective government. Indeed if we guess the total population of Europe at one hundred million, then nearly a fifth of them may have been Frenchmen.

How far the size of populations changed during the century is again controversial. Most historians incline to think that in spite of wars, revolutions, plagues and famines – the effects of which were sometimes exaggerated – a slow, unequally distributed increase took place. For example, the population of Spain declined, while that of England rose.

Europe was still devoted overwhelmingly to agriculture. 'Striped or irregular-shaped open fields, commons, pastures, wastes and forests made up much of the landscape from north-eastern France to the Ural mountains' (Heaton). The abundant rainfall and, in general, fertile soil, were conducive to farming; but when the weather caused bad harvests whole populations suffered even to the extent of starvation or of near-starvation. At the extreme ends of Europe Spain and Russia contained less fertile soil in relation to their total size than other lands; considerably less than half the soil of Spain was arable: it was given over mainly to pasturage with flocks of three to five million sheep; Spanish merino wool, introduced conceivably from north Africa in the Middle Ages, was considered the finest in the world. Only two possible exceptions can be made to the rule that European countries were dependent almost entirely on agriculture for their livelihood, the United Netherlands and England. Yet it must be remembered that the remarkable commercial and business achievements of the United Netherlands during their eighty years war with Spain and earlier were chiefly concentrated in the provinces of Holland and Zealand. Here the peasants benefited directly or indirectly from the affluence of merchants and tradesmen. In Friesland the tenant farmers were not so well off, while in Guelderland and Overijssel the soil was poorer and the inhabitants participated less in the prosperity of the north. In the north too the reclamation of land from the sea was a continuing process and the output of dairy products, like butter and cheese, for which the Dutch have always been famous, was substantial, while horticulture, notably the cultivation of the tomato and tulip, made progress during the century. But, by and large, the startling progress of the United Netherlands was founded on commerce deriving from a huge entrepot trade organised with sophisticated exchanges. This business activity fructified the whole of the Netherlands. Excellent communications by river and canal linked the Dutch people together and enabled them to avoid the economic calamities to which the bigger countries, such as France, Spain, Russia, and Germany, were too often subjected.

In England too and in France (as will be shown in more detail in a later chapter) commerce and industry were making headway. Industrially England progressed with the manufacture of woollen cloth ('divide your exportable commodities into ten parts', said Sir Edward Coke 'and that which comes from the sheep's back is nine points out of ten') and the mining of various minerals. A little advance was recorded in the Scandinavian countries, but Spain and Italy suffered a notable decline. Though to speak of the industrialisation of Europe in the century is to use incautious language, a commercial revolution was undoubtedly beginning, mainly owing to the opening up of new markets and sources of supply outside Europe, partly owing to a slowly growing population, partly because of higher standards of living at least in some sections of society.

Seafaring was an important source of livelihood in all countries with long seaboards. A remarkably high proportion of the populations of Great Britain, the Netherlands, France, Portugal, Spain, and Denmark was regularly employed at sea, though their work was generally ill paid, hazardous, and uncomfortable. Englishmen and Frenchmen sailed as far as Newfoundland to catch cod to be salted for the delight of the Spaniards and Portuguese. The rivalry between the English, Flemings, and Dutch over the herring fisheries was endemic, especially as the herrings had a propensity to migrate. So was the competition to obtain freights. Though the Amsterdam shippers boasted in 1629 that 'during the truce [with Spain, 1609–21] through our economic management and exertions we have sailed all nations off the seas, drawn almost all the the trade from other lands hither and served the whole of Europe with our ships', before the end of the century they were suffering sharp competition from French and English traders and merchant seamen.

In picturing the European community in this century therefore one must not be seduced by such colourful events as the rise of the coal trade in England, the establishment of state industries in France, the prospering silk manufactures in Italy, the development, say, of printing and engraving in Holland, or the eccentric activities of Pyëtr the Great in Russia at the end of the century, into imagining that a big industrial revolution had already started : at most it was a minor revolution, and science had hardly yet become the proud mother of technology. The bulk of mankind was absorbed either in some form of agriculture or in work connected with the sea. Of course there was much seasonal activity. During the summer the European seaports might be largely denuded of their male adult population, while in the winter no man went a-roving, preferring to live on the land. So too much of the weaving and spinning would be done in cottage homes where arable farming or pig-keeping was still the foundation of subsistence for the family. The peasant formed the broad basis of European society and therefore of its political structure which might still be described as feudal.

The agricultural classes were not homogeneous but ranged from day labourers who worked for a small wage and their food to comparatively wealthy farmers who owned their own freehold or tenants who held their land on long leases like the yeomen and copyholders of England and the *censiers* or *laboureurs* of France or the 'orphans' of Russia. Between these classes were many other shades such as *métayers* who shared the yield from their crops with their landlords. In nearly all countries the peasants had to pay to their landlord dues deriving from arrangements dating from time out of mind. In France, for example, they had to have their corn ground at his mill, make roads for him, and give him various payments in kind. In all countries they had to concede to their masters the right to hunt over many of the best lands. In eastern Europe vast estates or *latifundia* were worked by landholding serfs and landless labourers. The most backward peasants in Europe were those in Poland and in Russia where the boyars or rural nobles disciplined them with the knout. In the latter century too a great many serfs existed who, though they might buy and sell, could not move from their homes and might be sold along with them or even presented as gifts to other masters.

At the other end of the scale from the mass of the peasants were the land-owning classes, the nobility and the gentry. Their aim was to maintain the pomp of their station in life even if it meant perpetual borrowing. Fortunes could be repaired by judicious marriages. Also in several countries was to be found a bourgeois class who paid for what they bought out of what they earned; but many, possibly most of them, were liable to become landed proprietors themselves. Since an estate was a badge of prestige, successful business and professional men like lawyers, speculators, merchants and tax-farmers bought themselves houses with extensive grounds where they could ape the nobility: in France they became known as the nobility of the robe (or upstart lawyers) in contrast with the nobility of the sword. In England they bought themselves honours, but in most countries an 'inflation of honours', as it has been called, was characteristic of the first half of the century when rising prices often obliged impecunious peers to sell their landed properties to new buyers. Sometimes titles automatically went along with the purchases of large landed estates; at other times monarchs (like James I of England) provided estates from their own resources so that the titled nobility might be able to keep up the prestige of their order. In Sweden the king made grants of land to compensate the nobility for their former administrative powers in provincial government which he had taken away from them. Monarchs themselves were usually the biggest landowners in their kingdoms and used their estates as a capital fund out of which to meet their debts, reward faithful servants, or confer distinction on their favourites. In fact, they were all in that kind of social life together, and it would have ill become a king to let down his side.

Apart from the rising middle classes, whose incomes depended on other means than collecting rents or selling the produce of their lands, most countries supported an expensive high-ranking clergy and professional soldiers on the make. In some countries – Sweden, for instance – the clergy could be described as a distinct class between the aristocracy and the peasantry. The lower clergy usually approximated in status to the better-off peasants or to small tradesmen, and frequently had to pay taxes, as these did, to the Crown or else dues to their superiors; but the bishops in Lutheran, Roman Catholic or Christian Orthodox communities acquired estates as an adjunct to or perquisite of their offices and were frequently active landlords who took an energetic part in government. Army officers were usually the sons of the nobility or gentry (as in fact the higher clergy often were too) and for them the military career was not so much an adventure as an investment. They bought

C

17

their companies or regiments and then tried to make a living out of their soldiers, for whom the state paid them so much a head. By faking their accounts, by using dummy soldiers or 'faggots' at inspection time, and by cutting down on the rations, an army career could become quite profitable to officers. Most armies consisted largely of mercenaries and the men expected in any case to benefit more from plunder and pillage and from other advantages like requisitioning and billeting than from their pay. The professional soldier and the man of commerce represented expanding classes in this century and lent variety to the older and more static picture of society.

The paradox of this patchwork society was that it was the poor – the mass of the peasantry, the small shopkeepers, and artisans – who were expected to provide most of the yield from taxation for the upkeep of the state. Admittedly the government was supposed to 'live of its own' except in time of war, and with the rise of international commerce customs and excise duties became a valuable source of income for hard-up rulers. They also had the income from rents of their own lands and from the sale of offices and monopolies or patents. But in time of war – and wars, after all, went on most of the time – these financial sources were insufficient to buy arms and hire soldiers and so recourse had to be made to special taxes from which the nobility and privileged classes were invariably exempt. This rule applied throughout the whole of Europe. Not until the Interregnum in the middle of the century was there a regular, well-organised, and complete system of property taxation in England and that was dropped soon after the restoration of King Charles II. The gentry in the English House of Commons always voted down land taxes or kept them as low as possible: regressive taxes like the excise or hearth tax were preferred to land taxes. In France the *taille*, from which all the privileged classes were exempted, was notorious and was to be among the causes of the French Revolution. In Sweden it was said that the level of rents and taxes was so designed as to leave the bulk of the peasantry only barely enough to live on. Whether it was Moscow or Rome, it made no difference: everywhere the peasant was ground down by taxation payable either to the state or the Church; obviously the incidence of taxation might indirectly be upon the upper classes, for example by hitting their rents, or inducing farmers to hide their produce, but even sales taxes and other fiscal devices prevalent in Spain and elsewhere were always regressive in character.

Thus the gulf between the rich and poor grew wider throughout Europe, approved by governments and sustained by taxation. It is true that only in a few communities was there anything approaching a caste system and that some social mobility existed between classes (though the extent of it is controversial). The bourgeoisie, as we have seen, quite often converted themselves into nobility or gentry – as Molière's *bourgeois gentilhomme*. It was possible for the better-to-do peasantry or their sons to rise to relatively high offices in Church or state if they had influence, push, or outstanding ability. But the taxation system, the rent system, the tithe system all lent themselves to accentuating the gulf which is one of the principal characteristics of European society in this age.

Most of these class divisions came from historical patterns set up in earlier times, in days when kings and princes were mainly dependent on their nobility to fight their battles for them and to maintain internal security. But for various reasons the monarchs of the Renaissance had learnt to distrust this source of military manpower. The invention of gunpowder put an end to the usefulness of feudal modes of warfare; henceforward the maintenance of private armies became a menace instead of a support to law and order. In France where the princes of the Blood had been able to fight against the government during the religious wars of the sixteenth century the nobility had to be bought off or crushed as a means towards securing internal peace. They were to meet their Waterloo in the second war of the Fronde. The same thing had already happened in Tudor England and Stuart Scotland. But in France, in particular, the nobility were left with all their privileges – above all, their exemption from *tailles*, but were not permitted to perform any service other than fighting for their king (or against him, as the case might be). In Sweden the great Gustav Adolf bought off his nobility or created new peers who were exempted from taxation rather than let political control slip out of his hands. So the Swedish peerage enjoyed a golden age. In 1650 Swedish commoners petitioned Gustav Adolf's daughter, Queen Kristina, to save the Crown from poverty and to protect the peasantry from oppression by confiscating the estates of the nobility. She returned a dusty answer. In France the old nobility were allowed to serve in Louis xiv's numerous wars or to gamble away their fortunes at the tables of Versailles, but they were no longer expected to govern their country. In Spain the contrast between nobility and peasantry was even more marked. The soil yielded less food than that of England or France and there was not sufficient to go round. Many Spaniards even became monks or nuns in order to obtain enough food to eat.

While the monarchs allowed their nobility to maintain their wealth and their privileges, their tax exemptions, their immense rights over their tenants and servants, even, to some extent, their private jurisdictions, in fact the bulk of their feudal superiorities, which they had ceased to earn in terms of social equity, kings strove to prevent their aristocrats casting shadows over their thrones. Yet in spite of the destruction of the political powers of the aristocracy in many European kingdoms, in spite of the peace of Augsburg giving German princes authority over the religion of their subjects, in spite of the immensely strong positions attained by the Tudors in England or the Habsburgs in Spain, nothing is more erroneous than to imagine that the European monarchs at the outset of the century were yet absolute in the sense of being free from all restraints.

Certainly such a claim was made. For example, in 1604 James I of England told the House of Commons that he could command them 'as an absolute king'. But the doctrine that the authority of the king could not be questioned because his voice was the voice of God was one more honoured by lip-service than in actual practice. Moreover it really was a novel doctrine. Up till the sixteenth century the idea that a monarch was subordinate to a moral standard and a spiritual authority was generally accepted by political thinkers. Royal authority was limited by the 'laws of nature' and by customary or traditional rights, while in the realm of practical politics the kings had no automatic right to make new laws or impose new taxes on their subjects. In fact in the late sixteenth century and the early seventeenth Jesuits and Calvinists alike denied the necessity of obeying a wicked king. Parliaments or national assemblies also expected their opinions to be regarded and their traditional rights to be recognised; in some countries they actually elected the monarchs. When Felipe III of Spain tried to induce the cortes of Valencia and Aragon to vote him money, he met with the sternest kind of resistance, and so later did his son, Felipe IV. The Dutch rebels had justified their war against Felipe III's father on the ground that he had violated their ancient rights. Queen Elizabeth I had been obliged to listen, if not always impassively, to her loyal subjects in parliament criticising her handling of both domestic and foreign affairs; James I of England, whatever his boasts about absolutism might have amounted to, was compelled at the end of his reign to allow the House of Commons to debate his foreign policy. In France there were not only six *parlements*, headed by the *parlement* of Paris, which had acquired the right to register royal edicts and therefore by implication to question them, but as late as 1614 a states-general consisting of the three estates of nobles, clergy, and people (or the third estate), was invited to gather and express its views during the regency that followed Henri IV's assassination and did so in no restrained terms.

Indeed at the opening of the century most countries had national assemblies of one kind or another which were by no means devoid of political powers: in Spain the cortes, in France the states-general, in England, Scotland, and Ireland parliaments, in Germany the diet, in Poland a diet, in Sweden and Denmark riksdags, and in Russia the zemsky sobor. None of these were fully representative assemblies in a modern sense; their rights and duties varied from country to country. Generally they included leaders of the nobility and higher clergy – men of real influence – together with deputies from towns and sometimes from the peasantry; and they were not then deferential bodies register- ing votes of approval for whatever their leaders did, as sometimes happened in assemblies of a later age.

The relationship between kings and their nobility (including the higher clergy) was usually ambivalent: both were concerned to main- tain the existing social system. That was why in England at the time of the civil wars most of the nobility fought for the king against parliament. Such was the influence of the nobility in France that Henri IV at first thought it wiser to buy off its opposition rather than try to suppress it by force of arms. After the nobility fought against the Crown in the French civil wars (the wars of the Fronde) Louis XIV determined to strip it of all political power – he even removed the princes of the Blood from the council of state – but he did not think it right or possible to deprive them of their estates. They had to be soothed. For in fact throughout Europe the brothers and sons of monarchs were as likely to form a rally- ing point against the throne as to be loyal to it. Blood was no thicker than water. The history of the century is largely the story of how the monarchies strove to reduce the effective political influence of their nobles, suppress their national assemblies, and establish a workable bureaucratic form of government with the aid of the services of the middle classes.

One may detect this trend in every part of Europe. Before the death of Felipe IV the cortes of Castile were reduced to a cipher; after the states-general broke up under the regency of Marie de Médicis in 1614 they were not called to meet again until the eve of the French Revolution. The estates of Bohemia were crushed by the Habsburgs in the 1620s; the estates of Brandenburg and Prussia were later repressed by the 'Great Elector'. After Karl XI of Sweden became king in 1672 he set out to found a personal absolutism. The riksdag did not meet again regularly after 1680, the king's council became powerless, and the nobility was humiliated. Karl XI's heirs were declared 'responsible to none on earth for their actions' and when in 1697 the warrior Karl XII became king and embarked on his long period of wars he was able to boast 'the Swedes shall fight when I command them'. Almost simul- taneously the same train of events was occurring in Denmark. There Frederik III was recognised as an absolute monarch and the nobility was enfeebled; districts formerly administered by fief-holders were handed over to the government of salaried civil servants directly responsible to the king. Finally in Russia after the blood bath of 'the time of troubles' when the Romanovs were struggling to establish their authority a despotism was built up with the aid of foreign mercenaries embodied in a professional army loyal to the tsar. Between 1654 and 1682 no zemsky sobor was summoned. The duma of boyars (or council of state) even lost its power and the only threat to the tsar was his own palace guard or streltsy. The streltsy were suppressed by the Tsar Pyëtr I who at the end of the century became the most ferocious despot of them all. Even in England, 'the mother of parliaments', the political trend in the second half of the century was towards absolutism. No parliament met during the last four years of Charles II's reign and when his brother James II succeeded in 1685 the monarchy seemed unchallengeable. The new king relied on the 'passive obedience' of nobility and clergy. It needed a revolution in 1688 to restore the concept of 'parliamentary monarchy' which had prevailed earlier. In theory at least Willem III, the victor in the revolution of 1688, was still left with extensive rights in peace and war.

Apart from the traditional privileges of individual classes, like the nobility and clergy, or the special franchises accorded to towns or the accepted right of councils of state to be consulted on matters of policy or of national assemblies to be informed about reasons for raising fresh taxes, the real authority of central governments was limited by the political disunity inevitable in large states where communications between the seat of government and the localities were necessarily poor and slow. To take two examples from relatively small countries, England and the United Netherlands: in England the divisions in temper, habits, and degrees of civilisation between south and north were still considerable; they hardly spoke the same language; and since the wealth of the kingdom was concentrated in the south, the north was jealous and unruly. Kings had to rely upon lord deputies for the government of Ireland and on royal commissioners to control Scotland. But more than that: in every English county the king's representative was a lord-lieutenant, usually a very wealthy man who wielded more or less by right a determining influence upon local affairs. When in 1687 King James II attempted to pack a parliament dedicated to his own policies he vainly changed and changed about his lords-lieutenant, but could make no impression on the obstinate local loyalties of the English counties.

In the United Netherlands the original Union of Utrecht which bound together seven provinces in resistance to Spain was a loose confederation of independent republics. The states-general that met at The Hague was virtually confined to matters of peace and war and foreign policy. Even then the constitution required the unanimous agreement of deputies from the seven provinces to implement any important decision. It is amazing that a state so constituted should have held together while fighting wars against the two greatest kingdoms in Europe, first Spain and then France. The United Netherlands really survived because of the predominance of the state of Holland, which was the most prosperous and populous component community and paid over half the costs of the wars. When the chief executive officer of the Union, the stadholder, and the chief executive of Holland, the pensionary, were in agreement, which was by no means generally the case, then only did unity become possible: also the republic could stand together under the pressure of outside threats. Nevertheless the continuance of this loose confederation of provinces, without even common economic or religious characteristics, was a very remarkable fact. As Professor Geyl wrote of the first half of the century:

The medieval principle of the autonomy of small groups which was everywhere giving way to monarchical centralisation, and which in the loyal Netherlands now only slumbered on in petty local organs under the shadow of Spanish domination, was enjoying a remarkable hey-day in the republic born out of resistance to this very concept of the modern state.

If in these smaller states the problem of government was how to over-come fissiparous tendencies, how much larger were the difficulties that confronted the governments of Spain and France. The Spanish empire was a fortuitous conglomeration of communities, speaking different languages and possessing different local autonomous rights, acquired often merely by the marriage of princes and dukes into the Habsburg dynasty. Even in Spain itself Castile and Aragon, united by marriage in the sixteenth century, had not yet been blended together. Spain in Professor Elliott's words, was 'a confederation of semi-autonomous provinces'. Where the Spaniards genuinely colonised abroad then their culture took hold – as in Spanish America until this day – but where their authority depended solely on a small army or the occasional visits of a fleet, Spanish influence was and remained precarious. So during the century the resources of an impressive and indeed golden empire were overstretched. The enterprising Dutch and English attacked or under-mined Spanish-held territories in the West Indies, in Asia, Africa, and North America. In Europe the court of Madrid was confronted by the guile of French ministers like Cardinal Richelieu and Cardinal Mazarin determined to shake off the stranglehold imposed upon their country by the wide-flung possessions of Spain. Revolutions were to break out in Portugal, in Italy, and in Catalonia. Resistance to the levying of taxes was met everywhere except in Castile itself. Vainly Felipe IV's minister, Olivares pleaded with his master to make himself a real king of Spain instead of king of Aragon, king of Portugal, count of Barcelona and the rest. Then, he claimed, 'If your Majesty succeed in this, you will be the most powerful monarch in the world.' It was all a dream. In fact the Spanish Habsburgs never became the masters of the Iberian peninsula, let alone of the whole of their rickety empire.

France was somewhat more homogeneous than Spain. Most of its people spoke much the same language. But Henri IV, Louis XIII, and Louis XIV had to concentrate their energies on destroying not merely the independent power of the nobility and clergy but also the traditional privileges of the provinces in order to build up a centralised monarchy. The kingdom was divided, to start with, into *pays d'états* (like Languedoc and Brittany) which still retained their own estates and *pays d'election* (like Touraine and Maine) governed directly by crown officials. During the century resistance to the centralising ambitions of the monarchy therefore came naturally from the first category of provinces which covered about a third of France. Henri IV proceeded cautiously on his way by buying off local magnates and by granting concessions to his Protestant subjects, the Huguenots, in his far-reaching edict of Nantes of 1598. Louis XIII and the regency of Anne of Austria had to overcome rebellions and conspiracies against the Crown centred largely in the *pays d'états*. Louis XIV ended by governing all the provinces through Intendants directly responsible to himself, by depriving the nobility of all duties except soldiering, by setting up a really competent bureaucracy, and by suppressing the privileges of the Huguenots when he repealed the edict of Nantes in 1685. The history of France during the century is therefore of governments struggling to enforce unity while at the same time waging dynastic wars.

The pattern of development was the same in almost every country. Poland is perhaps the most notorious example in Europe of a disruptive state which failed to obtain really centralised government by the eighteenth century, though a spurious unity was given to it during the eighty-year rule of the Vasas. In the Scandinavian countries strong kings fought to overcome the obstacles to unity caused by geographical as well as political factors. Germany consisted of hundreds of rival electors, princes, dukes and estates which had to undergo the blood bath of the 'Thirty Years War' (1618–48) before gradually beginning to find some form of national consciousness in fighting the Turks on the eastern frontiers and the aggressive French on their west. It is possible that the very existence of the atrophied organs of the Holy Roman Empire militated against unity. In the north of Germany the great elector of Brandenburg began to fashion the kingdom of Prussia under the Hohenzollern dynasty and to the south in Vienna the emperors Ferdinand II and his brother Leopold I were to lay the foundations of Austria-Hungary. But many hindrances had to be overcome before the road to German unity was opened two centuries after the ending of the 'Thirty Years War'.

In view of the wide gulf between the rich and, in some cases, unserviceable and even unpatriotic aristocracy and the mass of the peasantry and common people living, for the most part, upon a minimum subsistence level under feudal conditions and doing what they were told except when driven to desperation, the employment by governments of nearly all countries of mercenary soldiers to wage wars, the gross unfairness both as to distribution and incidence of taxation, and the sale of most offices of central and local government not to trusted officials but to the highest bidders, and, above all, the dynastic views held by rulers and the local interests of magnates, dare one speak at all of 'nation-states' or of national unity in Europe during the century? As Professor Rowen has recently pointed out, if we define a nation-state as the actual or desired identification of the ethnic-linguistic nation and the political nation it emerged only transitorily and incompletely during this period. It has also been lately contended, however, that the century witnessed a transition from an age of feudal monarchies to that of absolute monarchies, sometimes enlightened and sometimes despotic and that this evolution was a necessary stage on the way to self-conscious nationalism.

One can certainly detect this evolution taking different forms, but one must be careful not to read the sentiments of the nineteenth or twentieth centuries into these earlier events. For example, the European dynasts all habitually engaged in foreign wars. Unprovoked aggression and undeclared wars or civil wars fomented or aided from outside were certainly not the invention of modern civilisation. In deciding to make war the kings of Sweden, Denmark, and Poland, for instance, or those of France, or even the popes of Rome had as their first objective simply the aggrandisement of themselves and the extension of their own existing possessions. Such rulers were rarely guided by motives of pure national justice or national self-defence. Reason was usually the servant of the instincts. It is possible of course that motives were at times more subtle than mere pride, greed, or jealousy, that rulers wanted to find occupations, relatively harmless to themselves, for their own more powerful subjects who might otherwise have engaged in intrigues or wars at home or else that such rulers wished to distract attention from purely internal discontents. These are motives frequently attributed to war-mongers, but, in general, statesmen tend to be simple rather than subtle in their motives and aims, if not always in their methods.

Looking back, national historians seek to endow past rulers of their own countries with the highest possible motives. For instance, French historians explain that King Louis xiv had to engage in preventive wars against the wicked Germans or Dutch or perhaps that he was merely seeking to secure the 'natural frontiers' of his realm to the north-east and to block up the routes by which his kingdom could be invaded by his enemies. Aggressive action for territorial advantage or personal glory, they argue, hardly passed through his mind. Again Karl xii of Sweden, like the French king, was merely endeavouring, when he waged war after war, to throw off the grip of his implacable enemies in Denmark, Poland, or Russia; he was never contemplating fresh conquests merely for their own sake. The Turks were moved by understandable religious aims when they attacked Poland or Austria and equally the Emperor Leopold i and King John Sobieski of Poland were being primarily religious when they planned to push the Turks out of Europe and help themselves to their territories. But impartial modern research casts doubt on such high-minded interpretations; and an English historian may as well frankly admit that not only King Charles ii but the English parliamentarians before him went to war with the Dutch largely for commercial reasons rather than for any obvious ideals or out of an urgent need for self-defence.

When the actual wars came, however, and especially if they looked like being lost, men were frequently called to the colours by the trumpets of patriotism. In 1709 when France seemed about to be overrun by a victorious coalition of her foes not only did the ageing king himself (normally no heroic soldier) volunteer to fight in the last ditch but so did many ordinary Frenchmen. When in 1672 the French and English, after one of the most cynical conspiracies of the century, threatened to conquer the Dutch Netherlands, many Dutchmen offered to supplement the meagre armies of the republic and hold off the assault from behind the water line. Even the subjects of the declining monarchy of Spain fiercely contested the attempt of the Protestant countries and the emperor to force an Austrian prince upon them as their ruler during the last stage of the war of the Spanish Succession, while earlier the people of Portugal had demanded to be governed by their own Portuguese Royal House rather than as a province of Spain, however honourably.

If then war contributed in some measure to a rising sense of patriotism, as it did too perhaps even in the England of William the Conqueror or the France of Jeanne d'Arc, one may detect certain growing points of national feeling also in times of peace. Clearly the smaller states were instances. England (especially when she was a republic), the republics of the United Netherlands and of Venice and of Switzerland earned many admirers abroad during the century and later as model states. Some of the Italian cities – Florence, for example – were also islands of early nationhood. The Florentine Machiavelli was, we are assured, inspired by patriotic motives when he wrote his book, *The Prince*. The

Frenchman Jean Bodin, one of the earliest exponents of the idea of sovereignty, also contributed to a nationalist mode of thinking. The more erudite looked back to the ancient Roman republic and to Athens and Sparta as city states where patriotic feelings once glowed and might be imitated, at any rate by the better-off. Capital cities too were possibly the nuclei of nation states: Paris certainly was once. Cities like London, Copenhagen, Paris and, to a lesser extent, Madrid and Moscow were centres of national customs, fashions, and pride. Certain regions too may have been breeding grounds of *staatsvolk*, as Mr Kiernan has suggested. London and the home counties of England, like the Ile de France, Old Castile, western Sweden are obvious candidates. Where the court, government, and parliamentary institutions functioned in close proximity there it was easiest for a sense of nationhood or at least national arrogance to flourish and find literary promoters. It may well be that the growing points of the nation-state are therefore to be found in comparatively limited areas in Europe.

None of the dynasts – Habsburgs, Bourbons, Vasas, Romanovs, Stuarts – were, as we have indicated, deliberately engaged in promoting the evolution of the nation-state. Much of what they did was for their own glory: they became symbols later. It is notable, for example, that though there was talk of the union of England and Scotland when King James I, who was also King James VI of Scots, came to his throne in Westminster in 1603, it was not consummated for more than another hundred years. Even when Willem III of Orange, the Dutch hero of the 1670's, was engaged in erecting barriers to prevent French aggression in northern Europe, he was also personally much exercised because his own patrimony of Orange, embedded in Southern France, was being filched from him. Men like Gustav Adolf of Sweden or Kristian IV of Denmark, when they came to their thrones, at once searched for paths of glory that war might open to them. Gustav Adolf wanted to rule over northern Germany as Oliver Cromwell did over Mardyke, Dunkirk, and Calais. Louis XIII's minister, Cardinal Richelieu, whose avowed aim was the strengthening and unification of France, was little concerned over the misery of the peasants or the crushing level of taxation that hit them, though there lay the central source of French weaknesses: he was too much absorbed in complicated intrigues to outwit the Habsburgs. It is wrong therefore to imagine that European monarchs always thought in terms of unification during the century.

To sum up, at the outset of the century Europe was a sparsely populated area with its inhabitants still largely absorbed in agriculture and with a mainly feudal structure. Though some mobility between classes undoubtedly existed, the course of events was determined by rulers with small regard for the welfare of the mass of the people. In those parts of

27

Europe where industry and commerce were beginning to modify the feudal and agricultural outlook the standards of living were higher and social barriers were breaking down. But if by the end of the century revolutionary changes were taking place, they were in political organisation and intellectual life rather than in social structure. These changes may be listed under four heads.

First and foremost in this century the history of European civilisation is that of the decline of Spain and the subsequent ascendancy of France; secondly, it is the story of how the small countries of Protestant Europe – England, the United Netherlands, Sweden, Brandenburg, and others– were the growing points of political thought, scientific discovery, artistic ideas, industrial progress, and more tolerant practices about religious beliefs; thirdly, it is the tale of the immense contributions made to the arts not merely by the virile Protestant countries but also in the large Roman Catholic countries like Spain, France, and Italy. Finally, the century saw the gradual, uneven, but none the less clear evolution from a predominantly feudal society, where kings were held in check by their nobility and the Church and were subject to traditional restraints of moral and customary laws as well as hampered by the obstructive powers of local autonomies, into a world in which centralised autocracy began to flourish and modern nation-states to take shape.

CHAPTER 3

TWENTY YEARS OF COMPARATIVE PEACE
1598–1618

The history of the world, wrote Colonel Repington in 1920, is the history of war. Many will be found to deny that. When Winston Churchill died in January 1965, one of his friends said that the kind of fighting with which Churchill had been concerned during most of his life had gone for ever; yet the world has seen enough fighting since then. The history of seventeenth-century Europe might in fact be told entirely as a history of war. But it was war fought along different lines from those wars fought in more modern times: in some ways it was more ferocious, but in many ways much less so. Towns were sacked and garrisons might be put to the sword if they refused to surrender after the walls had been breached. But armies at the outset of the century were generally little larger than one or two modern divisions and though occasionally the countryside was deliberately devastated, peasants, away from the battle area, might hardly be aware that a war was in progress; and, as a rule, fighting was left to professional soldiers.

Most armies consisted entirely of mercenaries. At the beginning of the century the English employed Dutchmen and Germans; the French recruited Germans and Swiss; the Spaniards hired Italians; later the Russians employed Scots; and so on. The principal weapons at first were the musket and pike, and the handling of these arms required some degree of training and discipline. The use of artillery expanded gradually (it was important in the armies of Marlborough and Pyëtr the Great) and bayonets and flintlock muskets were employed towards the end of the century. Though the infantry were needed to consolidate gains and hold fortresses, the cavalry then was queen of the battle. If one studies early seventeenth-century battle scenes in contemporary painting, one sees the climax was a confused *melée* in which the more vigorous mounted soldiers conquered. But mobile warfare was unusual. The famous Spanish *tercios* fought in closely massed squares, flanked by heavy cavalry. Siege and counter-siege was the characteristic method of fighting. Thus war was a career requiring skill and some training. Soldiers dismissed from one war would at once start looking for service

29

in others: they were tradesmen not patriots. The only amateurs were the high-ranking officers (in some countries nobles were either soldiers or were idle) or occasionally revolutionaries. When the parliamentarian armies went out to fight at the opening of the English civil wars they were armed largely with cudgels, while the Royalists, on the other side, relied on gentlemen fighting with their swords from the horses on which they normally went hunting.

But although the century was one of constant wars, of which the fiercest were the 'Thirty Years War' in Germany – the long war to halt French expansion which lasted from 1688 to 1715 – and the interminable struggles between Turks, Austrians, Poles, Russians, and Scandinavians, the first twenty years of the century, at any rate outside northern Europe, were years of comparative peace. Even in the north, after the peace of Knäred between Denmark and Sweden in 1613, the contests were of a somewhat spasmodic and desultory kind. King Sigismund of Poland was reluctant to abandon his hereditary claim to the Swedish throne or his interest in the affairs of anarchic Russia, but the kings of Sweden and Denmark wanted to put their houses in order after disputed successions before launching out upon fresh campaigns.

In western Europe the death of Felipe II of Spain, the internal problems confronting Henri IV of France and, five years afterwards, the death of Queen Elizabeth I of England all demanded a period of recuperation. Spain was reduced to financial distress owing to the prodigious efforts of Felipe II to maintain the integrity of his empire and to assert claims to the thrones of others. Bankruptcy had shaken the Spanish kingdom in 1586 and rudimentary forms of state borrowing had been introduced. Harvests had failed in 1595–8 and plagues had swept the peninsula in 1599 and 1600. The north of Spain had been reduced in population and a feeling of fatalism, exemplified in the writings of Cervantes, began to prevail. The taxation system, from which the hidalgos and clergy were largely exempted, was criticised in the works of economists known as *arbitristas*, while the selection, immediately after the death of his father, by Felipe III of a pretty worthless favourite, the duque de Lerma, as his principal minister, had promised neither revival nor reform.

France also had experienced poor harvests, plagues, and some famine. The peasantry were in a sullen mood. In 1594 at Bergerac twenty thousand peasants are said to have assembled and cried out '*Liberté! Vive le Tiers-Etat!*' Heavy taxation required by the war with Spain accentuated distress among ordinary people. The French king was determined to exert his authority and had concluded peace with Spain on unfavourable terms as well as yielding concessions to the Huguenots in order to give the kingdom a much-needed breathing space. In Maximilien de Béthune, duc de Sully, he discovered a minister of finance dedicated to reform. But peace was a first necessity.

In England the problems were as much political as financial, although here too the war against the Spanish empire had created difficulties for Queen Elizabeth's government and obliged her to put monopolies up for sale and to liquidate some of the royal estates. The war with Spain continued until the end of her reign. The queen's favourite earl of Essex was sent to Ireland in 1599 to suppress a rebellion led by the Roman Catholic Lord Tyrone. The Irish rebels invoked the aid of Spain. Essex failed in his mission, was recalled home in disgrace, and, after engaging in conspiracy against his queen, was executed. But the Spaniards once again failed at sea with an armada destined for Ireland and, although they succeeded in landing some troops there, who fought alongside the Irish rebels, the rebellion was suppressed in 1602 by the queen's lord deputy, another personable young man named Lord Mountjoy. When James I succeeded Queen Elizabeth I in 1603 he at once set about making peace with Spain. It was concluded in August 1604. The English promised to give no further help to the Dutch in their long struggle for independence; to cease trading with the Spanish Indies; and to accept the jurisdiction of the Spanish Inquisition over Englishmen in Spanish territories. Such a peace might have appeared humiliating to patriotic Englishmen – or at any rate to keen Protestants – but King James I of England, like Henri IV of France, felt the necessity of consolidating the position of the new dynasty; moreover he was also genuinely pacific, rejoicing in the title of 'the peacemaker'; and if he overestimated the determination and strength of Felipe III's Spain and was wishful to conclude a close alliance with her, that, after all, was a policy later to be followed also by France.

In any case the blaze of gold from Spain was still dazzling Europe. Her young king immediately sought glory by arms. His personal desires had promoted the hopeless Spanish campaigns in Ireland, somewhat confusingly called 'the English enterprise', and their failure, wounding to Spanish pride, had merely stimulated further and more desperate exertions. But for a variety of reasons the Spanish rulers had now to moderate their enthusiasm for regaining the Roman Catholic hegemony of Europe or at any rate they had to canalise it into somewhat more restricted channels. For one thing the king had discovered, after the death of his father, that most of the ordinary and extraordinary revenues for 1599 and 1600 had already been assigned to money-lenders. The various forms of taxation that sustained royal enterprises, such as an unpopular sales tax (the *alcabala*), the *millones* or communal taxes, and the various excises on commodities, besides the crude deficit-financing through the *juros* or funded debts, were calculated to damp down productivity. Real wages were then falling. King Felipe II had always, even at the worst of times, refused to debase the silver coinage, but the new king promptly authorised a debasement through the issue of vellón coins (copper or copper alloy) which yielded the Crown a profit of 100 per cent. The public debts nevertheless continued to mount and agriculture, commerce, and industry to flag. It has been estimated that the inflation of prices in Spain was then higher than anywhere else in Europe. The inflation continued throughout the first quarter of the century, partly owing to more debasements of the coinage. Under the circumstances the Spanish government had the greatest difficulty in raising money to pay for its wars: the cortes resisted royal demands; and it was because of these obstacles that the war in Ireland had to be abandoned and peace made with England.

The king himself fell at once into the hands of his favourites or *validos*, as they were called. Don Francisco de Sandeval y Rojas, marqués de Denia and duque de Lerma, was the favourite-in-chief and he had his own favourites, Don Rodrigo Calderon, count of Oliva, the king's secretary, and Don Pedro Franquero, the secretary of finance. The Grandees, who manned the council of state, were by-passed through the use of smaller committees or *juntas*. Though stern decrees were published forbidding luxurious clothing, Lerma and his cronies lined their pockets and preened themselves like peacocks while the poor starved. Lerma had the brilliant idea of removing the court from Madrid to Valladolid in order to stimulate the life of northern Castile, but that did little to mitigate the general economic depression in Spain.

After the peace with France and England the resources of the Spanish monarchy, such as they were, were concentrated upon the war against the Dutch. An able general had been acquired in the Genoese Ambrogio de Spinola who, with an army of Italians and Flemings, gave Prince Maurits a fright during the campaigns of 1603–7. The Dutch were victorious at sea, but in 1605 had to abandon Ostend and withdraw to carry on the fight in their own provinces. Spinola was handicapped by lack of arms, money and men. On a visit to Valladolid he saw that his employer was exhausted; he urged the conclusion of peace. Felipe III was unwilling to come to terms with rebels, but another severe defeat at sea jogged his elbow, and so in April 1609 the Archduke Albrecht signed a twelve-year truce, to which in fact Spain had been driven by another threat of bankruptcy.

But if the Spanish empire was thus unable to bring the boon of an all-embracing Roman Catholic faith back to England, Ireland or the United Netherlands by the force of its arms, it could make one little contribution to the religious welfare of its own subjects. Ever since the defeat of the Moors in the previous century some half million Catholicised

Moors or Moriscoes had dwelt in Spain, chiefly in Valencia. It was thought that these harmless peasants were in fact secret Mohammedans carrying on wicked rites. To purify Spain Felipe III, egged on by the duque de Lerma, decided that they must be expelled and pushed back into Africa whence they came. Soon after the truce with the Dutch had been signed, the resolution was carried out. The Moriscoes, thus expelled, remained Spanish subjects, but it is estimated that 275,000 industrious workers were lost to the mainland and that the effect on the economy of Valencia was disastrous.

Historians of Spain have disputed the exact significance and consequences of the expulsion of the Moriscoes. But one conclusion seems certain: in an earlier century the Jews had been expelled and the Spanish Inquisition had for years carried on an unrelenting campaign of persecution against those people of Jewish blood who remained even though professing Christianity, known as the *conversos*. The result was that Spain was left without any enterprising or industrious middle or lower-middle classes. And this accentuated the terrible division between the two extremes of very rich and very poor, aroused further discontent, contributed to idleness, and helped in the long run to bring about the decline of the Spanish empire. For these classes everywhere (almost without exception) the Huguenots in France, the nonconformists in England, the Jews in Germany and elsewhere, because they were deprived of political rights, concentrated on business and industry to the benefit of the kingdoms that so deprived them.

While Spain was dissipating her wealth on unhopeful ventures, France was having her house put in order for her by Henri IV and his minister Sully. Like Felipe III, Henri had found that he was encumbered with state debts and that the *parlements* were as restless over taxation as were the Spanish cortes. Without showing excessive originality as to methods, Sully proceeded to collect money wherever he could and to reduce the burden of debt. He sought gifts from the towns; he scaled down debts owed to the Crown by the rich in spite of their protests. He resumed Crown funds that had been alienated and used them to guarantee interest on loans raised at home and abroad. In order to encourage the peasantry the *tailles* that fell almost exclusively upon them were reduced, though no serious attempt was made to abolish them, while the salt tax or *gabelle* was actually increased. Another profitable source of income was the *paulette*, invented by Charles Paulet, the secretary of the king's Chamber. This was a refinement on the sale of offices by the Crown. When the holder of an office wished to sell it or bequeath it he could secure the right to do so provided that he undertook to pay a fixed sum to the royal exchequer.

By raising loans and taxes, scaling down debts, and reducing royal

D

expenses, Sully successfully re-established the king's finances; he found the kingdom in debt and left it rich with funds stored both in the Bastille and in the Treasury. He also promoted trade and industry according to the ideas of his day. The silk industry was encouraged; Dutch engineers were employed to reclaim marshland in the Bordeaux area; the export of wheat was permitted when the harvest was good. The manufacture of cloths and carpets, glass and tapestries was promoted. Instead of the vague and generally disregarded prohibitions of luxury imports that were introduced in Spain, Sully imposed prohibitive taxes upon them and endeavoured to secure the manufacture of luxurious goods, including silks and gold and silver thread, at home. Attempts were also made to improve transport and to stimulate foreign commerce. Finally exploration and colonisation were taking place overseas. In 1608 Quebec was founded and the intrepid Captain Samuel Champlain explored Canada as far as the Great Lakes. But Sully did not attach much importance to Canada: what he wanted, like other statesmen of his age, was to discover gold and silver mines that would rival the riches of Potosi.

The French king might therefore claim to be a benevolent autocrat. His ideas did not differ materially from those of other monarchs, but his methods were more efficient and his servants less corrupt. He kept his *parlements* in check; he promised but failed to summon the states-general; he used the royal authority to gain influence over municipal governments. He was also determined to show himself the master of all the great men of his realm. Henri's Achilles heel was women. His court, it was said, resembled that of the Great Turk and he knew no restraint when he fell in love with a pretty woman. Having got rid of his first wife, he intended (so it was believed at the time) to marry his beautiful mistress, Gabrielle d'Estrées and legitimise their children, but she died suddenly in 1599. Then he married the rich but unattractive Florentine princess, Marie de Médicis. To his new queen he introduced his latest mistress, Henriette d'Entragues, with these well-chosen words: 'This woman has been my mistress and today wishes to be your humble servant.' When Henriette did not bow sufficiently low to suit his wishes he threw her on to the ground. Henriette knew – or thought she knew – which side her bread was buttered. She had hoped to be made queen; now she entered into a conspiracy against the king with the aim of having their children succeed to the throne.

The principal figure in this conspiracy was another favourite of the king, the handsome and dashing Marshal Biron. Others, including some of the princes of the Blood, the king of Spain, the duke of Savoy, and an astrologer or two were involved. What the precise aims of all the conspirators were is obscure to this day, but their immediate purpose must have been assassination and the establishment of a new monarchy along the lines of previous successful *coups d'état* in France. In any case so many persons were concerned that someone was sure to blab, and blab he did. Biron was arrested, examined and executed. The net result of the conspiracy was to strengthen the Bourbon monarchy and humble the magnates of France.

Having established internal peace and put the royal finances in order, Henri IV's government looked to resume its contest with Spain. The treaty of Vervins had led to an uneasy peace and in fact Felipe III of Spain allowed himself to be drawn into Biron's conspiracy partly because he was angered by the support that the French had continued to give to the Dutch rebels. Henri IV had also tried by intrigues with the Grisons to cut the communications between Spanish Italy and her northern territories in Europe. In 1609 Henri took advantage of a dispute over the succession to the duchies of Jülich and Cleve, which abutted on the United Netherlands and Germany, to stir up trouble for the Habsburgs. He also entered into secret negotiations with the ever changeable duke of Savoy, whose geographical position invariably made him a turncoat. Foreign policy at the end of the reign was further complicated by Henri's amorous disposition. His latest mistress or would-be mistress, whom he had married to the prince de Condé under the mistaken impression that he would be complacent, had fled to Brussels under pressure from her husband who had proved to be less obliging than the king had hoped. Henri demanded her prompt return by the Spanish authorities. One of the French ministers gave a solemn warning that unless the Spaniards sent back the princesse de Condé to Paris there would be a rupture that 'could set on fire the four corners of the Christian earth'. Was there to be another Trojan war for the eyes of a new Helen? Or was this but a minor incident in a carefully thought-out plan whereby the Bourbons of France were to break the Spanish stranglehold for ever? No one can say with certainty. But the truth would seem to lie in a golden mean. The king of France, having settled his domestic problems, was ready to harass Spain and Germany in order to gain what advantages he could for his kingdom. But in politics one thing leads to another. Though he had in all probability no 'grand design', a European war might have come about as a result of his manœuvres when suddenly, on May 14 1610, this able but passionate ruler was struck down by a religious fanatic, François Ravaillac. Even the bourgeoisie, who had been shocked by his debauches and oppressed by his taxes, regretted the loss of 'the best of kings'.

The death of Henri IV imposed a pause on France's forward policy during the four years when Queen Marie de Médicis was regent until her son Louis XIII came of age in 1614. Spain was exhausted and glad of a breathing space, while in England King James I was more concerned over home affairs than foreign policy. But if in western Europe the establishment of new kings produced a spell of peace, in northern Europe changes in rulers brought long and confused, though sporadic wars. The difficulty in the north was that not one of the principal states felt in the least militarily secure: Denmark and Poland were the richest kingdoms, Sweden and Russia were continually threatened by their neighbours. The murder or sudden death of Boris Godunov, a tsar with a dubious title, aroused the cupidity of all Russia's neighbours, particularly of Poland, which was already absorbed in a war to her west in an attempt to conquer Sweden or at least to tear Estonia and Livonia from her. The Poles decisively defeated the Swedes at the battle of Kirkholm near Riga in 1605, but next year themselves were divided by a civil war aimed at reducing the royal powers of King Sigismund.

Meanwhile the time of troubles in Russia had spelt utter confusion. One of the first claims to the vacant throne was made by a candidate calling himself Dimitri, a supposed son of Ivan the Terrible. This Dimitri – false or real – was pushed forward by the Poles; a fortnight after his coronation he was murdered and replaced by Vasiliy Shuysky, supported, or at any rate approved, by the Swedes, who had for some time been dipping their hands into the bran tub of Muscovy. The Poles retorted by producing two more false Dimitris and, when they did not work out, induced the Russian diet to elect Sigismund's own son, Wladislaw, as tsar after Shuysky had wisely abdicated. The Royal Houses of Europe in those days were professional closed shops which were always ready with suitable candidates for any thrones that might happen to fall vacant. The Swedes also offered a candidate from their Royal House who was said to have the backing of 'God and Novgorod', believed to be an unbeatable combination. Before King Karl IX of Sweden died, a peace was patched up with Poland, and thus the Poles were able for a short time to devote their almost undivided attention to Russia. From 1610 to 1612 Polish troops actually occupied the Kremlin, the palace of the tsars, and successfully besieged the important town of Smolensk. But the people of Moscow rose against the Poles, the Polish and Swedish candidates for the throne were then dropped, and Mikhail Romanov, a native candidate for the tsardom, supported by the Cossacks or border warriors and by the smaller squires, was established as ruler. The Poles went on fighting and did not abandon their claim to the tsardom for another five years. But the dynasty of the Romanovs survived until ended by the Bolshevik revolution of 1917.

In Sweden the new young king also came to the fore at this time. Karl IX had a stroke in 1609 and associated his young son, Gustav Adolf, with him in the government of the country. Before Karl died in October 1611

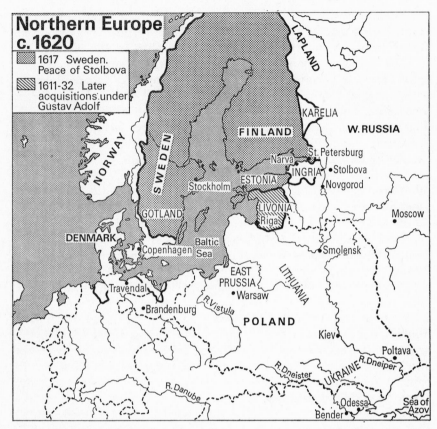

Northern Europe c. 1620

- 1617 Sweden. Peace of Stolbova
- 1611-32 Later acquisitions under Gustav Adolf

a war between Sweden and Denmark had broken out, known as the war of Kalmar. The Danes, who always resented the independence of Sweden, were the aggressors, although Swedish claims on Finland and Lapland had exacerbated relations between the two kingdoms. Thus Gustav Adolf, a prince who was to prove himself a military genius, was faced immediately he came to the throne with wars against Denmark and against Poland and with commitments due to the Russian embroglio. Gustav Adolf was only seventeen at the time, but he had the support and advice of an able representative of the Swedish nobility in Axel Oxenstierna, an imperturbable and adaptable man, then aged twenty-six. In order to ensure the succession of Gustav Adolf constitutional concessions were granted to the riksdag in the form of a royal charter. This amounted to a kind of oligarchic *coup d'état* reversing the situation under Karl IX, who had been able to keep the aristocracy under control. Gustav Adolf, as later events were to show, preferred, like Henri IV of France, to buy them off.

During his first year as king, Gustav Adolf struggled to maintain his head above water at home and abroad. In 1613 peace was made at Knäred with Denmark upon terms favourable to the Danes; all Swedish claims to expansion into Danish territory were renounced and the Danes were even allowed to display the crown of Sweden in their royal insignia; on the other hand, the Swedes received some solid concessions, among others the abolition of the tolls paid by Swedish ships passing through the Baltic Sound. The king of Denmark was now Kristian IV and his victory over Sweden made the other rulers of Europe look to the Danes rather than the Swedes as the leaders of the north; in any case there were more of them and they were better off. But Gustav Adolf was successful in his war with Russia. Taking advantage of the general confusion at the accession of Mikhail I, he obtained control of Ingria and eastern Karelia by the treaty of Stolbova in 1617 as well as opening up trade between Sweden and Russia. Thus by 1618 the king of Sweden and the tsar of Russia had established themselves upon their thrones.

Poland had little or nothing to show for her exhausting wars against Sweden and Russia. But Poland was burdened with many weaknesses. Lacking natural frontiers, she was constantly menaced by border troubles not only with the Swedes and Russians but also with the predatory Turks. She had a mixed population, consisting of peoples of different religions – Calvinists, Lutherans and Jews – in what was in name a Roman Catholic kingdom: Sigismund himself was actually called 'the king of the Jesuits'. Sigismund's attempts to change the anarchic Polish constitution had proved abortive and had merely caused civil war. Denmark remained the most admired of the northern kingdoms under a vigorous king who was personally devoted to the Norwegians and spent much of his time in Norway. But, as in Poland, the Danish throne was elective and thus much in the power of the nobility and so, in spite of the compact nature of his territory, the greatness of his capital, Copenhagen, and the valuable control he could exercise over the Baltic Sound, he suffered internal difficulties; and by the end of the century it was Sweden and Russia that were the rising powers in northern Europe while Poland and Denmark fell into a decline.

While the kings of northern Europe were fighting for their thrones or territories, the peace that had suddenly descended upon France and Spain was extended in greater or lower degrees to England, the United Netherlands and Germany. This comparative lull before the storm of the 'Thirty Years War' broke over Europe has been ascribed by one English historian to the general mediocrity of the rulers, it being assumed that in those days it was mediocre to preside over a country at peace. The more likely explanation is that countries could not stay at war indefinitely even in that age when war was less expensive and all-pervading than it was to become later. Secondly, internal affairs preoccupied the minds of most rulers. In England King James I was trying to come to terms with his parliament over finance. He saw himself as an enlightened statesman and a wise diplomatist when he was not engaged in killing stags. But the administrative machine was riddled with corruption, poisoned by greedy favourites, and endangered by royal extravagance. The king was a man of moods. At first he was of a Protestant frame of mind and allowed his favourite daughter Elizabeth to marry early in 1615 the Calvinist Elector Palatine Frederick, a marriage of fatal consequences for England. James had also been inclined to back the Protestants of Germany. But later, after a Spanish ambassador of persuasive qualities had arrived in London and James had proved highly susceptible to his flattery, he envisaged marrying his son, Charles, to the Spanish Infanta in return for an enormous dowry. Prolonged negotiations were opened with that end in view. James, who was a homosexual, was in the process of acquiring a new favourite in the handsome George Villiers, later first duke of Buckingham. Soon the king, Prince Charles and Buckingham settled down to the engrossing business of the Spanish match.

In the United Netherlands the Dutch were rejoicing in their freedom from the military attentions of Spain. Their trade was expanding and Amsterdam building up towards a population of 150,000 busy people. Prince Maurits, the stadholder of Holland and captain-general of the United Netherlands, deprived of his usual military occupations, turned his eyes upon domestic affairs. Religion was a delicate matter, for the Dutch Protestants were divided into two camps, Remonstrants or critics of extreme Calvinism – believers even in the freedom of the will – and Contra-Remonstrants, who preferred the pure undefiled waters of predestinarianism. Maurits himself ultimately became a Contra-Remonstrant, while Oldenbarnevelt, the patriotic pensionary of Rotterdam, was of Remonstrant sympathies. By 1609, after various theological conferences had broken up in confusion, Oldenbarnevelt had tried to work out a tolerant compromise by laying down that belief in predestination was not essential to salvation. But the city of Amsterdam was dominated by the extreme Calvinists who had not even wanted to make peace with Spain and were opposed to the supremacy of the State over the Church. Oldenbarnevelt played his cards badly; he alienated opinion by not sympathising sufficiently with the French Protestants and by annoying King James I of England. Prince Maurits was angered by a resolution passed in the states of Holland which he thought was calculated to reduce his authority over the army. Maurits exerted his influence in other states and then had Oldenbarnevelt arrested: in 1619 he was put to death on trumped-up charges of 'evil designs'. In the same year a synod, meeting at Dort, expelled the Remonstrants from the Dutch Reformed Church.

Germany was also perplexed by religious divisions. The Emperor Maximilian II, who succeeded the intellectual (or mad) Rudolf II in 1612, was a childless nonentity. Two of the strongest characters among the princes of Germany, Ferdinand of Styria, Maximilian's most likely successor, and Maximilian, duke of Bavaria, were convinced Roman Catholics, brought up by the Jesuits with the notion of reconquering the whole of Protestant Germany for the True Faith. In 1607 the duke of Bavaria employed his military might to subdue the small Protestant imperial city of Donauwörth and turn it over to Roman Catholicism. In 1608 some of the German Protestant princes, beginning to feel nervous, had formed themselves into an Evangelical Union with the support of the English and Dutch. The aim was to embrace Calvinism as well as Lutheranism in the religious settlement of Germany and to organise the defence of the Protestant cause. Inevitably the Roman Catholic rulers in Germany, headed by Maximilian of Bavaria, retorted next year by forming an opposing Holy League. For a moment it seemed as if the question of the succession to the Jülich-Cleve territories would form a *casus belli* in Germany and bring in other European powers. Both the claimants to these duchies were Protestants, but in the end a compromise solution was reached. Cleve went to a son-in-law of Maximilian of Bavaria, who promptly declared himself to be a Roman Catholic, and Jülich was assigned to the elector of Brandenburg, who conveniently turned Calvinist and thus pleased the Dutch. By that time Henri IV of France, who might have precipitated a European war by his intervention in the affair, had been murdered. But historians can now see in it a rehearsal for the 'Thirty Years War'.

The death of Henri IV led to a Franco-Spanish rapprochement, and therefore in effect to a truce between the Bourbons and Habsburgs. The regent Queen Marie de Médicis was lazy and let government fall largely into the hands of an Italian favourite named Concino Concini who married one of her ladies-in-waiting, Leonora Galigai. The able duc de Sully retired to write his memoirs in which he claimed rather more for his master and himself than they had either thought of or achieved. The Concinis had a Jewish doctor and believed in consulting astrologers about the future and therefore were regarded by the princes of the Blood, who were hopefully emerging from the shadows, as upstarts outside the pale, quite unsuited to governing France. But the queen had other advisers, such as the sieur de Villeroy, who advocated peace and an alliance with Spain. Perhaps Concini was not as black as he was painted, but in 1617 he was murdered, with the approval of the youthful Louis XIII, and his wife was executed as a witch. Cardinal Richelieu, the great French statesman, later defended Concini's memory (Concini had been good to him) and rewarded the most loyal of Concini's servants. A heroic conception of Marie de Médicis' life and regency may be seen in twenty superb paintings by Rubens, now in the Louvre. They will be admired long after the Concinis and Galigais are forgotten.

The Franco-Spanish marriage alliances were completed in 1612: Louis XIII was married by proxy to the Infanta Ana of Austria, the beautiful daughter of Felipe III of Spain, and Don Felipe of Spain was married to Louis's sister Élisabeth. External peace was necessary for France where discontent was rife. The nobility wanted the abolition of the *paulette* which they thought favoured upstarts, whereas the middle classes retorted by suggesting the abolition of the pensions paid to the nobility. These views were publicly expressed when the queen regent allowed the states-general to meet in Paris in 1614. As was the custom, *cahiers* or documents were produced expressive of public grievances mainly against the extravagance of the court and the nobility and in protest against the high and uneven incidence of taxation. Possibly the states-general overreached themselves; but in any case the three estates quarrelled with one another and it was easy for the government to return evasive answers to complaints and to wind up the meetings. It was then left to the parlement of Paris and to the princes to act as an opposition to the regency. Rebellions broke out and, soon after Louis XIII came of age and the Concinis were disposed of, his mother was obliged to retire into the country. Thither she was accompanied by the dexterous young bishop of Luçon, Armand Jean de Plessis de Richelieu, who by 1620 managed to reconcile the queen mother with her son, though another four years were to elapse before he himself became the chief minister of France.

During the regency the French Roman Catholic party was strengthened and the Huguenots became restless. In England the more extreme Protestants or Puritans were beginning to harry King James I at the very time when he was veering towards an alliance with Spain. In the United Netherlands the Calvinists had triumphed with the death of Oldenbarnevelt and the sentencing to life imprisonment of his learned and versatile friend, Hugo Grotius. In Germany the two religions were nervously facing each other across many frontiers. In northern Europe Sigismund and his Jesuit supporters were in the saddle in Poland, while Gustav Adolf in Sweden, having settled most of his external and internal problems, was revealing himself to be an exuberant Calvinist. Kristian IV of Denmark, with larger resources and a more compact territory, rivalled his younger colleague in Sweden as a possible champion of European Protestantism. On the other hand, the Habsburgs of Spain were still admired, courted and feared, and the younger branch of the family was girding up its loins. Thus during the twenty years of comparative peace in Europe – so fruitful for the arts and sciences – a sense of fear and uncertainty brooded over governments everywhere and the lines were being drawn for a major European war.

CHAPTER 4

ART AND SOCIETY: THE AGE OF BAROQUE

Art, like science, is international. Painters moved freely about Europe during the century. Architecture was also international, although buildings were modified by the character of the local stone and the local weather; but the same style might be seen from Austria to South America. Music crossed the frontiers too. French and Italian music was to be heard in London and Vienna. Lully, a Florentine composer, was to become the leading court musician at Versailles. Sweenlinck, the Dutch musician, learned his art in Venice. John Bull, the composer of the English national anthem 'God Save the King', became an organist in Brussels and Antwerp. Just as in modern times Paris proved a Mecca for artists from the whole of the aesthetic world, so at the outset of the century Rome was the artistic magnet. Even painters who never visited Italy, such as Hals and Rembrandt, were influenced by the work of the Romanists. Some French and Dutch artists settled for the whole of their working lives in Rome. Others went to Rome in search of understanding or inspiration or to renew their youth with the heady wines of Italian genius.

Art, again, throughout the ages has required patronage, and patronage tended to be cosmopolitan. In the first half of the century Queen Marie de Médicis, King Felipe IV of Spain, and King Charles I of England were acknowledged to be outstanding patrons of the arts. Rubens and other foreign artists were called to Paris to help with the decoration of the Luxembourg palace. Almost every day Felipe IV was delighted to go to the studio of Velazquez where he had a favourite chair. Rubens was invited to copy the king of Spain's collection of Titians. Charles I also had a celebrated collection of Italian paintings, as had his favourite, the first duke of Buckingham. Rubens received a knighthood from Charles I, while another superb Flemish artist, Van Dijk, also knighted, spent most of his life in England. We are familiar with the features and carriage of Charles I because of the paintings of Van Dijk, just as we remember those of Felipe IV and his family through the genius of Velazquez, though maybe Van Dijk was a flatterer. But in Italy, outside Venice, court patronage narrowed as compared with the glorious epoch of the Renaissance. The Index and the Inquisition made their impact on art. Music and architecture still flourished, but painting and literature declined.

In the later part of the century the centre of influence and patronage shifted to Versailles. But France imposed a kind of academic pattern upon art in a way that Italy and Spain had scarcely ever done. The French academicians were strict. Thus though the Italian sculptor and architect Bernini was invited to Paris, for various reasons he made little impression on the authorities and Nicolas Poussin, himself a Frenchman, preferred to return to Rome after a brief visit to his homeland. In the early part of the century patronage was pretty widely dispersed. At Brussels the court of the Archduke Albrecht and Princess Isabella offered encouragement to many artists; in Amsterdam rich merchants bought pictures and furniture for their homes and offices upon a lavish scale; in Rome the early popes offered opportunities to architects and decorators. It may be hazarded that in the Roman Catholic kingdoms the opportunities for the decorative arts were larger – for pageantry was as popish as religious imagery – while domestic furnishings, including easel paintings, were most in demand in the wealthy Protestant countries.

When the century opened the phase of art called Later Mannerism was in its hey-day. It is necessary to be careful in using such labels since art historians themselves are not always in agreement about the nature and duration of artistic phases nor over which artists to assign to them – and in fact the greatest masters can rarely be fitted into a convenient pattern. But unquestionably the behests of the council of Trent had made a profound impression on artistic Europe. The council of Trent had laid it down that 'the mysteries of our Redemption' might be portrayed, but required, first, clarity, simplicity and intelligibility; secondly, realistic interpretation, and thirdly an emotional stimulus to piety. The directors of the Counter-Reformation were highly sensitive to the Protestant criticism of Roman idolatry or image-worship and made it clear that the worship of images as such was proscribed and must not be stimulated either by painters or sculptors. Under this impulse the Italian artists of the latter half of the sixteenth century had practised a fantastic, anti-classical or anti-naturalist style or *maniera*. They were in fact reacting in a romantic manner to the perfectionist classical art of the Renaissance, so much so that some critics consider that they degenerated into affected elegance and sheer ugliness. On the other hand, the abandonment of any slavish adherence to classical rules by the Mannerist artists creates for them a certain sympathy in the modern mind. Thus Mannerism remains an attractive, if somewhat elusive, concept, but it certainly continued to exist among some lesser artists up till the middle of the century, although by then the Baroque style had reached its zenith.

Mannerism too may be thought of as a bridge between the Renaissance style and the Baroque. It has been said that the interpretation of the dictates of the council of Trent by the Jesuits and particularly by Pope Urban VIII (1623–44) was the real foundation of High Baroque art. Unquestionably the Jesuit church architecture with its cruciform pattern and rich decoration had a wide impact, starting in Rome and spreading out to all the Roman Catholic countries. But the strongest influence of all in pictorial art was undoubtedly the work of two northern Italians who settled in Rome, Michelangelo de Caravaggio and Annibale Carracci. Hence it is a mistake to write too facilely about a Counter-Reformation style or a Jesuit art. For these two men were uninhibited geniuses. Since neither landscape nor fresco was especially fashionable in the Rome of their times they concentrated largely on religious paintings which of course did aim to meet the requirements of the Roman Church. (Some artists got round a difficulty by dividing their work into religious and pagan themes: Rubens did that.) It has been said of Caravaggio that he sacrificed logical disposition and coordination of figures 'in favour of the emotional impact which he wishes to convey' (Wittkower). If Caravaggio was something of a revolutionary naturalist – as unconventional in his pictures as he was in his private life – Carracci was more of an eclectic, essentially in the classical tradition but with a penchant for dramatic effects. Nothing was too insignificant for these artists who were early masters of still life and *genre* painting. Both of them drew upon the life of the common people; both were lovers of the dramatic and the experimental; both of them revitalised Italian art and dealt a blow at Mannerism.

Much paper and ink have been expended on defining the characteristics of Caravaggio and Carracci. Was the first a realist, the second a classicist? Was the first a revolutionary, the second an academic? If one is to select any term, one might suggest that both tended to be 'romantic' painters, if we mean by romantic what the pundits of the council of Trent had in mind when they spoke of 'an emotional stimulus to piety'. In that sense Baroque was to be romantic and was linked with Mannerism: we can see it in its most extreme form in Salvator Rosa and more especially in the later work of Guido Reni (1575–1642), an able artist in the tradition of Raphael, who nevertheless produced standardised sentimental pictures during the last ten years of his life.

What then was Baroque? Like Mannerism, it was said by critics writing before our own times to have been an exaggerated or grotesque form of art. The word Baroque literally meant pearls imperfectly rounded – hence 'bizarre' art. (It has also been connected with a word used to mean a complicated figure in scholastic logic.) '*L'eccesso del ridicolo*' wrote a French encyclopedist of it in 1797; 'a savage dialect', claimed the historian of the Renaissance, Jakob Burckhardt. Technically a contrast with earlier painting has been found in its use of warmer colours: Professor Wittkower writes of 'a softer and warmer palette and a more sensitive characterisation of figures'. But Baroque was more than that: it was emotional, exuberant, often violent, and usually exciting: a creative revolution in the arts reflecting an expanding Europe. It is to be seen in the achievement of most of the leading artists in the first half of the century who had been influenced directly or indirectly by the School of Rome. It ranged from Hals's paintings of his fellow topers to the exotic wood-carving of church pulpits.

In architecture and sculpture Giovanni Lorenzo Bernini was the most powerful and influential of the Roman School. Born in Naples in 1598, he lived to the age of eighty-two. The High Baroque period of his art began in Rome in the 1630s when it is said that his sensibility increased. Bernini served the papacy and enhanced its glory. During the middle period of his career he produced his finest work in the tomb of Urban VIII and the colonnade of St Peter's. Though famed for his architecture, essentially he was a sculptor and before he attained the heights of his Baroque triumphs he suffered what has been called a classical recession. But most of his masterpieces in architecture were more ornate and highly coloured than the Renaissance churches: he loved to work with different coloured materials in association. Bernini's churches offered, writes Wittkower, 'the setting of a stirring mystery revealed to the faithful by sculptural decoration' – the romantic appeal. Whereas Bernini came from Naples to Rome, Domenichino left Rome for Naples where he died in 1641 and Guido Reni left Rome for Bologna. Salvator Rosa was both unorthodox and extravagant. But all of these Italian artists exemplified the trend towards elaboration. Even Domenichino, a classicist at first, drifted towards what is called Baroque.

Besides Bernini two other outstanding Italian architects were Francesco Borromini, who died in 1667, and Pietro da Cortona, who died in 1669, but more of the buildings of the High Baroque belong to the later part of the century when Rome remained the centre of this movement in art. French architecture, on the other hand, was more eclectic and less influenced by the Baroque spirit. The architects who were active at the time of Richelieu and his successor Mazarin were individualists, though each in his own way contributed to the evolution of the French classical style. In England too an architect of individual genius emerged at the beginning of the century in Inigo Jones. Jones was a self-made man, the son of a cloth-worker, who first made his reputation at court as the ingenious designer of stage masques. He visited Italy in the company of the second earl of Arundel, a patron of the arts, but was influenced by Palladio and examples of the Renaissance style rather than by the rising Baroque architecture. He helped the decline of Tudor Gothic in England. Among his few surviving master-pieces are the Queen's House at Greenwich and the Banqueting House at Whitehall. His piazza at Covent Garden in London also represented the Renaissance style at its best. But so far as native pictorial art was concerned, England was a backwater. Her artistic genius exemplified itself in the lyrical and metaphysical poets who wrote until the eve of the civil war.

In England, as in France, the first half of the century was an age of the theatre. The Elizabethan dramatists, headed by Marlowe and Shakespeare, established a tradition which was never to be entirely broken. They depended much upon the patronage of the court. But travelling companies covered much of Europe at the outset of the century. Both King James I's Danish queen and Charles I's French wife loved the theatre and enjoyed performing in the amateur theatricals, usually in the form of masques, some of which were designed by Inigo Jones and written by 'rare Ben Jonson'. In France Cardinal Richelieu was a notable patron of the stage, which was his one relaxation from a life of toil. Three companies came to Paris in the reign of Louis XIII, and the cardinal built a theatre in his hotel in the Rue Honoré. It was a friend of Richelieu, the Abbé D'Aubignac, who advocated the use of Aristotle's three unities, which shaped the classical style of French drama. This was the age of Corneille's *Le Cid*, a play as famous on the continental mainland as Shakespeare's *Hamlet* was to become in England. *Le Cid*, telling the tale of a clash between two generations, was a resounding success when first performed in 1637 and Corneille was acclaimed as a master and the father of French tragedy.

Ballet was based on mythology and poetry. *Don Quixote*, still per-formed today as a ballet by the Russian Bolshoi, inspired ballet as long ago as the early seventeenth century. Louis XIII, like King James I of England, was a patron of ballet. Indeed Louis took personal charge of the ballet at the French court and himself performed in it. But the theatre tended to suffer from the disapproval of the Church. The protection of Cardinal Richelieu saved it in France, but in England and the United Netherlands it fell before the blast of the Calvinist trumpets. Even in France Shakespeare was condemned as scurrilous. So towards the middle of the century the theatre was on the defensive, whereas in the later half of the century it was to be the rage of fashionable society.

In Spain, as in France, art depended on the active patronage of the royal court which set the example to the nobility. Whereas Felipe III gave his money to the Church by providing monasteries and convents, his son – under the impulse of his favourite, Olivares – spent generously on every form of art and entertainment. His pretty French wife also helped him along. In 1622 Queen Isabel herself appeared on the stage in a play, but unfortunately the theatre caught fire. Dramas were performed every Sunday and Thursday and these were interspersed with bull fights and auto-da-fés by way of popular entertainment. This has been described as 'the Augustan age of Spanish literature and Spanish art'. The most famous names were Lope de Vega, Calderon, and Cervantes, who died almost on the same day as Shakespeare. Lope wrote patriotic dramas, Cervantes amusing fables. Poetry became fashionable, masques were played in all the courts, and not even royal decrees could halt the ostentation and gaiety of this golden age in Spain.

It is a world that has been painted for us by Diego Velazquez, who was born in Seville in 1599 and summoned to Madrid when he was nineteen. He made little impression then, but later he returned at the age of twenty-four with his father-in-law, to whom he had been apprenticed in Seville, at the request of a court chaplain whose portrait he painted. The portrait was shown around the palace and by August, 1623 Velazquez was painting the king on a prancing charger, a portrait which was exhibited in the Lion's Walk, the heart of Madrid, for the admiration of its delighted and loyal citizens. As court painter Velazquez did portraits of all the famous figures of his time, such as the queen, Spinola, and Olivares. (Olivares, who also hailed from Seville, helped Velazquez on his way.) But the painter's genius lay above all in composition. In Italy he was much impressed by the Venetians, above all by Tintoretto. There too he encountered another distinguished Spanish painter, Ribera, who had settled in Naples, while Murillo, who also came from Seville, was his most successful pupil. On his travels too Velazquez met Poussin and Salvator Rosa; Rubens had admired his work when he was in Madrid. Thus Velazquez belonged to the cosmopolitan Europe of his day; but he remained essentially Spanish, commemorating as a victory the expulsion of the Moriscoes by Felipe III, and accompanying Felipe IV on his abortive visit to rebellious Catalonia. With Rubens and Rembrandt he was the foremost artist of his time.

Rubens (1577–1640), an older man, was also a loyal servant of Spain, although as a diplomatist he tried to heal the wounds of war. Rubens, even more than Velazquez, was influenced by Italian Baroque art. Rubens was, above all, a decorative painter – he dashed off his striking portraits with gusto, but they had neither the faithfulness of Velazquez nor the psychological insight of Rembrandt. Although he was an assiduous traveller and diplomatist and a man of inexhaustible energy –

he is credited with some three thousand paintings – Rubens spent much of his life in Antwerp where he gained a higher social distinction than most artists of his age. His work was the epitome of Baroque with its gorgeous colours and bold configuration. His studio was a factory where the master did the sketches and bestowed the final touches. Van Dijk and Snyders were among his collaborators as were also Vos and Jan Bruegel. A splendid organiser and administrator, Rubens estimated the value of his work at one hundred florins a day, but was always ready to take on more commissions in Paris, Madrid or London. He married twice: his second wife was the daughter of a silk merchant, and Rubens said that he chose her because 'she would not blush to see me take up the brush' – a revealing comment on the place of the painter in society. His versatility, like his energy, was immense. Emile Cammaerts wrote:

The whole stream of the Renaissance flows through Rubens' art, as the Scheldt flows through the Flanders plains; and while Satyrs pursue Nymphs along both banks, under the trees and in the light of the great landscapes, it bears towards the sea a fleet of barges full of praying Virgins, bleeding Martyrs and preaching Saints. And the Nymphs look like the women he loved and admired, and the Saints and the Wise Men like the friends with whom he exchanged remarks on antiquarian lore.

Rubens lived a full life and a noble one. He was fortunate in the hour of his death: he died in 1640, when the Spanish empire that he had served so well was about to collapse in revolution and war. One of the last paintings he did was for the altar in his memorial chapel with himself in the guise of St George – a moving epitome to an exuberant life.

Spanish art depended on the patronage of the courts, but Dutch painting was essentially popular. An English traveller when in Amsterdam in 1630 wrote:

As for the art of painting and the affection of the people to pictures, I think none other go beyond them ... all in general striving to adorn their houses, especially outer or street rooms, with costly pieces. Butchers and bakers are not much inferior in their shops, which are fairly set forth: yea, many times blacksmiths, cobblers, etc will have some picture or other by their forge and in their stall.

With such a demand for paintings artists were numerous, if of varying quality. Some of them made the pilgrimage to Rome, while others were indirectly subjected to Italian influences. Franz Hals (1580–1666), for example, studied painting under Karel van Mander, who had been in Rome and had then opened an academy in Haarlem with two other painters in which they propagated Italian ideas and styles. Rembrandt van Rijn (1606–69), who was born in Leiden, was first apprenticed to

E

Jacob van Swanenburgh, who had visited Italy and had an Italian wife, and later to Peter Lastman, a great admirer of Caravaggio, under whom he studied in Rome. It puzzled Constantyn Huygens, the poet and secretary to Prince Frederik Hendrik of Orange, one of Rembrandt's early patrons, why Rembrandt himself refused to go to Italy.

In spite of these Italian influences the Dutch painters were a rule to themselves. They enjoyed landscape subjects, which at that time in Italy were regarded as an inferior type of painting. Some of them discovered, as Professor Ellis Waterhouse has written, 'the shore, the estuaries, the dunes and the bleaching grounds of Haarlem as subjects worthy of love . . . ' They also lovingly pictured Dutch domestic scenes, most familiar to us in de Hoogh and Vermeer, and recaptured for posterity the daily life of the Dutch petty bourgeoisie. Hals pictured the regents of Haarlem, as de Hoogh was later to paint the important people of Delft. But Hals also portrayed the laughing children, the swash-buckling soldiers, the topers and the bawdy women of his adopted town. Born in Antwerp, Hals, it has been said, was a link between Rubens and Rembrandt. Certainly he was a colourist with an impressionist technique who caught the vigour, confidence, cheerfulness and optimism of the Dutch as they were emerging victoriously from their long war with Spain.

Rembrandt, for his part, pictured a more settled moment in the history of the golden century of the United Netherlands. Like Hals, he made his reputation by painting the civic guard. Hals's most famous early work was *The Archers of St George* in 1616: Rembrandt, who moved from Leiden to Amsterdam in 1631, did an equally famous painting of a company of musketeers about to go on parade which is usually (but inaccurately) known as *The Night Watch*. Rembrandt married a wealthy woman and was himself a keen Protestant, specifically a Mennonite. Hence though he is most celebrated for his introspective portraits of Amsterdammers, he also carried out a large number of religious paintings and etchings in a Protestant style, more realistic than those by the Roman Catholic artists of his time in Italy or Flanders. One can follow the career of Rembrandt in the sixty portraits he painted of himself: the eager and rebellious young artist, the very successful, married, portrait painter, then, after he became extravagant and was almost declared a bankrupt, an anxious middle-aged figure, and finally a drawn, neglected and largely forgotten old man, tended by his mistress and his son. In Rembrandt's paintings one perceives the industrious, professional and mercantile members of the community of Amsterdam and also, for a spell of his life, the scenery that surrounded the thriving city. Rembrandt searched deeply for the spiritual side in the personality of his sitters. There was an element of mystery in his work. He has been compared with Milton and Pascal: '*le coeur a ses raisons que le raison ne connait pas*'. Was he a supreme Baroque artist, as some critics argue, or a romanticist, who strove unsuccessfully to rival the grandeur of the Baroque? Though he lived his life in Holland, he was in contact with the world of European art, first through Caravaggio, then Titian, whom he deeply admired, and finally Poussin. As Sir Kenneth Clark has recently shown, he was also influenced by the Italian Renaissance and lifted Dutch provincial art on to a higher plane. A many-sided genius is not easily compartmentalised; but if the first half of the century witnessed the age of Baroque, then Rembrandt surely was one of its high priests.

In literature the first half of the century saw a gradual ending of a notable age and the beginning of a new one. Shakespeare and Cervantes died in May 1616. Italian sonnets and lyrics entered upon a period of decline as compared with the age of Tasso and the poets of the sixteenth century. Giovanni Battista Marino, a Neapolitan, and Alexander Tassoni of Modena experimented with the epic. The former was admired by Lope de Vega and by Cardinal Richelieu. Tassoni, for his part, was influenced by Cervantes as well as by Tasso and sustained a mock epic with skill. In Germany also it was a period of poetic decline, although Martin Opitz, a Silesian, has been described as 'the Ronsard of Germany', which also produced some celebrated hymn-writers. In Europe in general poets were still under the impress of the lyrical and dramatic poetry of the Renaissance. Just as the Italians acclaimed Marino as a master, so the Dutch were proud of Joost den Vondel not merely as a supreme lyricist but as a writer of versatility; but it was in England that poetry made the longest strides in the first half of the century. Only in France, under the direction of Malherbe, who dictated taste at court from 1608 to 1628, was lyricism frowned upon.

Shakespeare and Ben Jonson were the English figures who conferred fame on the court of King James I, but by the reign of King Charles I groups of poets were writing not only for the court in London but were also prolific in the universities of Oxford and Cambridge. Ben Jonson, a self-made man, was exuberant in all he did, but in his later years channelled his energies into the ephemeral art of the masque. Some of Shakespeare's finest poetry was to be found in his tragedies and *The Tempest* of his later days. The lyrical and metaphysical poets looked back to Catullus and Horace as models, but they were not all of a pattern. John Donne, possibly the most exquisite of them all (and also the master of rhetorical prose), wrote both sensual and spiritual poems, torn sometimes between his religion (he was a clergyman) and his emotions. Sir Herbert Grierson quoted this example of Donne in a Platonic mood from a poem addressed to his wife:

51

> Whil'st by pow'rfull love so much refined
> That my absent soul the same is,
> Careless to miss
> A glance or a kiss,
> Can with these elements of lust and sense
> Freely dispense
> And court the mind.

Robert Herrick, another great poet, was more of a simple countryman who loved the English ballad:

> I sing of brooks, of blossoms, birds, and bowers,
> Of April, May, of June and July flowers;
> I sing of maypoles, hock-carts, wassails, wakes,
> Of bridegrooms, brides, and of their bridal cakes.

In England prose was greatly influenced by Walter Ralegh's unfinished *History of the World* and by the translated authorised version of the Bible, two books which made a deep impression upon the Puritan movement and upon Puritan prose. But the essay was the most popular prose form throughout Europe. It stemmed from Michel Montaigne who retired in his château to write essays based on wide reading (he died in 1592): his essays were translated into English by John Florio, just as Shelton translated *Don Quixote*. Francis Bacon's essays followed those of Montaigne, as did the collection of essays entitled *The Anatomy of Melancholy* by Robert Burton. This essay form continued in France and culminated in the extreme brevities of La Rochefoucauld's wicked epigrams. At the beginning of the century too the tale was developing into the novel. *Don Quixote* is simply a collection of amusing tales, but threaded upon the characters of his hero and his servant, Sancho Panza. Honoré d'Urfée's long pastoral romance, *Astrée* is often considered to be the earliest European novel. But better novels were to come before the century was over.

We have been speaking here about imaginative literature not about prose with a didactive purpose – philosophy, politics, science, history. Descartes was a master of prose and so was the scientist Galileo and the political philosopher Hobbes, whom we shall be considering in later chapters. Historians were beginning to emerge; for examples, two of a different sort, Francis Bacon and Robert Cotton in England; in the United Netherlands Hooft, who was also a poet, wrote of the rebellion against Spain; France had De Thou and d'Aubigny and Italy Fra Paolo Sarpi. But it was not until the end of the century that one may detect a more general tendency to depart from mere conscientious chronicle or antiquarianism and to evolve something approaching scientific history.

May one write of a Baroque style in literature? If by Baroque we mean something that is elaborate, colourful, lively and exuberant, such a phrase may reasonably be applied to men as different as Cervantes and Donne. There was certainly, except in France, a reaction against classical simplicities; comparisons have been made, for example, between the paintings of Poussin and the prose of Milton since both tried to reconcile Christian morality with sensuality. But such comparisons can be far-fetched. Shakespeare, Jonson, Corneille, Cervantes were unique, and although literature to some extent crossed the frontiers and Latin was employed as an international language, probably less cross-fertilisation took place in literature than in the pictorial arts or in music.

In music the development of the Baroque spirit was remarkably parallel to that in painting and architecture; the music of the Renaissance had been dominated by austere techniques evolved mainly in connection with the Church, which reached their zenith in the sixteenth century; it was only in the French polyphonic *chanson* and in the madrigal that more worldly emotions found expression. The early seventeenth century did not discard the old essentially vocal and contrapuntal style in which the music matters more than the words, called by Monteverdi the *prima prattica*, but it rapidly produced a *seconda prattica* in which the music existed primarily as an expression of words. The music of the *seconda prattica* might be emotionally expressive melody or non-melodious declamation – *recitative* – but it floated on the surface of chords of which the bass-line – *basso continuo* – was played by one instrument while the harmonies were filled in by another (usually a keyboard instrument); it was not, as in the old style, one strand in a woven contrapuntal texture. Moreover the modern key system began to emerge more distinctly. All these new elements were combined in a new form – opera – which appeared first in Italy. The earliest opera, of which both music and libretto survive was Peri's *Eurydice*, staged for the festivities surrounding the marriage of Henri IV to Marie de Médicis at Florence in 1600. But the dramatic genius of this epoch was Monteverdi, whose *Orfeo* was performed at Mantua in 1607. Opera then spread to northern Italy, to Rome, and, twenty years afterwards, to Venice where the first commercial opera house was opened in 1637. Baroque music, though its roots lay in an 'affective' interpretation of words, not only required the cooperation of instruments – which often in the past had been merely *ad lib* – but also led to purely instrumental ensemble music including the concerto.

So the opera and the concerto were the products of the Baroque spirit. As with painting, Italy was the fountain at which the musicians of the century drank. Beside Claudio Monteverdi, Giovanni Gabrieli, who was the organist at San Marco in Venice, and Girolamo Frescobaldi, who was the organist at St Peter's, Rome, exerted considerable influence. Gabrieli's cultivation of vocal and instrumental Church music was carried on by the German Heinrich Schütz, who was not only apprenticed to Gabrieli, but later returned to Italy to sit at the feet of 'the sagacious Monteverdi'. In Holland Jan Pieterzoon Sweenlinck, like Gabrieli and Frescobaldi, was an organist (in Amsterdam); he was the acknowledged founder of the German organ school which culminated in Bach.

One characteristic of Baroque music which it shares with Baroque painting and architecture was its elaboration of ornament. Melodic line, whether for voice or for solo instrument, was lavishly embellished – if not by the composer then by the performer. The improving of ornamentation became an essential part of a musician's training. The combination of heightened emotional expression and profusion of ornament with the advance of the *basso continuo* and the purposeful progression of chords towards cadence points in definite key schemes all give Baroque music a dynamism and restless movement that contrasts with the floating, timeless serenity of the Renaissance masters.

Some historians have attempted to assign the Baroque style to specific political influences such as the Counter-Reformation or the rise of absolutism, but these attempts do not carry conviction. Many Baroque artists, composers, and writers were Protestants. The age of absolutism was not established until the later part of the century when French classicism arose and was its expression. Baroque was, above all, a fashionable style reflecting the exuberance of a golden age in European history. For fashion has always dominated the history of culture. And when men tire of one fashion, they invent another.

In considering the relations between the arts and society three questions may be asked. The first is what was the status of the arts in society; the second how far did the arts adequately reflect the society of the time; and the last is what was the historical significance of the arts within the broad history of civilisation. The position of the artist was an inferior one unless he happened to be a court painter, surveyor, or musician. Both the author and the artist were dependent on personal patronage for a livelihood. A painter like Rubens, who became a diplomatist, embraced the opportunity given him by his having a second career to gain access to important people in Europe and thus to climb to the top of Antwerp's social ladder. But Rubens was an exception and even he, we have noted, was pleased that his second wife was not ashamed that she had married a painter.

Once a royal court had set an example of patronage then commissions might come in quickly and it may well be that, measured in terms of the comparative value of money, painters did not then earn too bad a living so long as their work was in demand. Playwrights particularly needed royal patronage since theatres were few and small even in capital cities and they needed royal attendances to attract audiences; it helps today. It is said that Shakespeare earned less from writing his plays than he did from acting in them or by managing stage companies. His sonnets alone are sufficient evidence of his dependence on a patron. Corneille required the active support of Cardinal Richelieu, even though he made a name for himself in Paris with *Le Cid*. Outside the capital cities there were touring companies – for example both English and Italian comedians were to be found wandering round Holland, but theirs was not a respected profession: actors were regarded as little different from tramps and actresses were not expected to be better than they should be. Even in a home of popular art such as the United Netherlands was, painters could not be sure of a good living, however skilful their work. Franz Hals went bankrupt and died in an alms house; Rembrandt was poor in his last years, relying, it is said, on the sale of prints from his etchings and comparatively neglected by the city on which his art was to shed eternal glory. Painters were expected to enhance the prestige of the regents or Dutch ruling classes, and if the artists did not please them they might suffer deprivation.

As to the question how far artists reflected the society of their time, one may say first that our visual imagination owes much to them. Although modern research is at last beginning to illumine the lives of ordinary people, they rarely left written records and how they fared and what they suffered have to be pieced together from difficult and scattered statistics. But at least if one wants to know what they looked like one can turn to the paintings of artists like the Bruegels, the French brothers Le Nain – particularly Louis Le Nain – Georges de la Tour, Hals, Adriaen Brouwer, the Molenaers, Jan Steen, Caravaggio and El Greco (who died in 1614): from engravings and etchings we can visualise the kind of homes in which citizens and peasants used to dwell and labour. We owe much to the Dutch schools of landscape and seascape painters for our knowledge of what the United Netherlands and England and the waters in between then looked like. And for the upper classes we have an almost complete and continuous record. Rulers like Richelieu and Olivares, sovereigns like Felipe IV, Gustav Adolf, and his daughter Kristina are familiar through their portraits. In the marvellous paintings of Rubens and Rembrandt one can see precisely what the Flemish and Dutch of all classes were, how they comported themselves and how their homes were furnished. And in the plays of Shakespeare, Lope de Vega, and many lesser dramatists one can hear these people speaking. From the pages of Cervantes, say, or of a comparatively

55

unknown poet like Richard Brathwaite in England one may learn about life in the taverns and inns as ordinary persons travelled about their countries.

What is the historical significance of the arts in the civilisation of the century? To posterity it is paramount. But how much did it mean to contemporaries? To the kings and their nobility the work of painters and sculptors primarily increased their own prestige, paid tribute to their taste and wealth, gratified their families. Architecture was thought of as the art that gave permanence, glorifying some dynasty throughout the ages. Kings were able to build their own palaces as monuments: in Paris the Luxembourg, the Louvre, and the Palais Royale were resplendent in this era. As for the republicans, Amsterdam had its town hall, which still survives, but (ironically) as a royal palace. Most of the patrons, who were responsible for *hôtels* or country houses, which they planned and decorated with such care and pride, could hardly hope to live to see them completed. They remained for the delight, and sometimes the ruin, of their descendants and, like the famous cathedrals and churches, where they have survived, for the wonder of future ages and the glory of God.

But other manifestations of the arts – plays and novels, for example – must have appeared ephemeral. The poets themselves believed that their verses would never perish. But did Shakespeare or Corneille imagine that their plays, so closely wedded to the manners and tastes of their own times, performed only once or twice at court, would still be acted before groundlings in the twentieth century? The supreme object of the artist was to entertain – to practise *l'art de plaire*, as the French called it. But for us in our iron – or rather our nuclear age – we are glad to be able to recreate, as Don Quixote aimed to do, that age of gold.

CHAPTER 5

SOCIAL STRUCTURE AND ECONOMIC LIFE

The relationship between kings and their nobility, as we have already suggested, was ambivalent. On the one hand, kings feared their nobility, for in the days before standing or regular armies existed it still possessed the authority and resources to overthrow a monarchy. The civil wars in France and Sweden in the early part of the century demonstrated its threatening possibilities. Political stability therefore demanded that the nobility should at once be blandished and be kept in check. During the sixteenth century the influence of the nobility had begun to decline in most parts of Europe. With the development of musketry and the ability of royal governments to hire mercenaries it was no longer so important as a source of military strength, though nobles continued to lead or provide bands of retainers: the duc de Rohan, for example, offered King Henri IV fifteen hundred soldiers for his service, all of whom, he boasted, were his own relatives. Secondly, the net incomes of the nobility had been hit by the price revolution. For a time prices rose more quickly than rents, which could not easily or automatically be adjusted, while the extravagances of the aristocracy grew even more costly, for they were the principal consumers of manufactured goods and of imported luxuries. In France to meet their prodigal expenditure they had either to borrow or gamble or marry beneath them. Cardinal Richelieu, himself a member of the French aristocracy, thought that the nobility was becoming useless to the kingdom. Thus, once nobles were no longer needed to provide troops or had ceased to be unrivalled in their wealth or could no longer engage successfully in blackmail, they became less feared by the crowned heads of Europe and their ministers.

On the other hand, the monarchy and the nobility were bound up together. The king of France, observed Professor Tapié of Louis XIII, was 'only the first among gentlemen'. Where the monarchy was elective or a dynasty petered out, it was among the nobility that candidates for the succession might be found: in Russia, for instance, or in Portugal native nobles were preferred to foreign princes. The idea that prevailed in the days of Herodotus that the heads of the great men of the state should be sliced off by tyrants like ears of wheat in a cornfield was of course practised from time to time. Queen Elizabeth of England, a tolerant monarch, permitted her favourite, Essex, to be executed as a rebel; Henri III ordered the murder of Henri Guise; Karl IX of Sweden had Eric Sparre, an aristocratic leader, executed at the outset of the century; Prince Maurits of Orange disposed of the republican leader Oldenbarnevelt. But there were too many heads all to be conveniently cut off; and, after all, that would have meant open tyranny, a notion unacceptable, or at least surprising, in a still Christian society. For kings and nobility were, after all, part of the same social class, belonging to the predestined Great Chain of Being established by God to govern mankind. Some lines of Shakespeare from *Troilus and Cressida* (1602) have often been quoted:

> The heavens themselves, the planets and this centre
> Observe degree, priority and place . . .
> O! When degree is shak'd
> Which is the ladder of all high designs,
> The enterprise is sick . . .

To adopt a phrase from a different context, the natural view of monarchs was 'We must all hang together or we shall all hang separately.' The second alternative was chosen when the French Revolution came.

In most countries the nobility was a pretty extensive group. It ranged from a number of governing aristocrats who held sway over provinces, counties, or districts, but spent much of their time at court, to a relatively large number of country peers and country gentry who lived on their estates and looked enviously at their bigger brothers besporting themselves in the warm light of royal favour. In England at the outset of the century only some sixty peers were in existence (excluding church dignitaries), though within two generations the number had doubled owing to the 'inflation of honours'. As pillars of the court and of society, they were cherished and propped up by the Crown. But at the same time many families closely related to the peerage and owning substantial properties, 'the upper gentry', as they may be called, could be found living on their estates and wielding decisive influence both in society and in politics. In France the *hobereaux* constituted a very different class from the nobility *de l'épée*. In Spain the nobility ranged from the grandees to the humbler *caballeros*. In most countries under different names there was a *nobilitas major* and a *nobilitas minor*.

It is sometimes said that by the seventeenth century kings were deliberately seeking their ministers and advisers from another class than the nobility in order to destroy its political influence. This is not altogether true. In some countries – Spain, for example – no other class existed, except the higher clergy – and they normally came from the nobility – upon whom monarchs could draw for educated counsel and wise administration. It is true, as we have seen, that elsewhere in Europe there might be a rising bourgeoisie or even a professional class of self-made men who could reasonably be expected to provide more efficient and conscientious government servants than an enervated aristocracy. But one hesitates to say it can be proved that kings had yet consciously turned away from their established nobility for the general purposes of central government. Take the case of Henri IV of France. His principal adviser, the duc de Sully, was a leading member of the aristocracy; but he was not the king's only adviser on economic affairs; he equally depended on Barthélemy Laffemas, another Huguenot, but not out of the top drawer. But that balance of authority was scarcely deliberate. King James I of England made use of the services of the aristocratic Howard family for much of his reign, although the man who most helped to improve the royal finances was Lionel Cranfield, earl of Middlesex, a former merchant's apprentice: Middlesex was manoeuvred out of office after he had served his purpose. King Gustav Adolf of Sweden was from the very beginning of his reign dependent on the devotion of Axel Oxenstierna, a pillar of the Swedish aristocracy, though Gustav Adolf's father had preferred non-noble advisers, including a doctor. The Spanish kings had their upstart favourites, but drew on their aristocracy for advice. Kings could never afford wholly to alienate their nobility: it was contrary to tradition, to the *Zeitgeist*, to the vision of a class society. It was only in the later half of the century that one detects the beginnings of a clear policy of excluding the aristocracy from important offices and positions of real authority. The fact was that the aristocracy was capable of surviving a good deal of snubbing and temporary exclusion from power and also – as it did – a great deal of 'economic ruin'. After all, even in parliamentary England, the aristocracy continued to fill royal Cabinets right up to the end of the nineteenth century.

The bourgeoisie or burghers were the products of town life. Towns varied in their rate of development. Most capital cities were expanding. Antwerp was beginning to decline and Amsterdam was taking its place as the main port in the North Sea. The German Hanseatic towns, such as Hamburg, had also been damaged by the competition of Dutch and Danes. Venice, Milan and other Italian towns suffered a set-back and Seville did not retain its supremacy in the Atlantic for long. Though towns continued to be the sites of markets at which business was done, industry and manufacture were still carried on mainly in domestic units rather than in urban factories. The so-called industrious classes, smaller merchants, shopkeepers, artisans were probably better off than all but the richest peasants, but they did not provide the framework of a large industrial class anywhere in Europe. The most enterprising of these classes were often men who had been excluded from public life by their religion, such as the Jews and Protestants who left Roman Catholic countries where they had been subjected to severe restrictions or even persecuted. In the United Netherlands the Jews had been allowed to open their first synagogue in 1597, their second in 1639. In England the first synagogue was opened during the Protectorate of Oliver Cromwell. It is estimated that twenty thousand Jews were living in Amsterdam by the middle of the century. In Spain, in spite of the remorseless activities of the Inquisition, the *conversos* or Christianised Jews were employed in trade and the professions. But, in general, it was not from the mercantile or industrial classes that the monarchs drew their counsellors. They did, however, sometimes turn to the professions. For this was an age that also began to witness an expansion of these classes of the community. Lawyers prospered, for they now had litigation on questions of trade and industry as well as the interminable disputes over the ownership of landed property. In France the *parlements* consisted of lawyers of the Grand Robe, most of whom were officials of one kind or another. Doctors formed a rising class which was influential behind the scenes at court; because their services were so much in demand they were able to ask high fees and frequently became substantial citizens who could afford to buy estates and make investments. The increasing sale of offices by the Crown was gradually creating a new and in fact hereditary class of public servants.

In England and the United Netherlands the rise of these new classes led to some evening out of economic power in the higher-income brackets. In northern Holland few large landowners existed and wealth was well distributed among the bourgeoisie – merchants, financiers, insurers and the like. In England it seems that the landed gentry was expanding because new families were able to buy up property sold by the Crown, the Church and the nobility and were taking an active part in agricultural development, notably in sheep-farming for the sale of wool and meat. In Spain the owners of migrating sheep herds had formed themselves since the Middle Ages into a group known as the Mesta: this organisation paid a large sum to the Crown annually for the privilege of grazing their flocks all over the kingdom and thus exercised considerable political weight; it was sometimes able to prevent the use of valuable land for the efficient growing of food. (An edict of 1633 gave the Mesta jurisdiction over the whole of the pastoral industry, but it does not appear to have been enforced.) It was notable that in France when the abortive meeting of the states-general was held in 1614 it was the nobility who aimed to stop the creation of hereditary offices by the *paulette*, while the representatives of the third estate attempted to limit the number of pensions granted by the Crown to the nobility. Thus the bourgeoisie strove to check the extravagance of the nobility, while the nobility wanted to prevent the bourgeoisie from ousting them from positions of authority or profit. For it was through the sale of offices that the new nobility of the Robe was being established and expanded, while the old nobility of the Sword was realising that a political class was coming into being, astute, hard-working, ambitious, which could rival it in the favours of the monarchy. Gradually merchants, lawyers and other professional men, by their accumulation of economic power, by their willingness to concentrate on business, by their purchase of large estates and by their intermarriage with the nobility, were creating a more mobile form of society. By the second half of the century men like Colbert and Louvois in France or Clarendon and Shaftesbury in England were entering the field of government which had hitherto been largely reserved for the nobility and clergy. And since soldiers were becoming professional and the aristocracy was no longer needed to furnish troops for the royal armies, ruling society was changing its character and governments were coming to rely on an administrative and professional class that owed its position to its knowledge and experience of affairs rather than to royal whims. When Prince Willem of Orange came from the United Netherlands in 1688 to occupy the throne of England he turned for administrative experience and advice to men who had made their reputation in the service of the very king whom he had overthrown, simply because they were professionals. Earlier King Charles II of England had also found useful royal servants, such as the former merchant, Sir George Downing (after whom Downing Street in London is named) to occupy diplomatic and military posts who had earned their reputation under the regicide and usurper, Oliver Cromwell.

The new bourgeois classes were chiefly the products of commerce and industry. The United Netherlands, in spite of its lack of natural resources, comparatively small population, and limited territory was recognisably the most active centre of economic progress during the first half of the century and was the prime bourgeois achievement. Industry grew along with commercial expansion. As in most other countries, the textile or clothing industry was predominant. (One English historian wrote that 600,000 Dutchmen were employed in textiles, which is surely incredible.) Since the Dutch lacked raw materials, they concentrated on finishing processes. When the English government discovered the profits that the Dutch were making by finishing and dyeing English undressed cloth exported there, it tried to prohibit export which proved more serious for the English than the Dutch. It is said that Dutch industry flourished because high wages were paid and the workers were well fed. Sir Josiah Child, a successful English merchant, even commended the virtues of high wages on the Dutch model; so later did Daniel Defoe. But this was not the general view. Moreover in Leiden, the leading textile centre in the United Netherlands, much child labour was employed and since wages were kept down by the gilds, occasional strikes occurred, as in 1637, 1643 and 1648.

In England too the textile industry was the most important and its products ranged from heavy cloth manufactured in Lancashire and Yorkshire to the light draperies of Devon and East Anglia. In spite of setbacks the textile industries made considerable progress during the century and were the principal source of English exports. But England also possessed certain natural sources for industrial development, notably coal, iron and tin. In 1640 it is estimated that England produced more coal than the whole of the rest of Europe put together. The state had an interest in mining, especially of iron, and ever since the reign of Queen Elizabeth I had tried to enforce industrial regulation, particularly in regard to wage rates and rules of apprenticeship.

France was another country where industrial progress was recorded. She too possessed a variety of natural resources and in the reign of Henri IV the government intervened actively to stimulate industry. Besides textiles, metal, glass and tapestry manufacture flourished, although there was some dispute among the advisers of the king whether luxury industries ought to be encouraged. An ordinance of 1587 had attempted detailed regulation of the conditions of work in industry, and in a decree of 1597 this was extended to commercial undertakings. These regulations were probably honoured in the letter rather than in the spirit. After the United Netherlands, in proportion to its population and resources, England and France were undoubtedly the chief industrial countries. Professor Nef has written that by the reign of King Charles II England was on the point of becoming the leading country in Europe for mining and heavy manufactures, while France, though owning a number of light industries, produced less coal, copper or tin than England and relatively less woollen cloth. In England the nobility invested in industry and even intermarried with industrialists, whereas in France they were slower to demean themselves. On the whole, English industry – outside the coal and iron mines, and certain other businesses like brewing and soap-boiling – was carried on by a 'putting-out' or 'domestic' system in which the masters were usually considerate towards their work-people, ruling them, housing them, and feeding them. But many unapprenticed workers were to be found and the gilds were unable to exercise much control outside the towns. Both in France and in England wages at the outset of the century lagged behind prices, although later real wages improved. It was not practical to keep down wages by law when labour was in demand; and in fact in England the justices of the Peace, who prescribed wage scales, recognised as much. In France workers sometimes demonstrated against officials who tried to prevent wages from rising; but in England where wage rates were minimal 'workmen sometimes struck to remind officials of their duty' (Nef).

Industry in Spain had been stimulated by the growth of empire. In the sixteenth century metal, ceramics, leather, silk and textile industries existed as well as such specialities as Toledo blades. The textile industry was largely concentrated in northern Castile. But it was soon discovered that Spanish industry was insufficiently developed to meet all the needs of the home market or of the colonies. The exceptionally severe impact of inflation upon Spain in the early half of the century (owing in part to debasements of the coinage) meant that industrial wages became unattractive, while the Dutch and the English became able to compete with Spanish exports in markets outside Europe. In Italy a period of disastrous decline for industry set in during this century, even in the silks for which northern and central Italy were justly famous. For example, the number of bales of woollen cloth produced in Venice fell by one-tenth before the end of the century. In Milan the number of pieces of cloth fell to practically nothing. In Genoa the number of silk looms, which had reached eighteen thousand in the sixteenth century, was fewer than three thousand in 1675. It is suggested that Italian costs of production were too high, while former markets in Spain and Germany were lost owing to foreign competition and wars. Unquestionably Italian industry, which was dependent on exports, was hit hard not only by competition but also by import restrictions imposed elsewhere.

In the Scandinavian countries and Russia industry was not very far advanced. The success of the Dutch persuaded the governments of these countries to invite experts from the United Netherlands to help them with their economic development. In Sweden, for example, where the iron and copper industries were old established, a Dutch financier, Lodewijk de Geer, was welcomed and was highly successful. Armament industries were founded which helped King Gustav Adolf (and later Pyëtr the Great) in his military campaigns. France and England welcomed Dutch engineers to advise them on canals and land reclamation, while a Dutchman was allowed to lease royal mines in Uppsala. The products of the Swedish mines helped to pay for essential and non-essential imports. Norway was another country that had to export in order to buy necessities. Broadly we may compare Europe of that time with much of the world today which welcomes American experts to develop its industries.

Although the craft gild system had existed everywhere in Europe during the late Middle Ages, attempts were made to strengthen it in the first half of the seventeenth century because governments were unable to see any other method of controlling standards in expanding or large-scale industries, while freedom from regulation was thought to be socially irresponsible. The three most industrialised countries, the United Netherlands, France and England, all tried to invigorate the gild system. The idea was that craft gilds could ensure standards of workmanship and prevent wages from getting out of hand. In France the enforcement of gild regulations caused rioting and in large parts of England they were ignored. The gild regulations generally aimed at prescribing prices and wages, at insisting on the number of years of apprenticeship that had to be served (usually seven) and at preventing even men who had served their apprenticeship – 'journey-men' – from becoming masters for another three years or so and even then only if they had produced a 'masterpiece'. These rules often proved unworkable, caused industrial discontent, and handicapped economic progress, particularly, it seems, in Italy. But throughout Europe the gilds continued. They had originally been introduced into the Netherlands from Germany. In France they became systematised by the decrees of Henri iv. In England they were supported by the Act of Artificers of 1563. But they could only function successfully in towns and even there they often competed with one another. In a considerable number of industries, such as coal-mining and iron-mining, ship-building and brewing they were inapplicable and special regulations for these industries had to be laid down. But much industry remained domestic, carried on by small groups of people working in private houses. Thus during the century gild regulations became increasingly unpopular and unmanageable. And in the more advanced countries they were disappearing before the century was over.

Commerce also progressed during the century in spite of regulations and restrictions to which it was subjected by governments. England, France and the United Netherlands were now joining in the empire-building begun by Portugal and Spain. The prime object of empire was to lay hold of precious metals, such as had been discovered in Central and South America, but once colonisation had begun in earnest it was realised that other commodities were worth bringing over to Europe. Before the discovery of the New World the Baltic countries had been the sources from which the necessary materials for ship-building and war-making, such as timber, hemp and saltpetre, were drawn. The Danes and the Dutch largely controlled this valuable business – the Danes by their command of the Sound, the Dutch by the provision of merchant vessels suited to the Baltic trade. In 1602 the Dutch founded their monopolistic East India Company and profited substantially from the importation of pepper and spices. A West India Company followed in 1621. England also had its East India Company, dating from the beginning of the century, and various attempts were made to trade with the West Indies, although not much progress was achieved until after the capture of Jamaica from the Spaniards in 1655. The French later joined in the colonial scramble, but were never behindhand in privateering and piracy. The Swedes in 1626 planned a West India Company on Dutch advice. The Dutch not only showed immense enterprise, being the first to introduce the joint-stock principle in their trading ventures, while their commercial voyages reached out as far as Java, Ceylon, India and Japan; they also developed their shipping to such an extent that they became the carriers of much of the commerce of Europe. Amsterdam was the world's biggest entrepot where goods were bought and sold from everywhere, and by 1648 the Dutch were unquestionably the busiest traders in the world. But England did not lag far behind. A series of navigation acts was introduced to restrict the employment of Dutch shipping, and although British importers continued to depend on the Dutch for the Baltic trade, the number of Dutch ships calling at English ports diminished as the century advanced. After the middle of the century commercial rivalry led to war between the two countries, the first wars waged mainly for economic reasons in European history. English merchants began to import materials for ship-building from the North American colonies (to supplement those obtained from the Baltic) and also found sugar and tobacco profitable imports that could be resold. Gradually a big business in re-exports developed in London. By the beginning of the eighteenth century British exports had multiplied fourfold as compared with the middle of the previous century.

Other countries tried to sell their own specialities or superfluities abroad. France exported wine and brandy and since, except during periods of bad harvests, she was more than self-sufficient in foodstuffs, she did a good deal of business with Spain, whose arable land was limited, when the two kingdoms were not at war. The Dutch exported dairy products and smoked and salted fish. The Germans exported minerals and sold wheat to Holland. England sold spirits (aqua-vitae) abroad, beer to Germany and dried cod to Portugal, and sold cloth, tin and other minerals throughout Europe as well as outside it. Until their decline set in, the Italian silk industries exported to France, Spain, Germany and elsewhere. The biggest Spanish export was merino wool which was used both in England and Holland for the richer types of clothing.

It is difficult to measure the extent of commerce within Europe. It has been suggested that imports consisted mostly of luxury goods – or what were then regarded by governments as luxuries – such as silks, spices, wines, gold and silver lace and thread, and jewellery. Attempts were made to restrict such imports, but tariff wars, which were frequent, often ended in the negotiation of commercial treaties. These allowed, for example, the introduction of French, Spanish and Portuguese wines into England where they were widely drunk at court and by the gentry classes. If sherry and port spread all over the world, the non-alcoholic drinks of tea, coffee and chocolate also began to come in from the East Indies and Africa. Doctors at first recommended tea as a kind of medicine, while before the century ended coffee-houses were becoming popular in civilised countries. They were one of de Geer's sidelines in Sweden.

While most commerce remained in private hands, governments were not averse from encouraging exports and obtaining what profit they could from them, notably by the granting of charters, which meant in effect the conferring of monopolies, whether the companies concerned were 'regulated' or 'joint-stock'. In England King James I hoped to take money from the monopolistic scheme of concentrating textile exports on finished products; in France Cardinal Richelieu regarded commerce as a means for developing French shipping and raising the money needed for war. For the Dutch commerce was a life-line. Indeed even during their wars with Spain, Dutch shipping was used to assist in the trade between the Spanish homeland and its overseas empire and to bring in essential imports from the Baltic. The Dutch exchequer was replenished by the convoy-and-licence money that it charged for bringing its enemy's goods from the Scandinavian countries.

How far did governments contribute to the advancement of industry and commerce? On paper a great deal. Decrees were regularly published relating to the establishment and management of trading companies and to the upholding of the system of control by the gilds. But without good communications and a proper police force these rules and regulations were hard to enforce outside small and close urban settlements. Smuggling was widespread throughout Europe and could not be stopped; and it probably makes nonsense of such trading figures as we possess. Corruption was everywhere; it is clear, for example, that much of the Spanish silver from the Americas never reached the authorities at Seville.

The theory that lay behind many of the decrees of government was described by Adam Smith in the eighteenth century and by the liberal economists and economic historians of the nineteenth century as 'mercantilism'. Now it is true that in the seventeenth century the amassing of treasure by a single country became a conscious aim of policy. But a distinction is to be drawn between 'bullionism' – meaning clinging to such precious metals as a country possessed – and 'mercantilism' – meaning that governments encouraged such trade as brought in treasure and discouraged the purchase of imports that required its expenditure. 'The means of enriching a state,' observed Sully, 'is to draw in gold and silver and to prevent it getting out.' Hence French cereals were sold abroad for coin and the import of luxury goods was proscribed. This 'mercantilism' was, however, merely a less refined version of policies that all governments anxious to maintain their balance of payments practise today. 'It is always better to sell goods to others than to buy goods from them' : is that declaration not redolent of our own time? Nowadays high import duties are usually imposed throughout the world on luxury goods, which are at times even prohibited altogether. The same thing happened then. Not only was the importation of so-called luxuries restrained, but the wearing of rich apparel was frowned upon – even in prosperous realms like Spain and France – although such frowns were frequently ignored at royal courts. Foreign rarities were fashionable and conspicuous consumption never easily checked.

Intelligent writers on economic affairs realised that wealth could only be increased by an active foreign trade. Pieter de la Court in Holland noted that several countries, not only in the Far East but also in the Baltic, which supplied valuable goods, could not be traded with 'but by gold and silver' and in fact the Dutch imposed few restrictions upon the export of coin. In England Thomas Mun, writing in 1624, said that 'the ordinary means to increase our wealth and treasure is by foreign trade' and to trade with the East Indies required the export of bullion. This worked out in practice. Spain, whose export business declined, lost much of its precious metals by borrowing from abroad to pay for needed imports; the English and the Dutch, who had no precious metals, obtained them by buying scarce goods in Asia and selling them profitably elsewhere in Europe.

It has been contended that 'mercantilism' was a gospel of state power aimed at national unification. Rulers, it is said, adopted a nationalistic economic policy, involving the suppression of internal customs duties and the imposition of heavy duties upon imports as a method of building a nation. But if anything, the gospel was one not of power and plenty but of enforced scarcity. Professor Hecksher quoted the French economist Montchrétien, writing in 1615, to the effect that 'the brightness of the lamp is dimmed if it is too plentifully filled with oil' and later Nicholas Barbon who spoke of 'a dead stock called plenty'. The object was to cut down imports at all costs while people at home tightened their belts. It is likely that some governments permitted the export of foodstuffs while the peasantry were on the verge of starvation. Consistently with the doctrine of restricting consumption, mercantilist writers welcomed high prices. Consistently with it too, they pleaded for larger populations. The export of money, they believed, was a cause of depopulation and unemployment: more hands were needed to speed the plough at home and to produce goods for sale abroad. The state took action to promote 'infant industries', again so as to increase exports or diminish imports. Crude protectionism was a more or less universally accepted doctrine in seventeenth-century Europe.

If in theory the thinking of governments and their economic advisers was in agreement on the virtues of promoting exports and restricting imports, practising merchants mostly sought for greater freedom in buying and selling, although they looked to authority to prevent foreign competition. But everywhere merchants realised that peace was conducive to trade: that is clear from the writings and pleadings of most economic pamphleteers of the time. Governments, however, usually put war before trade. Only during the opening years of the century was Europe relatively free from wars, yet they rarely helped commerce as a whole and frequently interfered with industry. It is remarkable, in fact, how much economic progress did take place when not only foreign wars but civil wars were common.

Although the progress of trade and industry was one of the distinguishing marks of the century, the economy of practically every country was ultimately based on agriculture and therefore on the peasantry. As Professor Michael Roberts has justly observed:

> The power of the monarchy, the wealth of the aristocracy, the stipends of the clergy and the prosperity of the towns were all as dependent on the good management of the land and the vagaries of the weather as was the life and well-being of the tax-paying peasant farming his own few acres.

In most countries about half the soil was in agricultural use but invariably in a primitive way. Even the rich soil of France was subject to a three-year and sometimes a two-year rotation which required the land to be left fallow for long periods. In Spain and part of France and England arable farming was made to yield place to the needs of pasturage. Although the Dutch became expert in the reclamation of soil from the sea and their knowledge was borrowed elsewhere, notably in France and England, for work of this kind, the techniques for improving poorer lands did not exist and that was why large areas of Europe were left uncultivated. Comparatively few fertilisers were used – seaweed and ashes were among the commoner ones – and manure was always scarce. In spite of the new demand for agricultural produce created by the growth of trade and industry – and later by standing armies – it is doubtful if output increased at all, at any rate in western Europe; in the east the enlargement of servile estates may have increased production, but only to a limited degree.

The peasants, on whom output depended, were, except for a relatively few well-to-do freeholders or tenant farmers, generally living on a bare margin of subsistence. In Sweden their staple diet was porridge, coarse bread, turnips and beer. In Russia serf agriculture meant a minimum standard of living. In France rye bread, butter, beans, turnips, soup and thin wine, but more usually water made up a peasant's meal and that in a country where the peasants were energetic and the land good. In England bread, cheese and ale was the main diet, supplemented occasionally by poached game. In the United Netherlands bread, butter, cheese and vegetables comprised the normal diet and 'a fried egg was the consolation of a poor man'. Where the land was within easy reach of the sea or of well-stocked rivers, fish would be eaten – a painting by Nicolaes Maes shows an old peasant woman praying over a salmon cutlet – but nowhere in Europe did the peasants normally eat meat. In richer countries like England and France they might do so occasionally where a pig was kept, but the meat would not always be fresh and in winter was almost unobtainable. Food shortages or famines were frequent in rural areas, and in France in particular peasants revolted from time to time because they were not allowed to retain enough of their own produce. In Spain, writes John Elliott, 'the rich ate, and ate to excess, watched by a thousand hungry eyes as they consumed their gargantuan meals. The rest of the population starved.' Hunger was an ever-present menace elsewhere in Europe whenever harvests were poor. No wonder that little love was lost between the peasantry and the rising middle classes who could afford to preen and stuff themselves as they made their way up in the world. Charles Normand, the French historian, observed that the 'cavalier familiarity of the nobility was less insupportable to the poor and humble than the disdainful arrogance of the bourgeoisie solidly wrapped in their bleak clothes and prejudices'.

What effect had the 'price revolution' on the different classes of society at the beginning of the century? The revolution was one of the most startling facts about the economic history of the previous century, for it appears that in most European countries prices rose four, five and even sixfold between 1500 and 1600. The main cause was undoubtedly the inflow of precious metals from the Americas: prices first rose in Andalusia and then increased throughout Spain, and the Spanish empire in Europe, and finally throughout the rest of Europe. Another important factor was what has been called a 'population explosion' that took place in the later part of the sixteenth century. The growth of trade and industry also stimulated the demand for coins and currency and it cannot be doubted that moans about shortage of money were genuine. Financial difficulties caused governments to debase or devalue their coinage. The output of silver and gold reaching Europe attained its peak about the turn of the century, but did not begin to fall substantially for another thirty years. Prices continued to rise slowly throughout the first half of the new century, in England reaching their highest point in 1638, with severe fluctuations both in the 'twenties and 'thirties. The value of money was always complicated too by the bimetallic standard that prevailed.

This phenomenon of continually rising prices, or inflation as it is now called, was remarked upon by contemporary writers who tended to regard it as a bad thing. It does not appear, however, to have been injurious to the peasantry, the base upon which the entire social pyramid lay. The reason for this was that in most parts of Europe, as we have observed, the ordinary agricultural worker lived upon a marginal subsistence level. Thus when there was full employment and an increasing demand for food from the towns the earnings of the peasants naturally kept pace with prices. In England though real wages fell during the first decade of the century, they caught up later with prices and actually rose during the 1630s and 1640s. Why then the peasant revolts in France? The answer is that these were revolts against taxation: no doubt the peasants were even more conscious of the iniquities of the *tailles* and the *gabelle* at a time when the demand for their products was growing. Also, owing to poor communications (roads were bad everywhere) the peasantry in many European countries faced starvation whenever their own harvest failed because they could not be helped by supplies quickly brought in from more fortunate areas. If the French peasantry suffered famine from time to time, the situation was even worse in Russia and eastern Europe where famines were endemic. Frequent plagues were another cause of the misery of French and other peasants, for these, rather surprisingly, are said to have hit the countryside worse than the towns.

Writing about the price revolution in 1620, Scipion de Gramont in his *Le dernier royal* noted that 'the debtor gained what the creditor lost'. French historians tend to accept the view that the nobility suffered from the price revolution; and because what they bought cost them more while their rents were not easily raised (tenants crushed by taxation could not be squeezed) they were obliged to sell land to the rising bourgeoisie. In England rents were beginning to catch up with or even overtake prices in the first half of the century, but the extravagance of the nobility was more conspicuous in the reign of King James 1 than it had been in that of Queen Elizabeth 1. How far the aristocracy was selling its land is disputed, but that the bourgeoisie and the gentry were improving their economic position is quite clear. Perhaps it was governments, as the biggest creditors, who were most injured by the price revolution and that was why they tried to recoup themselves by selling land, raising taxes, and, above all, through auctioning offices.

Offices of every sort were lavishly sold by Henri IV of France and King James I of England instead of being given away as in earlier times. The middle and professional classes competed to buy them, both for reasons of prestige and possible profit, and thus their prices rose. In France the nobility in the states-general, in Spain in the cortes protested against the increasing sale of public offices, but the practice, so helpful to the finding of ready money for the Crown, was extended throughout Europe – in Paris, Madrid, London, Rome, Stockholm; only in the United Netherlands was there an exception to the rule. In France, in spite of doubts expressed by Richelieu and Mazarin, the practice was not halted until Colbert took over in the 1660s. It was said that 'as soon as the king institutes an office, God creates a fool to buy it.' K. W. Swart, who examined the practice throughout Europe in an essay on the sale of offices in the century, reached the conclusion that it 'became a systematic policy in Europe with the rise of absolutism'.

Sale of offices was one means of anticipating revenue. Another was to raise short-term loans, for example by tax-farming, or longer-term loans, such as the *rentes* in France, the *juros* in Spain or the *monti* in Rome. But methods of anticipating revenue used by governments in the first half of the century were primitive compared with later times. Interest rates were high (outside the United Netherlands) and state bankruptcy was faced because interest could not be paid when it was due. Much has been written about the difficulties of European governments in raising money to pay for their wars and about the burden of taxation that resulted. This burden owed less to its amount than to the fact that it was unfairly distributed. For though governments usually failed to balance their budgets – even in careful Holland – if the methods of raising taxes and anticipating revenues had been more efficient, there would have been no real problem about finding the money.

The historian has to realise and try to show that while the political, economic and social challenges of the past and the answers to them were not always so different from those of our own age, the character and the habits of the society about which he is writing and some of the assumptions upon which it worked were different. Inflation, high taxes, high prices, social inequalities are matters that are easy for us to understand and to sympathise with, for we have lived through them all. Even hunger is familiar to us not so much in Europe as in parts of Asia, Africa and Latin America. What is different is the huge gap that then

71

existed everywhere between the lives of the rich and poor – though even that may still be witnessed in some parts of Europe, say, southern Italy or Greece. Bad harvests, periods of starvation or near-starvation, widespread plagues and epidemics were common experiences in the first half of the seventeenth century. It was a gamble whether a new-born child would survive the age of one. Birth-rates and death-rates were high. The average expectation of life at birth was thirty or thirty-five years at most. Literacy was still confined to a minority and primary education was far from universal. Women and children were expected to work all day long to maintain a mere minimum standard of family subsistence. Wives had little or no education and were supposed slavishly to obey their husbands. Clever or ambitious women were frowned upon. Cardinal Mazarin once remarked how much better off the Spaniards were than the French because their women did not meddle, they only made love. But such remarks applied solely to the upper classes. For ordinary women love soon passed. They had to toil in their fields alongside their husbands till their health broke, except during the short period when they were bearing children. For all, disease and malnutrition were the enemies; only the well-to-do could afford doctors. The bulk of mankind was dependent on good luck and good weather to enjoy what life had to offer.

CHAPTER 6

SCIENCE AND RELIGION

'The modern world, so far as mental outlook is concerned,' wrote Bertrand Russell, 'begins in the seventeenth century.' The Europe of the Renaissance, he pointed out, would have been perfectly intelligible to Aristotle or to Aquinas. In spite of the humanistic discoveries which had such a revolutionary effect on the arts, the sixteenth century had been absorbed in theological questions and the divisions between the different kinds of Christianity, while the assumptions about the nature of the universe had remained much the same as in the Middle Ages. It was only gradually that the impact of inventions took effect – such as those of printing and the mariner's compass. The discoveries of explorers like Columbus, the Cabots, and Francis Drake, however, slowly opened men's minds to the size of the world and to the existence in it of a diversity of religious beliefs, while the telescope revealed the vastness of the universe.

It was in fact the rise of modern science that undermined the traditional scholastic conceptions and caused the hitherto virtually unchallenged authority of the Greek genius to be questioned. Among the sciences which brought about the change were astronomy and physics. Copernicus, by birth a Pole, who became a canon of the Roman Catholic Church, had first discovered or revived a heliocentric theory. He came to believe that the earth did an annual revolution round the sun. But this theory was not published until the year of his death, 1543, and was then said to have been purely an hypothesis. At the beginning of the seventeenth century, however, two other astronomers, Tycho Brahé, a Dane, and Johann Kepler, a German, who was for a time his assistant, brought the heliocentric theory into the realm of reality. Brahé employed instruments but not the telescope in making his calculations; Kepler, who was a mathematician and was influenced by the discoveries of William Gilbert, an Englishman, about magnetism, was able to show that the planets travelled on an elliptical course. His speculations about Mars were published in 1609. In the same year Galileo Galilei, who had heard of the invention of the refractory telescope in Holland, made one himself in order to study the stars and planets in the Milky Way and indicated that they obeyed Copernicus's laws. Not only was Galileo a practitioner of descriptive astronomy but he contributed importantly to the discovery of gravitation. Galileo corresponded with Kepler and together they mocked at philosophers of the old school who tried to conjure away the new facts of science. Thus before the middle of the century astronomy had made rapid progress.

In physics Galileo's outstanding innovation related to inertia; he maintained that a terrestrial body, once moved, continues in a straight line with uniform velocity unless interfered with. This principle was called by Newton the first law of motion. These two scientific discoveries, first that the earth rotated elliptically round the sun, secondly that a terrestrial body moved in a straight line with uniform velocity, were entirely contrary to the teaching of earlier times. Aristotle and Ptolemy, the Egyptian astronomer of the second century AD, had believed that the earth was the centre of the universe, that it lay motionless at the heart of a system of spheres and that everything circulated round it. The world of man consisted of four elements, fire, water, air and earth, but everything above the moon, which, it was believed, was attached to one of the spheres, consisted of a fifth element, mysterious and insubstantial. To the Greeks the celestial orbs were gods or related to the gods and to medieval Christians their God dwelt somewhere in the magical sky. Thus the idea that the earth was but one planet rotating in the universe was revolutionary and shocking. So too the law of inertia was a complete departure from scholastic conceptions. Aristotle had laid it down that bodies were dispatched on their way by a mover which did not itself move. When the mover ceased to operate and the initial impulse was exhausted the body dropped to earth or came to rest. The unmoved mover was God himself. The new theory of impetus did, however, admit that a projectile would drop after the impetus was exhausted; but in the case of the planets the impulse never did exhaust itself and thus they continued rotating. So God wound things up and they went on for ever. Such was the origination of the mechanical theories which were to become dominant in scientific thinking later in the century.

These revolutionary theories were not accepted at all readily by the Church. Militant Roman Catholicism, which had manifested itself at the council of Trent, was not lightly going to abandon a view of the universe that had been basic to it for centuries. Copernicus might have got away with his theories by explaining that they were mere hypotheses and by dedicating his posthumous book to the pope. But he died before their full impact was realised. Giordano Bruno, the Italian philosopher, who accepted the Copernican ideas and spoke of a plurality of worlds, was burnt by the Inquisition; Galileo was condemned privately in 1616 and publicly in 1633, and had to recant to avert being burnt. Kepler, a Protestant, was persecuted by the Theological Faculty of the university of Tübingen, while the university of Padua, where many of the scientists of the early part of the century were active, did not take at all kindly to the abandonment of Aristotelianism. Though William Harvey at Padua showed that another classical scientist, Galen, was as wrong over anatomy, or at least over the circulation of the blood as Ptolemy had been over astronomy, it was a very long time before Harvey's views were accepted and began to reshape medical science. But nevertheless the scientific achievements of the first half of the century were remarkable. Two Englishmen, Gilbert and Harvey, contributed much to the evolution of 'natural philosophy'. Dutchmen, Frenchmen and Italians were prominent as mathematicians and physicists. The scientific revolution was not confined to any one country or group of countries.

This period therefore saw the dawn of modern science, both theoretically in the advance of mathematics and pure physics, and practically through the invention, mainly in the United Netherlands, of the microscope, the telescope, the thermometer, the barometer and the pendulum clock. Science had repercussions not only on established religion but also upon philosophy in its modern sense. And it was above all in the virile Protestant countries, like the United Netherlands and England, that further philosophical progress occurred. For Spain and Italy still shuddered under the menace of the Inquisition. France gradually became uncomfortable for scientists. Germany was to be beset by the conflict of faiths in the 'Thirty Years War'.

Naturally the break with traditional concepts was neither sharp, easy, nor immediately complete. But some scientists began to look at the universe in an entirely new way. Galileo, absorbed in his experiments and calculations, was unmoved by the fact that his conclusions did not square with those of St Thomas Aquinas. Harvey was an indifferent Christian. Gradually the leaders of European thought abandoned the old scholastic controversies for a genuine search into the true nature of things, stimulated by the discoveries and inventions of recent times. In England Francis Bacon boldly asserted that 'the philosophy principally received from the Greeks must be acknowledged puerile.' The views of Bacon (1561–1626), who was not only lord chancellor of England but a master of lucid prose, had in the long run a profound influence upon the thinking of his contemporaries, although he was much more of a theorist than a practical scientist and had by no means entirely divorced himself from old-fashioned ways of arguing. He believed that generalisation could only be reached after a large number of experiments, but did not altogether recognise that the mere grouping of the results of experiments might be fruitless if they were not based upon a workable hypothesis. The form of induction that he advocated has been described as in fact resting upon the metaphysical assumptions of scholastic formalism. Nevertheless he laid stress upon the importance of investigating the corporeal world and taking nothing for granted. The mind, he said, must be washed clean of opinions; man's object must be 'not to conjecture and guess, but to find out and know'.

Though Bacon himself was less influenced than might have been expected by contemporary scientists, even by Englishmen of his time who were actually carrying out the experiments which he advocated, as were Gilbert and Harvey, it was the conscious development of modern scientific attitudes that had a decisive effect on the evolution of philosophy. Methodological reflection was opposed to the old scholastic assumptions. Emphasis was laid alike by Bacon and by the French philosopher, René Descartes (1596–1650) on a correct method of investigation, and thus a theory of knowledge arose. While Bacon pleaded for empiricism, Descartes preferred the deductive reasoning provided by a mathematical approach. But both aimed to start with a *tabula rasa*. Descartes adopted 'the method of doubt' which involved the provisional denial of whatsoever was not clearly and distinctly conceived. In using this method he concluded that the one indubitable proposition was 'I think, therefore I am'. He thus established the existence of the thinking self and from that proceeded to prove the existence of God. One proof consisted of the argument that only a perfect being could have caused the idea in his mind of a perfect being. Another proof was the famous ontological argument used earlier by St Anselm. This was that the very conception of a perfect being necessitated the existence of the perfect being since existence is a perfection. To pursue his reflections without interruption Descartes settled down in a stove-heated room in Germany 'undistractedly at leisure, moved to communing with his own thoughts'. Here during his period of apprenticeship he studied particular questions in mathematics and physics and reached his general views on intuition, clear and distinct ideas, and on the unity of science by a mathematical method. It was ten years later in Holland that he reached his final proofs of the existence of God, derived from the conception of distinct or 'innate' ideas.

Descartes was, like most seventeenth-century philosophers, also a good mathematician and a scientist. In mathematics he contributed to the invention of co-ordinate geometry; in science he welcomed the physiological discoveries of William Harvey. He believed that men's bodies worked according to the laws of physics but he never satisfactorily resolved the relationship between body and mind. Although he held that mind and body were distinct in essence, nevertheless in human beings they form a marvellous, intimate union arranged by God's will. His Dutch follower, Geulincx, invented an ingenious theory that the body and mind operated simultaneously but independently, both being set off like clocks by the orders of God. Thus though so far as his method went Descartes was a founder of rationalism, in much of his reasoning he differed little from the scholastics. Indeed, as we have seen, the ontological argument had been used by St Anselm. Though the Cartesian method gave the required result, it was the method which was more significant than the result. Indeed the sceptical method of Bacon and Descartes had one curious consequence. Some later thinkers like Pascal were able to argue that if empirical and rational methods were so unproductive of certainties, it was wiser to rely upon one's feeling rather than one's reasoning for the reality of religious faith.

The fact was of course that both scientific experiments and mathematical reasoning were necessary for the progress of knowledge. Christian Huygens, the Dutch scientist and, after Isaac Newton, probably the greatest in the second half of the century, criticised Bacon for failing to employ a genuinely mathematical method of reasoning and blamed Descartes for failing to carry out scientific experiments. But the inductive procedure which Bacon admired and the mathematical reasoning which Descartes and his followers pursued were in the long run to work together, if not in reaching convincing philosophical conclusions, at least in helping to advance physics. Before the century ended the majority of scientists accepted a mechanical explanation of the working of the universe and God had ceased to be Aristotle's unmoved mover and had become instead a divine clockmaker.

In the earlier part of the century the majority of European thinkers, however much they might have been persuaded decisively to break with scholastic teaching, were reluctant to admit, at least openly, that the concepts of traditional Christianity had been undermined by the discoveries of science. Instead they managed to separate what must be believed from what could be proved. Indeed many scientists have continued to do this ever since. It was not only Descartes who drew a distinction between the human mind which was innately convinced of the existence of God and a body that worked upon mechanical principles. Bacon sharply distinguished between religious revelation on the one hand and philosophy on the other. The first dealt, he thought, with religious truths, the second with knowledge that could be gained by rational and experimental methods: 'Sacred theology,' he wrote, 'must be drawn from the word and oracle of God not from the light of nature or the dictates of reason.' One must, he said, believe the word of God even if reason were shocked by it. Sir Thomas Browne, an English doctor and author, observed that 'many things are true in divinity which are neither inducible by reason or confirmable by sense'. Even in Descartes, the supreme rationalist, there was, as Bertrand Russell points out, an unresolved dualism between what he learned from contemporary science and what he had been taught at the Jesuit college where he had been educated. He remained a loyal Catholic and was proud of his proofs of the existence of God. Many of the finest minds of the century – in England a clergyman like John Donne or a Puritan poet like John Milton – became increasingly conscious of the divergence between the religious atmosphere in which they had been brought up and which it seemed so terribly important to get exactly right, and the scientific methods of thinking and reasoning that were rapidly destroying the teaching of the Middle Ages. Further there was also among some people a growing doubt whether the Christian God was the only God. Descartes, for example, was aware that other gods were worshipped by the Mexicans and the Chinese. Lord Herbert of Cherburg as early as 1626 put the case for deism as distinct from Christianity.

Yet theological divisions were still a matter of concern in themselves to Christian statesmen and leaders of European opinion. Taking the existence of God for granted, they were perplexed over the way in which he ought to be worshipped. Germany, which at the time of the treaty of Augsburg, was satisfied to split itself between Roman Catholics and Lutheran Protestants according to the wishes of the individual rulers, was now confused by the rapid advance of Calvinism. The differences between the various kinds of Christian religion (ranging as far as Quietism, Anabaptism, and Quakerism) which shaped late sixteenth and seventeenth-century history were as much organisational as doctrinal. Yet the organisational differences usually arose out of doctrinal preferences. Martin Luther, a German monk who was the original rebel against the Roman Catholic Church, had preached the doctrine that if a man had faith, he had all. The ceremonies of the Church, in his opinion, might be helpful for spiritual education, but priests and services could not of themselves make men good. Thus the true priesthood consisted of all believers. This doctrine therefore placed limitations upon the powers of the Church and thereby indirectly strengthened the hand of the state. And although logically Lutheranism might have seemed to spell out some kind of egalitarianism or democracy, in fact Luther was appalled at the peasant revolts in Germany and lent his influence to upholding the authority of those German governments that embraced his Protestant religion. Starting from the doctrine of justification by faith, Luther worked upwards to the thrones not only of God but of men.

John Calvin, a Frenchman, on the other hand, started from the majesty of the Almighty. Man, he said, was sinful by nature and if he were to be saved, it was purely through the grace of God. Man could do nothing to promote his own salvation, and therefore Calvin agreed with Luther over the superfluity of priests and of ceremonial services. Preaching and prayer were needed; but since it was God's decree that had fixed the number of those who were to be saved, his chosen people could show forth their salvation in their lives. Thus ultimately it was the chosen people who must rule. Therefore, surprisingly perhaps in view of the kind of dictatorship that Calvin himself exercised in Geneva, Calvinism proved to be a more democratic or at any rate more socially destructive influence than Lutheranism. The Calvinist saints were often rebel leaders. By beginning with God's sovereignty and working downwards Calvin conferred authority on the elect and on the rulers of the churches, for which he worked out a hierarchical pattern, and in consequence the Calvinist Church became a stronger and more effective force among European countries and in European society as a whole than the Lutheran did.

Luther, it has been said, pulled down the walls of Babylon, but Calvin built the ramparts of a new Zion. Calvinism was a more challenging, more radical, and more hostile faith. In Germany it made proselytes including three electors – the Elector Palatine, the Elector of Saxony, and the Elector of Brandenburg. It also became the ruling faith of the Dutch Reformed Church, of the Scottish Kirk, and among the Swiss. But Calvin's teaching penetrated even farther. The French Huguenots, who were a running sore in the side of the last Valois kings and of Louis XIII and his ministers, were Calvinists; and Calvinism made progress in greater or smaller degrees among the Poles, Czechs, Hungarians and Austrians. Lutheranism still prevailed in large parts of Germany, in the Scandinavian countries and in England. But while the Calvinist doctrines were more or less universally accepted in the English Church at the time of the death of Queen Elizabeth I, its organisational programme was not acceptable to King James I, although he had come from Scotland where Presbyterianism ruled. In fact it was because of the high claims of the Scottish Kirk in relation to the monarchy that the presbyters were anathema to the king in London. Because of the support given both by Queen Elizabeth I and by James I (and later by his son, Charles I) many remnants of Roman Catholic ceremonies, services and practices still existed and were subject to criticism by the more extreme English Calvinists who wished to purify the Church of them and were thus known as Puritans. But not all Puritans wanted to go so far as to abolish the bishops; some merely desired to deprive them of their secular rights. But James regarded the bishops, as he did his judges, as lions under the throne, and, so long as he reigned, the Puritans achieved only limited progress in England.

In the United Netherlands, on the other hand, the divisions which developed in the Reformed Church during the first half of the century, were doctrinal rather than organisational. A fierce controversy developed between two professors of theology at the university of Leiden, named Gomarus and Arminius. Arminius was a fairly mild man and the controversy did not reach boiling point until after he died in 1609. Then a number of his friends remonstrated against the prevailing doctrines of the Reformed Church. As the truce with Spain was concluded in 1609 a period of intense theological and political conflict within the Union became possible and it increased in bitterness until the synod of Dort was summoned in 1619. The meeting of the synod was preceded by the arrest of Oldenbarnevelt, the protector of the Arminians and a republican leader, who at the age of seventy was condemned to death for treason. His friend, Grotius, one of the finest Dutch minds of the time, a distinguished scholar and statesman, escaped with imprisonment. The Dutch Remonstrants questioned the doctrine that Jesus Christ had not died for all men but only for the elect. They admitted that man needed God's grace, but they thought that he required faith as well for his salvation; and they doubted whether God had chosen people for salvation who, however much they sinned, could never forfeit their state of election. The Remonstrants realised that they were a minority and sought toleration for their beliefs, just as the English Puritans, particularly those whose beliefs were the least extensively held, such as the Anabaptists and Quakers, also claimed that what they wanted was merely toleration and not supremacy in the kingdom. But in Holland the Contra-Remonstrants had firmer backing, that both of the House of Orange and of the ruling classes in the towns, as well as much popular support. They also, curiously enough, had the approval of the English Solomon, King James I who, for political reasons, was anxious for a Protestant union in Europe. Yet in England itself it was the parliament which backed the Puritans (whom Grotius compared to the Contra-Remonstrants) – particularly in their attacks on the bishops – and the House of Stuart and the Church hierarchy (which was of course threatened by their demands for reform) that were eager to suppress them. These facts became significant in the revolution of 1642 in England and the revolution of 1672 in the United Netherlands.

The controversy over grace and free will was not confined to the Protestant world. The Jesuits, members of the great missionary order which had been founded by St Ignatius Loyola in 1540, were keen advocates of freedom of will. St Ignatius himself had laid it down in his

Spiritual Exercises that 'we should not lay so much stress on the doctrine of grace as thereby to encourage the holding of that noxious doctrine which denies the exercise of free will'. But the question needed most delicate handling. For the Fathers of the Church like St Paul himself, St Augustine, and St Thomas Aquinas, had all asserted the supremacy of God's grace. It was always possible to fall into the error of the Pelagians; for Pelagius, by stressing the value of free will, was said to have questioned the omnipotence of God and the reality of original sin and had been condemned as a heretic. Towards the end of the sixteenth century Molina, a Jesuit professor of theology at the university of Evora in Portugal, had attempted to reconcile the ideas of grace and free will by suggesting that grace is only efficacious so long as the will cooperates with it. This doctrine, known as Congruism, was at once attacked by other leading Roman Catholic theologians in the missionary order of the Dominicans who claimed that it smelt of Pelagianism. The Dominicans themselves were content to belong to the Chosen People of God; the Jesuits did not see how they could carry on their missionary activities effectively if they were compelled to teach that Christ had died for the elect only and that Christians could not hope to acquire salvation by the exercise of faith.

Although the council of Trent had appeared to come down in favour of the Jesuit approach to Christianity, the popes at the outset of the century were *politiques* and not at all anxious to interfere in this tremendous theological controversy. But they found it difficult to remain aloof. For in 1640 a Dutch theologian, a Roman Catholic named Jansen, in his posthumous work, *Augustinus* brought the matter to the boil by arguing that St Augustine had stated that it was heretical to say that grace could be controlled by the human will. Jansenism, as it became known, was taken up with fervour in parts of France, notably by the abbé de St Cyran and by Antoine Arnauld, a leading theologian who had opposed the admission of Jesuits into the university of Paris. (The Jesuits had been recalled to France in 1603 and had founded colleges there.) St Cyran and Arnauld were closely connected with a newly formed convent and monastery known as Port Royal. The mother superior of Port Royal exerted considerable influence in French court society where for a time 'Jansenism' became fashionable. Two great writers, Pascal and Racine, were described as Jansenists. The controversy between the Jesuits and their opponents became increasingly complicated, divided and heated Parisian society, and was not resolved until towards the end of Louis xiv's reign.

One leading French figure who tried to keep out of the controversy, although he was a personal friend of St Cyran, was Vincent de Paul, a French Christian who devoted the whole of his life to the service of

charity. When he was a young man he had been captured by the Turks
and sold as a slave. After his escape from a terrible situation he took
advantage of his appointment as chaplain to the general of the galleys
to ease the lot of galley slaves and of prisoners in general. He was also
made aware of the miserable lot of the ordinary French poor, including
the peasantry, and induced charitable ladies of wealth to form themselves into groups known as Daughters of Charity to allay their suffer-
ings. It was significant that, like the Jesuits, he was unable to accept the
severe doctrines of the 'Jansenists', though because St Cyran was his
friend, he tried to save him from punishment when the French monarchy moved against him. Vincent de Paul was a saint whose story as
'Monsieur Vincent' has come down through the ages. But the French
Church was corrupt. Its state was worse than that of the Protestant
Churches, though, owing to an earlier concordat, it enjoyed more
freedom from temporal control than most other Catholic Churches. The
poverty of the lower clergy in France, as in Protestant England, was the
source of much that was lacking in the moral and spiritual welfare of
Europe and was highly damaging to the Christian religion.

In the end the Jesuits were victorious in the Roman Catholic Church,
just as the Contra-Remonstrants were in the Reformed Church. Possibly the virile Dutch were more conscious of their destiny. Though they
were severe towards their enemies, the missionary efforts of the Jesuits
were everywhere aimed at reconquering Europe for the Roman Church.
They used every resource including the cooperation of the Inquisition
where it existed. They were, it is true, frequently handicapped by the
purely secular policies of Roman Catholic princes. For example, the
Emperor Karl v had desisted in his attempts to suppress Lutheranism
in his realm when he found that he needed the assistance of the
Protestant rulers of Germany in his war against France. But Jesuit
confessors propped up his successor as emperor, his son as king of Spain
and a later emperor in Ferdinand ii. They helped to invigorate the
faith of the duke of Bavaria, the second most powerful Roman Catholic
prince in Germany. The struggle in southern Germany between
Jesuits and Protestants was accentuated during the first twenty years
of the century. Bohemia, Silesia and Moravia were all persuaded for a
time to expel the Jesuits from their territories. On the other hand, in the
Emperor Ferdinand ii, elected in 1619, and in Maximilian of Bavaria
the Jesuits had two trained and dedicated pupils, both statesmen eager
to reconquer the whole of Germany for the Roman Catholic faith and
never, however extensive their political ambitions were, willing to
compromise. It was because of the determination of these two Jesuitically-
educated men that the 'Thirty Years War' in Germany lengthened
and spread after a Protestant prince had been called to the throne of

Bohemia. This was the last big European war in which religious issues played a part. When the fire and fury died and the devastation ended, the advance of science and philosophy was found to have damaged rigid views about religion and to have paved the way towards toleration, liberty of thought and ultimately revolution.

CHAPTER 7

'THE THIRTY YEARS WAR'
1618–48

The 'Thirty Years War' in Germany, which broke out in 1618, was both a civil war and a political catastrophe that exposed the foundations of European society. It began in an international setting and by 1635 it converted Germany into the cock-pit of the European powers.

After a period of comparative peace in Europe during the early years of the century statesmen began to feel that war was certainly coming again. One reason for this was that the Spaniards had never acquiesced in their defeat by their Dutch subjects. While the fortunes of the Spaniards' empire, apparently so colossal, so extensive and so inexhaustible, were beginning to be endangered by governmental incompetence and habitual bankruptcies, they writhed with jealousy as they watched the commercial and financial progress of the upstart independent Protestant republic, led by Prince Maurits of Orange, an aggressive stadholder. Spanish pride had been affronted; and though King Felipe III, who was to die in 1621, was pacific, his son and heir was to be a more obstinate character. In the year when Felipe III was to die the truce with the United Netherlands, reluctantly signed by both sides in 1609, was due to expire and after that it was believed to be inevitable that the court of Madrid would marshal all its available forces to bring the Dutch to heel. To attain military success it would be necessary for armies to be brought across the face of Europe from northern Italy, Spain's richest source of soldiers and supplies, to the Spanish Netherlands, the obvious base for a renewal of the war. Thus 'the Spanish road' ran across Germany. That meant that Germany would sooner or later become involved.

A second cause of European unrest was the likelihood of a revival of internecine religious conflict inside the Holy Roman Empire of the German nation. In recent years the emperors had been either mad or doddery. But now the emperor-elect was Ferdinand, archduke of Styria, a prince carefully brought up at a Jesuit college, who was known to long to help in the work of the Counter-Reformation. In fact 'he declared he would sooner lose everything than tolerate the heretic' and he 'sincerely believed that the Habsburg dynasty alone could restore Germany to the Church'. The Catholic League in Germany, formed in 1610 in opposition to the rival Protestant Union, was headed by the other intelligent pupil of the Jesuits, Maximilian of Bavaria. It is true that the Roman Catholic states in southern and western Germany were cut off from one another; that the Habsburg emperors were always the objects of jealousy and suspicion to other princes; and that the peace of Augsburg had been a settlement which permanently accepted the religious division of Germany, guaranteed by the imperial diet. It has also to be remembered that the Electoral College which chose the emperor contained both Protestant and Catholic princes. Nevertheless, on the whole, the Roman Catholic powers in Germany were more united than the Protestant, who were themselves divided into Lutherans and Calvinists, hating each other almost as much as they hated the Catholics. Thus under the impulse of the Jesuits, it was likely enough that the first convenient opportunity would be seized to extend the sway of Roman Catholicism in Germany and strengthen the position and influence of the next Holy Roman Emperor.

The setting in which the conflict was to arise was the rivalry that was building up during the first twenty years of the century between the Bourbons and Habsburgs. National historians would argue that this was the product of mutual fears. Henri IV of France had been fully conscious of the grip exercised on his kingdom by the Habsburgs of Madrid and Vienna. His efforts during the last years of his life had been directed to prising loose this hold and in particular to cutting the life-line between northern Italy and the Spanish Netherlands by increasing the French influence in Italy and in that part of modern Switzerland then adjacent to the Swiss Confederation – the Grisons – that together with the republic of Venice, abutted on the Val Telline, the valley through which Spanish forces might march northwards across Germany.

But the immediate successors of Henri IV had been unable to pursue his aggressive policy because of internal dissensions in France, and the young Louis XIII, even after he established himself, was doubtful about the rectitude of supporting the Protestants in Germany against his fellow Roman Catholics. Thus though the French had long been the enemies of the Spanish Habsburgs and of their cousins in Vienna and for that reason had been the allies of the Protestant Dutch, it was not at first certain that the French monarchy would again want to intervene in the internal affairs of Germany. Equally, although the popes tended to favour the Bourbons at the expense of the Habsburgs, if only because the Spanish hold on Italy restricted the development of the papal states, it would be wrong to attribute to them any desire to hamper the recon-quest of Germany for the Roman Catholic Church. It was not in fact until after the German civil war had been in progress for some years that the French king and the pope exerted their influence against the emperor.

The spark which lit the war appeared towards the end of 1618 in Bohemia. Bohemia was a considerable state in south-east Germany: some historians indeed maintain it was not technically in Germany at all. But at any rate it was an electorate of the Holy Roman Empire whose king had traditionally been a member of the House of Habsburg. But the kingship was not hereditary and the people of Bohemia, who spoke Czech and not German, were proud and independent-minded. If, according to the Augsburg settlement, Bohemia was a Roman Catholic kingdom, it contained a substantial number of Protestants – not only Lutherans and Calvinists, but also Utraquists, who believed it right for the Christian laity to receive holy communion in both kinds – wine as well as bread. These Protestants of Bohemia were reluctantly tolerated by the Habsburgs who had in fact given them a written guarantee of their liberties in 1609, known as the Letter of Majesty. In June 1617, Ferdinand of Styria was elected king of Bohemia and hesitantly confirmed the Letter of Majesty. Meanwhile his cousin, the Emperor Matthias, who had replaced the mad Rudolf II in 1612, was tottering towards his grave. Ferdinand, besides being elected king of Bohemia, was thought certain to succeed as emperor. Thus this keen and devoted Roman Catholic monarch, whose territories not only in Bohemia but also in Austria and Hungary contained large numbers of Protestants, would hold sway over all south-east Germany and be likely to use his inheritance to assist the cause of the Counter-Reformation. In fact soon after his election in Bohemia the deputy governors appointed by him had forbidden the building of certain new Protestant churches on royal lands and had imprisoned Protestant burghers for objecting to the ban.

The Bohemian leaders were affronted by these actions of the imperial governors. They stood for nationalism, for independence, and for toleration and they refused to acquiesce in Austrian rule which they regarded as infringing their constitutional liberties. The leaders of the Protestant nobility therefore sought to reverse the election of their new king – claiming Ferdinand's election had been illegal – and looked for a Protestant candidate to occupy the throne. In March 1618 they organised a *coup d'état* against the deputy governors, two of whom were thrown out of a window of the Hradschin palace in Prague (landing safely however in the mud below) and invited the Lutheran elector of Saxony to become their king. When he refused their offer, they turned to a younger and less experienced prince, Frederick V, the Calvinist elector palatine, who was the son-in-law of King James I of England, having recently married his beautiful daughter, Princess Elizabeth.

Frederick, pushed on by his chancellor, embraced this glorious if dangerous opportunity. It was dangerous because it meant not merely defying his emperor, to whom as an elector he was bound by oaths of loyalty, but because to recognise the Bohemian Protestant revolt would rally the princes of the Catholic League against him without necessarily inviting the support of the other members of the Protestant Union, who were sure to be jealous of such a large extension of his territories through the addition of a wealthy kingdom, and the enhancement of his authority through the acquisition of a second vote in the Electoral College. Yet the risk seemed to him well worth taking. Frederick thought that he could count upon the sympathy of the Dutch and of at least some of his fellow Protestant rulers in Germany and also of his English father-in-law. If he were elected, the Bohemians would fight for him and he would command sufficient resources to raise a mercenary army. His rival, Ferdinand, on the other hand, had no army and would soon be occupied simply in establishing himself as emperor. So on 26 August 1619 Frederick allowed himself to be elected king of Bohemia. Two days later, the Emperor Matthias having died, Ferdinand of Styria was elected emperor (Frederick himself voting for him). But Ferdinand had not the slightest intention of giving up his claim to the Bohemian throne, a traditional and valuable part of the Habsburg inheritance, nor of allowing the Electoral College to pass into the hands of a Protestant majority. Moreover he knew that he could count on the active support of the Spaniards with whom he already had a secret understanding. So immediately he set about overthrowing the usurping king of Bohemia. And thus 'the Thirty Years War' began.

Frederick proved to be merely a 'winter king'. For Ferdinand was able to call upon two armies to depose the rebel against his imperial authority: the duke of Bavaria, as head of the Catholic League, raised an army of twenty-five thousand men under a capable general, Count Tilly, on the promise that he would be generously rewarded for giving aid to the emperor; the Spaniards were delighted to send another army of about the same strength to occupy the palatinate, left relatively unprotected by Frederick, which thus gave them a hold on central Germany. They undertook this expedition on the understanding that they would be allowed to move their troops across Germany from Italy to take part in their coming war with the Dutch. Against these forces Frederick had the assistance of a mercenary army under Count Mansfield, an unscrupulous and dangerous condottiere, who, however, soon suffered defeat and sat down at Pilsen to see which way the wind would blow next. Another adventurer who lent aid to Frederick was Bethlen Gabor, prince of Transylvania, a Calvinist, who found the Bohemian revolt an excellent excuse for attacking the empire from the east. Tilly's trained troops easily defeated the rebel Bohemians at the battle of the White Hill on 8 November 1620. Prague was thereupon surrendered and Frederick fled to Breslau and thence to Brandenburg. Meanwhile the Spaniards completed their occupation of the palatinate. The Elector Frederick had thus, almost in a flash, lost every one of his possessions and become an exile in a strange land; and the Habsburgs had triumphed.

The Bohemian rebellion was more significant in its consequences than its causes. Theoretically all that needed to happen now was for Frederick to beg humble pardon of the emperor for his insubordination and to seek restoration to his patrimony of the palatinate, while Ferdinand resumed the throne of Bohemia to which he had earlier been elected. But a dreadful revenge was immediately taken upon the Bohemians. Their capital was sacked by Tilly's mercenaries; the Letter of Majesty, which had given protection to the Protestants, was withdrawn; the expelled Jesuits were recalled; the Crown was declared henceforward to be hereditary in the Habsburg family. Furthermore the Protestant Union, which had failed to save Frederick, was dissolved. Thus Bohemia became a solid and regimented part of the Habsburg and Roman Catholic block in southern Germany.

But more important than any of these things, the emperor's allies began to clamour for their rewards. In vain Frederick sought help to secure his restoration to the palatinate. He had no army and virtually no allies. Mansfield, who had proved useless to him in Bohemia, now deserted his cause and went to help the Dutch against the Spaniards when the war in the Netherlands was resumed. The Spaniards thereupon evacuated the palatinate and Count Tilly occupied its capital, Heidelberg. Possession was nine-tenths of the law. In January, 1623 a special meeting or deputation summoned at Ratisbon confiscated the palatinate and handed it over to the duke of Bavaria for life. Thus what had previously been a Protestant electorate now became a Roman Catholic one and was given into the power of the leader of the German Catholic League. The Emperor Ferdinand, though he distrusted Maximilian of Bavaria, agreed to this as part of a deliberate policy of regaining the whole of Germany for the Roman Catholic Church. The mercenary armies brought with them not peace but a sword. The palatinate was treated as cruelly as Bohemia by soldiers always short of pay and living by requisitions. The Protestants were divided and helpless. The ablest among them, the elector of Saxony, had throughout refused his help to Frederick and had obeyed the emperor. The elector of Brandenburg, a weaker man, had his own absorbing problems. Frederick was unable to resist without an army and actually concluded an armistice with the emperor in the summer of 1624. Thus everywhere the Protestants were thrust on to the defensive. The Dutch were fully occupied in fighting the Spaniards. The English, who had hoped, by a marriage alliance, to persuade the Spaniards to favour Frederick's restoration, were humiliated by the snubbing of Prince Charles, King James I's heir, when he went eagerly courting the languorous but thick-lipped Infanta in Madrid. It looked for the moment as if the Habsburgs would overrun the whole of Europe and as if Germany would be lost for ever to the Protestant cause.

But slowly the Protestants outside Germany began to rally and unite. And they found an unexpected and remarkable ally in a cardinal of the Roman Catholic Church, Armand Jean du Plessis, Cardinal Richelieu, who in August 1624 was appointed by King Louis XIII of France as the head of his royal council at the age of thirty-nine. Richelieu's apologists have stressed that in all his policies he never for a moment intended to damage his Church. But he was a born enemy of the Habsburgs and was determined to carry on the programme of Henri IV aimed at containing both its Spanish and Austrian branches. He was helped in his policy by the fact that Pope Urban VIII, a famed patron of the arts, who was elected in 1623, was also no friend to the Habsburgs. The French concluded alliances both with the Protestant English (King Charles I married Henriette Marie, the sister of the French king in 1625) and with the Protestant Dutch. So eager was Prince Maurits of Orange for French support that he ordered Dutch warships to help suppress a rebellion by his fellow Calvinists at La Rochelle. Thus on both sides politics took precedence over religion. At the same time that a treaty of friendship was signed between the French and the Dutch, the Swedes and the Danes, so long deadly rivals, came to terms, while the elector of Brandenburg also allied himself with the United Netherlands. The king of Denmark, who had ambitions of his own in northern Germany (he wanted one of his sons to acquire bishoprics there) freed from anxiety in Scandinavia, prepared to intervene on behalf of the Elector Frederick, who was in fact his niece's husband. Gustav Adolf of Sweden at the same time concentrated upon a war with the Poles which he regarded in part at least as a crusade against the European Roman Catholic kings and a likely preliminary to intervention in Germany himself. Thus the triumphs that the Emperor Ferdinand and the Catholic League had achieved with such apparent ease were beginning, six years after the Bohemian revolt, to be challenged and the German civil war was becoming more and more an international conflict in which all Europe was directly or indirectly involved.

The years 1625 and 1626 were ones of immense political and military confusion. The king of Denmark in 1625 crossed the Elbe with ten thousand men. The Spaniards became anxious for the Habsburg emperor to protect their flank by extending his authority into northern Germany. That was the reason for the Danish intervention. The Emperor Ferdinand, not wishing to be solely dependent upon the duke of Bavaria and Count Tilly, now had a mercenary army of his own. The commander was Albrecht Waldstein or Wallenstein, a Bohemian tycoon, who had taken advantage of the aftermath of the Bohemian revolt to buy up property cheaply and had thus built himself a fortune, part of which he loaned to the emperor for his military needs. In return for his services the emperor gave Wallenstein permission to raise an army. For a time Tilly and Wallenstein cooperated in the service of the emperor. Wallenstein defeated Mansfield, now in the pay of the Dutch. Tilly defeated Kristian IV of Denmark at the battle of Lutter in August 1626, and within two years the Danish expeditionary force was compelled to disperse. Wallenstein was then employed by the emperor in trying to give indirect assistance to the Spaniards in their struggle against the Dutch.

At first the renewed war with the Dutch had gone extremely promisingly for the Spaniards, led by their exceptionally able Genoese general, Ambrogio de Spinola, who recaptured Breda from the Dutch in 1625, a military feat immortalised by the brush of Velazquez. From this setback the Dutch recovered under the leadership of Prince Friederik Hendrik, a younger brother of Prince Maurits, who died just before the surrender of Breda, and King Felipe IV of Spain begged the emperor to aid him by declaring war on the Dutch. That Ferdinand refused to do, but he ordered Wallenstein to recruit a fleet to be stationed in the Baltic. Wallenstein did not prove so successful an organiser at sea as he had done on land. 'Eagles,' it was said, 'cannot swim.' But the fact was that he had concentrated a well-equipped army of one hundred and twenty-five thousand men in northern Germany, had terrorised the Brandenburgers and slaughtered the Danes, and extended the authority of the emperor into the farthest confines of Protestant Germany. So, on the whole, by 1628 the Habsburgs felt conscious of victory. In June 1629 peace was signed between the emperor and the king of Denmark, who withdrew from the war. Flushed by his mastery of the situation, the emperor had preceded this by promulgating in March an Edict of Restitution in which, so far as Church property was concerned, the position at the peace of Augsburg was restored. Much Church property had of course changed hands since 1555 and the emperor's decree was unwelcome to many, to some Roman Catholics as well as Protestants. The edict was enforced on both parties alike by Wallenstein's army. Ferdinand, sustained in his policies by his Jesuit confessor, never felt more confident. But outside Germany his enemies were once more gathering against him.

The motives of statesmen are mixed. How far did religion and how far political ambition impel Olivares in Spain, Richelieu in France, and Gustav Adolf in Sweden to intervene in the affairs of Germany? Or could each of them have fairly claimed that he was forced into doing so for reasons of self-defence? Professor Michael Roberts has suggested that to seventeenth-century politicians such a question would have appeared improperly framed: 'It was not their habit to keep politics and religion in watertight compartments either in action or in thought.' Nevertheless such statesmen had to make it clear that they were not jeopardising the religious security of their fellow believers when they sided with their foreign rivals. It would ill have become a cardinal of the Roman Church like Richelieu to imperil the freedom of worship of German Roman Catholics. Nor could the king of Sweden in threatening the Protestant princes of northern Germany who were loyal to the Habsburg emperor acquiesce in the crushing of German Protestantism.

But, on the whole, the motives of these men were political. Olivares had devoted the whole of his life to restoring the prestige of the Spanish empire and fighting off its foes, whether they were Dutch Protestants or French Catholics. In the 1630s he still had hopes of overthrowing the Dutch and involving the emperor in his wars against them. The triumph of the emperor in northern Germany had appeared to open a way to hemming in the Dutch by sea as well as by land. At the same time Olivares was anxious to prevent the French from securing a foothold in northern Italy and thus interfering with Spanish supremacy there. In December 1627 the duke of Mantua had died and a French prince, the duc de Nevers, had the best claim to succeed him. Olivares encouraged the Spanish governor of Milan to send troops to prevent this succession and the emperor was persuaded later to lend his support by sequestering the duchy and by dispatching some of Wallenstein's troops into Italy to enforce his wishes. The Mantuan war, which lasted for three years, complicated the situation in Germany and also imposed more heavily upon the resources of Spain. These resources were further reduced owing to the capture by the Dutch of a Spanish treasure fleet – the first time that Spanish silver had fallen into Dutch hands. The Mantuan war produced another complication in that the emperor's interference in Italy provoked Pope Urban VIII and confirmed him on the side of the French.

Richelieu had by the end of 1630 defeated all his domestic enemies. At the end of 1628 the Huguenots of La Rochelle who had been in rebellion surrendered and not long afterwards peace had been concluded with the English, who, under the first duke of Buckingham had ineffectively attempted to aid the Huguenots. The French queen mother, who had intrigued against her son, Louis XIII, was disarmed and reconciled, and Richelieu had been proclaimed the king's principal minister. After he had finally crushed another conspiracy against him towards the end of 1630, on what was called the Day of Dupes, the cardinal could concentrate on what was to be his life's main work – his contest with the Habsburgs. His policy has been summed up under three headings: to stop the further advance of the Spanish Habsburgs in Europe (this applied particularly to northern Italy and the Netherlands); to reinforce the defences of France, that is to say to shake off the Habsburgs' strategic stranglehold; and 'to build bridgeheads into neighbouring states to guarantee them against the oppression of Spain if the occasion should arise'. Hence he at once engaged in elaborate diplomatic manoeuvres to embarrass the Habsburgs by concluding alliances in Germany, Italy and the United Netherlands. Later he was also to turn to the king of Sweden.

Gustav Adolf was no man's puppet. He too could claim that the object of his policy was to shake off the stranglehold of his neighbours and to build bridgeheads into northern Germany with the object of establishing a semi-permanent base. His aims were above all strategic. In the decade since he had become king, he had carried out internal reforms, he had exerted control over his nobility, and he had outfought both the Danes and the Poles. It had long been his intention to wage war in Germany and it may be that his true ambition was to make himself the master of northern Germany and thus convert his kingdom into the mightiest Baltic Power. He had also been angered by Wallenstein's attempt to support the Spaniards against the Dutch by extending the imperial power into the Baltic. In October 1629 Gustav Adolf had informed his council that the cause of his coming war was the imperial designs against Sweden and the Baltic. But at the same time it was asserted that the object of the king's proposed campaign in Germany was to free the Protestants in the empire from the Habsburg yoke. He had, as we have seen, regarded his Polish war as part of a crusade on behalf of his fellow Protestants and, as Professor Roberts has written, 'it is futile to deny the importance of the religious motive in shaping Gustav Adolf's policy'. But it was certainly not his only motive. And historians have disputed until this day how far-reaching was the scope of his plans when he disembarked his expeditionary force in Pomerania in July 1630. He was a highly emotional man, still young and glorifying in his own capabilities. Possibly he did not then know where he was going. But he came of his own volition; he was not called in by the Protestant rulers of Germany. Both the elector of Saxony and the elector of Brandenburg, the two most powerful princes in northern Germany, boasted of their continuing loyalty to the Holy Roman Emperor. Yet many ordinary German Protestants, conscious of the miseries they had suffered at the hands of Wallenstein's and Tilly's mercenaries, rejoiced at the coming of the Lion of the North.

At first the king of Sweden had not figured prominently in Cardinal Richelieu's complicated political calculations. But he badly needed allies to carry out his designs, for as yet he had neither a large army nor navy. Diplomacy and subsidies were his weapons, and he hoped to play off the German princes against one another and thereby stop the progress of Spain both in northern and southern Europe. But it was not at all easy. For in 1630 war no longer prevailed in Germany itself; Wallenstein's genius had destroyed the German Protestant rebels and their ally, the king of Denmark, and his soldiers were enforcing the edict of Restitution. In the summer the Emperor Ferdinand had summoned a meeting at Ratisbon in the hope of establishing German unity after the prolonged but now apparently ended civil war. He wanted to persuade the leaders of Germany to acknowledge his son, Ferdinand, king of Hungary as his ultimate successor upon the imperial throne under the title of king of the Romans and to enlist support for his cousin in Spain. It was at Ratisbon that French agents, headed by Richelieu's Capuchin confidant known as Father Joseph, began to engage in their complex diplomatic intrigues. They had their eyes on Maximilian of Bavaria who alone possessed the military resources to contend with the emperor. Maximilian, for his part, as a price for his loyal services and, enthusiastically backed by his fellow princes, demanded of the emperor the dismissal of the unpopular Wallenstein, while the Protestant electors clamoured for the rescinding of the edict of Restitution. Maximilian triumphed. No promises were given about the imperial succession or about aid for Spain, but on 3 August 1630 Wallenstein was dismissed. That was precisely a month after Gustav Adolf landed in Germany.

The emperor, who had thus dispensed with his best general and had dispatched many of his troops to Italy, was however, not unduly worried by the Swedish invasion. He had long expected it. Germany was at peace, if not entirely united. Why should not the experienced Tilly dispose of the king of Sweden, just as earlier he had overthrown the king of Denmark? Gustav Adolf was therefore at an initial advantage because his capacity and strength were underestimated and the forces of the emperor were dispersed. He was able quickly to build up his bridgehead in Pomerania; he found that he could increase the size of his army by recruiting among the mercenary soldiers released from the German civil war; he had a large number of easily portable three-pounder guns and soon had a substantial cavalry force which made his army extremely mobile. His aim was first to surround and intimidate Brandenburg, whose ruler, Georg Wilhelm, was his own brother-in-law.

He sought other allies, including the Protestant city of Magdeburg, which guarded the strategic crossing over the River Elbe. Unlike most generals of his time, Gustav Adolf did not suspend operations during the winter. Soon after Christmas he brushed off the first imperialist resistance to his advance and was knocking at the gates of Brandenburg. By January 1630 he had done enough to make Richelieu realise where his best hopes lay and on the 23rd a treaty was signed at Barwälde near Frankfurt-on-Oder whereby the French monarchy agreed to subsidise the Swedes on condition that they allowed freedom of worship to the German Roman Catholics and left the duke of Bavaria alone: for the French were hoping also to reach an agreement with him. But the treaty of Barwälde was a triumph for the king of Sweden; he had more than exacted his own terms. Moreover it was an open treaty. And the French were thus compelled to acknowledge that their object was to humble the German emperor. It was indeed the first stage in a direct Franco-German conflict which was to continue until modern times.

So Germany became the battle ground of a European war. After Gustav Adolf had established his bridgehead and come to terms with Pomerania, he moved his forces into Brandenburg, frightening the timid elector, and then occupied Frankfurt-on-Oder. But he was unable to move fast enough to save his Protestant allies in Magdeburg, which was conquered by Tilly with terrifying consequences: the city was burnt to the ground and five-sixths of its inhabitants perished. The sack of Magdeburg, though but one of the many tragedies of the war, sent a thrill of horror through the Protestant world. The two Protestant electors of Brandenburg and Saxony, who had so long and loyally stood by the idea of German unity, came to terms with the king of Sweden. The forces of the king of Sweden and the elector of Saxony joined together and on 17 September 1631 a big battle was fought at Breitenfeld near Leipzig. The inexperienced Saxons fled from the field, but the Swedes destroyed the imperial army, killing nearly eight thousand men and taking six thousand prisoners. Not long before this the Dutch had inflicted a bloody defeat on the Spaniards in Zealand. Thus 1631 was a dark year for the Habsburgs. But Cardinal Richelieu did not rejoice in the victory of his ally, the king of Sweden; he had no wish to see the Protestants overrunning Germany. His purpose was simply to construct a coalition against the Habsburgs to restrain them; and for a time he held as large hopes of the alliance of the Catholic duke of Bavaria as he had of the Swedish king. Ultimately Richelieu's aim was to unite the Swedes with the Catholic League so as to stop any further Habsburg advance. But Gustav Adolf was already virtually the master of Germany. With his rear secured by his German Protestant allies he moved south to Frankfort-on-Main and thence, when the next campaigning season started, turned towards Bavaria and, in spite of the commitments he had made in the treaty of Barwälde, harried the duchy from end to end.

Nobody knows with certainty how high the ambitions of Gustav Adolf soared: it is doubtful if he knew himself. He had now raised no fewer than five armies which occupied different parts of Germany. He had money, supplies, allies. Did he wish to become a Protestant emperor and 'liberate' the Protestants of southern Germany or did he merely hope so to frighten the Emperor Ferdinand and his allies as to secure recognition as the lawful protector of northern Germany? It may never be discovered. Nor can one gauge the motives of Wallenstein, to whom the emperor was compelled to turn for help in his hour of peril as the only general capable of gathering an army large enough to defeat the Swedes. It is possible that if earlier in 1632 Gustav Adolf had marched on Vienna, he would have triumphed decisively. But he left it too late. At the end of May Wallenstein was in Prague and moving forward to threaten the rear of Gustav Adolf's main army which had gone north to Nuremberg. After much manoeuvering for position during the summer the two armies met in battle at Lützen west of Leipzig on 16 November. Wallenstein's new army, supported by that of the Bavarians, outnumbered the Swedes. The Swedes won the battle, forcing Wallenstein to withdraw from the field, but Gustav Adolf himself was killed, dying of many wounds. Soon afterwards Prince Frederick, the Elector Palatine, whose acceptance of the throne of Bohemia had sparked off the German conflict, died of plague somewhere on the Rhine. So another phase of the 'Thirty Years War' had come to a dramatic end with the disappearance of two of its leading actors.

Germany lay shivering and exhausted. Towns were completely destroyed, the countryside depopulated, starvation rife, and plague rampant. But many persons were interested in continuing the awful war. Axel Oxenstierna, the effective ruler of Sweden, since Gustav Adolf's successor was a baby girl (the future eccentric Queen Kristina), wanted to pursue his dead master's plans at least to the extent of acquiring territory in northern Germany and of forming a firm alliance with the German Protestants (which he did at Heilbron), and eventually a new treaty was concluded with France. Wallenstein also secretly entered into negotiations with France, apparently seeking to acquire the throne of Bohemia, his native land, as the price for changing sides. Once again the emperor was persuaded to dispense with Wallenstein, who, always eccentric and guided in his action by the stars, was losing his military genius and trembling upon the verge of madness. In January 1634 he was again dismissed and a month later he and his entourage were murdered by English and Irish mercenaries who claimed that they had executed him as a traitor on orders from Vienna. Ferdinand, king of Hungary, the eldest surviving son of the emperor, was at the age of twenty-six appointed in his place commander-in-chief of the imperial army.

Thus new figures were appearing upon the European scene. In the Spanish Netherlands another Ferdinand, known as the cardinal-infante, brother of Felipe IV of Spain, took over as governor in succession to his aunt Isabella. Bernard of Saxe-Weimar, a German princeling built along the lines of Count Mansfield, a mercenary chieftain with no fixed motives other than his own advancement, commanded a Swedish army. Bernard quarrelled with the other Swedish generals and with his paymasters. In September 1635 King Ferdinand crossed the Danube at Donauwörth and was joined at Nördlingen to the north of Donauwörth by the cardinal-infante (who was his brother-in-law) with a Spanish army which he had brought across from Italy. The two out-numbered the Protestants under Bernard and wiped them out. The battle of Nördlingen and the advance that followed it have been described as 'the rejuvenation of the [Habsburg] dynasty under two young princes' but at the same time as being 'nothing but the sudden flaring of a guttering candle' (C. V. Wedgwood). At any rate for the moment the Habsburgs were triumphant and Cardinal Richelieu abashed. He had to pick up the pieces. After years of underhand war he was driven out into the open. He offered another treaty to Sweden, promising to send a French army into Germany. But Oxenstierna refused the terms and the Saxons and a number of other Protestant states made peace with the emperor at Prague in view of the Swedish defeat at Nördlingen. Cardinal Richelieu now decided openly to inter-vene. In the spring of 1635 Oxenstierna went to Paris and signed a definitive treaty. In accordance with its terms, on 21 May of that year King Louis XIII declared war on Felipe IV of Spain, using a specious but insignificant pretext.

Yet the years 1635 and 1636 proved disastrous for the French Bourbon and Swedish Vasa cause. Towns in northern Germany were occupied by the Spaniards and the French were not welcomed in Flanders. On 14 August 1636 the cardinal-infante crossed the French frontier and occupied the town of Corbie, south of Calais, while an imperial army penetrated the Belfort Gap to occupy Franche-Comté. Another Imperial general reached Compiègne and nearly the whole of Germany was once more hopeful and united under the old emperor. His dynasty's authority was confirmed when in December 1636 his son, King Ferdinand of Hungary, was elected king of the Romans or imperial successor. On 18 February 1637 Ferdinand II died, at peace with his world, having fought off so long and so victoriously all the enemies of the Habsburg power and of the cause of the Roman Catholic Church in Germany, though at the price of enormous devastation and suffering for his peoples.

But if the Austrian Habsburgs survived the onslaught – the policy of the new emperor, Ferdinand III, was an Austrian rather than a German policy – the Spanish Habsburgs were nearing the end of their tether after years of constant and expensive wars. In October 1637 Prince Frederik Hendrik of Orange-Nassau, the Dutch stadholder, retook Breda. Bernard of Saxe-Weimar began to win victories in Germany, aided by a rising French soldier, Marshal Turenne. The Spanish threat to France then evaporated and in December 1638 the town of Breisach, the key to the Lower Rhine, fell to French arms: the news of this victory is supposed to have been the means by which Cardinal Richelieu consoled the dying hours of his faithful servant, Father Joseph. By 1640 the Spanish empire was not only undergoing military defeat, but was riddled by revolution.

The European war was to drag on for another eight years and even then it was not completely ended, since the French, who had not entered it officially until 1635, went on fighting the Spaniards until 1659. But more of the leading actors were disappearing and being replaced. Bernard of Saxe-Weimar died in 1639 still a young man. The cardinal-infante followed in November 1641. Richelieu, whose dedicated mission to overthrow or confine the Habsburgs had been responsible for the war's prolongation – a hero to the French, a villain to the Germans – died in December 1642, confounding his enemies until the end and still scheming for himself and his master, Louis XIII, who followed him to the grave a few months later. In January 1643 Olivares was dismissed by the Spanish king and retired to his estates to vindicate his policies. Then Pope Urban VIII died in 1644 and his successor was not pro-French but more sympathetic to the Habsburgs. The new actors included the Swede, Lerab Tortensson, a skilful pupil of Gustav Adolf, who gained a victory over the imperial troops at the second battle of Breitenfeld and the Duc d'Enghien (later known as the great Condé) who crushed the Spaniards at the battle of Rocroi in 1643.

Under the impact of these defeats the new Emperor Ferdinand III began to think of peace. The French also had reasons to promote it since Cardinal Mazarin, Richelieu's successor, was confronted with civil war before he had established his own position during the minority of Louis XIV. But it took more than four years before the settlement was completed. By the group of treaties comprised under the name of Westphalia the Franco-Swedish alliance came off best: the French obtained important territorial gains on their eastern frontier (including Alsace, Metz, Toul, Verdun, Breisach and Philippsburg) and in north

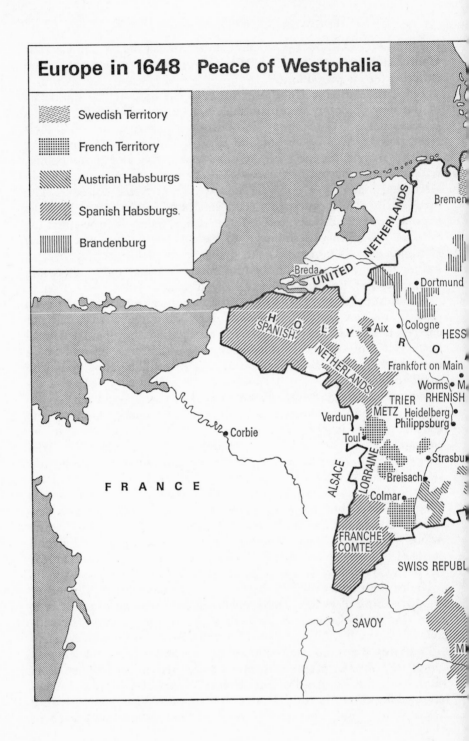

Europe in 1648 Peace of Westphalia

Swedish Territory

French Territory

Austrian Habsburgs

Spanish Habsburgs

Brandenburg

Bremen

NETHERLANDS

UNITED

Breda

Dortmund

SPANISH

HOLY

Aix

Cologne

HESS

NETHERLANDS

Frankfort on Main

Worms M.

TRIER RHENISH

METZ Heidelberg

Verdun

Philippsburg

Toul

Strasbu

ALSACE

LORRAINE

Breisach

Corbie

Colmar

F R A N C E

FRANCHE
COMTE

SWISS REPUBL

SAVOY

M

Italy, while the Swedes acquired large parts of Pomerania which increased their population by one third. The Spaniards admitted defeat by the Dutch, who finally sealed their national independence by the treaty of Münster. The new elector of Brandenburg, Friederich Wilhelm, to be known to history as the Great Elector, strengthened his power in north-east Germany where he had acquired Pomerania by inheritance (but was obliged, to his disgust, to yield the richer part of it to the Swedes) while the duke of Bavaria was confirmed as an additional German elector and the sovereign of the upper palatinate. Bohemia stayed with the Habsburgs, but Frederick's son was restored to his electorate and to the lower palatinate. Germany, as a whole, lacerated by the wars, was left to lick her wounds.

The 'Thirty Years War' takes a significant place in the evolution of European civilisation. French and Germans had fought before, but Richelieu's coldly calculated exploitation of German differences left an indelible mark of hatred. The battle over Alsace and other frontier territories was to continue into the twentieth century. It is difficult to say that the war caused the disintegration of Germany because it was, after all, a deeply divided community even before the war began. At times, it is true, it had appeared to be uniting politically in the face of its foreign enemies, but then religious differences and particularist aspirations prevented unity. Nevertheless the greater Protestant princes had long remained loyal to the emperor and to the imperial institutions and traditions; gradually after the war these institutions began to lose all meaning except as ghosts sitting on a grave. Henceforward the French were able to intrigue almost at will with the various German rulers against the Austrian Habsburgs: French cultural leadership received an impulse and the French language became international. And the final division between Germany and Austria had been foreshadowed during the last stages of the 'Thirty Years War'. The emperors were themselves largely to blame for the lack of German unity; for Ferdinand III deliberately chose the path of Austro-Hungarian expansion rather than a search for an effective confederation of Germany.

It was in fact the diversity of political ambitions rather than religious bigotism that in the end precluded the growth of German unity. For the Habsburgs had been compelled to abandon their edict of Restitution and to accept the splitting up of the former possessions of the Roman Catholic Church in Germany. After 1648 Calvinism as well as Lutheranism was officially recognised throughout Germany and in the second half of the century a more tolerant religious attitude began to prevail. But it took Germany a long time to recover from her wounds, partly self-inflicted, in the 'Thirty Years War'. No historian can gauge all the suffering that it brought.

It is perfectly true that measured in longer terms the material damage inflicted on Germany can be exaggerated. Modern economic historians have shown that the northern German ports had already been damaged by Dutch competition before the war began and that the war in some respects stimulated their trade. Populations were forced to shift about as the fire and sword fell upon them, so that while some parts of Germany were depopulated, other parts were filled by emigrés. Nor was the cultural life of Germany affected more than was customary in war-time. But when all these arguments are taken into account, it does not mean that there was no suffering. German historians have occasionally tried to gloss over the events by statistical ingenuities or by asserting that some of the warrior chiefs were battling for a faint but genuine notion of German nationalism. But it is difficult to see men like Mansfield, Tilly, Wallenstein, Bernard of Saxe-Weimar and their imitators as more than ambitious adventurers or professional soldiers on the make. They let loose their mercenaries and their camp-followers to devour the land like locusts, to destroy towns and villages, to spread the germs of disease, to create hunger, and to batten unmercifully on the German peasantry. Maybe Wallenstein would have liked to set himself up as king of Bohemia but that was to foreshadow Czech not German nationalism. For the rest it is hard to show that their real aim was a united and peaceful Germany. In so far as German nationalism was promoted by the war, it was by the menace of the invaders – the French, the Swedes, even the Spaniards – than by condottieri with their mixed armies of hired soldiers from many lands. In fact it was chiefly in the purely Protestant countries – in the Sweden of Gustav Adolf and his daughter, in the United Netherlands of Prince Maurits and Prince Frederik Hendrik, in the England of Oliver Cromwell – that the beginnings of the modern national spirit may be detected. The Spanish empire itself was threatened with disintegration by manifestations of nationalism in Portugal, Catalonia, and southern Italy, as it had been previously in the United Netherlands. The German emperor, having overcome the outburst of Bohemian nationalism at so enormous a cost, had soon to contend with Hungarian nationalism. Indeed the larger part of Europe was shaken by revolutionary aspirations – partly nationalistic – in the middle of the century. To these we shall now turn.

CHAPTER 8

THE MID-CENTURY REVOLUTIONS

Most modern historians are in agreement that a 'general crisis' occurred in Europe during the seventeenth century and that it was reflected in revolutions or rebellions that took place about the middle of the century. The crisis has been variously described as political, social, or economic in character. The revolutions have been attributed to an underlying malaise in European society. That they were all brought about by precisely the same causes or partook of the same nature would be hard to substantiate. Clearly the 'Thirty Years War' that shook the foundations of political and religious life was, directly or indirectly, an important factor in all the mid-century revolutions. But can they also be traced to economic or financial circumstances – such as the 'price revolution'? Were they products of changes in class structure, such as the expansion of the gentry (the land-owning classes below the rank of the nobility) and of the bourgeoisie (the merchants, industrialists and professional men)? Or did religious alterations, following upon the reformation of the sixteenth century – an upheaval in established ideas that ought not to be overlooked in concentrating on economic or class history – create a convulsion in society, throwing up 'revolutionary saints', single-minded in their dedication to new dreams of power? Or was there a breakdown in society because of the dislocation between the growing financial requirements of governments, stemming from the prolonged wars, and populations living for the most part on a bare margin of subsistence? Some of the suggestions have already been sketched out, and they will be re-examined. But let us first consider the nature of the revolutions to which the general crisis is said to have given rise.

The central government of the Spanish empire was confronted during the 1640s by revolutions in Catalonia, Portugal, Sicily, Naples and Andalusia, while the revolt of the Netherlands continued until the peace settlement in 1648. In England a constitutional revolution began in 1640, developed into a civil war in 1642, and changed the form of government from a monarchy into a republic in 1649. France underwent two civil wars after the death of Louis XIII, known respectively as the parliamentary Fronde, which lasted from 1648 to April 1649, and the Fronde of the princes, which continued until 1653. In the United Netherlands a bloodless revolution followed the death of Prince Willem II of Orange in 1650, which was caused in part by his own behaviour before he died. Political disturbances also took place in Switzerland and the Ukraine and no doubt in other parts of Europe. Unquestionably these revolutions had repercussions on one another. The Frondes were influenced by the English revolution, and the establishment of a republic in England impressed the Dutch. The French stirred up internal trouble in Spain and were repaid by the Spaniards. The revolution in Portugal was directly brought about by the insurrection in Catalonia, which denuded Portugal of Spanish troops. The Portuguese revolt intensified the revolutionary ardour in Catalonia. The Neapolitans revolted because the Spanish monarchy was known to have been weakened by internal difficulties elsewhere.

The Spanish empire, as we have seen, in spite of its diversity of members, each possessing constitutional privileges, had held together in a remarkable manner during the long reign of Felipe II. It had experienced grave pressures under his son, Felipe III, whose ministers, the duque of Lerma and his son the duque of Ucedo (who overthrew his father in 1618), had not been men of much ability. During the reign of Felipe III the Moriscoes had been expelled at the price of damaging the economy of Valencia, while the economic position of Castile, which was responsible for most of the taxation levied by the Spanish Crown, had been undermined. When Felipe III died in 1621 at the age of forty-three and was succeeded by his sixteen-year old son, authority soon fell into the hands of Olivares, who wished not only to restore the greatness of the empire, but also to reorganise the resources of the monarchy. The receipts from the American silver mines had declined; the people of Castile had found increasing difficulties in bearing the burden of taxation; and since new wars were coming, particularly the fresh struggle against the Dutch, Olivares aimed to carry out political and fiscal reforms. Why should the empire not be genuinely united? Why should not each part of it assume a share in upholding the grandeur of the Habsburgs of Madrid? For example, the kingdom of Portugal and the principality of Catalonia were both supposedly rich, rejoicing in commerce and maritime trade. Olivares adumbrated a Union of Arms in which he proposed that each of them should furnish and support sixteen thousand men to serve in the Spanish armies, while other parts of the empire should be called upon for smaller contingents. That would not only enable him to maintain the glory of Spain but help to relieve the severe pressures on the loyal Castilians. Such a plan, however, required the approval of the regional cortes, which proved unenthusiastic,

although Aragon and Valencia did agree to make a regular contribution to the imperial coffers. Catalonia, proud of its independent
rights, offered neither men nor money.

In Catalonia it had long been accepted that supreme political
authority and jurisdiction were divided between the king and the three
estates which met in the cortes. And since the king rarely visited
Catalonia, the Catalans were able to safeguard their constitutional
privileges or *fueros*, being represented by a standing committee of the
cortes, known as the Deputation (*Diputacío*). In order to secure
occasional grants of money Felipe III had on his accession confirmed the
Catalan privileges, but during the course of his reign, these privileges
had been neglected by the Spanish governor or viceroy who used drastic
emergency powers because of the pressure of internal disorders.
Catalonia was full of bandits, and these bandits, the viceroy asserted,
could be suppressed only at the price of ruthlessly trampling upon local
rights and immunities. The members of the deputation, or *diputats*,
protested and Felipe III ordered the viceroy to respect those privileges,
which to some extent he did. His successor was less tactful. Not unnatu-
rally he asked for money from the Catalan towns, including Barcelona,
in order to maintain law and order. But he met with resistance and
complained that 'only the torments of hell can be compared with
governing Catalonia'. The next viceroy, the bishop of Barcelona,
appointed after the death of Felipe III, was actually boycotted for a time
by the Catalan nobility. Thus nationalist feelings had been aroused
among the Catalans and when in 1632 Olivares induced the king to
appoint his brother, the cardinal-infante as viceroy in order to seek
subsidies from the cortes, they were again refused.

Such was the background to the revolution in Catalonia. Its immediate cause was a consequence of the Spanish war with France which
began in May 1635. The French, who had long been anxious to regain
the frontier districts of Rosellón (Roussillon) and Cerdaña (Cerdagne)
had invaded Catalonia in the summer of 1639 and Olivares had hoped
that the Catalans would demonstrate their loyalty by fighting alongside
the Castilians in the imperial cause. In fact the bulk of the fighting was
done by Castilians, Flemings and Italians and when the French were
finally repulsed in January 1640, the imperial army was ordered to stay
in Catalonia so that it could operate on the French frontier in the next
campaigning season. The Catalan nobility were indignant and the
Catalan peasantry were soon at loggerheads with the Castilian soldiers
who confiscated their animals and their crops. When one of the
diputats protested, he was arrested and thrust into prison in Barcelona;
thereupon the peasants, who had already spontaneously banded
together to resist the Castilians, formed an army, forced their way into

the capital, and released the arrested diputat. Too late Olivares and the royal junta in Madrid tried to be conciliatory. The whole of Catalonia was ablaze. The rebel army moved from town to town creating havoc and in June 1640 the viceroy, himself a native Catalan noble, was murdered. Though some of the Catalan nobility, fearful of the monster that had been unleashed, were now willing to come to terms with Madrid, the principality was out of control. The effective leader of the deputation, a canon of Urgell named Pau Claris at first declared Catalonia an independent republic under the protection of France and then acknowledged King Louis XIII as count of Catalonia, thus breaking away from Spain.

That was the high point of the Catalan rebellion. In 1642 the French completed the conquest of Roussillon and the Castilian forces, organised under the direction of the king himself, were defeated. Next year the king dismissed Olivares, who died in 1645, a victim of his imperial vision. For a time a French-controlled government ruled Catalonia. But the Catalans found the French no easier masters than the Castilians. Moreover the upper classes grew increasingly conscious of the unruly and anarchic elements among the Catalan rebels. In 1651, after the ending of the Dutch war, Felipe IV found the Catalan nobility and merchants were becoming more sympathetic to Spain than to France and sent his illegitimate son, Don Juan of Austria, as commander-in-chief of an army, to recover the principality for the Crown. In October 1652 rebel-held Barcelona surrendered to him after a siege of fifteen months. Peace was made on the understanding that Catalan constitutional privileges would in future be respected by the Spanish monarchy. But ultimately in 1659 the Spanish monarchy had to pay the price of war and revolution by ceding Rosellón and much of Cerdaña to France.

The revolt in Catalonia sparked off a rising in Portugal. Although Portugal had been part of the Spanish empire for sixty years, its leading subjects looked back with pride to the long years of independence during which it had built up its own language, literature, flourishing commerce, and overseas empire. Portugal had been an independent kingdom since the twelfth century and its boundaries with Spain were established in the thirteenth. The outstanding events of its early political history had been military victories over Spain. When in 1580 the House of Aviz came to an end Felipe II had acquired the Spanish throne through his mother, the daughter of Emmanuel I, but he was not recognised as king until he had guaranteed to maintain Portuguese liberties. He undertook that the viceroy of Portugal should either be a member of the royal family or else a Portuguese noble. He was true to his promise. But the Portuguese benefited little from their union with Spain. Much of the commerce of Lisbon was lost to Cadiz and because of the Spanish involvement in war with the Dutch the Portuguese empire in Asia, in west Africa, and in South America was threatened with disruption, particularly by the newly formed Dutch West India company. The Portuguese, for their part, refused, like the Catalans, to take any part in their own defence and even the Portuguese fleet and the warfare in Brazil against the Dutch had to be paid for by Castile. Inevitably jealousies were aroused between the Portuguese nobility and the Castilians who came to the kingdom in search of profitable offices; while Princess Margarita of Savoy, the sister of Felipe IV, who had been appointed viceroy in 1634, proved herself considerate (as the Archduchess Isabella had been in Brussels), Miguel de Vasconcellos, who was the personal representative of Olivares, was exceedingly unpopular. The imposition of a five per cent property tax, nominally to pay for the defence of Portugal, was regarded as a violation of the constitution and resulted in a rising in Evora in 1637. Gradually economic and political discontents gave rise to a plot for an insurrection of which the reluctant figurehead was João, duke of Braganza, egged on by his Spanish wife, a sister of the duque de Medina Sidonia, one of the most eminent grandees of Andalusia. Cardinal Richelieu is said to have dabbled in the Portuguese conspiracy with promises of help, while Olivares, fearing the nationalist appeal of João of Braganza as a descendant of the House of Aviz, tried to tempt him with a variety of offers of offices and rewards. How far it was really the intention of Olivares to destroy Portuguese liberties and to assimilate the kingdom to Spain is not clear. But both sides feared the intentions of the other. When João of Braganza was ordered out of Portugal to take part in the war against Catalonia, he retired to his country estates. A French fleet appeared off Portugal and in December 1640 the conspirators struck. The viceregal palace was invaded and Princess Margarita hurried to the frontier; Vasconcellos was assassinated. The people of Lisbon proclaimed King João IV, and in January 1641 the Portuguese cortes confirmed the choice of the new monarch.

The Portuguese rebellion was carried out with remarkable ease. The armies of Spain were absorbed elsewhere, in the Netherlands, in Germany, in Catalonia. The only riposte was a counter-conspiracy against the new House of Braganza. Encouraged by the success of his brother-in-law, the duque de Medina-Sidonia himself was induced to head a revolt against Madrid in Andalusia, but Olivares got wind of the plot and the chief conspirator was put to death. After Olivares was dismissed, Felipe IV attempted in 1644 to lead an army against the Portuguese but was repulsed and for a time a Portuguese rebel army crossed the frontier and menaced Badajoz. The maintenance of Portuguese independence was assisted by alliances with France and

England. Pressure was exerted against the Dutch to prevent them from pressing their attacks on the Portuguese overseas possessions. Internal dissensions inside the United Netherlands contributed to irresolution, and by 1654 Brazil, which for a time had been largely in Dutch hands, reverted to Portuguese allegiance. It was not until after the end of the 'Thirty Years War' that the Spaniards contemplated resuming their war with Portugal, for in the meantime they were also occupied with revolts in Italy and the continuing war with the Dutch. Ultimately, after peace was concluded between Spain and France in 1659, King Felipe IV again ordered campaigns against Portugal. The Portuguese armies were then actually assisted by a contingent of three thousand men from England; for, with full French approval, King Charles II of England had married a Portuguese princess, Catharina of Braganza, and concluded a treaty with Portugal. The Spanish armies were thrice defeated in the years 1665–7 and by a treaty in February 1668 Portuguese independence was finally recognised.

The Portuguese revolt was the only one that broke out in the middle of the century which was permanently successful against the might of Spain; and it was really a war of national independence by a people conscious of a glorious historic past. Revolts in the centre of Spain were abortive. Castile, which was overtaxed and overburdened by the demands of the imperial wars, did not revolt. Catalonia had to call in French assistance, which it did not enjoy, and received no support from either Valencia or Aragon. In fact, in spite of all the centrifugal tendencies of the Spanish empire, it held together in an extraordinary way during these years of crisis. In Sicily, again, attempted revolt failed. In Naples it was the lower rather than the upper classes that were provoked to rise against Spanish rule. Naples had been acquired for the Spanish Crown through Ferdinando of Aragon and it possessed none of the effective constitutional liberties that were enjoyed in other parts of the Spanish empire, including Portugal and Catalonia. Hence the viceroys governed with an iron hand, promoted Castilians over the heads of Neapolitans, and imposed taxes without meeting resistance from the local parliament. Inevitably the financial difficulties of the Spanish Crown in the 1640s had resulted in fresh exactions and created a series of problems, such as the attempted revolt in Sicily, while the depredations of pirates from Africa had required the enlistment of more troops. A new tax on fruit imposed by the viceroy, the duke of Arcos, in 1647 was the occasion of the revolt. A fisherman of Amalfi, known as Masaniello, found it extraordinarily easy to create a rebel army by arousing the town mob and breaking into the prisons of Naples. The viceregal palace was sacked and the duke of Arcos barely managed to escape with his life.

Masaniello was a remarkable character both in real life and in subsequent fiction – he is the hero of an opera by Auber. For a time he ruled by terror but was soon murdered by leaders of his own mob. Neither the nobles nor the middle classes were at first sympathetic to the insurrection which engendered so much violence and wholesale destruction of property. But for a time the peasants forced the hands of their feudal overlords and obliged Prince Massa to take over the leadership of the revolt. In October 1647 a Spanish fleet under the command of Don Juan of Austria arrived in Naples bay, but when troops were landed they were repulsed, though Massa himself was killed. The rebel leaders then declared Naples a republic and – like the Catalonians – invoked French aid. But the republic was shortlived. By the following February Don Juan of Austria had returned and restored Spanish rule.

Thus the rebellion in Naples lasted a year, that in Catalonia a dozen years, and the revolt in Portugal was not decided for twenty-five years, while the revolt of the Netherlands had endured for eighty years. All these revolts, though they did not substantially reduce the extent of the Spanish empire were injurious to its resources and left Castile, the heart of the empire, morally and materially bankrupt. Because of the respect that Felipe II and Felipe III had shown for the constitutional rights of the different parts of Spain it held together at any rate as long as the Habsburgs governed. But Olivares's attempts to put the empire on a united and paying basis and to reconquer the United Netherlands proved costly failures. For more than twenty years Felipe IV, that proud unhappy prince whom we know from the paintings of Velazquez and Rubens, was vainly engaged in patching together his kingdom and its dependencies which had fallen apart under the provocation of the far-reaching, but by no means ignoble ambitions of Count Olivares. When Felipe IV died in 1665 and the throne of Spain was inherited by Carlos the Bewitched, the last of the Spanish Habsburgs, the strength and effectiveness of Felipe II's empire had declined to a point of no return, though Europe at first did not realise that this was so. But, whatever the precise long-term causes for the decline of Spain were, it did not become a reality until nearly a century after the defeat of the Spanish armada by Elizabethan sailors. In fact when one considers the separatist characteristics of its constituent parts, the varied languages, traditions, and interests of its peoples, the political ineptitude of some of its rulers, it is astonishing that it endured quite as long as most European empires.

On the face of it the revolution in Great Britain – or the great rebellion, as it is now popular to call it, had little in common with those that shook the continental mainland. The islands of Britain and Ireland were protected by choppy seas which had over the years secured them from invasion by their enemies. Nevertheless travel by the aristocracy and by merchants or sojourns abroad by religious exiles brought home new ideas, and during the reign of Queen Elizabeth I almost the whole of the Church had succumbed to Calvinist tenets that had swept the continent. Although it is no longer fashionable to speak of a Puritan revolution, religion had its part in the political convulsion of the middle of the century. The people of the islands were divided into different religions. The majority of the Irish were Roman Catholics, though there was a Protestant enclave in the north and Protestants ruled from Dublin. In Scotland the majority were Presbyterians, following Calvin's pattern of Church government in which the laity played an important part, but in the highlands there were Roman Catholics. England itself was subject to a compromise. The Elizabethan Church retained the structure of the old Roman Church and many of its rituals, but the bulk of its members were Calvinist in their theology. For example, Archbishop Whitgift, the scourge of the Puritans at the end of Elizabeth's reign, himself was a convinced Calvinist.

In the reigns of James I and Charles I two significant minorities had grown up within the English Church: the Puritans who aimed to destroy all Catholic rituals and, for the most part, wanted to abolish the bishops, and the Arminians, headed by Archbishop William Laud, who did not accept the full Calvinist theology and aimed at enforcing uniformity of worship in the Church. Gradually the Puritans' influence increased, particularly in the towns; their preachers were not, as many English clergy were, 'dumb mouths', but inspired their listeners with radical notions. Since the very beginning of Elizabeth's reign a vociferous Puritan minority had existed in the House of Commons and reached notable proportions by the time that Charles I came to the throne in 1625. Most people had grievances against the Church hierarchy: the bishops were often wealthy property-owners; ecclesiastical jurisdiction covered all sorts of moral behaviour and extended to testamentary dispositions; oaths were enforced by the Church which could punish by excommunication; and payments of tithes and fees by the laity to the Church were a long-standing grievance. Hence even members of parliament who had no pronounced Puritan sympathies were antagonistic to the leaders of the Church and wanted to reduce or abolish their secular powers. Finally it was widely suspected, especially after the king married a French wife, that a movement was on foot at the court to bring the kingdom back into the Roman Catholic fold. Thus there were stirrings against the government not dissimilar from those that brought about the Bohemian revolt.

Another cause of grievance against the English goverment, which was common to the revolutions in Spain and in France, was the imposition of new kinds of taxation. These were directly related to the monarchy's involvement in continental affairs from the time when James I was reluctantly drawn into them by his son-in-law, the Elector Palatine. During the first part of James's reign and the last part of Charles I's England was at peace and financial problems then were the least pressing. But when at the end of his reign James was at war both with Spain and with France, and when at the outset of his reign Charles I tried to avenge himself on the Spaniards for his personal humiliation in Madrid, matters of public finance became paramount. The kings could not wage war without grants from the House of Commons which was unwilling to give them unless it were conceded greater control over policy. Not that the gentlemen of England really disapproved of the war against Spain or of succouring the German Protestants, but they thought it could be done on the cheap, as it had been, to some extent under Queen Elizabeth. Charles I was driven to reviving out-of-date feudal impositions, to increasing customs duties, and to levying ship money, for none of which he needed parliamentary consent. But in 1639 and 1640 he was drawn into a war with his Scottish subjects on whom he had foolishly tried to fasten a version of the Church of England prayer book and then, after an interval of eleven years, during which he had managed to govern without calling a parliament, he was obliged to appeal to the House of Commons for help. The calling of two parliaments in 1640 precipitated civil war, just as the refusal of the cortes of Catalonia to grant money to Felipe IV of Spain had been preliminary to a civil war in that principality.

Another important factor in the causes of the English revolution was the rise of new and influential classes in the community, particularly a wealthy gentry class and a bigger mercantile class. The gentry dominated the House of Commons; the merchants were less strongly represented there, but often intermarried with the gentry or became gentry themselves by buying estates. Some English historians have argued that the rise of the gentry may be traced far back into history, at least to the fifteenth century, if not earlier. But it can scarcely be doubted that the sales of Church lands at the time of the Reformation and the sales of Crown lands, for example, by Queen Elizabeth I, had given the class below the peerage a chance to improve their fortunes and extend their influence. Yeomen or tenant farmers rose to become landowners and the younger sons of the aristocracy and high clergy established themselves as proprietors of large estates. From at least the beginning of Elizabeth's reign these gentry had been making their mark in the House of Commons and, in alliance with members of the legal profession, had become critical of the conduct of the monarchy. The first parliament of James I's reign had been no less, though perhaps no more, opposed to the government than had been the Elizabethan parliaments. The rise of the gentry, like the rise of the House of Commons, is not a historical theory but a historical fact.

But when all has been said and done, it was not merely a changing class structure that explains the English revolution. The leaders of parliament honestly believed that the Stuarts had by their behaviour during the first forty years of the century disobeyed accepted laws – above all the Common Law of the realm – and endangered the Reformation. The king was condemned for imprisoning members of parliament without showing cause, for levying illegal taxes, for flirting with the Roman Church. The commons seized the opportunity afforded by the king's desperate need for money in 1640 to insist on constitutional changes, notably the abolition of some of the royal prerogative courts which had existed since the time of the Tudors, a declaration that ship money was illegal, an agreement to hold regular meetings of parliament. Charles I gave way, but a crisis came over the control of the militia. Parliament was afraid that if it let the king raise an army or control the militia at home he would use his power to reverse the concessions he had granted them and rule again, as before, in an arbitrary manner. Charles did in fact attempt to arouse the Scots against the English and later invoked the aid of the Irish. The commons passed a Grand Remonstrance outlining their grievances; but the fact that a substantial minority of the members voted against it gave encouragement to the king. At the end of 1641 he tried to arrest five of the leading opposition members of parliament; when they escaped, he left London for the north and began recruiting an army to bring parliament to its senses. Parliament also enlisted an army, and in August 1642 the civil war began.

The first civil war lasted until 1646. Charles I was beaten and taken a prisoner. A second civil war broke out in 1648 and culminated in the trial and execution of the king. But by that time the leaders of the parliamentary army had quarrelled with the 'rump' of the parliament which ruled the kingdom after the royalist members had left it and was 'Presbyterian' in its religious views. This was largely, but by no means entirely, a religious dispute. Many of the soldiers were not Presbyterians and believed in the independence of individual congregations. The army overthrew the parliamentary leaders and established an oligarchic republic. After royalist movements in Ireland and Scotland had been suppressed, the commander of the parliamentary army, Oliver Cromwell, became lord protector of the three kingdoms in 1653. He ruled the country in a constitutional rather than an arbitrary way until his death in 1658. Wars against the Dutch and the Spaniards brought glory to the protectorate and when Oliver died the regime seemed so strong that the royalists did not at first believe that the Stuart monarchy could be restored. Oliver Cromwell had refused to become king himself, but when his son Richard succeeded him as protector the royalists were hopeful of coming to terms either with Richard or the army commanders. They did in the end succeed in inducing the general in command of the army in Scotland, George Monck, to come over to their side. Thus Charles I's son, Charles II, returned to London as king in 1660. The revolution made a profound impression not only on English but on European opinion. For Charles I had not been assassinated (like Henri IV of France), but had been publicly tried by a revolutionary tribunal appointed by parliament. Many of the procedures of government followed by the Tudors and early Stuarts were therefore abandoned forever by the English monarchy. And although by the end of his reign of twenty-five years Charles II did in fact open a path to absolutism, another successful revolution against a Stuart king in 1688 reduced the chances of the English monarchy becoming despotic like that of France or Spain, Russia or the Scandinavian kingdoms in the early eighteenth century.

The revolutions in France arose after the death of Louis XIII and because of the weakness of the government during the minority of his son. The nobility, or at any rate the French princes of the Blood, had long resented their treatment by the dead Cardinal Richelieu and were determined, if possible, not to be humiliated by his successor, Cardinal Mazarin. Mazarin, an astute Italian adventurer of modest parentage, owed his position not only to his skill as a politician and diplomatist but also to the love and trust of the queen mother, Anne of Austria, who, in defiance of her husband's will, had been appointed sole regent of the kingdom. But the wars against Spain and the Austrian Habsburgs were continuing and their expense demanded new financial expedients, just as Charles I's wars had done in England. So long as the French government could subsist by turning the screw upon the peasantry, it had only to contend with sporadic revolts. When, however, it dared to attack the interests of the nobility of the Robe and the bourgeoisie it met with fierce resistance. The administration of Mazarin and of the finance minister, Particelli d'Hémery, was condemned in a flood of pamphlets known as the 'Mazarinades': in them the Bourbon monarchy was upheld, but despotism censured. The parlement of Paris, a corporation of more or less irremovable lawyers (the hereditary character of their offices was secured by the existence of the *paulette*), aware of the achievements of the revolutionary parliament in England, protested to the regent against the government's financial policies which included a forced reduction in the value of the *rentes* (or loan stock) and an attempt to tax newly-built houses in Paris. In June 1648 representatives of the four sovereign courts in Paris met together in the Chambre de Saint-

Louis and put forward a far-reaching programme of reforms, requiring, among other things, that in future no taxes should be levied except by edicts freely registered by parlements. For a time the queen and Mazarin were forced to give way, but in August they ordered the arrest of a number of leaders of the Paris parlement, including the venerable Pierre Broussel. The retort to this was a rising in Paris and in October 1648 the regency yielded and conceded virtually all the demands put forward in the Chambre de Saint-Louis. In the winter, however, these concessions were revoked and the prince de Condé, who had won victories in Germany (he had succeeded his father in the title in 1646) blockaded Paris on behalf of the regency. But neither Condé nor his brother, Conti were wholeheartedly on the side of the government; they were jealous of the influence of Mazarin and eager to supplant him. Thus the position of the government was weakened and finally in March 1649 it was again obliged to come to terms with the leaders of parlement in the treaty of Rueil. The so-called *Fronde parlementaire* ended therefore in a victory for the French middle classes over the monarchy, much as the first civil war had done in England.

The word fronde derived from a catapult or sling which boys used to fire at strangers before they ran away. The second Fronde or *Fronde princière* was such a confused and futile revolution that the word was an appropriate one. It was started in January 1650 by the decision taken at court to arrest the three princes, Condé, Conti, and their brother-in-law, the duc de Longueville, for treasonable conspiracy. In Paris there was no reaction, but trouble broke out in the provinces. Marshal Turenne, seduced by the wiles of Madame de Longueville, returned from Germany and the princess de Condé set up a rebel government in Bordeaux. Nearly all the higher nobility conspired against Mazarin, including even the king's uncle, the duc d'Orleans. Their ideal, it has been said, was a combination of interested cynicism and refined Machiavellianism. By February 1651 the regency government had been compelled to release the rebel princes and Mazarin himself had fled abroad. But then the various frondeurs began to quarrel among themselves, as the Puritans did in England. Condé and Turenne, the two ablest French generals of their time, fought one another, and to strengthen their hands the rebel princes conspired with Spain, still at war with France. Gradually many French people realised that their choice was between anarchy and loyalty to the monarchy. In October 1652 the court returned to Paris. Condé was exposed as a traitor to his king and country. The feelings of relief in Paris were similar to those felt in London when Charles II returned in 1660. In March 1653 even Mazarin was tepidly welcomed back in the French capital and finally in August 1653, Bordeaux, which had set up a kind of revolutionary republic, capitulated to the royal forces. The reaction was so fierce that the concessions won by the *Fronde parlementaire* were lost and the monarchy became firmer than ever. Louis XIV never forgot his childhood memories of the Parisian revolutionary mob.

The failure of the revolution in France was due to the fact that the classes who had grievances against the Crown never combined effectively against it. The aims of the nobility of the sword appeared to be purely selfish; the bourgeoisie distrusted the nobles; the peasantry, whom crushing taxation had so often angered, took little or no part in the revolutionary movements. It was in no sense a popular revolution; in fact in some parts of the kingdom the court found sources of support against the feudal princes and the dominant classes in Paris. All the revolutionary leaders accepted the idea of an absolute monarchy; what they wanted was simply to overthrow the regime of Mazarin and d'Hémery. But when it was realised that the real choice for France was between anarchy and a stable, if despotic government, the majority of the property-owning classes turned with gratitude back to an institution which at least worked both under Henri IV and Louis XIII. They rejoiced therefore in the idea of strong government; what they resented was the despotism of the first minister, whether it were Richelieu (who, after all, was one of their own aristocracy) or the upstart Mazarin. As David Ogg wrote, 'the fronde prepared the way not for the French Revolution but for the absolutism of Versailles'.

The revolution in the United Netherlands stemmed from the peace settlement of 1648 and was bloodless only because of the sudden death of the chief protagonist, Willem II, prince of Orange. During the war Willem's father and uncle as military leaders under the titles of captain-general and admiral-general and stadholders or chief executive officers of most of the provinces had been a centralising force in the Union, which originally had been no more than a loose confederation of republics. But the province of Holland provided most of the sinews of war and because of its widespread commercial interests usually inclined to peace. Willem II, however, wanted to continue the war in alliance with France in order to win back other parts of the Netherlands from Spain. He also wished to help his father-in-law, Charles I of England, in his conflict with parliament. But Holland insisted on peace being concluded and a reduction in the size of the Dutch army. Relying on the prestige of his family name and the support given to him in the other six provinces, Willem II had attempted to carry out a *coup d'état*; he had arrested and imprisoned six of the deputies of Holland and laid siege to Amsterdam, forcing the magistrates to come to terms with him. The arrest of the six deputies may be compared with Charles I's vain attempt to arrest the five members of parliament or with the arrest of the French parlementaires. The assault on Amsterdam may be compared with the march of the English royalist army on the city of London in 1642, from which it was repulsed, or, better, Condé's siege of Paris in 1649. But Willem's death of small-pox in November 1650 enabled the powerful leaders of Holland to reverse the trend towards centralisation and monarchical governments. Willem, wrote Professor Geyl, 'was the exponent of the monarchical principle which was then prevailing all over the continent: centralising and militaristic, no longer leaning on the nobility as an independent power, but using it all the more as an instrument and for its own more resplendent lustre.' Europe looked upon the events that followed the Dutch prince's death almost with incredulity. Just as Willem had tried to compel the states of Holland to accept his direction of policy, now the regents took their revenge. They persuaded the other provinces to abolish the post of captain-general and themselves abolished the stadholderate. Though Willem's cousin remained stadholder of two provinces, the others had none and the next twenty-two years became known as the stadholderless period in Dutch history. A Grand Assembly of all the provinces, a revolutionary body, organised by Holland, met at The Hague in January 1651 and decontrolled the management of the army and virtually decentralised the Union. The Orangists were forced underground and somehow or other this gimcrack political arrangement held together during two wars against England. It was not until 1672 when the French monarchy launched an unprovoked assault on the Dutch that Willem II's posthumous son, a youth of twenty-two, was recalled to the offices of captain-general and stadholder of Holland and the whole of the Dutch provinces were for a time firmly united.

Clearly the points of view of the two sides in the United Netherlands were so diametrically opposed that had it not been for the death of Willem II a long civil war, like those in France and England, might have taken place. As it was, the nation, created by eighty years of war against the Spanish empire, was out of line with the rest of Europe, repudiating all traces of monarchy and centralised government and carrying on as a political entity mainly because of the predominance of the wealth of Holland where the oligarchial leadership was able to determine decisions in the states-general, the confederate assembly responsible for the conduct of foreign affairs.

What do we understand by a revolution? If we mean the overthrow by forcible means of an existing government or form of government, then it is clear that all the events of the middle of the century which have been outlined can fairly be described as revolutions or attempts at revolution. The Portuguese revolution was a complete success; the English revolution contributed significantly to the development of

English political and constitutional ideas. In fact the later Stuart kings were taught a lesson by the public execution of Charles I after an open trial. His son, Charles II, for a long time followed a constitutional or at least semi-constitutional course of behaviour; his other son, James II, panicked at the critical moment in his reign and fled the country, fearful of suffering the fate of his father. Two of the revolutions in Spain failed because their leaders could find no alternative to accepting the rule of the Habsburgs except only by offering their allegiance to the French Bourbons. The frondes were also ill conceived. Their aim was to overthrow an unpopular minister and not a government; lacking an alternative to the monarchy (indeed the Mazarinades were not critical of the monarchy as such) in the end the revolt against the regency collapsed in anarchy. The revolution in the United Netherlands was not a lasting success since twenty-two years after it took place the Dutch people turned with relief to the prince of Orange as their leader and symbol of unity.

It has sometimes been argued that economic discontent – the birth pangs of a civilisation about to deliver 'capitalism' – which prevailed throughout Europe in the first half of the century produced a general sense of social unrest that erupted into revolutions. It is true that the price revolution caused difficulties at any rate to some sections of the community. It had been brought about not merely by the influx of precious metals from the New World but also by increases of population during the period of comparative peace, and by the debasement of the coinage, notably in Spain. But the price revolution had slowed down by 1630 and in any case if it had been a source of general crisis, why did this not explode into revolution in the sixteenth century when prices rose four, five, or six times? It is also true that periodic bad harvests and outbreaks of plague accentuated the habitual miseries of the mass of the people; but one would suggest that the principal way in which the price revolution gave impetus to unrest was through its repercussions on national finances because customary sources of revenue diminished in value. Governments were more and more driven to seek new methods of raising income and in nearly all countries these were regressive in character, hitting poorer people the most. But the basic cause of the demands for increased taxation was the high cost of war. It was certainly no mere coincidence that the revolutions broke out when governments had been involved for a long time directly or indirectly in the 'Thirty Years War' and had to pay for the hire of soldiers, sailors, ships and all the weapons and supplies of war. Ship money, more than anything else, helped to create the widespread sense of dissatisfaction with the monarchy in England. Willem II's persistent opposition to the idea of reducing the size of the Dutch army gave rise to the revolution in

Holland. The demand by Olivares that Portugal and Catalonia should pay their share towards the expenses of the Spanish armies fighting the Dutch or the French or serving in Germany was a direct reason for the revolutions there, while Masaniello's revolt in Naples was sparked off by the tax on fruit. As Professor Charles Wilson has rightly said, the idea that 'oppressive taxes' should give rise to revolutions or bring about the decline of empires is nowadays regarded as 'an unfashionable theme'. People today accept very high taxation to pay for national defence as a necessary or at least unavoidable part of their way of life. But most people did not think like that at all three hundred years ago. And taxation is also far more fairly distributed in European countries now than it was then.

In France the numerous peasant revolts against taxation, notably against the *taille*, which took place in various parts of the kingdom, are well documented. To some extent the peasants were encouraged to protest by the landlord class, for if the peasants paid their taxes in full, they could not also manage to pay their rents and leave themselves enough to live on. Modern research in fact has shown, as Mrs Prestwich has pointed out, that 'the revolts were largely instigated by the local bourgeoisie and office-holders and that the nobility were often involved'. Thus a connection of a sort can be traced between these sporadic revolts and the frondes which were essentially the work of the nobility and bourgeoisie. In Catalonia and Naples, on the other hand, the revolts were largely engineered by the lower classes and in fact the possessing classes were perturbed by their violence. In England and in the United Netherlands, however, the revolutionary leadership came from the well-to-do. In England the gentry were divided for or against the king, though the nobility for the most part sided with him; Cromwell's army was said by himself to consist of fewer gentlemen than that of the Cavaliers whose soldiers were largely recruited from the outdoor staffs of the peerage and large landowners. Yeomen and members of the 'industrious classes' tended to sympathise with parliament and when a professional army was raised to fight the royalists in 1645 the infantry consisted partly of pressed men. But the mass of the peasantry were the victims of the war, not its protagonists. In the United Netherlands the bulk of the people inclined to favour the Orangists and so did many of the orthodox ministers of the Reformed Church. It was the regent class, the prosperous bourgeoisie which advocated disarmament and separatism.

It has been suggested by Hugh Trevor-Roper that the 'general crisis' in Europe in the first half of the century can be attributed to a breakdown in the relationship between the courts or the state and society as a whole. Those people who did not bask in the favour of the monarchs, who did not benefit from gifts or fees or the advantages that accrued from the purchase of offices of one kind or another resented the influence of those who did; the aim of revolution was to 'jettison a top-heavy bureaucracy' and 'to return to a responsible mercantilist policy'. But the difficulty about this theory (though it can certainly be supported by examples from England), his critics have observed, is that in France it was the office-holders themselves who started the parliamentary fronde and in the Iberian peninsula it was those parts of the country which suffered least from the burdens imposed by a bureaucracy that revolted, whereas the Castilians who did suffer remained loyal to the monarchy. What, however, is undoubtedly true is that the extravagances of courtiers and officials were everywhere a source of grievances and helped to undermine the authority of governments. The 'sumptuary laws' passed by governments in Spain and elsewhere in the early part of the century to check extravagance and ostentation were intended to assuage very real resentments. Moreover men who made their own way up in the world by competitive processes came to believe that leading ministers were despotic and corrupt, and that again created unrest and disloyalty. Those kinds of emotions were aroused against James I's favourites and ministers in England, against Richelieu and Mazarin in France, against Lerma and Olivares in Spain. Since corruption, or what today would be called corruption, was rife, it was always possible to lay the finger of guilt upon men at the top, though the finger might easily be pointed that way by men who would have been equally corrupt themselves had they enjoyed equal opportunities. Whether that kind of feeling was novel, whether it was symptomatic of a 'general crisis' may still be debated.

How far were such emotions peculiar to monarchies? It might be questioned whether republics proved themselves more efficient, more economical, or more incorrupt than monarchies, but some men believed that they might be so. The foundation of the republic in England and the abolition of the captain-generalship in the United Netherlands were hailed as the beginnings of a new era. For a moment a republic was mooted in Catalonia and Naples. At the height of the second fronde Bordeaux declared itself a republic. Educated men looked back to the republics of Greece and Rome as models to be followed. Venice and Switzerland were admired. Thus a republican movement existed. But the majority of the revolutionaries in England, France and Spain accepted the idea of monarchy as such and were only eager to overthrow wicked ministers. Experience tended to show that successful attacks on monarchies or the proclamation of republics did not lead to a better state of society but only degenerated into anarchy. The Catalan and Neapolitan republics turned hastily to the French monarchy to sustain them; England soon faced anarchy after the strong hand of Oliver Cromwell was removed; the Dutch in the end had to call back the House of Orange to power.

The seventeenth century was not an age of revolution in the sense that the nineteenth and twentieth centuries were to be. For a time the revolutionaries infected one another, but revolutions did not arise out of the striking contrasts between wealth and poverty that certainly existed throughout the whole of Europe. There was of course much economic distress and financial worry, but, after all, few historical periods, including our own, have, since the invention of money, been free from depressions and inflations or have unveiled the secret of economic stability. Governments three hundred years ago had yet to discover an efficient means of borrowing on a national scale: indeed it was the mishandling of the *rentes* that provoked the fronde, while the forced loans in England, Spain and Rome were fruitful causes of discontent among the propertied classes. But the original source of these financial difficulties in every case was war. When for a short period Europe was at peace, exhausted by the 'Thirty Years War' and the long struggle between Bourbons and Habsburgs, revolutionary outbreaks subsided. Though new and revolutionary intellectual ideas were then developing, especially as science opened surprising vistas to European minds, politically most countries turned not to republicanism or democracy, but to even more absolute governments that could enforce order, command obedience and maintain internal peace.

CHAPTER 9

THE REVOLUTION IN MEN'S MINDS

The greatest revolution in the century was in the minds of men. Descartes was the first outstanding modern philosopher. By abandoning the assumptions of the medieval scholastic thinkers and adopting a mathematical or geometrical method of reasoning, derived from a few simple ideas, Descartes and his successors examined the problems of human existence in ways that were untrammelled and entirely novel. They believed that deduction from clear and distinct ideas would lead them infallibly to the ultimate truth about things. Spinoza was convinced that ethics could be as surely demonstrated as the propositions of Euclidean geometry: 'in the true philosophy the order of ideas ought to be the same as the real order of things'. The German Samuel Puffendorf undertook to deduce the entire system of natural rights by a geometrical process based on the needs of society. Leibniz set out many of his arguments in a mathematical form, complete with corollaries. Thomas Hobbes thought he could rely on definitions and the irrefutable necessary deductions he drew from them.

But if they followed their logic wherever it took them, these rationalist philosophers understood that they were exploring dangerous territory. Though, as we have seen, Descartes was himself a Roman Catholic his 'mechanistic despiritualisation', as it has been called, was shocking to many of his immediate contemporaries, and in 1663, after his death, his works were officially condemned by being placed on the Index of the Roman Catholic Church. His followers, like Geulincx and the Abbé Malebranche, strove to make Cartesianism respectable in the Christian world. Malebranche thought there was a universal reason in all minds which was a divine attribute and thus was able to argue that philosophy taught that 'we behold all things in God'. Nevertheless the Jesuits for the most part opposed Cartesianism as mechanistic and materialist. Benedict de Spinoza (1632–77), a Jew of Portuguese extraction, who preserved his personal independence by earning a living as a lens-grinder in Holland, published under his own name during his lifetime only an exposition of the philosophy of Descartes: his own even more revolutionary ideas appeared anonymously. In fact he gave instructions that his *Ethics* was not to be published until after his death and he was very reluctant to allow Leibniz, an equally daring thinker, to see the manuscript. Spinoza, because he was a Jew with the reputation of being an atheist, understandably needed to be careful even in the tolerant Netherlands. So did Thomas Hobbes, who, with rather more reason, was attacked as an atheist in his own country. Leibniz, on the other hand, devoted much of his life to trying to heal the breach between the different Christian confessions and his philosophy was aimed at reconciling the mechanistic and teleological views of the universe and at uniting the scientific and religious outlook of his time. Yet he was extremely anxious to avoid being censured by ecclesiastical authority, even by the Roman Catholic Church, of which he was not a member and although he spent most of his life in Protestant Germany. He was much perturbed when Antoine Arnauld, the French theologian, criticised him for being heretical and he told the Landgrave of Hesse that 'it is always well to be on one's guard', for 'touch the mountains and they will smoke'. John Locke also preferred to do much of his writing anonymously, including his political treatises. By these cautions and anonymities one can measure the awareness of the intellectual revolution that was taking place.

Yet nearly all these philosophers were in fact profoundly religious men in their own ways. It has even been argued recently that Thomas Hobbes, the writer who was the most frequently accused of atheism, was a believing Christian and a moralist. But where these thinkers could not be induced to compromise was over the facts revealed by science. The pure scientists themselves – the 'natural philosophers' – were usually content to acknowledge that the universe – from the bodies of men to the stars in the heavens – worked upon recognisable principles or according to physical laws and left to theology the interpretation of the mind of God, the creator of all things.

But what distinguished the outlook of men like Descartes, Spinoza, Leibniz and Locke, who were philosophers in the widest sense of the term, was that they drew their pictures of the universe directly from their definition of body and mind and therefore found it difficult, if not impossible, to separate science from theology.

Spinoza was more audacious than Descartes. Not only did Spinoza reject the Old Testament of his ancestors as incompatible with the facts of science and the methods of logic, but he wrote a polemic against the anthropomorphism of teleology. Unlike Descartes, Spinoza thought that there was only one 'substance'. To him God and Nature were identical, constituting the universal world essence. God was therefore not the transcendent creator, separate from the universe, but the immanent cause of all things. Everything in the universe was determined and nothing was contingent. Thus the Spinozan metaphysics were the expression of the ideal that had been established by a unified science. From this conception of the universe was deduced Spinoza's system of ethics. Man, he thought, must understand the nature of his passions and by understanding free himself from them. Moral problems (as Professor Hampshire has explained) could therefore be treated as clinical problems, much as Freud was to do later. Man could be said to be free in so far as he acquired a clear and distinct understanding of the causes of his own physical and mental states; his happiness therefore consisted in identifying himself with nature and his wisdom in meditating not on death but on life.

It was no wonder that these notions as they spread were deemed revolutionary and heretical. Spinoza was a determinist, but a metaphysical determinist; a materialist but not a crude materialist; a pantheist but in an extremely subtle sense of the term. Thus in his lifetime he was believed to be the destroyer of all established religion and morality. But later generations came to regard him much more as an idealist who saw life in terms of a divine essence. And his philosophy in fact made him the champion of intellectual and political freedom, caused him to live a life of independent thought and ascetic practice, and gave him the courage to face death with equanimity.

Leibniz tackled the problem of body and mind in a different way from either Descartes or Spinoza. Since many of his metaphysical thoughts were published long after his death, it is difficult to be sure exactly what he did believe, and to the modern mind his theories may seem fantastic. But he was a busy and versatile man: a universal genius like Newton. He was an outstanding mathematician, inventing the infinitesimal calculus at about the same time as Newton. He wrote on mathematics, physics, jurisprudence, theology and logic. For a time he was the librarian of the duke of Brunswick and was occupied in writing an official history of that country, but he had only reached the eleventh century before he died. He spent some time in Paris and tried to persuade King Louis XIV to divert his attentions from western Europe to Egypt. He once spent a month with Spinoza, but was anxious not to be tarred with the brush of his atheism. Unlike Spinoza, he believed that, though the universe was built on scientific lines, it had an ultimate purpose. The world, he thought, did not consist of one 'substance', but of many 'substances' or 'monads', as he called them. Life was variety and at the same time unity. To him each substance or monad was the world substance but in a particular form: it was unity in plurality. The monad was not physical but quasi-psychical in its nature. The universe consisted of a hierarchy of monads progressing from mere matter to the central monad or God. Thus all the monads harmonised or corresponded with each other (though they had 'no windows': they were 'metaphysically impenetrable'). This pre-established harmony was due to God. Thus God the creator was reintroduced into the scheme of things and the problem of the dualism of mind and matter was solved. 'In Leibniz', observed Windelband, 'all threads of the old and new metaphysics run together.'

Leibniz was an optimist. He thought that 'every soul was a world apart, independent of everything else except God'. God, he thought, had made men free: there was a 'principle of sufficient reason' which 'inclines without necessitating'. The existence of sin was necessary in order that man might have a free choice between good and evil. God is good and has created the best of all possible worlds – a notion that was later to be mocked by Voltaire. Such at least were the theories that he expounded openly in his lifetime, but it has been suggested by Bertrand Russell that another Leibniz is to be discovered who was less optimistic and more of a determinist.

Spinoza was a pantheist and a metaphysical determinist; Leibniz was an optimist; the Englishman, John Locke, the contemporary of Leibniz, was, above all, an empiricist, the common-sense philosopher *par excellence*. He took certain ideas for granted, such as his own existence and the existence of God, and preferred credibility to consistency. For Locke the proper study of mankind was man and he thought that the grounds of probability were 'conformity with our own experience and the testimony of others' experience'. Empirical psychology was the basis of his theory of knowledge. He rejected the innate ideas of Descartes because he thought that knowledge could be derived from experience attained by sensation or reflection. There could be nothing in the mind of which the mind knew nothing. Both Locke and Newton rejected the metaphysical hypotheses of their contemporary European philosophers. To them the various notions of 'substances' used by Descartes, Spinoza and Leibniz, which were obtained from the logical categories of subject and predicate, were medieval nonsense. Thomas Hobbes, too, was an empirical psychologist who rejected all high-flown metaphysics. He was also a materialist. Another earlier empiricist who influenced Locke was the Frenchman Pierre Gassendi (1592–1655): like Hobbes, he was a critic of Descartes: he found the source of knowledge in sense perception, not innate ideas. But unlike Hobbes, he believed that theories needed to be confirmed by observation and that man's outlook ought to be based on probabilities.

There were therefore in seventeenth-century Europe two main strands of thought: first, the metaphysical which explained the universe by mathematical reasoning based on a few logical hypotheses and produced the dualism of Descartes, the pantheism of Spinoza, and the 'wondrous monads' of Leibniz. Because this method of thinking did not stem from religious faith or divine inspiration it was condemned by most Churchmen. Secondly, there were the empiricists, chiefly Englishmen, beginning with Bacon and culminating in Locke, who rejected innate ideas and metaphysical arguments and laid the foundation for a psychological form of reasoning. But both these different strands contributed to a revolution in the European mind; for they each of them prepared the way for the ideals of reason and humanity that were to be met in the eighteenth century.

These two strands were plain enough to see: it is an exaggeration to claim that Cartesianism swept over Europe in the second half of the century; it was rejected not only by the empiricists but by Spinoza and Leibniz and their followers and by influential writers who were not philosophers. Though few questioned the idea of a purposive God, there were growing doubts about the truths of Christianity. Cartesianism had shaken faith, even if in fact it was intended to bolster it up and numbered Christian philosophers among its disciples. Deism had been advocated in England in the century both by Lord Herbert of Cherbury and by John Toland. Such men were impressed by the stories about the variety of religious beliefs that were brought back from the New World by explorers and adventurers. Herbert of Cherbury in his *De Veritate* (1624) argued the case for 'natural religion': he claimed that moral judgments are eternal truths which were valid in their own right without any prescribed authority. Not only Hobbes but French authors like La Rochefoucauld and La Bruyère presented a case for morality based on psychology. One of the most influential figures towards the end of the century was Pierre Bayle (1647–1706), a French Huguenot who, after various adventures, settled in the United Netherlands. He criticised all forms of blind faith or superstition. Not only did he attack astrology, a very popular superstition, seductive, it seems, even to the great Newton, but he declared that atheism was not prejudicial to morality. In his *Historical and Critical Dictionary* (1697), which has been described as 'the bible of the eighteenth century', he belittled Old Testament heroes, questioned the reality of miracles, and expressed doubts about much accepted ethical teaching. He was indeed the type of free and independent thinker who gradually emerged during the aftermath of the 'Thirty Years War'. He did not acquire his scepticism through his knowledge of science, for he was not much of a scientist. But, like other influential European thinkers of his time, he realised that the old order of ideas, founded on Aristotelianism and orthodox Christianity, had been completely undermined and that the facts of ethics and history stood in need of reinterpretation.

The general use of mathematical or rational methods of argument in metaphysics and ethics inevitably had their impact on political theory.

These methods led, as in philosophy, to the redefinition of commonly-used phrases, such as natural law and contract, and also to the deduction of new ideas from these definitions. The most striking of these new ideas was the conception of sovereignty, first put forward by the Frenchman, Jean Bodin, at the end of the sixteenth century and developed by English writers including Parker and Hobbes, whose thoughts were turned in this direction by the civil wars. Earlier political thinkers may be said to have been dominated by two concepts, first that of the Great Chain of Being, secondly, the supremacy of the law. Theirs was a static world in which every member of society had his appointed place from the pope and king down to the father and child, master and servant. But the king was not thought of as an absolute ruler; he was subject to the law, which generally meant God's law or the moral law, although it might also mean the customary law or common law of the land. In the Middle Ages European kings were also considered to be subject to the pope so far as spiritual matters were concerned; and since spiritual matters were believed to be more important than material ones, in the last resort popes could and did overrule kings.

The Reformation strengthened the hands of Protestant rulers who were no longer the servants but had become the masters of the Church. However, they were still thought of as being obedient to the law, while in most countries they were also obliged to consult their estates, who had their place in the Great Chain. Thus, as has already been observed, monarchs, at the outset of the century, were nowhere regarded as absolute; and if they did not accept the customs and laws of their realm, they were condemned as arbitrary and liable to be resisted. Traditionally kings swore oaths or granted charters when they were crowned, and so it could be claimed that they were not necessarily merely governing by divine right granted from on high but also in terms of contracts made with their own subjects. The author of the *Vindiciae contra tyrannos* and the Jesuits, Mariana and Suarez, both used contractual phraseology to prove that monarchs were limited in their rights. Althusius argued that an association was formed by the people to set up magistrates and a contract made between the association and the magistrates.

The idea of it being the duty of the king to obey the laws both of God and man died slowly. Though Bodin argued that the existence of a sovereign power was the essential characteristic of a fully formed state, he did not break away from the older view that princes were subject to divine and natural laws. In the last resort he thought that a subject could disobey if a ruler did not respect the sanctity of the family and of private property. During the sixteenth century too the Scottish

Presbyterian leader, John Knox, Sir Thomas Smith, the English political writer, and others employed 'populist' arguments for controlling the Crown. Richard Hooker wrote that 'the seat of the law is in the bosom of God', while Johannes Althusius insisted that the natural law to which all governments were subject was based on the Ten Commandments and he also advocated sovereignty for the estates.

Machiavelli was the first well-known author to look at the state in a purely material and practical way, free from medieval notions of divine laws and duties. He wanted his native state of Florence to be free, independent and strong. Machiavelli, Bodin and Grotius all tried clearly to separate human and divine rights. They emphasised the social responsibilities of government. Grotius based the law of nature on human reason alone and regarded natural right as subservient to social needs. In his work on international law, for which he is best known in European history (although in fact he was a versatile thinker, like so many of his great contemporaries), Grotius urged that it was necessary to formulate rules of conduct to cover the position of civilians in war time since otherwise they were at the mercy of the military. International law was to him a law of nature at the service of the community. And the principles of contract law were applicable to a society of individuals as much as to a society of nations.

The evolution of the doctrine of political sovereignty was therefore due partly to the separation by empiricists of the divine from the human sphere and partly to the practical need for a clear and unqualified source of authority in the state. In England up to the eve of the civil war the doctrine of 'mixed monarchy' prevailed among the majority of political thinkers: they inclined to the opinion that the king, the parliament, and the judges all had their rights and duties in political society. But civil wars and revolutions threw doubts on the value of such divided authority. Bodin, employing what has been called the argument by correspondence, thought that the king must be absolute as God is absolute. In England that kind of argument was used by Sir Robert Filmer, the most influential of royalist apologists. Althusius based his case for sovereignty upon the natural law. Grotius and Hobbes, on the other hand, believed that sovereign authority was founded on contract. But in Hobbes both contract and natural law received new connotations.

Thomas Hobbes (1588–1679) was influenced in his political theories by the scientific discoveries of his time, notably the work of Galileo, by his knowledge of contemporary history, and by his general philosophy. He was an empiricist, a materialist and a nominalist. Like the anatomical scientists (such as Harvey) he aimed to break up society into individuals and study their natures and needs. This has been called the 'resolutive-compositive' method. Be that as it may, Hobbes was convinced that men because they are naturally envious of each other are born into a state of war of all against all. The laws of nature are rules of prudence which require men, in order that their persons and property may be secured, to surrender their individual rights (except the right to self preservation, which is fundamental) and agree to obey an absolute sovereign, the Leviathan. They therefore make a contract or convention with each other to carry out this surrender of their natural rights; but they sign no contract with the sovereign, for if it were to be subjected to rules it would not be sovereign and therefore would not be able to preserve the peace. Hobbes's sovereign therefore owed nothing to divine right or popular election. But he was man-made, deriving ultimately from the psychological needs of men, a mortal god. Many of Hobbes's contemporaries understandably regarded him as an atheist, whose political theories were subversive of a Christian society.

Hobbes's theories have fascinated twentieth-century thinkers who never cease to write about them. Some modern critics have maintained that they are not as straightforward as was once thought; that his ethical views are not dependent upon his egoistic psychology; they say that he thought it was the moral obligation of subjects to obey the Leviathan as a duty to God as well as because of a contractual agreement among men. But however much Hobbes may appeal to present-day scholars, there is little evidence that his ideas played much part in the practical politics of his own time. In England he was generally repudiated, even by leading royalists like the first earl of Clarendon who infinitely preferred the reasonings of Filmer about government, derived mainly from the argument by correspondence. John Locke, the great English political philosopher of the Enlightenment, seems scarcely to have read Hobbes and devoted his efforts to refuting Filmer. Only Spinoza appears to have read and been impressed by the teaching of Hobbes, though it is said that he reached his own political opinions independently of him. But like Hobbes, Spinoza was regarded as an atheist-materialist whose views were shocking and immoral.

Spinoza thought that political science must be based on a clear understanding of human nature as it really was. This much he had in common with Hobbes, although Spinoza's view of human nature was less pessimistic. He thought that political consent and obedience could be justified as rational self-interest. A political organisation ought to be judged by whether it prevented or assisted a free man's understanding of nature. Laws and conventions, Spinoza thought, were only valuable so long as they were useful. If they threatened the safety or happiness of an individual, then he was not called upon to conform to them. Moreover if a sovereign power employed its authority to subdue opposition to its unreasonable wishes, then it forfeited its rights. Security and intellectual freedom were the criteria of good government and if a government did not provide them, then revolt against it was permissible. Spinoza therefore attached supreme importance to individual liberty, freedom of thought and religious toleration. In this he differed completely from Hobbes for whom the safety of the state was the supreme law. Though a man might resist public authority in order to save his own life, Hobbes regarded a general rebellion or revolution as the worst of all evils. To him despotism was preferable to anarchy.

It is important to remember that two main schools of political thought existed during the century: first, those who were so fearful of the civil wars and revolutions that had divided France and England and had devastated Spain and Germany that they were anxious at all costs to sustain a case for a strong and absolute government – generally envisaged as a monarchy. Even the liberal-minded Grotius had ranged himself with Bodin, Barclay and other advocates of monarchy in its most potent form, and Grotius, like Machiavelli, thought that politics should be independent of religion. Even 'social contracts' and 'natural laws', which are associated in many minds with the origins of liberal political philosophy, were used as arguments for absolute monarchy. The contract that Hobbes wrote about was a contract to set up an all-powerful sovereign, not a contract of government. But, secondly, to many others, mainly English writers, a contract was a guarantee of individual liberty. To John Milton magistrates were always the deputies or agents of the people, not their masters. Their power was delegated to them and could be taken away from them if they violated the broad principles of liberty, such as freedom of conscience and the freedom of the press. John Locke, writing thirty years after Milton, made his contract the very foundation of individual liberty, which meant to him, above all, the sacred right of private property. Like Hobbes, Locke spoke of a state of nature from which men emerged into political society; but whereas Hobbes allowed only the right of self-defence to be retained from this state of nature, Locke thought that individuals in society kept intact their own private rights against the government which they set up. Thus if a government transgressed property rights, it could be overthrown and replaced by another one.

The German Samuel Puffendorf (1632–94) attempted to reconcile Hobbe's authoritarian views about the state with the concern for individual rights which, like Locke later, he derived from the principles of contract law. To Puffendorf the state of nature was not one of war but of general peace. Men, he believed, were rational beings and the law of nature consisted of the dictates of right reason. The first law of

Monarchs

In 1598 when Felipe II died, Spanish power and culture financed by the wealth of the New World, dictated to western Europe; a century later the glory of the 'Sun King' symbolised the supremacy of France.

1 (*above*) Felipe II, king of Spain from 1555 to 1598, painted by Titian in 1550.

2 (*below*) The Escurial, the monastery-palace of granite from the seclusion of which Felipe ruled the Spanish empire.

3 (*above*) Louis XIV (*seated*), who reigned over France from 1643 to 1715, painted
with his son, grandson and great-grandson, by Largillière.

4 (*below*) Versailles: the royal palace, and centre of the French Government; Le Vau's
classical design for the garden façade with J. H. Mansart's additions.

5 Gustav II Adolf, king of Sweden
from 1611 to 1632, whose victorious armies
conquered northern Europe
until his death in battle.

6 The Habsburg features of Felipe IV are flattered by Velazquez.
Felipe's reign from 1621 to 1665
brought a golden age of Spanish arts
but a collapse of wealth and power.

7 Charles I came to the English throne in 1625; in 1649 after two civil wars
he was brought to trial and executed. His Flemish court painter Van Dijk
gave a romantic character to the man who was an inept ruler but a
great patron of the arts.

8 The seven-foot tall Pyëtr I, Peter the Great, from 1696 to 1725 tried to force
Russia into a European mould. His passion for ships, which he studied
on a visit to England in 1697, is hinted at in this portrait
by the English painter Kneller.

Statesmen

9 Count Axel Oxenstierna, chancellor of Sweden,
helped Gustav Adolf strengthen the power
of the Swedish Crown at the expense
of his own class, the nobility.

10 and 11 During the ministries of the
Cardinals Richelieu and Mazarin, 1630–
1661, France was established as a
leading European power and an enemy
of the Habsburgs. The triple portrait
by De Champaigne (*above*) shows
Richelieu, the far-sighted statesman;
(*opposite above*) Mazarin, the subtle Italian,
opens the door of the Temple of Peace,
an engraving commemorating
the Peace of the Pyrenees
made with Spain in 1659.

12 (*opposite*) Louis XIV inherited Colbert
from Mazarin; until his death in 1683
he was indispensable to the king as
the superintendent of finance and of
virtually everything else.
In this painting he is shown in the
foreground (with stick) supervising
the building of Versailles.

13 Johan de Witt, grand pensionary of Holland from 1653 to 1672, helped
to consolidate the prosperity of the United Provinces. The French invasion of
1672, however, gave the excluded Orange party the opportunity to overthrow
de Witt, who was murdered.

Nobility and Gentry

14 and 15 (*above*) Recreation: a ball at the court of Don Juan of Austria in the late 1650s; and a boar-hunt for the gentlemen of the Spanish court.
16 (*below*) Responsibilities: the estate, supported many dependants; English peasants were better off than most, and in this painting the poor of Tichborne receive the dole distributed by the gentry.

Bourgeoisie

17 and 18 (*below*) A Dutch merchant and his wife, symbolic of solid bourgeois
wealth, watch the return of an East India Company ship to Batavia (now Jakarta)
in Java, the trading centre for the East in the seventeenth century.
Dutch trade made the burghers of the United Provinces the élite of the
European middle class. (*bottom*) Rembrandt painted the quiet self-assurance of the
Syndics of the Cloth Drapers' Guild in 1662.

19 (*above*) Two families of the French 'nobility of the robe' (the lawyer class equivalent in wealth and respectability to the Dutch merchants) draw up a marriage contract, an engraving by Abraham Bosse.

20 (*below*) A family group of the Dutch middle class painted by Franz Hals.

Workers and peasants

21 An old French carpenter working by candlelight is the model for
Georges de la Tour's portrayal of St Joseph.

22 and 23 The sketch of a hard-working ferryman contrasts with the idealised gaiety of Italian peasants fishing.

24 French peasants, their faces resigned to poverty and frequent famine, share their bread and wine with a beggar.

25 An old woman says grace over her salmon cutlet, unaware of the cat's attempts to steal her meal. Fish and meat were rarely part of the workers' diet.

The recreations of the poor:
26 and 27 (*above*) dancing at the village
fair by Jan Bruegel;
games outside an inn, by Adriaen
Ostade, and 28 (*below*) bawdy scenes
inside, by Jan Miense Molenaer.

Women

29 (*left*) The learned and
eccentric Queen Kristina of
Sweden, daughter of
Gustav Adolf, was one of
the few women in
seventeenth-century
Europe who wielded power.
She abdicated in 1654.
30 (*below*) Ladies of society
often wrote letters and
diaries, but rarely ventured
so far into the world of
literature as Mme de la
Fayette, whose *La Princesse
de Clèves*, published in 1678,
was the first and greatest
French novel of the century.

31 A Dutch housewife in her courtyard directs a maid preparing fish.

32 and 33 Constant toil in the fields and in the home prematurely aged the women of the poorer classes. *Left:* a kitchen maid, coarsened by work. *Below:* an old woman working at home in her cottage.

Art and Artists

Mannerism, reflecting the spiritual emphasis of the Counter-Reformation, reacted against the classical rules and calm of Renaissance art. 34 The elongated forms and nervous drapery of the style can be seen in El Greco's *Baptism of Christ, c.* 1600.

35 Caravaggio, who died in 1610, laid the foundations of much seventeenth-century painting by his revolutionary use of naturalism and dramatic chiaroscuro. His *Christ and His Disciples at Emmaus*, c. 1597, shows the vigour characteristic of Baroque art.

36 Carracci's frescoes, painted 1597 to 1604, were commissioned by Cardinal Farnese, and this panel shows Jupiter welcoming Juno to the marriage bed.

37 Guido Reni's fresco of Aurora, 1613, shows the romantic influence of Carracci on Italian painting in which classical myth was used to lend pageantry to religious allegory.

38 and 39 Urban VIII, 1623–44 (his monument, left, by Bernini), and Innocent X 1644–55 (right, by Velázquez), two of the popes of the first half of the seventeenth century whose patronage made possible the development of Baroque art in Italy.

40 Bernini, sculptor, architect, painter, was the universal artist of the Baroque period. His sculpture, creating a painterly effect with light, illusionism and coloured materials, was especially influential. *The Ecstasy of St Teresa* shows the fluid movement and emotionalism of his style.

41 Rubens, the Flemish painter, is an example of the cosmopolitanism of the art of his time. He studied in Italy, worked for Albrecht and Isabella in the Spanish Netherlands, and executed in heroic style for Marie de Médicis of France the cycle of her life. *Above:* the queen disembarking at Marseilles, a painting in which exuberance and pomp are effectively merged.

42 Velázquez, appointed painter to the Spanish court in 1623, gradually evolved from his early Caravaggesque manner into the less sculptural style of this painting of the court dwarf 'El Primo', showing a concern over human frailty and solitude.

43 Rembrandt, the greatest of the Dutch painters indirectly influenced by Caravaggio, painted this group of civic guards (incorrectly called *The Night Watch*) in 1642. The dramatic use of light and shade and the diagonal composition make this the climax of his High Baroque manner.

At least sixty self-portraits of Rembrandt are known; they record
the developments in his style and in his character.

44 (*below*) Aged 34, 1640, rich and successful, the stress on horizontals rather than
curves in the composition shows Rembrandt's increasing interest in a more
classical style.

45 (*opposite, right*) Rembrandt, aged 21, *c.* 1629,
an aggressive use of deep shadow on the face, the confident young man.

46 (*below right*) Aged 53, 1659; his popularity as an artist waned and in 1656 he
was threatened with bankruptcy. Rembrandt's deeper emphasis on the spirit
is reflected by this troubled self-portrait.

47 (*far right, below*) Aged 57, 1663, the artist as an old man faces the world serenely.

48 Franz Hals' brush technique and use of the play of light gave his portraits
of his fellow topers of Haarlem the impression of a fleeting instant
caught by the artist.

49 Vermeer's calm interiors owe much to the Dutch tradition, but the natural
effect of his paintings come from a strict sense of composition and the use of
side lighting which he learned from the Italians.

50 and 51 The façade of Il Gesù, Rome, (*top*) the founding church of the Jesuit
order is of the more austere period of the Counter-Reformation. The style was used
for Jesuit churches all over Europe (for instance, at St Germain des Près (*above*)
and was to expand into the more voluptuous lines of Baroque architecture.

52 The interior of S. Ignazio, Rome, 1626, like all
Jesuit churches, follows the cruciform pattern
of Il Gesù with the predominance of nave
and dome; the rich decoration is Late Baroque.

53 and 54 (*opposite*) Bernini's colonnades for
St Peter's, Rome, 1656, combine the Roman
grandeur of the massive columns with the
openness of the oval, a form much favoured in
Baroque architecture.

55 and 56 The oval form, which lent movement
to the centralised plan, was used by Borromini for
the small church of S. Carlo alle Quattro Fontane,
crowned by the dome (*left*). The same delight
in undulating forms, characteristic of Baroque
architecture, can be seen in the façade of the
same church (*below*) built in 1667, the year
of Borromini's death.

57 (*above*) In England, Inigo Jones turned away from the sensuousness and rich
decoration of Italian Baroque architecture and looked rather to the Italian architects
of the sixteenth century, particularly Palladio. The Queen's House, Greenwich,
begun in 1616, is very like an Italian villa of the early Renaissance in the
plain symmetry of its loggia façade.

58 (*below*) The magnificent town hall of Amsterdam was begun in 1648 when Spain
formally recognised the independence of the United Provinces. The classical
façade, influenced by Italy, is combined with northern verticality,
steep-pitched roofs and large cupola.

59 and 60 The intellectual
and classical side of
Baroque art as opposed to
the emotional, was
developed in Rome by the
French painter Poussin, and
the Italians Sacchi and
Sassoferrato and their
school: (*above*) *The Arcadian
Shepherds* by Poussin, *c.* 1650,
one of the paintings much
admired by the French
intellectuals of his time.
(*left*) Sassoferrato
Madonna in Prayer.

62 (*overleaf*) Sacchi's
The Vision of St Romuald,
c. 1638.

61 (*right*) Claude, also a
French exile in Rome,
painted serene landscapes,
inspired by the Italian
countryside and Vergil's
pastoral poetry, in contrast
to the Stoic philosophy
which permeated Poussin's
most classical works. *Right:
Classical Landscape*.

63 and 64 In
Louis xiv's France
the classical
movement was
transformed into a
cold academic
pattern which
became the fashion
in European art.
(*above left*) the
marble bust of the
king by Bernini, 1665 :
Baroque grace.
(*below*) Louis xiv by
the French sculptor
Coysevox, *c.* 1680 : art
glorifying regality.

65 (*below*) Charles Le Brun, the director of the French academy through which Colbert kept a close supervision of French art, accompanies the king on a visit to the Gobelins factory; one of the Gobelins tapestries designed by Le Brun.

66 and 67 The palace of Versailles (see also illustration 4) and its formal gardens (*opposite*) designed by Le Nôtre, formed the setting for Louis XIV's court. (*left*) The ambassadors' staircase designed by Le Vau with Le Brun's decoration of painted figures and imitation architecture and tapestries.

68 and 69 Pierre Mignard's portraits of the king's mistresses as classical goddesses
(*above*) Mme de Montespan and her eldest son by the king, set a fashion in European
courts. Mme de Maintenon, (*below*) who eventually became the morganatic
wife of the king in 1683, was painted by Mignard in a less pagan manner in
accordance with the more sober mood of her reign at court.

Literature

70 William Shakespeare (this painting from the
National Portrait Gallery is believed to
be of him), the greatest poet in an age
of magnificent English poetry.

71 A scene from Cervantes' *Don Quixote*, first published in 1605 and rapidly translated into every important European language. Contemporary Spanish society was brilliantly satirised in the tales of an old Spanish gentleman obsessed with chivalry.

72 *Le Cid* by Corneille, the father of French tragedy, was first performed in 1637. (*Above*) The frontispiece of the 1663 edition, love versus honour: the heroine demands from the king vengeance on her lover for her father's death.

73 Racine, whose tragedies rivalled Corneille's in classical purity, but in his plays men were moved by passion rather than honour.

74 Molière (*extreme left in this painting of the characters of farce*) was compared to Terence by French intellectuals. His comedies attacked middle class complacency for the enjoyment of his courtly audience.

Gul. Faithorne ad Vivum · Delin. et sculpsit ·

Joannis Miltoni Effigies Ætat: 62.
1670.

75 English poetry more or less escaped the dominating influence of French
classicism. Milton's religious epic *Paradise Lost* was written
and published during the Restoration.

Music and musicians

76 The 'war' scene from *La Finta Pazza,*
one of the earliest comic operas.
It was imported by Mazarin from Italy in 1645
and delighted the French court which had
acquired a taste for musical spectacles from
Louis XIII's *ballets de cour*.

77 Opera was even performed in England during Cromwell's Protectorate.
(*Above*) a backcloth designed for *The Siege of Rhodes* produced at Rutland House in
London in 1656.

78 The interior of the Opera House, Vienna, during the performance of
Il pomo d'ora, written by the Venetian Cesti for the wedding festivities of
Emperor Leopold I and the Infanta Margherita of Spain.

Religion and Science

Heretics and witches were still persecuted in the seventeenth century, and the Roman Catholic Church particularly saw the great philosophical and scientific advances as a form of heresy.

79 (*Above*) the hanging of four witches in seventeenth-century England. 80 (*Left*) An impenitent heretic in the costume in which he was consigned to the flames by the Spanish inquisition, from Limborch's *Historia Inquisitionis*, 1692, 81 (*below*) The popular conception of the witches' sabbath.

82 (*above*) Monks in the quiet peace of the
refectory by the Spanish painter Zurbarán.
In Spain, poverty forced many into the Church.

83 (*opposite*) Galileo's discoveries in astronomy and
physics contradicted the ancient authorities,
Aristotle and Ptolemy;
the Church, feeling threatened, condemned him
for blasphemy in 1616 and 1633, and forced him
to recant.

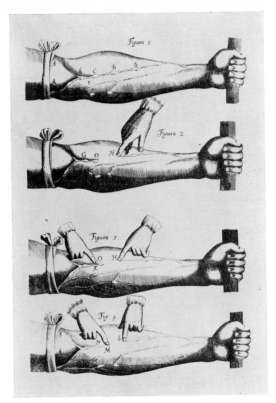

84 (*left*) William Harvey's work at Padua on the circulation of the blood in the early years of the century were not published until 1629 in Frankfurt. His diagrams demonstrating the function of the valves of the veins from the first edition of *De motu cordis*.

85 (*below*) Rembrandt painted this anatomy lesson in 1632. The growing acceptance of the necessity to dissect the human body in order to understand its functions reflected the concern of seventeenth-century science with observation and experiment.

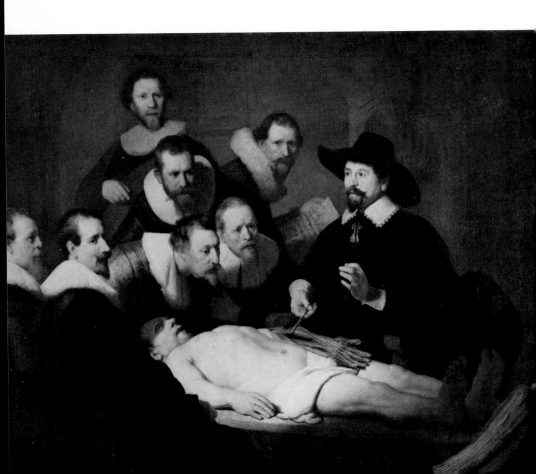

86 and 87 Descartes' basically sceptical approach to philosophy and science was condemned by some of the Jesuits as materialistic and mechanistic, (*top*, portrait of Descartes). He found a home in the Protestant United Provinces and there in 1637 published his *Discours de la Méthode* (*above*) A diagram of the mechanics of the telescope from the first edition.

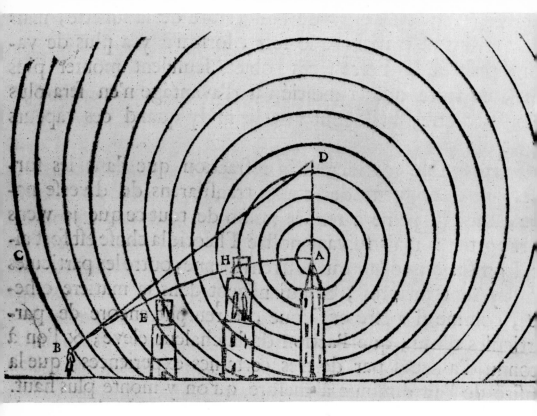

88 Christian Huygens questioned the Cartesian deductive methods of reasoning, turning to experiments for his conclusions. (*above*) a diagram of an illusion created by the refraction of light from his *Traité de la lumiere*, written in 1678 and published in Leiden in 1690. The Dutch scientist worked on astronomy, optics, acoustics, the air pump and pendulum clock.

89 and 90 Huygens patented the pendulum clock in 1657. (*below left*) general view and (*right*) back view showing the pendulum 'cheeks' of a bracket clock made in The Hague *c*. 1675.

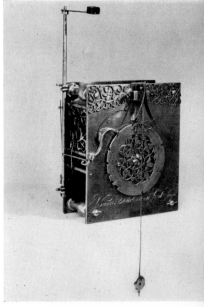

91, 92 and 93 The telescope was invented in Holland about 1608 and greatly improved by Galileo and Kepler. Huygens started the practice of lengthening the distance between eyepiece and object lens so much (for greater magnification) that no tube was used, and these were called aerial telescopes. Isaac Newton, the intellectual genius of the second half of the seventeenth century, invented a reflecting telescope which did not need to be of such enormous length.
(*above*) Tube telescope in use at the Royal Observatory, Greenwich, (established 1675) (*below right*) Newton's telescope. The compound microscope, invented in 1590, was improved during the seventeenth century by Kepler and others. (*below left*) a compound microscope used by Robert Hooke from his *Micrographia*, published in London in 1665.

94 (*right*) Grotius, imprisoned by the
Contra-Remonstrants of the
United Provinces, found refuge in
France and then Sweden. His work on
international law separated the concepts
of human and divine rights, and paved
the way for the doctrine of political
sovereignty.

95 (*below*) The English philosopher,
Thomas Hobbes, thought, like Spinoza,
that political science should be based on
an understanding of human nature.
To prevent a war of all against all
he advocated absolutism. Above the
title page from his *Leviathan*,
the first edition of 1651.

96 (*right*) The German philosopher,
Samuel Puffendorf (*right*, his portrait
from *De jure natura* published in 1684),
deduced his system of natural rights by
a geometrical process based on the
needs of society. Like Locke and unlike
Hobbes, he believed in a contract between
government and people as circumscribed
by the individual's inalienable rights.

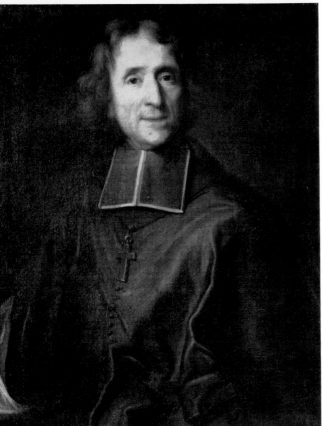

97 and 98 Bossuet
(*above left*) taught that the
authority of the monarchy,
the most natural and
therefore the best form of
government, was sacred
and absolute, a theory
fitted to appeal to his king,
Louis XIV.
Fénelon (*below*) on
the other hand was more
doubtful about the
desirability of despotic
government.

99 The Revocation of the edict of
Nantes by Louis XIV at Fontainebleau
(shown in this Dutch engraving)
was out of step with the growing
atmosphere of toleration in Europe; the
expulsion of the French Protestants arose
from the king's determination to
complete the unity of the kingdom.

War and Warriors

100 The Genoese Ambrogio de Spinola was employed by Spain as general of the forces attempting to crush the Netherlands' bid for independence. In this painting (*above*) by Velezquez, he is shown receiving the keys of the city of Breda after its capitulation in 1625.

101 Albrecht Wallenstein, a Bohemian tycoon, raised and led an army for Emperor Ferdinand in the Thirty Years' War. His successes were offset by his intrigues and ambitions, and in February 1634 he was murdered by English and Irish mercenaries who claimed they were acting on orders from Vienna.

102 (*above*) Cromwell, a country squire, discovered his genius as a soldier in the English civil wars. The Puritan troops he raised formed the basis of the New Model Army who finally defeated the Cavaliers.

103 and 104 (*opposite*) Two of Louis XIV's ablest generals: (*above*) Turenne, killed in 1675 in the war against the Dutch. (*below*) Marshal Villars, who fought with distinction in the war of the Spanish Succession.

C.I.H.M. DUC DE VILLARS ....

105 Prince Eugen of Savoy,
resenting his treatment in
France, left to become the
hero of the Emperor's wars
against the Turks, winning
a magnificent victory at
Zenta in 1697. He was one
of the famous commanders
who fought against France
in the war
of the Spanish Succession.

106 John, duke of
Marlborough, was
appointed commander-in-
chief by Queen Anne in
1702 soon after the
conclusion of the Grand
Alliance against France.
He is shown in triumph in
this allegory
commemorating the victory
of Ramillies in 1706.

107 and 108 This battle scene (*above*) of 1622 shows the Spanish *tercios*, the closely massed squares of pikes and muskets protected by heavy cavalry. These formations meant that the climax of the battle was a confused close combat in which the mounted soldiers had the advantage. The battle of Lützen in 1632 (*below*), one of the decisive battles of the Thirty Years' War, was won by the strictly organised army of Gustav Adolf, whose methods helped to bring the military revolution of the second half of the century.

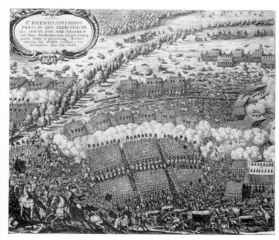

109 By the time of the battle of Malplaquet in 1709 (*above*), warfare had changed. Armies had become professional; uniforms were in regular use; improved muskets and the invention of the bayonet made the infantry, supported by cannon, more mobile; the cavalry were faster, no longer weighed down by heavy armour.

110, 111 (*left*) The correct use of the musket and the pike, taken from an English edition of a Dutch manual of arms, of 1607.
112 (*below left*) two pike heads.

113 (*above*) An armoured cavalryman with arquebus from a 1640 French edition of the manual illustrated in 111 and 112.

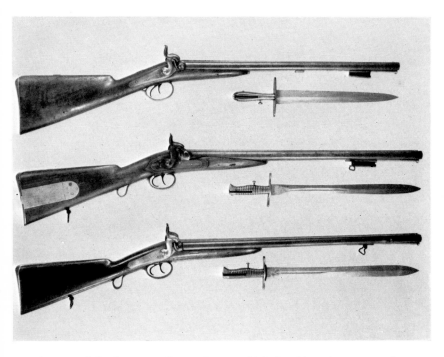

114 A group of plug bayonets of around 1700, which, fitted into the guns, made the infantry far more efficient.

115 (*top*) In spite of the improved warships in use during the seventeenth century, sea battles still demanded hand-to-hand fighting. This painting shows English and Dutch sailors in the Anglo-Dutch wars.

116 The mid-century saw outbreaks of revolution and civil war; (*above*) the barricades erected in Paris during the *fronde parlementaire* in 1648. The standing armies of the second half of the century were as useful for keeping down unrest at home as for aggression abroad.

nature was that a pacific social life must be maintained. Private property, he believed with Locke, was necessary to the well-being of society and rested upon a kind of contract between property-owners and the community at large. But he agreed with Hobbes that men are naturally selfish: hence the need for the formation of a government by an agreed contract. Puffendorf considered that there was a social contract and a contract of government. The sovereign power was supreme, but it was not absolute, for it was restrained by the ends for which it had been created. Thus both to Puffendorf and to Locke the fiduciary contract between an organised society and a government was a limiting one. Grotius, on the other hand, said that while a people could by contract choose what government it would, once it had chosen, it must accept subjection. His view of the right of resistance to a tyrannous government was more circumscribed than was that of Locke.

Thus phrases like social contracts, states of nature, laws of nature, and natural rights were given different meanings by different thinkers. Spinoza, for example, said bluntly: 'big fishes devour little fishes by natural right'. But the dividing line was between those writers – mainly English – who regarded contracts and natural laws as the protection for individual liberty and property and therefore (as with Locke and others, Algernon Sidney, for instance) in the last resort sanctioning rebellion against a tyrannous government and those who, like Hobbes and Spinoza, and to a lesser extent Grotius and Puffendorf, felt that the supreme power of the government was the surest guarantee of peace and security and that rebellion was tantamount to the breakdown of organised society. One must not forget, however, that both Hobbes and Spinoza were regarded as atheists and as men who preached deplorable and subversive doctrines. Though their works were undoubtedly read by contemporaries, it was not their arguments that were most commonly used in justification of the absolute state.

In fact it seems clear that most of the political philosophers who wrote during the century were not opening up new paths at all but were striving to justify a state of affairs which was already in being. Grotius tried to justify and uphold the position of a republic which was dependent upon the effective freedom of the seas and the recognition of an international law, and also to defend and maintain the position of a confederation of states in which different groups of individuals retained independent rights. Hobbes defended the absolutism alike of a Charles I during his so-called 'eleven years tyranny' or an Oliver Cromwell during his so-called period of dictatorship. Milton, Sidney and Locke thought in terms of an oligarchy of virtuous men of a Platonic kind that had tried unsuccessfully to rule England before and after Cromwell died. Machiavelli spoke for Florence, the Jesuits writers for the pope of

Rome, Bossuet for Louis XIV. Thus political science was assumed to exist and to justify current forms of government, though sometimes by arguments that were novel as compared with those of earlier times. Yet probably the most influential writers about politics were not those who elaborated upon complicated and imaginary concepts of natural states and social contracts, but men who claimed that monarchy had been ordained by God from time out of mind and fulfilled the needs of men's natures. Louis XIV, like the Tudors before him and the Hohenzollern dynasty after him, was convinced that he ruled his people by divine command for their own good. Bossuet taught that monarchy was the most natural form of government and therefore the strongest and best. So did Filmer who insisted that its value had been demonstrated by history. The authority of kings therefore was both sacred and absolute. The people must fear their prince, but if the prince were to fear his people, all would be lost. The king was the image of God's majesty. A monarch's duty was to maintain religion and to dispense justice. Subjects might respectfully protest if they considered that his policies were unwise, but in no case should they revolt.

Thus the thinkers who most effectively put the case for absolute monarchy during the second half of the century were not those who used the method of quasi-mathematical deduction but those who wielded an old-fashioned dialectic stemming from the Old Testament patriarchs. The more liberal views about government belonged, at any rate so far as their influence extended, not to the seventeenth but to the late eighteenth and nineteenth centuries. In France men like Vauban and Fénelon might have begun to express doubts about the unqualified virtues of absolutism, but it was absolutism that represented the intellectual climate of their times. And where indirectly the new philosophers contributed to this climate was not by their political reasoning so much as by their scientific approach. For once it became accepted by men as varied in their outlook as Hobbes, Spinoza, Grotius and Puffendorf that material and social problems could and should be separated from religious ones, that, in the words of Grotius, the law of nature was founded on reason alone, then governments could be organised on realistic Machiavellian lines, society could be protected from subversion or revolution not because the monarch was a divine authority, sanctified by the Church, but because he was indeed a mortal god whose supremacy was the essential guarantee of peace, order and property. The greatness of the state depended on a well-defined and unrestricted leadership, not on a divided balance of power.

Yet older and less empirical concepts took a long time to die. As Dr Greenleaf has pointed out in a recent book, it was not found easy to set aside the doctrines of the organic nature of society with its hierarchy of unequal men. They even contributed to the mystique of absolutism. Thus absolutism received support from many intellectual sources, and moved towards its time of ascendancy in most parts of Europe, from Spain to Sweden, from France to Prussia. Only a few countries, such as England, the United Netherlands and Switzerland did not obviously fall into that category. But certainly the powers of the English monarchy remained very large until the reign of King George III. The power of the Dutch stadholder Willem III grew until his death in 1702 without an heir. And though the Holy Roman Empire might have become, in the words of Puffendorf, a 'monstrosity', it could scarcely be doubted that the sovereign's powers were also growing inside the Habsburg dominions.

The appeal of absolutism was understandable. Men could see how contests between governments and parliaments had led to chaos and civil war. Life was short and frighteningly insecure. Perhaps historians have insufficiently investigated the problem of the maintenance of order in early modern Europe. We live today in an age of law-making or decree-making and tend to assume that the laws will be obeyed because they can be enforced. But in no European countries was there anything like a modern police force. (A French 'lieutenant of police' was, it is true, appointed in 1667, but he was really an examining magistrate and Paris, like London, never appears to have had more than a small night watch.) The peace was still the king's peace as in the Middle Ages. In the last resort it was royal armies or central bodies of troops – like the French gendarmerie or the Russian streltsy – who were the guarantors of peace and stability, above all, in the capital cities. When King James II fled from London in 1688 and disbanded his army the English capital was so menaced by disorders and attacks on private property that the Dutch troops who came with William of Orange had to be called upon to restore order. After the frondes the unpopular Cardinal Mazarin was welcomed back to Paris because his return promised the restoration of order there. So it is clear why up to the time of Locke political thinkers were more exercised by the problem of order in a state than they were by that of individual liberty. The king of France became admired because he not only symbolised but ensured law and order. The anarchy that philosophers like Spinoza and Hobbes dreaded was no imaginary danger. Though daring speculations about the nature of the universe were made, it was recognised that an effective government was above all needed to provide the conditions in which men could enjoy their possessions and follow their thoughts wherever they might lead them.

CHAPTER 10

SCIENTIFIC ADVANCES AND
PHILOSOPHIC DOUBT

The period of comparative peace and stability that prevailed in Europe after the ending of the 'Thirty Years War', the death of Cardinal Mazarin in France, and the restoration of King Charles II to the throne of England, proved fruitful to philosophers and scientists who communicated ideas to each other and moved freely around the civilised world. It has been said that the mechanical philosophy of which Descartes was the master was 'the heart of the new scientific outlook' and in the words of Professor Butterfield, 'the idea of a clockwork universe' was 'the great contribution of seventeenth-century science to the eighteenth-century age of reason'. Gradually the Ancients – the last-ditch disciples of medieval Aristotelianism – were defeated in argument by the Moderns. Dr John Wilkins, who combined the surprising attributes of being Oliver Cromwell's brother-in-law and (later) an Anglican bishop, espoused the Copernican theory and attacked Aristotelianism in England. So did the sceptical Thomas Hobbes and Joseph Glanville, author of *The Vanity of Dogmatising*, while Robert Boyle, 'the father of modern chemistry' and a sincere Christian, wrote to uphold *The Usefulness of the Experimental Natural Philosophy*.

But if in England and other Protestant countries the new mechanical physics and heliocentric astronomical ideas were becoming supreme, some differences of opinion existed about which were the proper methods to follow in pursuing scientific research. At first it looked as if Cartesianism would sweep everything before it, and so far as the mechanism of the body was concerned it did. But, as we have seen, purely deductive methods of reasoning were questioned by the more practical scientists, for example, by the Dutchman Christian Huygens and the German Leibniz and in England in particular Bacon's persuasive plea for the primacy of experiments was taken up with enthusiasm by the Royal Society half a century after he was dead. Boyle urged the value of experiments in relatively small fields of research and exalted Bacon at the expense of Descartes. Robert Hooke, a fertile experimenter, attacked what he called 'the Brain and the Fancy'. Then Thomas Sprat, another bishop, published his history of the early days of the Royal Society in which his theme was the defence of experimental philosophy and his appeal was for the virtues of collecting data.

That in fact was what was largely done in the new scientific academies, whose appearance was such a feature of the second half of the century. It has been disputed which was the earliest of these academies, but the notable fact is that they all sprang into existence at about the same time, during the years of comparative European peace. In Italy an academy of experiments was founded by two disciples of Galileo in Florence and was supported by the ruling Medici family. This Academia del Cimento published its proceedings under the title of *Saggi di Naturali Esperanzi* which was translated into English in 1684. The Florentine academy flourished from 1657 to 1667; it was said to have been closed because Leopold Medici was created a cardinal of the Roman Church. The Royal Society in England traces its origins back to a so-called 'invisible society' which met at Gresham College in London during the early years of the Interregnum. Subsequently scientists gathered together in Oxford, while in 1659 a number of intellectuals conversed regularly at a coffee house in the capital city. But a royal charter was not conferred on the society until 1662. The kind of persons who met to talk and to witness experiments varied. Some of them were more interested in statistics and foreign trade than in physics or anatomy, while others, like Samuel Pepys the diarist, were pure dilettanti. Thomas Hobbes, though he prided himself upon being a mathematician as well as a political philosopher was never a member of this society, but the astonishing intellectual achievements of Isaac Newton owed not a little to the encouragement of its members.

In France the Académie Royale des Sciences also traces its origins back some years before it was officially instituted by Louis xiv's chief minister, Colbert, in 1666. Like the Florentine and London societies it published its proceedings in a *Journal des Savants* which became a state publication in 1701. Colbert's most active collaborator was, surprisingly enough, the Dutchman Christian Huygens, who was an immensely versatile figure. Between the death of Galileo and the emergence of Newton, Huygens was accepted as being the leading scientist of his age. He visited London in 1661 to obtain information from Gresham College. When he was twenty-six he met the Italian astronomer Gassendi in Paris. He corresponded with Robert Boyle. He worked not only in astronomy with an improved telescope (though not a regular observer of the skies, he discovered the Ring round Saturn) but also on optics, acoustics, the air pump and the pendulum clock, which he patented in 1657. Other foreigners who were active in the Paris academy were the Italian Domenico Cassini and the Dane Olaus

Roemer. Astronomy in particular made big strides at this time. In 1675 the Royal Observatory was established at Greenwich and later an observatory was set up at Paris. But, like the other academies, the one in Paris declined after the initial impulse. Huygens returned from France to Holland because he did not approve of the militaristic policies of King Louis xiv, while Louvois, who succeeded Colbert as the patron of the academy after Colbert's death, was less attracted by theoretical experiments. None the less the Paris academy received a stimulus from the royal government in that pensions were paid to its members and they were also granted financial help in their researches; in England Charles ii confined his interest to experimenting himself in his own laboratory. It is perhaps a measure of the intellectual freedom that prevailed in the United Netherlands that they did not go in for academies, though their contributions to science and technology were outstanding.

The great Leibniz, who, like Huygens, was a qualified admirer of Descartes (he is 'admirable,' he once said, 'at explaining by beautiful guesses the causes for the effects of nature') was impressed by the Paris academy and eventually succeeded in persuading the elector of Brandenburg to set up a similar academy of science in Berlin, in 1700. All these academies were therefore the products of international enthusiasm and exemplified the evolution of a European scientific mind. The mathematician Borelli and the astronomer Cassini went from Florence to Paris; the Royal Society elected foreign members. Papers were usually written in Latin or French, the two international languages, and in the *Philosophical Transactions* started by the secretary of the Royal Society, Henry Oldenburg, there was virtually an international scientific journal.

Science became both popular and fashionable. Kings and their ministers patronised it and dabbled in it. Wealthy men had their own laboratories just as they had their own libraries. The rising middle classes realised that scientific theory might lead to technical advances and social benefits. Professor Butterfield has drawn attention to the achievement of the secretary of the French Academy of Science, Fontenelle, as a populariser: '[he] consciously set out to make science amusing to fashionable ladies and as easy as the latest novel.' Fontenelle's most successful book, *The Plurality of Worlds* appeared, a little unfortunately, in 1686, the year before Newton published his *Principia*, 'the most perfect treatise on mechanics that can be imagined', as another Frenchman called it. No doubt popular scientists, like popular historians, are always a little out of date.

In spite of the rapid expansion of scientific activity and scientific publicity after 1660, it was realised that 'proofs' of the 'new philosophy' were still required. It is, as has already been suggested, an exaggeration to say that Cartesianism swept all before it. Nevertheless even those like Boyle who criticised Descartes's methods of deductive reasoning in fact accepted his mechanistic principles: Boyle himself applied mechanism to chemistry, while Alfonso Borelli applied it to biology. It was in the field of gravitation that Descartes's theories proved misleading. Descartes thought that heavenly bodies were dragged around by large whirlpools of invisible particles. Newton refuted this theory as being incompatible with Kepler's laws. Newton's own theory of universal gravitation was garnered from a large number of sources, beginning with William Gilbert's work on magnetism. Gilbert's book was published as early as 1600. He demonstrated the earth's magnetism and connected it with motion round the sun. Kepler had accepted Gilbert's theories and drawn attention to the fact that tides were influenced by the magnetism of the moon. In 1665 Borelli put forward the hypothesis of the existence of a centrifugal force and Huygens later worked out its mathematics. Newton calculated the mathematics of a gravitational pull independently ('I deduced,' he wrote, 'that the forces which keep the Planets in their Orbs must be reciprocally as the squares of the distances from the centres about which they revolve') making use of measurements of foreign astronomers who were able to watch the skies through improved telescopes in their observatories. Although Newton achieved a remarkable synthesis on gravitation and destroyed Descartes's theories of whirlpools, the *Principia* or *Philosophiae Naturalis Principia Mathematica* (1687), which was no easy book, written in Latin and employing classical geometry as its method, did not at once command general acceptance. Indeed both Huygens and Leibniz, the greatest of Newton's contemporaries, criticised his views about universal gravitation, preferring the Cartesian notion of mysterious forces operating mechanically to a mere mathematical description of relationships between particles of matter. Newton admitted that he did not pretend to know the causes of gravitation – he had searched for them in vain – but he did establish that the universe could be reduced to one fundamental system of scientific law; it was fifty years before his arguments conquered, but they had a profound effect upon the minds of men.

Scientific methods were now being applied not merely to astronomy, chemistry, biology, zoology and the like but also to such subjects as history, biblical criticism, politics and economics. The Benedictine monk Mabillon was the inventor of diplomatic – the scientific study of medieval documents – and another French monk, the Oratorian Richard Simon, published a critical history of the Old Testament in 1678. England lays claim to the invention of statistics, Sir William

Petty arguing that statesmanship would benefit from an objective knowledge of social facts, an argument that has not always been accepted even in modern times. The statistics of population produced by Gregory King are the vademecum of modern economic historians. But it is surprising how slow was the pace of technological progress in this intensely scientific age. For example, railway lines were tried for the movement of iron ore and a Parisian doctor attempted to build a steam boat. But steam boats and steam trains did not emerge for many years. Similarly many books and pamphlets were written about methods of improving agriculture (for example, by Samuel Hartlib and Robert Boyle); yet, broadly, old methods of two-course and three-course rotation and the fertilisation of land by dung and marl were retained unaltered throughout Europe. A lighter plough is about the only positive discovery attributed to the century by modern historians. Men in society still sought after the philosopher's stone and ladies accepted the guidance of astrologers, while old-fashioned clergy deprecated pre-occupation with material standards. Curiosity, admittedly, was at a premium and experiments all the rage. 'I prefer,' said Leibniz, 'a Leeuwenhoeck [the Dutch microscopist] who tells me what he sees to a Cartesian who tells me what he thinks.' But in fact many obstacles had to be overcome before scientific theories translated themselves into practical achievements. Most technical advances had to await the next century.

The extraordinary intellectual discoveries of the later part of the seventeenth century were therefore mainly concerned with fundamental scientific principles. Newton's genius extended not merely to the theory of universal gravitation, but to the infinitesimal and integral calculus, to optics (he published his work on light in 1704) and metallurgy. Newton was a unique and paradoxical character: reluctant to publish and liable to squabble with other scientists; modest about his achievements but confident of his conclusions; a disinterested and solitary investigator who yet sought profitable public employment and died a wealthy man; a scientist of genius who at times became bored with what he called 'philosophy' and devoted much of his life to other pursuits; a thinker who proclaimed that hypotheses must be derived from experiments yet reached many of his discoveries by intuition. Newton was, it is true, but one of a group of European scientists making rapid progress after the middle of the century. It seems that Hooke, Huygens, and Halley (the English astronomer) all arrived independently at the inverse square law. Leibniz also invented the infinitesimal calculus. It is disputed who first invented the microscope, the pendulum clock and the air pump. What all these men shared in common was the research attitude of mind. There was, on the whole, a growing reaction against Descartes's methods of deductive contemplation in a warm room. Gassendi proclaimed that theories must be confirmed by facts. Biology and zoology were mainly descriptive of what had been observed without any large theoretical conclusions. Experiments were often undertaken for the mere pleasure of experimenting. Only Thomas Hobbes confessed that he was not interested in the experimental verification of truth, but then he was no real scientist.

How can one account for this astonishing outburst of scientific progress in the later half of the century? It is notable that much of it took place in Protestant countries, above all, in England and the United Netherlands, but also in Protestant Germany and in the Scandinavian countries. There were some distinguished French and Italian scientists; but, on the whole, the Roman Catholic Church and the Inquisition were discouraging. The execution of Bruno and the persecution of Galileo were remembered and one Italian scientist committed suicide. Althusius did his work in Protestant Germany, first as the servant of the count of Nassau and then in the city of Emden in Frisia. Descartes, as we have noticed, left his native France and produced his finest work in Germany and Holland; he died in the service of the queen of Sweden who did not appreciate his quality. Spinoza, a Jew, was born in Amsterdam and despite his daring ideas, the character of which became known, was left alone by the authorities. Leibniz lived and wrote in Protestant Germany, having been born in Jena and having found employment in Hanover. Puffendorf also worked in Protestant Germany, the United Netherlands and in Sweden. John Locke, chased from England for political reasons, found refuge in Amsterdam and Rotterdam where he wrote his most famous books. Pierre Bayle left France for Geneva when he was eighteen and compiled his famous dictionary in Holland. The only apparent exception among the distinguished thinkers of the latter part of the century to the rule that their habitat was a Protestant realm are Pascal, Grotius and Hobbes. Pascal was scarcely an organised thinker, but he was an unorthodox Roman Catholic who was fortunate enough to be protected by influential French aristocrats. Grotius was imprisoned by his fellow countrymen for political and religious reasons, but managed to escape and found refuge in France. Later, however, he was welcomed in Sweden and actually became a Swedish ambassador; before he died he was allowed to return home to Holland. Hobbes, fearful of the coming civil wars in England, went to Paris and it was there that he first propounded his political theories. But afterwards he returned to England; King Charles ii gave him his personal patronage; and, in spite of the accusations of atheism and immorality levelled against him, he died safely in his bed.

Lavisse pointed out that French science was mediocre except when aided by foreigners like Huygens, Roemer and Cassini. After Descartes a century passed before French science revived. When the body of Descartes was brought back to his native land from Sweden, Louis XIV refused to allow laudatory obsequies to be pronounced over it. Some modern historians have linked European intellectual progress with Calvinism, just as earlier historians, like Weber and Tawney, attributed the rise of business enterprise or 'capitalism' to it. Here the controversy goes on. But even Professor Michael Walzer, who has recently resuscitated the Weber-Tawney thesis, admits that 'Calvinism was not a liberal theology, even though congregational life was surely a training for self-government and democratic participation.' No one who studies the history of Geneva when Calvin was supreme there can seriously talk about liberal democracy or intellectual freedom. Calvin may have been, as Friedrich Heer has claimed, 'a political thinker of the greatest stature' and Calvinism may have led indirectly to the modernisation of political thought, just as the Puritan doctrine of men's being 'called' to office by God undoubtedly lent strength to individual economic enterprise. But Hugh Trevor-Roper has recently argued persuasively that no precise connection can be established between Calvinism and scientific or philosophical progress, at any rate until after the great dispersal following the expulsion of the Huguenots from France in 1685. Professor Haase observed that Protestantism in France produced no statesman (can he have overlooked Sully?), philosopher or poet of distinction and that after a century of spiritual sterility the French Protestants in exile found a weighty role to play in the republic of letters. (Incidentally recent research appears to suggest that the Huguenots' economic achievement owed more to their being excluded, like the Jews, from political life than to the nature of their religion.)

It was in fact the atmosphere of freedom in countries whose governments permitted different religions – or different brands of the Christian religion – to be practised that stimulated scientific thought. Men like Descartes, Spinoza, Locke and Bayle found a haven in the United Netherlands, while Huygens, like Grotius, eventually returned home. So perhaps it is fair to say that it was indeed the blow inflicted on monopolistic religions by the terrible blood-letting of the 'Thirty Years War' that prompted scientific advance. Original political thinking also owed much to the stimulus offered by growing religious toleration. Thus when the Scandinavian kings decided to intervene in Germany to prevent the forces of the Counter-Reformation from overwhelming Protestantism and when Calvinism established its rights in Germany equally with Lutheranism, the way was paved for intellectual daring. Yet the extreme caution of many of the leading philosophers and scientists, even in the later half of the century, in publishing their real opinions (indeed it may be that Leibniz never did) shows how they were still aware of the shackles of the past.

There was then a remarkable international scientific revolution, which was indeed the outstanding characteristic of European history in the second half of the century, though it remained true that astronomy, physics and mathematics stayed ahead of biology and chemistry and that the practical application of the new knowledge was delayed. How far did this flood of light that Newton and his contemporaries threw upon the fundamental mechanical laws of the universe undermine religion? Did God become for the men of this century a remote clock-maker instead of a God of Love who intervened actively and intimately in an individual's daily life? It can be argued that the discoveries of science both strengthened and weakened religion and that even professional practitioners of Christianity were uncertain which way to take it. For example, some Jesuits attacked Cartesianism, while others used mechanical theories as the basis for their text-books. Descartes himself believed that he had irrefutably proved the existence of God. Newton, wrote Professor Butterfield, seemed to think 'gravitation represented an effort that had to be produced by God throughout the whole of space – something that made the existence of God logically necessary and rescued the universe from the over-mechanisation that Descartes had achieved.' Newton himself wrote that 'such a wonderful Uniformity in the Planetary System must be allowed the Effect of Choice.' And he himself did not exclude the possibility that God continued from time to time to intervene in the working of nature. Leibniz said that Newton's God was an imperfect workman constantly tinkering with the universe.

But many people who thought closely about the question reasoned that the new scientific laws which had been discovered, whether demonstrating corpuscular mechanism or atomism or the mathematically exact force of gravity, proved conclusively that the universe had been planned by a single intelligence on purposive lines. Life was not, as Shakespeare had written, a tale told by an idiot, but planned by a genius. Its mathematical tidiness was impressive. Geometry in fact proved extremely attractive to theologians. Newton applied his magnificent mind to tracing a pattern woven by theology and history, devoting particular attention to the prophecies of Daniel who, he seems to have thought, anticipated the coming of the Roman Catholic Church. What, however, the scientists and other thinkers of this age often found difficult to grasp was the doctrine of the Trinity; and it seems clear that men like John Milton, Huygens, Newton, Locke and Leibniz doubted if Jesus Christ was divine.

On the whole, therefore, it would appear that although the leading scientists themselves were theists (if Hobbes was an atheist, he certainly was not a scientist), natural philosophy did tend to undermine traditional religion and disquiet theology. Men had, after all, been brought up with a world picture that stemmed from Aristotle and Aquinas. When Galileo demonstrated the identity of celestial and terrestrial phenomena and later Isaac Newton proved the existence of universal scientific laws, then it became clear beyond the shadow of a doubt that the world in which men lived was not unique, that the place where Christ had dwelt was not in fact the centre of the universe. Mysterious forces were gradually being dispersed and superstitions undermined. Those who studied the new ideas honestly believed that their acceptance could lead to atheism: the earth had shrunk and men were at the mercy of mechanical laws. In England Dr Henry Stubbe, a physician, attacked the Royal Society for this reason. Leibniz, though himself, to outward appearances, an optimist and a theist, feared that science was bound to fortify atheism and naturalism. As Professor Hall has written, 'for physics the practical answer was that God had been driven from the universe with the planetary intelligences'. On the whole, towards the end of the century the separation of science and religion advocated by Bacon and, to a lesser extent, by Descartes, was no longer believed to be possible. Yet God seemed inevitably to have become more remote from the facts of everyday life. And those scientists, like Robert Boyle and Blaise Pascal, who felt vehemently about Christianity, were forced to the conclusion that it was now necessary to make a fresh effort in order to reconcile science with religion.

The early half of the century had seen the rise of Puritanism in several guises; it had two aspects, first the emphasis that it laid upon the individual's direct relationship with God, secondly the importance it attached to a high and consistent standard of moral behaviour. This was linked with and derived from the belief that an all-powerful God had chosen those on whom he conferred his grace, for the chosen had to set an example to the reprobate. Perhaps in recording the history of Jansenism in France and in the Spanish Netherlands one tends to give too much thought to its theological aspects. It was claimed, for example, that one of Jansen's propositions was that it was heresy to say that Christ died for all men without exception. But the 'Jansenists' denied that this proposition was in Jansen's book. Fundamentally the Jansenists were not so much predestinarians as Puritans. Like many of the English Puritans (and like Calvin) they condemned dancing, the theatre, and extravagant dress. They insisted on a recognisable code of behaviour and on rigid principles of daily conduct. They believed that the doctrines of the Jesuits were so lax that they undermined Christian morality.

The Jesuits retorted, in line with the teachings of Loyola and Molina, that God conferred sufficient grace upon all alike and men could find their salvation by cooperating with it. They held that sins might be forgiven to the penitent, that salvation could be attained by all, and they even thought it legitimate to adapt pagan practices to Christian services so long as the fundamental belief in God the Saviour was accepted. Naturally the Jesuits, who were striving to spread Christianity throughout the whole world and to maintain and expand the authority of the Roman Catholic Church in Europe, condemned their critics as heretics. In that sense it has been argued that the Jesuits invented Jansenism.

Blaise Pascal, himself in his youth not only a mathematician of outstanding ability but also a sceptic, experienced a conversion like that of Oliver Cromwell, John Bunyan and many other Puritans. He then came to be associated with the so-called Jansenists and lived with his sister in the Port-Royal, the centre of the Jansenist leadership. In 1656 he began writing his *Lettres Provinciales*, a supreme example of elegant invective, in which he criticised the laxist principles of the Jesuits. But the pope and the French monarchy stood four-square behind the Jesuits who had done so much for the Roman Church. Pascal's book was placed upon the Index, and it seems that towards the end of his life in 1662 he himself became doubtful of the wisdom of what he had done in attributing wicked motives to a religious order. Be that as it may, in his other celebrated book, his *Pensées*, published posthumously, he concentrated upon a more constructive task – that of converting men to, or affirming them in, a religious way of life and thought. In fact it was clearly necessary and desirable for believing Christians to close their ranks in face of the growing scepticism among educated men and women with which they were infected by the findings of the philosophers and physicists. Hence what Pascal drew up in the last years was an apology for Christianity, 'an antidote to the poisons and paralysing indifference of the free-thinkers who swarmed in Paris at that time' (H. F. Stewart). Pascal therefore set on one side the scientific deductive reasoning of the kind that he himself had practised as a mathematician in his youth and appealed to men to embrace the truths that they found in their hearts. He argued that metaphysical proofs of God were so remote from men's range of reason and so involved that they failed to grip the imagination. Men could understand the realities of religion only by means of their instincts and by their experiences, not by the use of their reason. For God was a being of love and truth, not a mathematician.

Thus in Pascal, as distinct from the other so-called Jansenist thinkers is to be found a strong element of mysticism; and it was in mysticism that much of the active Christian reaction against seventeenth-century rationalism was exemplified. Among its manifestations were Quakerism, Quietism and Pietism which were not confined either specifically to Protestant or to Catholic countries. The founder of Quietism was Miguel Molinos who taught in his *Spiritual Guide* (1675) that Christianity is a purely personal experience, independent of priests and doctrines, and that ultimately the soul is absorbed in a state of utter quiescence in God. Another mystical figure to arise in the heart of the Catholic Church was Madame Guyon who, after having had a husband and five children, decided that life ought to be a long act of pure contemplation and of love. God, she thought, was incomprehensible to the intellect, but she believed that a mystical union with Him could be attained after years of self-mortification culminating in a state of perfection. Madame Guyon attained some influence in France because she managed to impress François Fénelon, an exceptionally able member of the French ecclesiastical hierarchy, who had been appointed tutor to the duke of Burgundy, Louis xiv's eldest grandson, for whom he wrote a famous text-book called *Télémaque*. Through Fénelon Madame Guyon's teachings reached Madame de Maintenon, the morganatic wife of the French king. But Bossuet, an even more influential hierarch in the French Church (Fénelon had been one of Bossuet's favourite pupils) thought Madame Guyon was bogus, that her voices, unlike those of Jeanne d'Arc, were not genuine. Ultimately both Molinos and Madame Guyon were deemed heretical. Her doctrines were condemned by the archbishop of Paris and Fénelon, who was appointed archbishop of Cambrai in 1695, abandoned her. There was, he explained, both a true mysticism and a false mysticism. After the death of the duke of Burgundy in 1712 Fénelon turned to writing a French grammar.

The only thing that may be said with certainty about the religious movements of the last half of the century is that it is dangerous to generalise about them. Pascal, for example, was Jansenist in his sympathies but also a mystic and to some extent a Cartesian. The Jesuits were active participants in public and social life, yet keen missionaries and capable of producing a mystic like Molinos. Some of them condemned Cartesianism, others used it. The Order was condemned for casuistry and laxity and yet its members were admittedly often as austere and dedicated as the most extreme Puritans. The Puritans themselves were frequently men of fervent political and commercial interests and yet could furnish mystics like George Fox and his Quaker followers. Spain was at once the stamping ground of the Jesuits and the breeding ground of mysticism.

The official Churches did not care for unorthodoxy and unrest among their members. Not only King Charles i but Oliver Cromwell, the master Puritan, had vainly striven to impose some kind of organised

Christianity throughout the British Isles, and during the reign of King Charles II parliament had tried hard to suppress nonconformists with Test acts and penal laws. In France the king had invoked the assistance of the papacy against the Jansenists, who he thought were subversive, though a compromise solution agreed in 1669 failed to work. Later the Protestants or Huguenots were outlawed, Louis XIV abandoning the policy of toleration pursued by his grandfather in the edict of Nantes. Until the accession of Innocent XI in 1676 the prestige of the papacy had fallen low and this had tended to strengthen the position of governments in relation to the Church, even in Roman Catholic countries. But it became increasingly difficult to maintain uniform orthodoxy and obedience to church government. That may be said in part at least to have stemmed from the rise of science and rationalism during the century and especially from its acceleration after the end of the 'Thirty Years War'. In fact the intolerance exemplified by Louis XIV's revocation of the edict of Nantes was out of tune with his times.

One group of thinkers, not primarily mystics, but with a mystical bent, who tried to adapt philosophy to religion were the English rational theologians or Cambridge Platonists. They respected science and admitted the supremacy of reason. To them reason was 'the candle of the Lord' or 'the eye of the soul'. They preferred Bacon and (to some extent) Descartes to Aristotle and the Schoolmen, but also looked back to the teachings of Plato and, above all, his disciple Plotinus, who founded Neoplatonism in the third century after Christ. Plotinus was not himself a Christian, but invented a metaphysical doctrine of a holy trinity consisting of God, Spirit, and Soul. His was essentially a subjective religion: human beings are capable of becoming conscious of a great power within them that enables them to know the divine mind. Men can have ideals and hopes: they are not the mere recipients of grace from above. The Cambridge Platonists, who followed Plotinus, therefore regarded God as 'the ocean of light in which human spirits move'. They were not concerned over historical criticism or the constitution of the Church. Their outlook was broad and tolerant; they thought that the essentials of faith were few, and reason and religion totally compatible. Hence their contemporaries dubbed them 'latitude-men' or 'Arminians' (since, unlike the Calvinists and Jansenists, they believed in free will). On the whole, they laid stress upon the moral teachings of the Bible, but different theologians employed different kinds of emphasis – Benjamin Whichcote on tolerance, John Smith on spirituality, Ralph Cudworth on the inexorable moral conscience, and Henry More on a rational mysticism.

The Cambridge Platonists were not the only group that upheld the merits of rationalism and toleration in the later half of the century.

Indeed it can be said that Bodin and Grotius had anticipated them. Bodin considered that because he could find no certain criterion for true religion, the state should tolerate all religions, while men could use their own reason to discover the way to earthly bliss. Grotius was also a religious rationalist who considered that the really important thing was that men with a short time on earth should discover the right way in which to live. But Bodin distributed his views in secret, while Grotius was imprisoned for being an Arminian. The Cambridge Platonists, for their part, exercised genuine influence upon the ruling classes in England. Archbishops like Tillotson and Tenison were rational theologians and they were extremely powerful in the English Church during the reigns of William and Mary and Queen Anne. Other thinkers, such as Leibniz and Locke, were protagonists of toleration towards the close of the century. In many parts of Europe after the 'Thirty Years War' it was recognised that the doctrine of *cujus regio lius religio* laid down at the peace of Augsburg was becoming hard to sustain. King James II of England, himself a convinced Roman Catholic convert, tried to promote and indeed impose civic equality for all Christians. The extreme Dutch Calvinists put up a prolonged fight to maintain a religious monopoly, even to the extent of persecuting the unorthodox, like Grotius; yet Prince Willem III of Orange, himself a strict Calvinist, had in the end to promise toleration of beliefs both in the United Netherlands and in Great Britain. The great elector of Brandenburg – a Calvinist ruling over a largely Lutheran state – extended his brand of toleration widely even to include the Jews in Berlin, the Roman Catholics in Prussia and the Socinians who did not accept the divinity of Christ; Johann Friedrich, ruler of the Protestant state of Hanover, like James II of England a Roman Catholic, struggled to obtain relief for his co-religionists. Finally, a number of intellectual leaders, like the Germans, Georg Calixtus (who died in 1660) and Gottfried Wilhelm Leibniz, advocated what was called Syncretism, that is to say a reunion between the Roman and Protestant Churches. Quite distinct hopes were felt at one time that a scheme for the comprehension of all Christians in one Church might be worked out in England and France. But Louis XIV's treatment of the Huguenots, which by no means pleased the pope, was really a death-blow to this movement.

To sum up, one may detect three significant aspects of European religion which manifested themselves coincidentally with the triumph and spread of science in the second half of the century. First were the mystical movements which ranged right across Europe from the Quietists in Spain to the Pietists in Scotland. Secondly, 'rational theology' had its beginnings with its advocates emphasising the ethical teachings of the Bible and reducing theological beliefs to a few essentials. Thirdly, more and more practical statesmen and worldly philosophers were being attracted to the idea of a wider toleration or even a reunification of the Christian world. All the blood shed in the 'Thirty Years War' had taught a grim lesson. Thirty-five years after it ended the Mohammedan assault on Vienna was to furnish a reminder that Christian Europe was still not secure and that a case could be made out on political grounds alone for Christian union and unity. Though attempts to achieve such unity, in which Innocent xi, ablest of the seventeenth-century popes, participated, broke down, the trend towards toleration of different forms of religious thought continued; and it may be attributed in no small measure to the impact of science and philosophy on the minds of thinking men.

CHAPTER 11

FRANCE AND EUROPE
1661–78

On 9 March 1661 Cardinal Mazarin died, after a last fond look at the treasures he had accumulated on earth, and King Louis xiv, now twenty-three years old, announced that he would be his own first minister. From that date roughly one may speak of the preponderance of France in Europe. It was not because Louis himself was a genius, although such a claim has been made for him by some French authors. But he had entered into a promising inheritance and he knew what he intended to do with it: he wished to make his country admired and feared. 'There is not today in the world without any exception a better House than ours,' he told his son, in words suitable to a Victorian merchant banker, 'nor a monarchy as old, nor a power that is greater, nor authority more absolute.' Though Louis had not enjoyed much of a bookish education (not as good, for example, as that of his famous rival, Prince Willem of Orange) he had benefited from the political instruction of the wily Italian Mazarin, who was, in effect, if not in name, his step-father. Louis had sowed his wild oats and realised that a monarch must be dignified and hard-working. He identified himself with his kingdom. 'When one has the state in view,' he explained, 'one is working for oneself. The good of the one makes the glory of the other.' And glory was what he strove for: glory was 'a noble mistress'. Magnificence, order, beauty – these were the aims of the refurbished Bourbon monarchy.

Louis owed his opportunity for magnificence to his predecessors who ruled the French kingdom, Henri iv, Richelieu, Mazarin. They had first by devious means humiliated, obstructed and thrust back the House of Habsburg in Madrid and Vienna. They had extended the influence of France into Germany and to a lesser extent into Italy through alliances with the dukes of Savoy. They had even allied themselves with the rising Protestant countries: Mazarin had concluded a treaty with the Puritan usurper, Oliver Cromwell, when fighting the Spaniards. Secondly, they had gradually established the authority of the French Crown over the nobility and had held in check the growing power of the bourgeoisie. Henri IV had been obliged to proceed carefully; Richelieu had waged a ceaseless war against the French aristocracy who vainly tried to overthrow him; Mazarin had won the two wars of the fronde, the first largely against the bourgeoisie, headed by the parlement of Paris, the second against an irresponsible and turbulent aristocracy. But even these victories would not have enabled a centralised France to become predominant in Europe if it had not been for the possession of generous natural resources and a hard-working population. Whereas the population of Spain was declining in the first half of the century, that of France was growing. In spite of heavy and unfair taxation, of occasional famines and epidemics, French agriculture flourished because of the richness of the soil and the dedication of the peasantry. Although preoccupied with foreign affairs and internal administration, Richelieu did what he could to promote commercial and colonial enterprise. Thus Louis XIV was able to raise the financial resources that he needed to sustain the politics of glory.

Moreover, as Louis XIV himself noted when he took over the reins of government, Europe was virtually at peace: 'everything was calm everywhere'. That was largely because Europe was exhausted after long and intense years of internecine war and internal conflicts. The French monarch thus found a clean sheet on which to write his plans. The Habsburgs, the main rivals of the Bourbons during the past hundred years, were the most exhausted of all. Though Spain had lost less than she might have done to France by the terms of the treaty of the Pyrenees in 1659, she had in the following years suffered severely in her ill-starred war against Portugal. This costly war was financed, to begin with, by yet another debasement of the coinage which disrupted the economic life of Castile. The recent history of Spain had been punctuated by a succession of royal bankruptcies. Neither the manipulation of the coinage nor the repudiation of debts nor the lavish sales of offices solved the perennial financial problems of the Spanish monarchy: 'On many days the households of the king and queen lacked everything including bread.' Felipe IV, who was a feeble ruler, when he died in 1665 left an even feebler successor in his sickly baby son, who was to become known as Carlos the Bewitched or Carlos the Sufferer.

The Habsburgs of Austria were sturdier figures. Their authority had not been diminished by the 'Thirty Years War'; Leopold I, who succeeded his brother Friedrich in 1657, was the King of Bohemia as well as of Hungary, and in 1658 was elected Holy Roman Emperor. Leopold's difficulty was to be that he was to become the constant victim of war, or at any rate military menace, on two fronts. On the one hand, the Vienna government had been openly attacked by France as well as by Sweden and had been involved in conflicts with the Dutch because of the emperor's standing alliance with his cousins of Madrid. At the same time he was regularly threatened on the east by the Turkish hordes which surged forwards and backwards in vast waves. They had never abandoned their ambitions in eastern Europe. Though the Habsburgs claimed to rule over the whole of Hungary, two-thirds of it was in fact in the hands of the Turks. None of the Habsburg territories was easily defensible against a determined enemy. Transylvania, lying to the east of Hungary was also to be subjected to the Turkish power. Austria itself was thus always menaced from the east, as Germany was by the growing French armies in the west. Moreover the German princes, who were nominally Leopold's subjects as Holy Roman Emperor, frequently allied themselves with his foes to obtain advantages at his expense. But the Austrians did not allow themselves to be unduly worried by all this. Leopold was a mild and pious man, dependent on his confessors and on his ministers of state, the latter of whom were highly competent. He was likened to a watch which had to be periodically wound up. When he escaped disaster he touched his hat even to the humblest priests. And a proverb said that in the Danubian lands it was always Sunday.

Peace had descended for a while upon northern Europe: while France had been fighting Spain after the end of the 'Thirty Years War', the Swedes had been engaged first against the Poles (1655–7) and then against the Danes (1657–60), the Poles had been attacked by the Russians as well as by the Swedes, while the Brandenburgers had been absorbed in a set of complicated manoeuvres to increase their territorial possessions. After the death of Gustav Adolf Sweden had been successfully governed for a time by his former chancellor, Oxenstierna. Then in 1648 the eccentric Kristina, daughter of Gustav Adolf, had become queen and created an international furore. In 1654 Kristina, who was a lesbian, handed over her throne to her cousin Karl x, whom she had refused to marry, and retired to become a centre of intrigues in Rome, after she had joined the Catholic Church. Sweden itself, like Denmark and Brandenburg, was Lutheran, though this fact did not conduce to peace in northern Europe. Karl x was an ambitious man who regarded war as his trade, but he had neither the military nor the political skill of Gustav Adolf. Friedrich Wilhelm of Brandenburg (1640–88), on the other hand, might claim political genius. He built up a standing army of twenty-six thousand men and a substantial war chest, but aimed to gain his ends by diplomacy rather than war, ever ready to sell himself to the highest bidder. As a result of his manoeuvres he gained full control of eastern Pomerania (in 1648) and later of Prussia (in 1660) which he first held under Polish and then Swedish suzerainty. Tsar Aleksey of Russia (1645–76), a relatively enlightened and attractive ruler, also had his ambitions and aimed to extend his sway at the expense of the Poles. Poland, then with John Casimir (1648–68), brother of Ladislas IV, as its king, was thus attacked on all sides and was threatened with the partition to which it succumbed in the eighteenth century. Denmark under Frederik III (1648–70) also had difficulty in defending itself, but neither England, France nor the United Netherlands wanted Swedish predominance in northern Europe and tried to damp the martial ardour of Karl x. After a life of war Karl died in February 1660, to be succeeded by a minor and a regency, and peace in the north was patched up in the same year by the three treaties of Oliva, Copenhagen and Kardis.

The results of these treaties were mainly to the benefit of Sweden and Brandenburg. Sweden gained in territory and population and the Baltic was now in the process of becoming a Swedish lake, largely at the expense of the weakened kingdom of Denmark. Brandenburg acquired territory chiefly from Poland. Russia was also obliged to make concessions to the Swedes, finally admitting their claim to Livonia. The Tsar Aleksey, however, managed after a prolonged struggle to establish himself as the protector of the Cossacks of the Ukraine, thus cutting southern Poland from the Black Sea. But later in 1663 the so-called Cossack wars between Russia and Poland were resumed and by the treaty of Andrusovo in 1667 the Ukraine was divided along the line of the river Dnieper.

While a pacification was thus worked out for a time in northern Europe, the only immediately disturbing factor for the continent as a whole was the attitude of the Turks in the east which remained uncompromisingly aggressive. At the beginning of the century it had been reckoned in Christian Europe that the Ottoman empire had entered upon a period of decline. A prolonged frontier war with the Persians had debilitated it; its officials were corrupt; and the Janissaries, originally Christian mercenaries, were a source of unrest. Yet the Sultan Murad IV was a strong personality who managed to keep the Janissaries under control and during the reign of his son Ibrahim (1640–8) Azov was recovered from the Russians and an attack launched upon the island of Crete as an operation in a war with the Venetian republic. In 1648 Ibrahim was deposed and during the minority of Mehmed IV a struggle for power took place between his mother and grandmother, thus demonstrating that even in Muslim Turkey women could exercise political influence. (Murad IV had drunk himself to death in spite of the Prophet's ban on alcohol.) Eventually the elder of the two ladies was murdered and the sultan's mother called upon an illiterate Albanian named Mohammed Kiuprili to become grand vizir or chief minister at the ripe age of seventy-one. Kiuprili did remarkably well during a short term of office when he reorganised the administration and improved the finances at the cost of a wholesale slaughter of officials; he was succeeded in 1661 by his able son, Fazal Ahmed, who virtually ruled Turkey with the help of the sultan's favourite wives for a period of fifteen years. This has been called a golden age in Turkish history. That the reserves of the Ottoman empire in men and money were still formidable was proved by the fact that not only was the siege of Candia in Crete pressed but the Habsburgs were scarified in Hungary and Transylvania. But in 1664 a Turkish army was defeated by General Montecucculi at the battle of St Gothard and a truce concluded between the two empires for twenty years. And though the diplomatic relations between France and the Turkish empire had been delicate at the accession of Louis xiv and though the Most Christian King had actually dispatched a small expeditionary force to the aid of the Holy Roman Emperor in Hungary, the sultan was seen by the realistic French diplomatists to be a sovereign worth cultivating in the contest between Bourbons and Habsburgs that lay ahead.

England and the United Netherlands rejoiced briefly in the period of peace that followed the death of Oliver Cromwell. Cromwell had disapproved of the first Anglo-Dutch war, but had insisted on the exclusion of Willem of Orange, whose mother was a Stuart princess, from all positions of authority as the price of peace in 1654. When Charles ii was restored to the throne of England six years later, his sister naturally hoped that her son's exclusion would be ended. But the leading Dutch republicans, headed by Johan de Witt, the grand pensionary or chief officer of Holland, were determined to continue to rule and to keep the youthful Willem of Orange out of office. In spite of Charles ii's return, the Dutch still distrusted the English, for although Cromwell had sought a close political alliance with them, the two countries were rivals on the high seas, in matters of commerce and shipping, and in such outlying parts of the world as the East and West Indies, North America and West Africa. So it was that de Witt and his friends looked to an alliance with France as a means of security – security both against a renewed war with England and trouble with or through their neighbours in the Spanish Netherlands. A Franco-Dutch defensive alliance was therefore signed in 1662.

The English royalist government also sought support from France. Charles ii had regained his throne through being recalled by a parliament and not through force of arms: he had no loyal army on which to rely: hence he could not be certain of maintaining his position (although he adopted, on the whole, a conciliatory policy towards many of the former rebels) and he had no wish to be exiled again by discontented subjects. He owed the French government a debt because until Mazarin made his treaty with Cromwell it had treated him and his brother James with generosity, while his mother, the widow of the executed Charles I, had found a permanent home in France, which was her native land. Thus from the beginning of his reign Charles II was subject to French influences which Louis XIV was glad enough to reinforce. It was with French approval that he had married a Portuguese princess. To France he sold the valuable port of Dunkirk, which Cromwell's soldiers had helped to capture from the Spaniards. But whereas the French king has signed a defensive treaty with the Dutch, he only extended the hand of friendship, lined with gold, towards his English cousin. According to the letter of the Franco-Dutch treaty the French were obliged to help the Dutch if they were attacked by the English. But it was hoped that the occasion would not arise.

In fact a war between England and the United Netherlands broke out in February 1665, arising from quarrels over commerce and colonies. The two sides were evenly matched and French assistance, reluctantly given to the Dutch, in accordance with the treaty of 1662, proved of importance. The Dutch had the better of the argument at sea, the ultimate humiliation for England being when a Dutch squadron sailed up the Thames in 1667 and destroyed the naval base of Chatham on the Medway. The treaty of Breda that ended the war in July of that year did not have any decisive significance except that the English retained control of the New Netherlands in North America and of its chief town, New Amsterdam, which had been renamed New York after the title of the younger brother of the king of England, a name which the city has retained until this day. That was the second war between the English and Dutch during the century and a third was to come. At the same time the rivalry between the Swedes and the Danes remained fierce and wars between them were continual. Thus religion was gradually ceasing to count as a main consideration in international relationships. Oliver Cromwell had insisted on ending the first Anglo-Dutch war as he did not approve of a contest between Protestant brethren; he had also aimed to create a European Protestant union. On the other hand, he had allied himself with Roman Catholic France, just as the French government had assisted the German Protestants in their war against the emperor. Moreover the French monarchs regarded themselves as the natural foes of the Habsburgs, of whom Louis XIV was intensely jealous. He was even to hesitate a second time to lend his help to them in the event of a Turkish assault from the east. So during the century there evolved, or perhaps was confirmed, the concept of a balance of power among rival groups of states in Europe; and realistic economic and strategic considerations became paramount in the relations between governments.

The war between the English and the Dutch ended in July 1667. In August 1664 the war between the Turks and Austrians had ceased for the time being after the truce of Vasvar. By 1668, three years after the death of Felipe IV, the Spanish monarchy had finally conceded independence to Portugal after a war that had lasted intermittently for many years. Thus Europe paused in the sixth decade of the century, awaiting, as it were, even if this were not fully realised, to see in which direction the politics of glory would beckon the French king who had assumed power in a rich and populous country. Already he had demonstrated his pride of place by humiliating both the Spanish king and the pope, meticulously insisting on diplomatic precedences. The French ambassador must occupy the first place at the court of St James in London; the French ambassador at Rome must be treated with respect by the papal guards; the French flag must not admit to any deference even to English warships sailing on English waters. But leaving aside these rather childish demonstrations, Louis XIV had to consider four possible courses of action in his search for glory. He could aim to extend the frontiers of France so that they corresponded with those of ancient Gaul. Richelieu had inaugurated such a policy, being particularly anxious for aggrandisement on the north-east so as to give strategic protection to Paris. Or the king could concentrate upon obtaining for France a large slice of the Spanish empire if it collapsed. For in 1665 Felipe IV had been replaced on the throne by an only son who was not expected to live. Might not France claim the right to the whole or at least part of the Spanish inheritance through Louis XIV's wife, who had renounced her right of succession only in return for a dowry that was never paid? Or again Louis could aim to humiliate both the pope and the emperor and seek recognition as the mightiest monarch in Europe. Finally he might devote his resources to commercial, industrial and colonial expansion, imitating the smaller countries like England, the United Netherlands or Portugal in acquiring wealth through trade.

The last choice was never seriously considered, although it was to some extent pressed upon the French king by his able superintendent of finance, Jean-Baptiste Colbert. It was made clear to Colbert that although it was his duty to improve the economic position of the kingdom, and to build a navy as well as finding pay for a huge army, Louis XIV intended to attain glory by means of war or the threat of war. French historians have argued that no government in the century ever thought otherwise than in terms of war and therefore the king's decision was entirely natural and understandable. Certainly the politics of power depended on armed forces. Gustav Adolf had fashioned a modern army and on this basis his kingdom had become the leading power in the north. Though neither England nor the United Netherlands had a standing army, each of them possessed a navy which enabled them through command of the sea to make rapid progress in the New World and to be useful allies in Europe. The French monarchy therefore set about creating a large army and navy. By the 1670s it had constituted an army of 120,000 trained men and a navy of over a hundred warships, plus an equal number of frigates, fireships and auxiliary vessels. A group of capable ministers inherited by Louis xiv from Mazarin, Le Tellier, Lionne, Colbert worked indefatigably for their young master; and not only did the French king acquire an impressive armed force but soon he had also the most efficient and comprehensive diplomatic service in Europe.

With these weapons at his disposal Louis xiv aimed to extend the frontiers of his kingdom. But there is no evidence that it was his considered intention to embody in France all territories where the French language was spoken, to achieve 'natural frontiers' or concentrate exclusively on securing the succession to the Spanish throne for a member of his family. Yet always at the back of his mind was the possibility of obtaining territorial gains through claims he could put forward in the name of his Spanish wife.

In 1667 he threw his first dice. He claimed that as the local laws of Brabant and Hainault gave females the right to inherit property in preference to males who were younger members of the family, his wife, as the daughter of the king of Spain by his first wife, should have precedence in inheritance in the Spanish Netherlands over his son by his second wife. Louis xiv sent an army over the frontier to enforce the queen's rights. The Spaniards were too exhausted or too preoccupied to fight, but the governor-general of the Spanish Netherlands, Castel Rodrigo, resisted the French demands with a delaying action, while a subscription list was opened in Madrid to help him. Not only did the French armies seize a line of fortresses, but they also occupied Franche-Comté, south-west of Alsace, in the middle of the winter of 1667–8. The Dutch, though nominally the allies of France, would have preferred the French to keep Franche-Comté to their becoming uncomfortably close neighbours in Flanders. The grand pensionary therefore, in January 1668, concluded a treaty with his former enemy, Charles ii of England, offering to mediate between France and Spain but in reality aiming to bring pressure on Louis xiv not to open his mouth too widely. About the same time, however, the French king had signed a secret treaty with the Habsburg emperor, who, having been weakened by the Turkish war, was willing to agree to terms by which the Spanish empire should be divided up in what was regarded as the likely event of the swift death of the little Spanish King Carlos ii. This vast and splendid prospect persuaded the French king to be more accommodating than he might

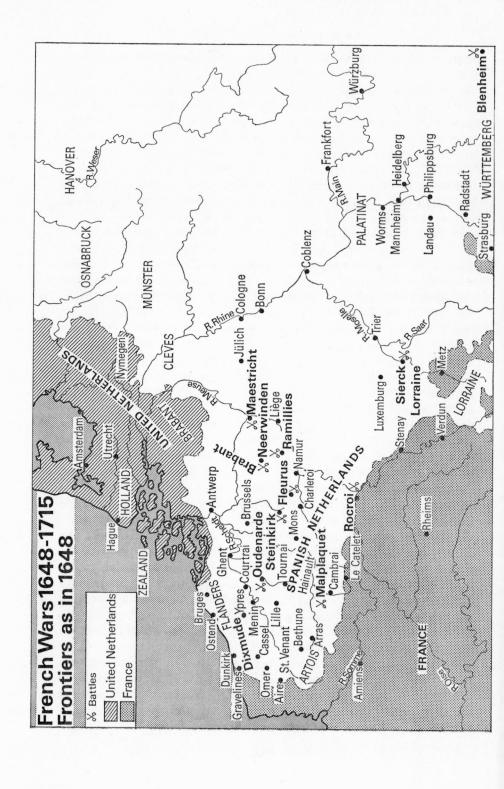

French Wars 1648-1715
Frontiers as in 1648

Battles

United Netherlands

France

HANOVER

OSNABRUCK

MÜNSTER

R.Weser

Amsterdam

Utrecht

HOLLAND

Hague

ZEALAND

UNITED NETHERLANDS

Nymegen

CLEVES

BRABANT

R.Meuse

Brabant

Antwerp

R.Scheldt

Brussels

Ghent

FLANDERS

Bruges

Ostend

Dixmude

Ypres

Menin

Cassel

Courtrai

Oudenarde

Steinkirk

Tournai

Lille

Menin

Bethune

St. Venant

Aire

Omer

Dunkirk

Gravelines

ARTOIS

Arras

Cambrai

Le Catelet

Malplaquet

Hainault

Mons

SPANISH NETHERLANDS

Charleroi

Namur

Fleurus

Ramillies

Neerwinden

Liège

Maestricht

Jülich

Cologne

Bonn

R.Rhine

Coblenz

R.Moselle

Trier

R.Saar

Luxemburg

Stenay

Sierck

Lorraine

LORRAINE

Verdun

Metz

Rocroi

Rheims

FRANCE

R.Somme

Amiens

R.Oise

R.Main

Frankfort

PALATINAT

Worms

Mannheim

Heidelberg

Landau

Philippsburg

Radstadt

Strasburg

WÜRTTEMBERG

Blenheim

Würzburg

otherwise have been; so he brought the war in the Spanish Netherlands to a rapid end, satisfying himself in the treaty of Aix-la-Chapelle, much to Dutch indignation, with a line of frontier fortresses including Lille and returning Franche-Comté to Spain. For why bother with a small portion of the Spanish empire if, in no time at all, a very large part of it was coming his way by mutual agreement with the other interested party? Nevertheless Louis resented the Dutch attempt to force his hands by their treaty with England, to which Sweden had also acceded in May 1668, forming a triple alliance. Louis xiv gave instructions to his diplomatists that the English and Swedes were to be detached from the Dutch and he decided as his next move in the policy of glory to abase the upstart republicans of the United Netherlands.

The preparations for the annihilation of the Dutch were elaborate. In May 1670 a secret treaty was concluded at Dover between the kings of England and France. In this treaty Charles ii stated that he was convinced of the truth of the Roman Catholic religion and that when the time proved suitable he would hope to incline his people to follow his 'august example'. In case any difficulty arose he would expect the support of French money and French troops. Pending the realisation of this wonderful design, he also agreed, in spite of existing treaties, to a joint assault on the Dutch. Historians even today are not in complete agreement about what Charles ii had precisely in mind when he agreed to the first clause of this astonishing treaty. His brother, James, duke of York, averred in his memoirs that Charles had in reality been converted before the signature of the treaty; certainly he was to die in the arms of the Roman Catholic Church. But Charles was a realist and, as Sir Keith Feiling has argued, may have thought this a good, if slightly complicated and risky way of screwing more money out of the French, as in fact he did. French agents were also successful in buying over the Swedes after an auction against the Dutch for their alliance. Many of the German princes too accepted French pay. The emperor, still distracted by events elsewhere, finally promised his neutrality, provided that the coming war was kept out of Germany.

In the United Netherlands the blow was expected, though only with reluctance did the burghers of Holland agree to provide money to raise an army in their defence. Clearly the policy of Johan de Witt had failed. He had hoped by allying himself with France in 1662 to ward off war from the Dutch frontiers. Instead of that he had first been obliged to acquiesce in the French invasion of the Spanish Netherlands; then he had watched his allies of the triple alliance being detached from him; finally he had seen his country blackmailed in a tariff war directed by Colbert. It was plain that Europe had been terrified by the French king and his new army and that his intention was to partition the bulk of the United Netherlands with their old English enemies. Prince Willem of Orange, the nephew of Charles II of England, who had been deliberately excluded from authority by De Witt, was offered the bribe of becoming king of a truncated nation if he would betray it. Willem refused the temptation and was named captain-general, the post held by his ancestors, for a period of one year only. But when the French struck with a big army that crossed the Rhine on 11 June 1672 Willem took over full command. Johan de Witt paid the penalty for the failure of his policies, above all for his alliance with France, which had failed to save his country from the aggressor. He and his brother were murdered by an enraged mob. Marshal Turenne, the ablest of the French generals, overran much of the United Netherlands, but Holland and Zealand stood firm, protected by the flooded watercourses.

The war did not prove to be a parade-ground exercise for the French soldiers, as the invasion of the Spanish Netherlands had been in 1667. The heroic defence of Willem of Orange, alone against the world, gained time for his country to acquire allies. In February 1674 the English government was compelled by opinion expressed in parliament to withdraw from the war, after its navy had been repulsed at sea. Though the great elector of Brandenburg, the uncle of Willem of Orange, who sided with him, was temporarily forced out of the war, the rest of Germany slowly plucked up courage to aid the Dutch. The emperor, fearful that the war might engulf Germany, signed treaties with Spain and the duc de Lorraine in the summer of 1673. After six years the two main protagonists fought themselves almost to a standstill. Turenne was killed in 1675, De Ruyter, the best of the Dutch admirals, was killed in 1676. In the close the French were left with only one ally, Sweden. At the end of 1677 an Anglo-Dutch agreement was concluded, sealed by the marriage of Willem of Orange to King Charles II's elder neice, and plans were made to compel the French to seek peace. After nearly two years of negotiations treaties were signed in the second half of 1678.

The treaty between France and Spain, concluded at Nijmegen in September, obtained for France a line of strong places stretching from Dunkirk to the river Meuse and also gave the French Franche-Comté. On the other hand, they surrendered some of the fortresses nearer the Dutch frontier which they had gained by the earlier treaty of Aix-la-Chapelle and they granted valuable trading concessions to the Dutch in a separate treaty. Thus in fact both the original contestants in the war had something positive to show for it. The duc de Lorraine, who had fought against the French, was eventually restored to his throne, but for the time being his duchy remained in French occupation. The French king insisted that the only ally who had been consistently loyal to him,

Sweden, should be generously treated, even though her armies had been surprisingly defeated by the Brandenburg troops at the battle of Fehrbellin in 1675. The emperor agreed to surrender Freiburg and Breisach to the French, but Phillippsburg was restored to him.

Louis xiv was delighted with the results of the war in which he had been engaged against half of Europe. He had managed to extend the frontiers of his kingdom both to the north and south of his eastern borders. His army and navy had conducted themselves with skill. His army was battle-hardened and could be expanded still further to support his foreign policy. He had been loyal to his treaties, standing by Sweden, as earlier he had stood by the United Netherlands. Thus both his generals and his diplomatists had distinguished themselves and it appeared as if the ascendancy of France in Europe had been procured. The peace of Nijmegen was actually regarded by Louis xiv as a springboard for fresh conquests. Commenting upon it at the time Madame de Sévigné observed: 'The king's triumph is so complete that in future he will only have to say what piece of Europe he wants. People will be glad to give it him without his having the trouble of marching at the head of his armies.'

Though the United Netherlands had not emerged too badly from the war and Prince Willem of Orange had gained international prestige after repulsing the Anglo-French assault in 1672, the climax that the country reached under Willem has been described by a modern Dutch historian as 'the beginning of the decline'. 'Before 1680,' writes Professor Kossmann, 'the creative geniuses of seventeenth-century Holland had already died. . . . The inspiration of Dutch civilisation seemed to change.' Oligarchic abuses, he says, increased and French classicism began to permeate Dutch culture at the very moment when French imperialism had been checked. Not all historians would agree that the decline of the Dutch republic began so soon. Under Willem ii the Dutch were again successfully to resist French pretensions to dominate Europe. Professor Boxer, for example would put the social and economic decline as much as a hundred years later when the golden age of the Dutch yielded to that of the periwig.

For Germany too it was a significant moment in history. Both at the time when the league of the Rhine had been formed under French patronage and later on the eve of the war of 1672–8 many German princes had been happy to be allies of France: it had then seemed as if the Germans were completely disunited and indifferent to the leadership of the Holy Roman Emperor or the functioning of the German diet; but now the blatant aggressiveness of the French, who had not merely attacked the Dutch without warning but had violated Lorraine and thrust across the Rhine, forced the German rulers to realise their own perils, to recognise the virtues of unity, and even to look with more respect upon the emperor. They could see that through the strengthening of his frontiers where fortresses were at once improved or newly constructed the king of France had immensely enhanced his strategic position and that his next moves were likely to be not against the Spaniards or Dutch but against the Germans themselves.

For the king of England the lessons of the war were that the French were dangerous, cunning and resilient. Twice Charles II had been forced into resistance, in 1668 and 1678, under the pressure of his parliament, but on each occasion the French had ignored the threat and defiantly gone on their own way. Parliament was now proving itself obstreperous to the English monarch even though it was still the same royalist parliament that had been elected in an atmosphere of romantic loyalty in 1661. By 1678 the House of Commons was demanding that Charles II's heir presumptive, his brother, James, duke of York, should be excluded from the throne because he was an avowed Roman Catholic. Murmurings were heard about a 'popish plot' against Protestant liberties, which were not so far from reality in the light of the first clause of the secret treaty of Dover. But Charles II, though eager to avert rebellion, feared that if he agreed to the exclusion of his brother, the Stuart monarchy would be overthrown for the second time and a republic reconstituted. So he decided to reduce all his foreign commitments, no longer to defy the French, but, on the contrary to seek, in return for his neutrality material and moral support for the maintenance of his throne.

For the great elector of Brandenburg the war of 1672–8 had been a golden opportunity. A man of iron will and violent temper, he had managed by changing sides and making good use of his army to consolidate his position in northern Germany. Had it not been for Louis XIV's loyalty to his ally, he would have gained western as well as eastern Pomerania. He swallowed his resentment for the time being, but he did not forget or forgive and before he died he was to contribute to the resistance mobilised against the French advance into Germany. He also turned to putting his own house in order and because a coarsened version of the absolute monarch. Sweden equally was not grateful to France, from whom she had gained little enough in return for her alliance. The result of the war was indeed to throw the Swedes for a time into friendship with their old enemies, the Danes. A secret treaty was concluded between the two Scandinavian kingdoms in 1679 and this was sealed by the marriage of King Karl XI of Sweden to the sister of the king of Denmark. Moreover the war gave an impetus to absolutism in Sweden. The government of the regency was blamed for Swedish failures in the war, including the defeat by the Brandenburgers. Karl XI claimed that it was no longer necessary to consult his council on matters of state and this was followed by a reduction in the rights of the riksdag which was, as a rule, called only when the king needed money. No *coup d'état* took place. The estates were ready to yield before a monarch whom they regarded as patriotic and wise.

Thus in different ways the treaties of Nijmegen constituted a historical milestone. Absolutist tendencies were strengthened in England, Brandenburg and Sweden; the prestige of Willem of Orange had been heightened in the United Netherlands, though personally he disapproved of the making of peace. The lessons of the war, underlining the restless ambitions of the French monarchy, gave an impulse towards German unity. The emperor was alerted, while the appetite of the king of France was stimulated for more extensive conquests. From the scheming of Richelieu and the open cupidity of Louis XIV may be traced the Franco-German enmity that was to endure until the twentieth century.

CHAPTER 12

A CRISIS FOR GERMANY
1678–88

In the 1680s the Holy Roman Emperor, a lover of music and the gentler pleasures of life, seated in his capital of Vienna, was disturbed by the menace of war on two fronts. Since Leopold 1 had come to the throne in 1657 a recovery had slowly taken place in the mixed and ill-defended lands – Austria, Styria, Carinthia, Silesia, Bohemia and Hungary – that made up his rickety dominions. They had suffered severely in the 'Thirty Years War', though it is not possible to estimate precisely whether their population had declined or how much destruction of property resulted from it. Bohemia, where the war started, was devastated. The landlord class exploited the opportunities provided by markets that were opening up for food, drink and other supplies purchased by the ever-embattled armies. But the peasants, whose labour was required by their landlords to increase production, were hit by interference with their own customary subsistence agriculture. Town life had been damaged by the war too. At the same time attempts to recatholicise parts of the Habsburg dominions had created resentment and confusion. Such was the internal situation.

Abroad the new emperor's difficulties at first came mainly from the east. Karl x of Sweden ʌnd inherited the ambitions of Gustav Adolf in Germany and even aspired to the throne of Bohemia. To harrass the emperor he had concluded an alliance with George Rakoczy II, prince of Transylvania, the area to the east of Hungary and south of Poland, of which the Turks claimed to be the suzerains. But Karl x and the Transylvanian prince quarrelled. The emperor was able to form an alliance with Poland against Sweden. Then the Turks attacked Transylvania and eventually Rakoczy had to appeal to the emperor for help against them. This brought about the war that was ended by the battle of St Gothard, only fifty miles east of Vienna, and the subsequent truce of Vasvar (1664). Although the truce left the Turks in control both of Transylvania and much of Hungary, the emperor had obtained temporary security from an assault from the east. And he was thus able to turn his attention to the other growing threat to Germany that was held out by the rising 'Sun King', Louis XIV.

At first, as we have seen, the emperor – and the empire, as represented in the imperial diet – turned a blind eye upon the French assault on the Spanish Netherlands. Whether these provinces were or were not technically of concern to the empire was a moot point. At any rate Leopold signed what historians call the first partition treaty with Louis XIV by which he was promised French agreement to his acquiring a substantial part of the Spanish empire if the Spanish Habsburg dynasty was extinguished. But when in 1672 the French attack on the Dutch Netherlands spilled over into Germany itself, Leopold had second thoughts about acquiescing in French ambitions. His capable ambassador count de L'Isola (who died in 1674) had warned him earlier that the French attack on the Spanish Netherlands was 'the beginning of the march of the enemy towards the gates of Vienna'. Hence the emperor was drawn into an alliance with the Dutch and the Spaniards against the French. But though he had generals and diplomatists of genuine ability at his disposal, he was uneasily aware that he had no army that could possibly compete either with the one hundred thousand or more Frenchmen to his west or the one hundred thousand or more Turks to his east. It was not until later that the diet, alerted at last to Germany's peril, voted in favour of creating an imperial army of forty thousand men.

So during the 1670s the emperor concentrated on securing his rear and preparing to face his western foe. After an abortive conspiracy had taken place in Christian Hungary in 1670-1 an army of occupation and an Austrian administration were established there which imposed ruthless order upon the Hungarians. Hungarian political liberties were abrogated and pressure exerted to convert the Protestants in the area to Roman Catholicism. These methods aroused discontent which burst into flame in 1678. Another Austrian army was stationed on the Upper Rhine because it became painfully clear that the treaties of Nijmegen had not satisfied the appetite of Louis XIV and that his next acts of aggression would be directed against Germany.

The reason why the emperor had been freed from immediate anxiety over the Turks was that after the truce of Vasvar their warlike attentions had been diverted elsewhere. It was not until 1669 that they obtained the surrender of Candia, which they had been besieging for twenty-three years, and at last came to terms with the Venetian republic. The foreign policy of the Ottoman empire was now directed by the grand vizir, Fazil Ahmed, since the sultan himself was quite happy so long as he was allowed to spend his days in hunting. Once Crete had been occupied, affording the Turks, in theory at least, control of the Mediterranean (though in fact the Beys of Tripoli, Tunis and Algiers were extremely independent of Constantinople) Fazil Ahmed turned to

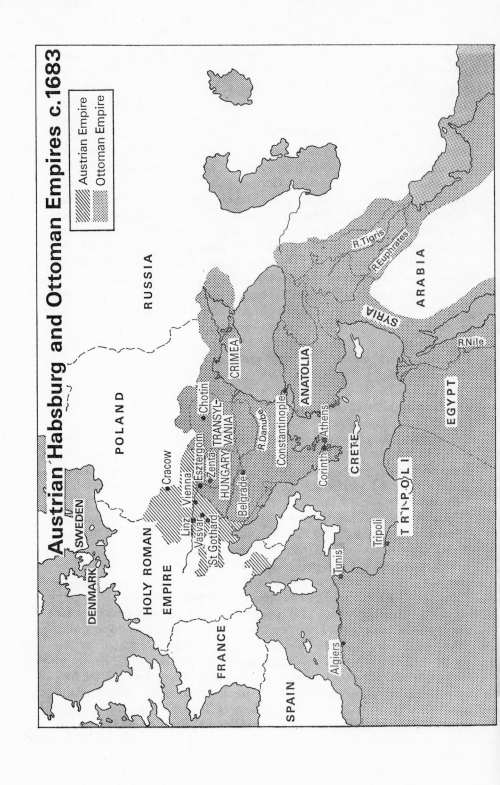

Austrian Habsburg and Ottoman Empires c.1683

Austrian Empire
Ottoman Empire

SWEDEN

DENMARK

HOLY ROMAN
EMPIRE

FRANCE

SPAIN

POLAND

RUSSIA

Cracow

Linz Vienna
Vasvár
St Gothard

Esztergom
Zenta
HUNGARY
TRANSYL-
VANIA

Chotin

Belgrade

R.Danube

Constantinople

CRIMEA

ANATOLIA

Corinth Athens

CRETE

Tunis

Algiers

Tripoli

T R I P O L I

EGYPT

SYRIA

ARABIA

R.Tigris

R.Euphrates

R.Nile

another enterprise – an assault on the Ukraine, previously the battle-ground of the Russians and Poles. A Cossack hetman sought the protection of the sultan and offered to defend the Ukraine against both the Russians and the Poles; a large Turkish army was thereupon sent to the Ukraine to support the Cossacks, but was defeated by John Sobieski, soon to be elected the king of Poland, at the battle of Chotin in 1673. This battle was not as conclusive as that of St Gothard and in fact for a time the Ottoman power was allowed to retain its hold on the Ukraine north of the Black Sea. Peace was made with Poland in 1676 and in the same year Fazil Ahmed died, to be succeeded as grand vizir by his brother-in-law, Kara Mustafa. In 1681 the new grand vizir signed a peace treaty with Russia and abandoned the Turkish claim on the Ukraine. It was then decided that the Ottoman armies should once again be launched against the Habsburg emperor so that the defeat of St Gothard might be revenged.

An opportunity had been presented to the Turks by the discontents of the inhabitants of Christian Hungary. The latter had grown increasingly resentful of their oppression by the Austrians. They discovered a leader in Imre Thokoly, a Magyar aristocrat of twenty-five, who raised the standard of rebellion in 1678 and aimed to drive the Austrians out of northern Hungary. The emperor at that time, though he had just concluded peace with France, was distracted by internal problems. Plague and famine were sweeping through his dominions and in Bohemia he was confronted with a peasants' revolt. Thokoly was able to arouse his people to fever pitch because they had religious as well as political grievances (the Jesuits had attempted to deprive the Hungarian Calvinists, of whom Thokoly himself was one, of their customary liberties). With the help of French officers and Polish mercenaries military progress was achieved and by 1680 Thokoly had control over much of northern and western Hungary. The Turks, though still bound by the truce of 1664, were glad to fish in these troubled waters, and gave help to the Hungarians. The Emperor Leopold, for his part, still more concerned over French intentions in Germany than the disturbances to his east, tried to come to terms with Thokoly. In May 1681 he promised to restore all the customary Hungarian liberties and to allow Calvinist pastors, who had been forced into exile, to return to their offices. But Thokoly did not really want peace with the Habsburgs: his ambitions were enflamed by his success; early in 1682 he was to reach an agreement with the Pasha of Buda and later in the same year be recognised as king of Hungary by the Turks.

There were various reasons why the Ottoman empire now decided to make war on the emperor even though the truce had not yet expired. The grand vizir, Kara Mustafa, had not thought well of his predecessor's

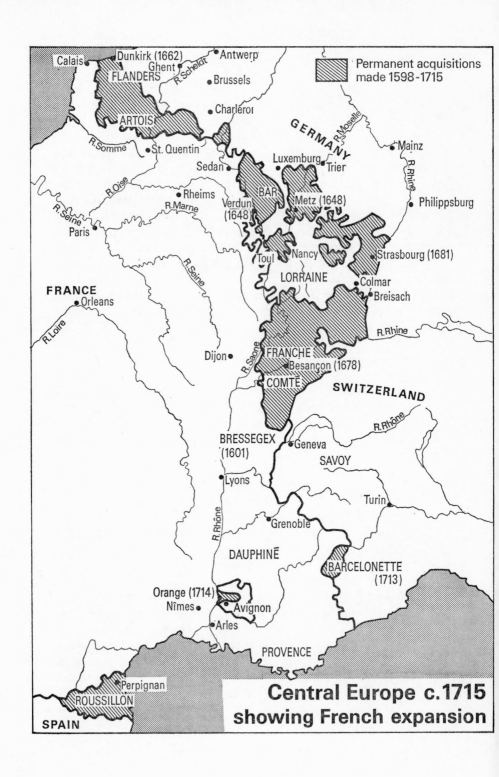

Central Europe c.1715 showing French expansion

wars in the Ukraine. Yet the Turks lived by war and wars were necessary for his own personal prestige and survival. The Janissaries were always liable to rebel if they were not profitably occupied and the subject princes of Moldavia, Wallachia, Transylvania and elsewhere were generally restless. Moreover the grand vizir had enemies at court. But supposing he could bring off the magnificent coup, frustrated earlier in the century, of conquering Vienna itself? Then his enemies would be abashed; the subject princes would rally behind him; the Janissaries would have spoils to share; and a holy war against the Christians could be invoked. In August 1682, the resolution was taken. The sultan ordered that a huge army – no one quite knows to this day how huge – should concentrate in Belgrade in the spring of 1683; and thence the march on Vienna should begin.

Grave though the peril was, it was with considerable reluctance that the Emperor Leopold averted his eyes from the west of Europe. Up till the very last moment he attempted to do a deal with the Turks, for during the past four years he had been absorbed as titular leader of Germany in countering the menace of Louis XIV. The French king had been by no means satisfied with his gains from the treaties of Nijmegen. He aimed to extend his empire by means of legal ingenuities backed by force. He still had available an army of one hundred and forty thousand men. His idea was to make use of certain loopholes in previous treaties to extend his sovereignty on his newly acquired frontiers in Flanders, Franche-Comté and Alsace. For this purpose Chambers of Reunion, consisting of lawyers predisposed to the wishes of the king, were created to determine which territories belonged to France. The first of these chambers was set up at Metz in December 1679 to trace what 'usurpations' had been made from the three bishoprics of Metz, Toul and Verdun which had been assigned to France by the treaty of Nijmegen. (One must remember, as Sir George Clark has pointed out, that this was a stage of transition between decadent feudalism and modern notions of sovereignty.) Similar tribunals were created at Besançon, Breisach and Tournai. These interested bodies decided that various lands, some of which had been under the sovereignty of other princes, including the king of Sweden, rightfully belonged to France. As a result of such 'acts of reunion' by the summer of 1680 Strasbourg was the only independent state left in Alsace. But Strasbourg too was claimed by France, though it regarded itself as a free city within the Holy Roman Empire; it was therefore besieged and occupied by French troops in September 1680. That was done on the ground that the Chamber of Reunion in Breisach interpreted the treaty of Westphalia to mean that Strasbourg was French. In any case, so French historians have observed, it had been insufficiently neutral.

The seizure of Strasbourg appeared to be a blow at the heart of Germany. The emperor had vainly protested and sought a conference over this latest French claim. But by a mixture of bluff, threats of force, and offers of bribes – such as the restoration of Freiburg – the emperor was induced to acquiesce in the French coup. Thus a great Protestant city fell into French hands; a Roman Catholic cardinal, Fürstenburg by name, became its bishop; and Louis xiv himself paid a ceremonial visit to the city to celebrate a bloodless victory. Casale in northern Italy, a strategic town hitherto under the sovereignty of the duke of Mantua, was also seized by another French expeditionary force. And two months later the French laid siege to another key town in Europe, Luxemburg, a fortress belonging to Spain, which guarded the route linking the Spanish Netherlands with Germany.

The French king fortified these acts of aggression not merely by legal arguments but also by a masterly display of diplomacy. When not only the emperor and Prince Willem of Orange but even the English government expressed anxiety over the fate of Luxemburg, French troops were withdrawn for the time being. Again the French king did not, at any rate openly, encourage the Turks against the emperor, though he certainly lent his support to the Hungarian rebels. He used bribes to keep the king of England on his side and he concluded treaties with Denmark and Brandenburg. Thus though a Dutch-Swedish treaty was signed at The Hague in September 1681 with the intention of resisting French pretensions (the Swedes were particularly angry about the acts of reunion) there was as yet no effective method of stopping the progress of Louis xiv unless the Holy Roman Emperor was able to rally the whole of Germany against him. But the emperor, as we have seen, had his distractions elsewhere.

For Willem of Orange too these were years of frustration. He had been opposed to accepting the terms offered by the French at Nijmegen and had been willing to continue fighting the French even after six years of exhausting struggle. But the peace terms had not been costly for the Dutch: indeed they had received commercial concessions. So Willem's wishes were disregarded by the states-general. Moreover he experienced another setback. At the time when he had married the niece of the king of England in 1677 he had good reason to suppose that he had succeeded in detaching the English government from France. But when in 1681 the Dutch, recognising the new dangers from the French claims in Flanders and elsewhere, attempted to persuade England to agree to a renewal of the triple alliance of 1668 with Sweden, the king of England refused to do more than offer to mediate over the question of Luxemburg (though in the very same year a treaty was concluded between England and Spain). The reason why the English king was reluctant to extend his continental commitments was that he was perturbed by events at home. It seemed to him as if a new civil war might take place if he did not give way to demands made in parliament either for the exclusion of his Roman Catholic brother from his right of succession to the throne or the acceptance of constitutional limitations on the hereditary rights of the monarchy. While almost everywhere throughout the rest of Europe monarchies were being strengthened into absolutism, the idea that the English monarchy should voluntarily inflict such wounds upon itself appeared fantastic. Hence Charles II preferred to come to a secret agreement with the French king, protecting himself against his own parliament, rather than fall into line with the martial plans of his nephew.

In spite of the refusal of England to join in the anti-French alliance the Dutch persisted in building up diplomatic resistance to Louis XIV. In February 1682 the emperor acceded to the Dutch-Swedish treaty aiming to uphold the terms of the treaties of Nijmegen and in May the Spanish Habsburgs also joined in. In September 1682 a number of German princes met in Vienna and also promised their help in maintaining the existing European settlement. But Europe was not solid in its resistance to France. Brandenburg was still in the pocket of the French king and England also remained so until the death of King Charles II at the beginning of 1685. Some of the other German princes in the north were so fearful of the might of the French king that they preferred to reach an understanding with him. In the end in fact it was only the enfeebled monarchy of Spain that plucked up the courage actually to fight the French. The Dutch, in accordance with their treaty obligations, provided the Spaniards with a force of eight thousand soldiers, but without the help of England they refused to join in the war themselves.

The emperor could not have fought the French even if he had wished to do so; for before the end of 1682 it had become clear to the Austrians that they were going to be faced with a massive assault from the east. It is true that in November 1682 a brief truce was concluded with Thokoly but all the signs were that in the following spring the Turks would advance through western Hungary along with the discontented Magyars. The emperor had therefore to concentrate all his efforts upon raising troops, collecting money and finding allies. It is estimated that he had at first only some thirty thousand trained men as compared with the Turks who had at least one hundred thousand (some historians speak of three hundred thousand). Fortunately one ally offered itself as a result of the Turkish menace. The Poles were fearful that if the Turks advanced into Hungary, they would fan out and threaten Cracow and its neighbourhood. So with the help of Pope Innocent XI, who, since his accession in 1675, had been eager to arouse Christian Europe against the infidel Turks, a Polish-Austrian agreement was negotiated and signed whereby the court of Vienna promised to put sixty thousand men into Hungary and to subsidise a Polish army of forty thousand. The Poles were to be led by their soldier king, John Sobieski. But the Emperor Leopold himself was no soldier and after some hesitation it was decided to invite his brother-in-law, a refugee prince, Charles of Lorraine, 'with an aquiline nose like a parrot's', to take charge of his armies. But before all these arrangements could be completed the Ottoman hordes had struck. Early in July 1683, before the Poles were ready, the Turks and their Magyar allies thrust forward through Hungary, outmanoeuvred Charles of Lorraine, and by the middle of the month were at the gates of Vienna. A week earlier the emperor and his ministers had fled from the capital, leaving the garrison under the orders of the capable Count Rüdiger von Starhemberg. The siege of Vienna lasted for just two months. In early September the Polish army arrived and joined that of Charles of Lorraine whom the Turks had chased from Hungary. The garrison had held out gallantly and on 12 September 1683 a great battle took place to the west of the city in which the Turks were crushed and Vienna was relieved. That was a notable and often forgotten date in the history of European civilisation. The Turks retreated into Hungary and on Christmas day the grand vizir, Kara Mustafa, paid the price of failure: he was strangled at the order of the sultan.

The emperor and his advisers were now confronted with a choice: should they press on relentlessly against the fleeing Turks who had not merely been driven off Austrian soil, but had been compelled to surrender the valuable fortress of Esztergom to the pursuing Poles, Austrians and Germans? Possibly the whole of Hungary could be reconquered and the Christian peoples of the Balkans freed for ever from the Turkish yoke. Or, on the other hand, should the Holy Roman Emperor order the concentration of his armies in western Europe (where only ten thousand of his men were then stationed) and try to put a halt to the attacks of Louis xiv and thus preserve the integrity of Germany? At the same time that Vienna was being relieved the French had launched a fresh assault on the Spanish Netherlands, occupying Courtrai and Dixmude and laying waste parts of Hainault and Flanders. These events had perturbed the Dutch as well as the German princes. Even the elector of Bavaria now joined up with the defensive alliance against France that had been originated in 1681. Willem of Orange was still anxious to resist the French, but he tried in vain to persuade the emperor to give teeth to the alliance by at once recalling his troops from Hungary.

Thus the Spaniards, now but shadows of the fighting tercios of Felipe II, were left to carry on the hopeless contest alone, since their appeals for help to their fellow Habsburgs fell on deaf ears. The French easily overcame all resistance and in the spring of 1684 they again laid siege to Luxemburg. Even before then the emperor had made up his mind. Under pressure from the pope a Holy League was formed with Poland and the republic of Venice for a combined war upon the Ottoman empire. Poland and Austria hoped to extend their frontiers eastward, Venice to regain Crete. The treaty of alliance was signed at Linz in March 1684. Efforts were made to induce the Russians and the French, and even such Protestants as the Dutch and the English and the Moslems of Persia to take part in the war. The pope invited Louis XIV, the Most Christian King, to lend his fleet to the enterprise, but he refused. He had other plans, and contented himself with playing his part by harrassing the Turkish possessions in north Africa.

Nevertheless the Holy Alliance was soon activated. In the years that lay ahead the Turks were driven from Hungary and even attacked by the Venetians in Greece. The sultan himself, who had ordered the strangulation of his grand vizir, was deposed in 1687. 'Without much exaggeration,' Mr Stoye has written, 'the war of 1683-99 against the sultan can be called the last of the crusades.' In September 1686 Budapest, 'the shield of Islam', fell to the Austrians. In the following summer the Venetians took Corinth and bombarded Athens, destroying much of the Parthenon in the process. Ten years later a magnificent victory over the Turks was won by Prince Eugen of Savoy at Zenta in 1697 and by the treaty of Carlowitz that concluded the war in 1699 the Ottoman empire was much reduced, the Turks surrendering in particular nearly the whole of Hungary to the Austrians. Thus from the end of the century it could be said that the Austro-Hungarian empire came into being, to endure until 1918, while the Turk had become 'the sick man of Europe'.

For Louis XIV the emperor's choice was too good an opportunity to be missed. For some time the king of France had been holding out the suggestion that a truce should be concluded between him and the Habsburg powers for twenty or thirty years whereby he was to be allowed to remain in occupation of the lands he had acquired by the acts of reunion, but the question of their ultimate sovereignty was to be left in abeyance. To his previous acquisitions he now added Luxemburg, which fell to French arms in June 1684. The diet at Ratisbon accepted the proposed truce for a period of twenty years. The Dutch states-general, realising, after an abortive conference at The Hague in February 1684, that effective opposition to the French was out of the question and believing that a general war must be averted, also acquiesced in the truce, and Spain was obliged to follow suit. Thus France was left in possession of Strasbourg, Luxemburg and Casale, a large part of Alsace and Lorraine, and a number of fortresses in Spanish Flanders. Louis XIV appeared to have reached the apogee of his success. But in fact he was less secure than he had been after the treaties of Nijmegen six years earlier. His triumph was due to a number of fortuitous and temporary circumstances. The English and Dutch had been distracted by internal political problems. The emperor was absorbed in the war in Hungary. But the lines had been prepared for a grand alliance against France. Fear, as Rousseau was to argue, governs the relationship between states. Sooner or later the Dutch and the Germans were bound to feel that their security was endangered by the progress of Louis XIV's armies. In fact the counter-blow was to come sooner than the French reckoned. For long before the emperor's war against the Turks was over and long before the truce of Ratisbon expired Willem of Orange was to become the architect of the Grand Alliance.

After the signature of the truce Louis XIV concentrated particular attention on the state of his own soul and on the Christian unity of his kingdom. Hitherto his religious policy had had two aspects: on the one hand, he considered that because he was the divine choice to be the ruler of his country he was responsible for the religious welfare of all his subjects; on the other hand, though the Church of France was a part of the universal Roman Catholic Church, it had long asserted its right to a position of independence under the monarchy. So from the beginning of his reign Louis XIV had shown himself quick to resent any claims to superiority by the papacy. He thought of himself as a good son of the Church, but a son with well-defined and recognised rights of his own. For example, he asserted his right to exercise by royal prerogative the temporal and spiritual powers of the French bishoprics from the time that the incumbent died until the time when his successor was instituted. That enabled his government to nominate to many benefices; the king's ministers, such as Colbert, took full advantage of the opportunities offered for nepotism. This right – known as the *régale* – had not originally been applied to all the dioceses in the kingdom, but only to half of them. But in 1675 the *régale* was extended to all; some bishops protested and were backed by the pope. In the summer of 1681 the king called an assembly of the clergy who were persuaded not only to uphold the *régale* but to pass four resolutions redefining the relationship between the Church of France and the papacy. Thus a quarrel between Louis XIV and the determined Pope Innocent XI followed. In 1687 a squabble over the rights of the French ambassador in Rome resulted in his excommunication by the pope. Louis XIV retorted by seizing the papal estates at Avignon.

Yet this quarrel did not lead, as it might well have done, to a complete rupture. Louis XIV did not wish to be a schismatic nor to follow in the footsteps of Henry VIII of England. On the contrary, he wanted the assistance of the pope not only in his long-drawn-out contest with the Jansenists (which did not finally reach a settlement until 1710) but also in the measures that he was proposing to take with regard to the French Protestants or Huguenots.

There were about one million Huguenots living in France, whose rights were guaranteed by the edict of Nantes, promulgated by Henri IV in 1598. They were for the most part industrious and useful subjects and some leading Huguenots had served the monarchy with loyalty and ability. But the assembly of French clergy had constantly pressed Louis XIV to lend his support to the conversion of these Protestants in the midst of his kingdom, to back their own propaganda efforts, led by the gifted Bishop Bossuet, with all the strength of his secular arm. The king, who had originally acquiesced in the existing arrangements, was persuaded to change his policy for a number of reasons. First, he was concerned over the unity of his kingdom in the face of an increasingly recalcitrant Europe. Secondly, in his middle age he gradually became more conscious of his own sins, for he had led a sexually exuberant life. He was pressed to take action not only by his confessors but also by Madame de Maintenon, a pious widow without claim to royal blood whom, after the death of his Spanish queen, he secretly married in 1683. 'Fear of death and anxiety to expiate the sins of his past life, fear of the judgment of God and blind acceptance of the wishes of the directory of his conscience,' observed the Brandenburg envoy to France, 'were capable of making him take resolutions which were bound to be followed by serious consequences.' To some extent that was speculation. But Louis XIV was convinced that the Huguenots were rapidly yielding to the prolonged conversion campaigns to which they had been subjected. In fact the maximum pressure had been brought to bear upon them, organised largely by Louis's minister of war, Louvois, temporarily deprived of his normal occupation of attacking the weak abroad. Many of the Huguenots' places of worship were demolished; they were excluded from offices and professions; they were bribed to change their religion with promises of money and exemption from the *taille*; finally they had to submit to the 'dragonnades', that is to say deliberate bullying by the French soldiers or dragoons compulsorily billeted upon their homes. So in October 1685 the French king was persuaded that the edict of Nantes could be revoked because it had become superfluous. The decree of revocation ordered the destruction of the Protestant temples, the cessation of all Protestant services, the closure of all Protestant schools, and the baptism of all those born in the Protestant faith.

The news of this far-reaching measure was welcomed with delight by the Roman Catholic clergy. Men as intelligent as Bossuet and Fénelon hailed it as a divine miracle. The king's wife and confessor were enthusiastic. The new decree was harshly enforced. Inevitably many Huguenots accepted conversion at any rate in name. But in spite of persecution the secret practice of the Protestant religion continued in France and resentment against the ecclesiastical hierarchy became one of the factors that contributed to the devastating movement against the French Church even before the revolution of 1789.

About two hundred thousand French Protestants managed to escape abroad and found refuges in the United Netherlands, in Protestant Germany, notably in Brandenburg, in Switzerland and in Great Britain. There their industry proved useful, while, freed from the restraints from which they had suffered in France, they were able to make intellectual contributions to European thought. It is sometimes said that in enforcing the policy of unity Louis XIV was doing no more than was customary: the right of princes to choose the religion of their subjects had been accepted since the Reformation and been upheld by the treaties of Westphalia. Yet not only in Protestant countries but also in parts of Poland and the Austrian empire the idea of permitting liberty of conscience to all Christians was beginning to take a hold. Though Roman Catholics were excluded from many political rights in England and in the United Netherlands by 1685 they were generally allowed to attend Mass without molestation. Louis's action was therefore contrary to the spirit of his times, just as the Holy Roman Emperor's had been in Hungary. And it made many statesmen outside the French kingdom realise that they were dealing not merely with a dangerous aggressor abroad but also with an intolerant despot at home.

The expulsion of the Huguenots therefore played a part in helping to build up an alliance, hitherto shadowy and ineffective, against French ambitions in Germany. In northern Europe the absolute monarchs of Sweden, Denmark and Brandenburg were beginning to come together. They resented the policy of the reunions and feared renewed acts of aggression in spite of the truce of Ratisbon. In August 1685 Brandenburg, so long the ally of France, signed a defensive treaty with the Dutch. In January 1686 Brandenburg followed this with another defensive treaty with Sweden and a treaty with the emperor. The treaty with Sweden definitely envisaged the possibility of a threat by France to the Lutheran religion. In 1687 the Danes, who had also signed a treaty with the Brandenburgers agreed to submit the question of Holstein-Gottorp, so long a bone of contention with Sweden, to a congress in Altona. In July 1686 a number of princes in western Germany, including the king of Sweden, for his Germans possessions, formed a league at Augsburg to maintain the existing treaties. This league was not as important as some historians later made out, but it nevertheless impressed Louis XIV and his ministers as indicating a growing resistance movement in Germany.

Throughout these uncertain years Prince Willem of Orange was concerned lest an Anglo-French alliance should be reconstructed, following the lines of that of 1670, aimed against the Dutch republic which had earlier impeded the French drive to the east. In fact Willem underestimated his father-in-law, James II, who had become king of England in 1685. James was a proud and obstinate man, and although he was anxious to proselytise his Protestant subjects to his own strongly held Roman Catholic faith if he could, he neither approved of the methods used in France forcibly to convert the Protestants before the revocation of the edict of Nantes nor was he willing to become a servant of French policy. But Willem feared James's intentions and so did the states-general. The Dutch government had been shocked by the revocation and was also fearful of the fresh threats to the Rhineland. Thus it was decided early in 1688 that if Prince Willem received an invitation from leading Englishmen, he should be allowed to head an expeditionary force over from Holland to England and compel his father-in-law to enter the anti-French camp. Louis XIV was not unduly disturbed by this plan, for he believed that if Willem went over to England, a fresh civil war would follow and thus both Great Britain and the United Netherlands would be neutralised. Indeed these very facts encouraged him to pursue his policy of intimidating the Germans.

Fear, as we have remarked, is the dominant factor in relations between governments. Louis XIV was afraid – in spite of the truce of Ratisbon – that as soon as the emperor had overcome his Turkish enemies he would turn his attention back to the west and aim to upset the European settlement. But for the moment the Austrians and the Poles seemed fully occupied in the eastern war. England and the United Netherlands, suspicious of one another, appeared to be committed to a long war. Though undoubtedly the important electorates of Brandenburg and Bavaria were no longer friendly to French interests and Sweden was no longer a French ally, the league of Augsburg could be considered a paper tiger. But it might be argued – and has been argued by some French historians – that Louis XIV struck again in 1688 in self-defence in a preventive war. Equally, however, it can be and has been argued that the French assault on the palatinate, which then took place, and the sending of troops towards Cologne were parts of a policy of deliberate intimidation that had worked effectively before in 1681–4. The government that is willing to go to war in the last resort to enforce its ends and possesses a trained army in readiness to move is always at an advantage compared with governments that are trying to patch up alliances and to recruit armies. That at least has invariably been the case throughout modern European history. So in the autumn of 1688 Louis xiv published a manifesto declaring the reasons why he was now going to war with the emperor. He described the conduct hostile to him in Germany; he said that the truce of Ratisbon ought to have been converted into an enduring treaty; he condemned the formation of the league of Augsburg; and he explained the rightfulness of his claims to interfere in the palatinate and in the electorate of Cologne. His army then laid siege to Philippsburg, a key fortress in the palatinate, while another smaller French force occupied the territory of Cologne, apart from the city itself, where the elector of Brandenburg had sent an army. Thus the whole of the Rhineland was menaced by French aggression.

But for once the French advance was to be barred. 'Louis xiv,' it has been said, 'was the architect of his own ruin.' Not only did he assault the empire, but on 26 November 1688 he declared war on the Dutch republic. After French troops had occupied the left bank of the middle Rhine, leading princes of northern Germany met at Magdeburg to raise an army against him. The new elector of Brandenburg (the 'great elector' had died earlier in the year) broke off negotiations with France. The king of Spain, whose French wife had just died, aligned himself with the Austrian Habsburgs. Willem of Orange accomplished a bloodless revolution in England and at the end of 1688 his father-in-law had taken refuge in France. So in May 1689 England joined the anti-French coalition. Under its new monarch England declared war on France and concluded an offensive and defensive alliance with the United Netherlands. Other princes including the duke of Savoy, adhered to the Grand Alliance. Thus Louis xiv, who had attempted to blackmail the Germans into conceding to him a frontier on the Rhine by a threat of force or a short, sharp campaign, found himself committed to a war against half of Europe.

This was the war that was to shape and dominate the political history of Europe (with a short interval) until Louis xiv himself died in 1715. Up till 1684 France had progressed smoothly enough to the leading place among European powers. She was admired and feared. Her king's example as an absolute monarch, her culture, her intellectual and aesthetic ideas had impressed people everywhere and had been widely imitated. That is why the second half of this century is rightly regarded as epitomising the preponderance of France. In the next chapter we shall discuss what that meant.

CHAPTER 13

THE CLASSICAL MOMENT

On 6 May 1682 Louis XIV moved his entire court into the palace of Versailles which was to be the heart of his kingdom for the remainder of his reign. Altogether the palace took fifty years to build, to decorate and to fit into the setting of its gardens. When the court arrived it was not yet completed: the masons were still at work. The king's daughter-in-law, the dauphine, who at that time was big with child, the child who was to be the promising duke of Burgundy, was obliged to change her apartments the second day after she reached Versailles because the noise prevented her from sleeping. The palace had been built on marshy ground and many thousands of workmen had died of fever. But whatever criticisms might be made of the site or of the departures from the original plan of Le Vau, the grasp of the principles of classical architecture and the sense of magnificence displayed epitomised a new spirit in European art.

Of what did the French classical spirit consist? A whole battery of adjectives has been used to describe it: it was clear and yet subtle, heroic yet restrained. Those who were guided by it aimed to eliminate all inessentials from their art and to embody in it '*le bon sens*'. The end was perfection; the French classicists had no belief in progress. The aesthetic rules were laid down and meticulously followed. Grace, elegance, purity, clarity, order, good taste and exactitude were sought after. In literature the classical movement bowed before the gods of reason, order and Nature. Theoretically such ideas might be thought to contrast violently with those of the Baroque spirit which was so characteristic of the first half of the century. For Mannerism and, to a smaller extent, Baroque had been reactions against the classical spirit: the keynotes of Baroque were exuberance and romanticism. Yet some writers on aesthetics speak of *le style Louis Quatorze* as a compromise, as equivalent to 'high Baroque classicism'. The argument has been so far stretched that even Racine's *Phèdre* has been called Baroque. It is indeed dangerous to become bogged down in such generalised terminology.

What is plain is that the French classical style was in the making before Louis XIV assumed personal authority and before the plans for the palace of Versailles were agreed. It was during the years 1630–60 when France under Richelieu and Mazarin was establishing her position as a great power in Europe that some of the finest exponents of French art and literature flourished. Corneille, Poussin, Claude, Descartes, Pascal and François Mansart all helped to originate French classicism. Louis XIV obtained the conception of Versailles from the château belonging to Nicolas Fouquet, the ministerial colleague of Mazarin, at Vaux-le-Vicomte which he visited on the eve of Fouquet's disgrace for financial speculation. But the style was systematised and imposed by the king and his chief agent, Colbert. 'The period of Richelieu and Mazarin,' writes Sir Anthony Blunt, 'was in French architecture, as in other fields, one of great individualism.' François Mansart, Louis le Vau, and Jacques Lemercier, builder of the Palais Royal and the Sorbonne, were architects who were not only creative in their own way but left a mark upon succeeding generations; all of them contributed to the French classical style, but their contributions were distinctive. In fact creative artistic achievement at this earlier stage was ruled by a search for enjoyment rather than the need for 'uniform excellence' postulated during the personal rule of Louis XIV.

Although Bernini's proposals for the Louvre were rejected by the court and those of Le Vau ultimately preferred, the French classical spirit owed a good deal to Italy. The detachment and even coldness of Poussin, who spent most of his life in Rome, exemplifying a restrained version of the Baroque spirit, impressed native French artists and Parisian society. Claude too, though he also worked in Rome and was influenced by the southern Italian landscape and by the poems of Vergil, assisted in shaping the ideas that were practised in the France of Louis XIV. 'At the moment when Dutch painters were applying to nature their principles of realism,' writes Sir Anthony Blunt, 'Claude showed that the methods of French classicism can also be used to extract the poetry of inanimate nature.' In French literature too it was largely the Latin rather than the Greek spirit (except in the case of Racine) that was dominant. Molière was compared to Terence, Fénelon was soaked in Horace and Vergil. Latin remained the language in which most European scholars wrote their books. Before and after the age of Louis XIV, it has been suggested, Frenchmen wrote in a more exuberant and virile way – de Retz, La Rochefoucauld, Corneille, Pascal before, and afterwards Saint-Simon, the principal critic of the reign of the Sun King. On the other hand, the writings of Descartes, who owed nothing to the patronage of the French court, with their precision and lucidity, also helped to formulate the French classical literary style.

Under Colbert, who since 1664 held among his other offices that of superintendent of buildings and was a man of some taste and judgment, a close and complete control over the French arts was imposed. He aimed so to inspire and direct the arts that they reflected in a uniform manner the glory of the king. Although the French Academy originated in 1637, it was reorganised by Colbert as its protector and by Charles Le Brun as its director. The Gobelins was created as a factory to produce tapestries and other artistic objects and also to serve as a school of the arts. Le Brun had received part of his training in Rome and had grand ideas which accorded with the spirit of his times. He was a second-rate painter, but a skilful decorator and designer, though not comparable with Rubens and his followers in the first half of the century. He was also an excellent organiser of other people. Under the inspiration of Le Brun what has been called 'Italian Baroque tempered by *le bon goût*' or else 'a compromise between Baroque and classicism' gradually became the accepted artistic style throughout the whole of France. The colonnade of the Louvre was one of the earliest examples of this style and it was further developed in the buildings of Versailles. French artists began to look back to the Italian Renaissance painters as their models and to avert their eyes as far as they could from the Baroque masters. Charles Le Brun and Pierre Mignard (his successor at the Academy), Coypel, de la Fosse, Largillière and Rigaud demonstrated the classical French style in painting. The king's mistresses were transformed into Latin goddesses not only in France but also in England. Thus it can hardly be said that the French autocracy did much for painting. Rubens's magnificent cycle of paintings carried out for Marie de Médicis exerted practically no influence during this period. It was not until after the deaths of Colbert and Le Brun that a more original spirit was manifested. Then the colour of Rubens and the Flemings and the naturalism of the Dutch School began to modify the dominant Latinism. Louvois, the French war minister, who followed Colbert as superintendent of buildings, was less concerned with the patronage and shaping of the arts than his predecessor. Six years before Louis xiv died the genius of Antoine Watteau, which embraced a feeling for the French countryside, began to shine in Paris and French artists shook off the restrictions of the court and helped to evolve the gaiety of the early Rococo.

If French painting suffered from the rules laid down by the academicians, French literature and drama enjoyed the patronage of the court without being suffocated by it. 'The great dramatists and poets and prose-writers of the epoch,' observed Lytton Strachey, 'were in the position of artists working by special permission for the benefit and pleasure of a select public to which they themselves had no claim to belong.' Another commentator has observed that whereas the painters and decorators were under the obligation of being directed by the court, since the plum commissions came from it, authors were more dependent on society as a whole for their readers and playwrights for their audiences Nevertheless authority prevailed over literature; the rules of 'reason' were accepted; and the limitations required by the exercise of '*le bon sens*' in a circumscribed society were acknowledged. The critic Boileau carried at least as much weight in the later half of the century as Malherbe, the official poet of Henri IV, had done in the first half. Both were admirers of poetic laws and enemies of preciosity:

> Quelque sujet qu'on traite [wrote Boileau] ou plaisant ou sublime
> Que toujours le Bon Sens s'accorde avec la rime.

Martin Turnell has argued that what we perceive, above all, at this classical moment, was a 'regulated tug of war' between reason and passion. In Corneille, a limited genius, whose best work was done during the first half of the century, France had a heroic dramatist writing plays in which moral values, held with complete certitude, were raised to a high level of poetic intensity. He had a sense of society as an ordered whole where man must choose between love and honour. In Racine the conflict is of a different order. His heroes were not men of honour but men of passion; they were always at the mercy of their emotions and found reason an obstacle to life. That was the essence of his tragedies. For Corneille there was always a possibility of a settlement to the human conflict; but Racine recognised that the victory of the passions was assured. Corneille was a pupil of the Jesuits and believed in free will, while Racine was a 'Jansenist' who acquiesced in the inevitable: 'In all Racine's plays,' says Turnell, 'reason is powerless to resist the swirls of passion.'

If Corneille was a man of honour and Racine a man of passion, Molière, born in Paris in 1622 under the name of Jean-Baptiste Poquelin, concerned himself mainly with the 'natural man'. For many years he learned the art of the theatre while acting with wandering players in the French provinces. It has been pointed out that his first play in Paris, *Les Précieuses Ridicules*, was performed before Louis XIV began to rule in person. Molière was a satirist, but was careful whom he satirised: he did not aim to undermine the society of his time any more than William Shakespeare had done. He examined the position of women, the state of religious belief, the place of medicine in society, and pictured them with a vivid and delicate wit in order to amuse his audiences, not to bring about a revolution. He did not attack the aristocracy, but aimed to puncture middle-class complacency. His comic characters denounced a world they did not expect to change. It was much the same with Molière's friend, the fabulist poet Jean de la Fontaine. His fables were intended to entertain rather than to criticise. His poetry was beautiful, his morals were simple, and his criticism was of the foibles of ordinary beings, not of the society which he served. Like most of the writers of their time, Molière and La Fontaine were content to record and comment upon the atmosphere of French society, much as Mme de Sévigné did in her letters or Mme de Motteville in her memoirs. At this classic moment in French literary history authors obeyed the rules and accepted life as it was.

The French classical spirit, as it revealed itself in literature, was, on the whole limiting. Jean de la Bruyère, who appeared late on the scene, wrote in his book *Les caractères* (1688): '*tout est dit*'. French prose, he thought, was already perfect, though it might be made more alert. In fact the classical movement had streamlined the French language which was in the sixteenth century rich in earthy, concrete images. Corneille rooted them out when he touched up his early comedies, while La Bruyère criticised Molière for 'jargon' and 'barbarism'. Purity was all.

The poets, the dramatists, the writers of criticism, epigrams and memoirs did not exhaust the literary achievement of Louis XIV's France. There were too famous prosodists and novelists whose work endured. Mme de la Fayette's *La Princesse de Clèves*, published in 1678, was the first and possibly the only great French novel of the century. Mme de la Fayette (whose own marriage was not a success: her husband lived in the country while she stayed in Paris) wrote, like Racine, about human love. She lived in the same house as La Rochefoucauld and they taught each other something about the art of prose. If one contrasts her work with that of her predecessors, Honoré d'Urfé and Mme de Scudéry, who wrote enormously long romances, such as *Clélie*, one can detect a more classical approach and a subtler psychology. But romantic novels were a product of the century (Aphra Behn's books are the best known in England) and they were widely read. Nearly all of them were written by women (Paul Scarron, first husband of Mme de Maintenon, was an exception) and educated women of leisure often proved themselves to be the creators of a splendid natural prose style in their letters and memoirs. By contrast in prose were the majestic periods of Bossuet or the moralising of Fénelon. Bossuet is less read now than Mme de la Fayette or Mme de Motteville. His funeral orations, like the *Eloges* of Fontenelle, the nephew of Corneille, proved valuable contributions to historical biography. Fenelon's *Télémaque* which was written for the benefit of the young duc de Burgundy and went into many editions, and his *Traité de l'Education des Femmes* throw light on the educational theories of his age. With all his

179

eccentricities Fénelon had a fine mind and his letter to Louis xiv, written in 1699, but not then published, reveals that he – unlike Bossuet – was in advance of his time. With Vauban, Saint-Simon and others he was to be cited by Sainte-Beuve as a 'reforming spirit' at the end of the reign of Louis xiv which 'had endured too long'.

In much of the literature of the age – particularly in the writings of Bossuet and Fénelon, La Rochefoucauld, and Mme de la Fayette, Boileau and La Bruyère the atmosphere of Versailles is recreated. Although the court did not move there until 1682, before that Louis xiv used it as his principal country house. His father, Louis xiii, had what Saint-Simon called 'ce petit château de cartes' at Versailles where he hunted and pursued his chaste love affairs. Louis xiv fell in love with it when he was a boy and employed the architects and decorators of Fouquet's Vaux-le-Vicomte – Le Vau, Le Brun and the landscape gardener, André Le Notre – to embellish the estate with terraces, fountains, balconies, sculptures, and classical temples. New buildings, known as the Château Neuf, enveloping Louis xiii's chateau, were begun in 1668 by Le Vau, but after Le Vau's death, Jules Hardouin Mansart used this three-storey château as the centrepiece of a far more ambitious scheme. The new scheme, which included the Hall of Mirrors (not finished until 1684) and two staircases, erected on either side of the original palace, threw out the proportions. At the same time the gardens were extended and the Grand Canal built. Thus Versailles, though impressive in its classical simplicity, is not one of the perfect buildings of the century. Its attraction lies in its setting – the lakes, the statues, the gardens, the latter now somewhat neglected as compared with those high moments of glory. Nor should visitors to the palace today imagine that it is the palace of Louis xiv they are looking into; for much of its furniture and the arrangement of the rooms, as well as the recently reconstructed theatre, belong to the age of Louis xv.

Colbert did not approve of Louis xiv's decision to move the court to Versailles; he thought that the monarch should have stayed at the rebuilt Louvre. The expense of Versailles was colossal, for roads and a town were also built there as well as ancillary palaces such as the Trianon and Clagny to house the king's mistresses and friends. But the creation of Versailles was a deliberate act of policy. The king's object was to keep the leaders of the aristocracy there under his own direct control so as to prevent the kind of conspiracies that had been engineered against his father and grandfather. Moreover he recalled the rebellious Paris of the Fronde and had no compunction about detracting from its historic greatness by removing the court from it. Colbert died about the time that the move to Versailles took place and, as we have seen, his successors were less concerned over the patronage of the arts. Artists began to rejoice in their greater freedom and were less hide-bound than they had been by the precepts of Le Brun or Boileau. It is therefore difficult to attribute to the court of Versailles, except indirectly, the literary and artistic triumphs of Louis xiv's reign. What Versailles offered was the concept of magnificence, even if at times it was over-done. The duc de Saint-Simon, whose memoirs are a chief source for the later part of Louis xiv's reign, was its bitterest contemporary critic. He spoke of Mansart's 'horrible elevation'; he also wrote that the site was 'the saddest and most ungrateful of all places, without a view, without woods or water or good soil' and Mme de Sévigné described it once as a 'favourite without merit'. But art had fashioned what nature could not provide. This 'sumptuous dwelling place' has been described by one of its historians as 'a treasury of art' which Louis xiv 'opened largely to his subjects' (or some of his subjects) and continued to enrich. Whatever its overall defects, it was never in bad taste. Its wooded vistas, dignified courtyards, and wide roads that link the palace with the town of Versailles survive to this day to bear their witness to the classical grandeur of the Sun King.

French classicism spread with remarkable rapidity throughout Europe and made its impact on painting, architecture and literature. After the deaths of Rubens and Rembrandt art in the Netherlands declined. As we have seen, Rembrandt was neglected and even depreciated at the end of his life; Vermeer, who died in 1675, was neither prolific nor influential. Jordaens in the Spanish Netherlands was a shadow of Rubens and as a portrait painter Nicolaes Maes was a shadow of Rembrandt, though he made a good living when he dis-covered that 'young ladies would rather be painted in white than in brown.' Dutch landscape and marine painting, however, endured in its own right. Jacob van Ruisdael (1629–82) was a superb painter of trees, Meyndert Hobbema (1638–1709) of water mills, and Aelbert Cuyp (1620–91) of cows. The two Willem van de Veldes were the most famous painters of seascapes. But after 1661, writes Wilenski, 'the Dutch upper classes, like the rest of Europe, modelled their taste, culture, and fashion on the taste and standards of Paris . . . rich Dutchmen were conspicuous in Paris by their over-elaborate clothes bedecked with lace and ribbons.' Gerard de Lairesse, who was born in Liège, but settled in Amsterdam in 1665, remarked in the year of Rembrandt's death that he was a 'master capable of nothing but vulgar and prosaic subjects'. Lairesse himself admired Poussin and Le Brun and engaged in classical allegory on a large scale; his work was much admired by the Dutch. In the end he went blind through debauchery and is now largely forgotten. But his success was typical of the popularity of French culture in Holland.

The theories of art [writes Professor Geyl] which Hoogstraten, Pels, Lairesse had imported from France cancelled everything that in Dutch art had been most characteristic, and for that very reason most valuable . . . . There was no future except for the academic or drawing-room manner. France, whose armies had been arrested by the Water Line, saw in spirit overrun the field of art in the unvanquished land of Holland.

Even in Italy – even in Rome itself, so long the cynosure for European painters and sculptors – French influences began to take hold after the great age of Bernini, Borromini and Cortona. The foundation of the French Academy in Rome in 1666 and the death in 1667 of Pope Alexander VII, whose patronage was much missed, accelerated the change of taste. Andrea Sacchi (1599–1661), who had been a pupil of Cortona and was especially impressed by the latter's painting *The Massacre of the Innocents*, turned against his old master. Sacchi pitched his work in a lower key than that of the early Baroque painters, aiming to recapture the tragic essence of the classical world by simplicity and unity, by psychological penetration, and by the use of a few figures. A long controversy over the question of good taste in allegory raged between the Moderns and the Ancients (much as it was doing in philosophy) and Sacchi's views were victorious. He had a number of successful followers, such as Sassoferrato (1609–85) and even converted the aged Bernini. So potent was the French classical style in Italy that French artists were able to compete with native artists, and Paris vied with Rome as 'the most dynamic art centre of the western world' (Wittkower).

In Germany too the French artistic and literary influences were far-reaching. This was partly owing to Leibniz, who spent four years from 1672 to 1676 in France, and afterwards corresponded with Bossuet. The French novelists like Mme de Scudéry were much imitated in Germany. The only original German literary talent at this period was a humourous writer known as Simplicius who wrote somewhat in the style of Daniel Defoe in *Moll Flanders*. The fact that King Charles II of England, Queen Kristina of Sweden, and the Tsar Pyëtr the Great of Russia had all been subjected to French influences made an impression upon their kingdoms. Two of the biggest Swedish buildings of this era directly owed their character to the French classical style and not to the Baroque: the palace of Drottningholm in Stockholm, built for the widow of King Karl x, and the Riddarhus for the Estate of Nobles. In England there was under the later Stuarts a substantial demand for translations from the French. Descartes made a big impact on England and Sweden. English dramatists admired Molière, even if they could not imitate him. But the English novel was completely submerged by French fashions. In Italy too French literature was at a premium. Spain, however, continued to find native artists and writers, like Murillo and Calderon.

Although there was constant intercourse between the cultures of France and England and English painting owed almost everything to foreigners – Germans, Swedes and Dutch as well as French, ranging from Lely to Kneller, English literature – and particularly poetry – remained aloof. The leading poets were Milton, whose *Paradise Lost* was published in Charles II's reign (the royalists realised that this republican propagandist was England's greatest poet) Andrew Marvell, Samuel Butler, Edmund Waller, John Dryden, and Alexander Pope: a noble list. Marvell and Butler were essentially satirists and Butler owed a little to Cervantes. The heroic couplet became the characteristic verse form, which attained its supremacy in Dryden and Pope. Dryden, who was appointed Poet Laureate but later lost the post because he was a Roman Catholic, was the outstanding and most versatile author of his time, writing besides poetry, plays, prose, satire and criticism. He read both Corneille and Boileau, but only in his emphasis upon the value of lucidity was he indebted to French taste. The satirists were political commentators and played a part that would hardly have been possible elsewhere in Europe. Jonathan Swift was to help topple the great duke of Marlborough from his eminence in the reign of Queen Anne. Playwrights were clever, witty and unrestrained. William Congreve was a master of the comedy of manners and at his best might be compared with Molière. The rest of the Restoration dramatists, such as Rochester, Etherege, Wycherley and Vanbrugh reflected a society and morality very different from that of Shakespeare and Marlowe. The theatre, as in France, was extremely dependent on the court. Only a few performances of each play took place and success was problematical. In the reigns of William and Mary and Anne the theatre tended to be frowned upon. English drama, especially comedy, then entered upon a period of decline. But, as in France, it was a splendid age of prose that ranged from the writings of the Bedfordshire tinker, John Bunyan, whose *Pilgrim's Progress* appeared in 1678, to that of the aristocratic marquis of Halifax. In the reign of Queen Anne authors like Addison, Defoe, Pope, Steele and Swift – some of whom found inspiration in Boileau – created an Augustan age of literature. But the French style was not easy to imitate. Nor was the English. Broadly speaking, as a modern art critic has remarked, England has never been the home of the pure classical spirit. In the seventeenth century the greatest English writers like Burton, Milton, Bunyan were laws unto themselves. Boileau in fact condemned Milton because he thought that poetry did not lend itself to the treatment of the Christian religion. And no two playwrights could be more poles apart than Shakespeare and Racine, the most renowned in their respective kingdoms.

If in the France of Louis XIV Le Brun was the dictator of art and Boileau of literature, Jean-Baptiste Lully (1632–87) was to be that of music. Lully was a Florentine by birth but arrived in France when he was a boy and entered the service of the French court when he was twenty. In the first half of the century Italian opera had come into being and this novel and exciting form of entertainment spread gradually throughout Europe. As in painting, so in music the Italians, headed by Monteverdi in the new dramatic style, acquired a high reputation and composers from all over Europe flocked to Italy to learn and admire. If ballet did not, like opera, entirely owe its origin to Italy, the first notable *ballet de cour* was in fact devised in 1581 by an Italian, Baldassarino de Belgioso (known as Beaujoyeulx) and the outstanding composer of *ballets de cour* under Louis XIV was Lully. The *ballet de cour* was not what was meant by ballet in modern times; like the English masque, it embodied songs and recitatives. Nevertheless dancing was the most important ingredient. In his earlier ballets Lully collaborated almost solely with Benserade, but when Louis XIV assumed personal power and Lully was appointed superintendent of the king's music in 1661 he began to work with Molière and once or twice with Corneille. From ballet he turned to *tragedie-lyrique*, a form of opera closer in spirit to Corneille and Racine than to Italian opera; for his recitative was based on French tragic declamation. In 1672 he received a patent conferring upon him a monopoly of opera in France and thus he became the real founder of French opera. His librettist for fourteen years was an inferior dramatist named Quinault who probably fed his genius better than a Corneille or Racine would have done.

Lully 'brought Baroque music in France to an acme of stylisation,' writes Bukofzer, 'which none of his successors was able to surpass.' The 'sweetness' of the French music at the time of Lully was contrasted with the 'violence' of the Italian style. But French music did not have the same overwhelming impact as did French painting and architecture on the rest of Europe. In England, it is true, King Charles II encouraged the importation of French music and sent Pelham Humfrey (1647–74) to study in France. But the younger and greater genius, Henry Purcell (1659–95) was a master of every style: Lully's in his only true opera, *Dido and Aeneas*, the Italian in his trio sonatas, and the old English polyphonic style in his string fantasies. Purcell wrote both Church and secular music, much instrumental music, anthems, masques, so-called operas (really plays with music interpolated) and bawdy songs and catches.

In Germany too music developed rapidly in the later half of the century. Here Italian influence was powerful. Many Italian operas were performed in the German courts, particularly those of Agostino

Staffini (1654–1728), an Italian by birth, who lived and worked in Hanover, but his operas were also performed in Munich, Vienna and elsewhere. German operas began to be written and produced in the later half of the century, especially in Hamburg, 'the Venice on the Elbe'. In 1685 three outstanding composers were born, Johann Sebastian Bach, Georg Friedrich Handel, and Domenico Scarlatti. With them may be associated François Couperin (1668–1733), the latest and greatest of a famous family of French musicians. All of them quickly matured. Handel served a period of apprenticeship in Italy, during which he and Scarlatti became friends and rivals, and when he succeeded Staffani at the court of Hanover in 1710 he was already recognised as a master. But in 1711 he left Germany for England, where he produced *Rinaldo*, the sixth of his forty operas, which took London by storm. Bach became court organist at Weimar in 1708 and soon was famous as an organist throughout Germany. Bach was the master of the organ, as Scarlatti and Couperin were of the harpsichord. Bach learned a great deal from Italian composers such as Vivaldi, celebrated for his concertos, and the Danish musician, Dietrich Buxtehude. But the major achievements of Couperin and Scarlatti, Bach and Handel belong to the eighteenth century rather than the seventeenth. By the later half of the eighteenth century it was believed that in the history of European civilisation music was the characteristic art of Germany, as painting was of Italy, and poetry of England. French art was always eclectic, prolific and versatile, and this nature may perhaps be traced back to the reign of Louis XIV.

With the eighteenth century Europe entered into an age of rationalism and Rococo. In the later half of the seventeenth century one may detect in the arts, as in the sciences, a movement of conscious change. A battle was being fought out between the Ancients and the Moderns, as happens during almost all vigorous phases of history and, naturally enough, the Moderns won. During the exciting period of early Baroque exuberance, enthusiasm, even violence were the keynotes of art. Men still believed passionately in the Christian tradition and were deeply concerned about how best to present it, particularly in large-scale painting. We can see that concern in the work of Velazquez, Rubens and Rembrandt and in the lively debate between the Italians Cortona and Sacchi. But after the Spanish wars were over and the 'Thirty Years War' had ended in Germany, a cooler breeze began to blow. Painters looked back beyond Caravaggio and Carracci to the masters of the Renaissance, to Leonardo or Raphael. In French writing a classical style – simple, unified, clear – was deliberately constructed. In the theatre the unities of Aristotle were admired. Even in England the heroic couplets of Dryden and his Augustan age successors were a contrast with the metaphysical style of Donne or the passionate epics of Milton (though Dryden considered that Milton had failed as an epic poet). By the reign of Queen Anne tastes had changed completely and perhaps become more refined : comedies of manners were preferred to the 'ranting' of Shakespeare; but truly heroic poetry was dead.

Some historians have used the word Baroque as if it were applicable to the whole of the seventeenth century. But unquestionably a new classical spirit, deriving from Poussin and Descartes, transformed art and literature at least for a time. That transformation reflected a genuine change in men's outlook on life. It was not merely imposed by the French academies; in fact, after the death of Colbert, rules and restraints were gradually relaxed. In the last resort, after all, the finest art is the product of individual genius. In this golden century history moved from an epoch of magnificent painting to that of a splendid literature and ended in the dawning of the greatest age of music that European civilisation was ever to know.

CHAPTER 14

THE ECONOMY AND WAR

One thing that the drama and poetry of the seventeenth century show, as Sir George Clark has observed, is that 'war was taken for granted as a fixed necessity of life'. But wars could not be fought all the time: they were too exhausting for the delicate machinery of state finance. Thus, after the 'Thirty Years War' and the revolutionary period which followed it or coincided with its later stages were over, Europe slowly recovered and even enjoyed a short pause, as it were, before the eternal battle was resumed. At first the social and economic outlook was precarious. Populations declined or stagnated not so much because of the losses of men in war (as a rule the professionals preferred to manoeuvre rather than to kill) but owing to the spread of disease, to crop failures such as those which produced a famine in France in 1661–2, and to epidemics, like the Great Plague that reached London in 1665.

If, as is sometimes argued, the unrest of the middle of the century was connected with the 'price revolution', that had now come to an end. In France, for example, the price of wheat fell after 1662 and by 1670 stood at about a third of what it had been in 1660. Prices in general increased slightly after 1680, but fell slightly after 1700. But except in famine years, such as 1661–2, 1693–4, and 1709–10, there were henceforward no big fluctuations. In England the price level remained comparatively steady during the same period and even Spain managed to avoid the sudden and violent changes of the early part of the century. In 1686 the Spanish currency, now on a copper or vellon standard, was stabilised after a twenty per cent increase in the price of silver. French merchants had also been pressing for the devaluation of the currency by raising the price of silver, although its price in France was already said to be the highest in Europe.

In fact a general shortage of gold and silver prevailed throughout Europe in the later part of the century. The French managed to attract precious metals from the Spanish empire, partly by keeping their prices high and partly by having a favourable balance of trade with Spain and Portugal, which regularly bought French wheat and textiles. About three million pesos' worth of gold and silver were exported to France from Spain during the last thirty years of the century, while

187

even supplies for the Spanish treasure fleets had to be paid for with vellon 'and often the gold and silver that flowed in from the Indies never entered into circulation in Spain' (E. J. Hamilton).

Although war was everywhere taken for granted, it is doubtful if governments consciously assessed wars in economic terms. Sometimes wars were fought largely for economic reasons – the Anglo-Dutch wars, for instance, though even there questions of prestige were involved – and sometimes wars stimulated trade and financial activity, at any rate for the countries that did not take part in them. To give one example: the European price of lead usually rose whenever a war was about to begin. The Dutch sold their services and goods to both sides during the Scandinavian wars. When Charles II's second parliament met after the second Anglo-Dutch war several members protested against joining in the alliance in restraint of France on the ground that it was wiser to stay out of European wars and profit from trade. Undoubtedly war interfered with commerce and some governments – the English government at any rate – did not approve of its subjects and allies trading with its enemies, although it found it hard to stop this. Moreover it was beginning to be recognised that one way of winning a war was to injure the trade and shipping of the other side.

European historians have held rather varied views about the economics of war during this period. On the one hand, it is said that since wars were endemic, governments realised that they must not be allowed to interfere too seriously with ordinary life. For wars were not total, merely the continuation of policy by other means. Moreover commercial intercourse was in any case rarely peaceable at sea; piracy, privateering, and smuggling were so common that even in times of so-called international peace trade was a gamble. On land bandits and highwaymen flourished almost everywhere; for there were no police. On the other hand, it is argued that in fact war was employed as a deliberate instrument of economic gain now that the age of religious wars was over. But it is doubtful if most ordinary merchants regarded warfare as helpful to their business even when it was being waged against their competitors; they accepted the idea of perpetual war, but they did not like it.

Nevertheless one must not forget that war nominally stimulated industrial demand. For example, armies were becoming bigger. In the 1690s the French army numbered over four hundred and fifty thousand men. Soldiers wore uniforms (a practice not common before the middle of the century) which helped the textile industries. They also required supplies and weapons. A larger need for gunpowder grew up and that proved of particular benefit to Sweden, a principal source of saltpetre. In fact the prices of all raw materials of war rose substantially between 1688 and 1715, a period of almost continuous fighting both in central and in northern Europe as well as in Italy and Spain. Warships were becoming bigger and carried more guns. The prices of all naval materials rose, notably hemp, pitch, tar and timber. Skilled workmen found well-paid employment in the military and naval arsenals. That was one side of the picture. On the other, a heavy strain was placed on the finances of governments. This not only involved a burden on agriculture through land taxes or taxes on produce, but also on commerce: for a new tax, the excise, originally invented by the Dutch, was now levied in some form or another in most other countries: it was a cause of grievance not only among tradesmen but among all classes of the community since it fell on some of the necessities of life from candles and soap to ale and cider. Even for the Dutch, whose finances were better organised than those of any other country, the debts inherited from the prolonged periods of warfare proved crippling in the end.

If industry benefited from the demand created by war, that did not apply to the same extent to agriculture. The fact that grain prices had ceased to rise so much during the second half of the century meant that agriculture lacked sufficient inducement to improve its efficiency. The comparative stability in the size of populations – even a decline in some parts of Europe – also prevented the stimulus of increased effective demand. The exports of wheat from eastern Europe fell off, though the Dutch imported food for their own population and, as we have noted, the French exported food to Spain and Portugal. England was generally self-sufficient in food, but in times of good harvests was able to export mainly to the Dutch and to the American colonies. But nowhere was the demand really substantial. And the tendency was not only in Great Britain but in other parts of Europe for more pasture to be sought to feed sheep and cattle for meat and clothing. Indeed the parlement of Paris forbade new methods of cultivating the arable for fear it should interfere with sheep-farming on which the capital was dependent. It is interesting that although historians of agriculture often quote ideas put forward by theorists, not always practising farmers themselves, they offer little positive evidence of technological advance. Apart from the enclosure of wastes and commons, now generally accepted, and the employment of new types of ploughs, the evidence of agricultural advance is small. It appears that in Lombardy a course of cultivation which included forage crops and omitted the period of fallow was followed but, wrote Marc Bloch, 'the Italians found few imitators north of the Alps'. Turnips, it is true were grown as fodder in some parts of the United Netherlands and of England, while the idea of using clovers and artificial grasses to enrich pasturelands was advocated. But the indications are that even this was not widely practised.

Broadly the old rotations and the old methods of sowing seed, manuring and ploughing were followed. It is probable that in the rising countries, such as Great Britain, the United Netherlands, France, Sweden, Denmark, and Switzerland, where towns were growing, industries developing and populations slightly increasing, efforts were exerted to make better use of the land. The rising bourgeoisie though they often bought estates, if only to increase their social prestige, expected them to pay their way and to yield a reasonable return on their investments: they were, it is thought, more rapacious than the nobility. The freeholders or tenant farmers were invariably hard-working but not necessarily enterprising and suffered from the competition of larger estates. The reclamation of land in the English fen country and the flooded areas of the United Netherlands continued throughout the century. In eastern Europe, on the other hand, the falling off in the demand for exports of grain, the oppression by the big landlords of their tenants, and the ravages inflicted by the wars all helped to discourage agricultural progress. Moreover taxation to pay for the war invariably fell most heavily on the peasantry. Even in France where Colbert (like Sully before him) attempted to reform the administration of the *taille*, rates had to be raised when warfare was intensified after 1672. Thus while agricultural labourers possibly benefited in their standard of living from this period of comparatively stable prices, small landowners and tenant farmers had frequently to battle against low prices for the products on one side and high taxes on their earnings on the other.

If agricultural progress remained modest, industrial advance was uneven. Industry in Spain and Italy, for example, continued to decline, while the Spanish Netherlands, constantly the site of battlefields and the subject of fierce Dutch competition, lost much of their former prosperity, notably in Antwerp and in the textile industry situated at Hondschoote. Dutch industry benefited from the needs of commerce, while in England the traditional textile centres manufacturing woollen cloth were supplemented by calico printing and the production of taffetas, linen and some cotton goods. State control over industry was relaxed and the creation of monopolies effectively resisted. One may hazard the guess that on the whole industrial output was increasing in England by the end of the century. It received an impulse from the expansion of commerce and from the activities of Huguenot settlers and from the better credit facilities following the establishment of the Bank of England in the reign of King William III.

In France, on the other hand, industry was directly subjected to closer state control, just as the arts were. As early as 1653 Colbert had written a memorandum to Mazarin urging the creation of industries by the government even for the manufacture of luxury goods. Of course textile industries had long been established in France as in most other parts of Europe. According to David Ogg, 'in Europe the making of cloth was as common as the baking of bread and there were nearly as many spinners as unmarried women'. But French industry was minutely regulated by Colbert. Even the workshops of dressmakers and silk manufacturers were highly supervised. Woven cloth was stamped upon one side with the words: '*Louis* XIV *restaurauteur des manufactures de France.*' In 1663 a court of commerce was set up which imposed some fifty regulations upon the French cloth industry alone. Later a naturalised Italian was appointed inspector-general of manufactures and state finance was poured into industry ranging from the making of silk stockings to lace and tapestries. Monopolies were created and 'royal manufactures' were exempted from the local regulations.

In the Scandinavian countries and Russia too industrial advance was recorded by the end of the century. This was largely owing to the demands of war. Sweden, as we have noted, was a most important source both of naval and military raw materials. Here technology was applied to the mines: Christopher Pohlan, who was born in 1661, acquired a high reputation as a mining engineer. The output of copper, iron and lead remained at a high level in Sweden while Finland and Norway were valuable suppliers of timber for ship-building. In Russia too copper and iron were mined and smelted with charcoal from the forests to manufacture guns and other weapons of war. Pyëtr the Great is said to have 'discovered the Urals' where a large number of foundries were established. Labour for manufacturing has always been cheap and plentiful in Russia, just as it has been for cannon fodder.

Still it is questionable if any notable changes were taking place in the organisation of industry during this period of European history. In no country were there any large factories in the modern sense and indeed the word factory was used to describe a place where merchants gathered, not where labourers toiled. Capitalism was developing fairly rapidly. Both private financiers and governments (in countries like France, Sweden and Russia) were investing more largely in industry than before. Merchants, in particular, found themselves able to save and invest. Tax farmers were often mainly financiers. And perhaps for the first time capitalists were beginning to be faced by trade unionists. In 1688 the journeymen feltmakers of London combined to enforce an increase in their wages; on the other hand, trade combinations were severely penalised in Holland. In France town workers would get together secretly to exercise pressure on their employers. There were a few fairly large concerns, such as mines and iron foundries, but, in general, manufacturing industry was still conducted mainly as a 'putting-out' system. For instance, in France one monopolistic company engaged in lace manufacture employed 5,500 workers, but they were scattered about over a dozen different towns.

In foreign commerce it was still predominantly the age of monopolistic joint-stock companies, which were granted charters by the state. France under Colbert followed in the footsteps of the Dutch, English and Swedes. The French East India Company (based on Madagascar) and the West India Company were both founded by the state in 1664 and given capital provided by the government. Yet by 1674 the West India Company had failed and in 1682 the East India trade had been thrown open; in 1669 a French Northern Company had also been brought into existence and in 1670 a Levant Company. Yet none of these companies obtained much success. The other countries which had set up chartered companies earlier had too much experience to be ousted. The Dutch East India Company had been built up during the first half of the century under the masterly direction of Jan Pieterzoon Coen, a self-made man, who became governor-general of Netherlands India, with his headquarters first in Bantam and later in Batavia. He was a dedicated man who thought his fellow countrymen drank too heavily: in Ceylon, it appears, they began their day with gin and tobacco. The Dutch traded largely in Java and Sumatra, Borneo, Malacca and Ceylon (conquered from the Portuguese) and elsewhere in the Far East, while the English merchants concentrated more on India. In 1652 an expedition from the Dutch company under the command of Jan van Riebeeck founded a settlement at the Cape of Good Hope in Table Bay to facilitate the long sea voyage from the United Netherlands to the Eastern Indies. This small, almost incidental colony was the forebear of the South African republic.

The English East India company, which had been in existence since the beginning of the century, had its ups-and-downs and during the Cromwellian protectorate the trade was for a time thrown open; but that did not prove satisfactory and the company received a new charter. When King Charles II married a Portuguese princess in 1662 he handed over Bombay, which he acquired as a part of her dowry, to the East India Company. The company necessarily continued as a monopoly both under Cromwell and Charles II because it provided the forts and factories essential for trade in India. Though the government, under pressure from interloping merchants, permitted the creation of a second company in the reign of William III, in the end the old and new companies amalgamated and laid the foundation for the conquest of India by British arms in the eighteenth century. The Dutch East India Company continued to flourish throughout the century and to extend its activities as far as New Guinea, Formosa and Canton. It competed effectively with both English and French merchants, but paid a price for the long wars with Louis xiv. By the middle of the eighteenth century the Dutch East India Company had gone bankrupt.

The East India companies successfully established settlements and promoted trade which helped to raise the standard of living, at any rate of the wealthier classes in Europe; the West India companies for most of the century were engaged chiefly in battening on the Spaniards. The first big success of the Dutch West India Company was when, after the ending of the twelve-years truce, Piet Hein captured the Mexican silver fleet in 1628, which enabled the company to pay a dividend of 75 per cent in the following year. Similarly the English occupation first of Barbados and then of Jamaica facilitated, and was intended to facilitate attacks on the Spanish treasure fleets operating from the Americas from the time when England was at war with Spain during the Cromwellian protectorate. From the 1650s onward the Greater and Lesser Antilles became havens of buccaneering and freebooting mostly by the English based on Port Royal in Jamaica and the French based on Tortuga in St Dominique. Although during the Anglo-Dutch wars the English had an excuse for attacking the Dutch West India Company in West Africa and North America, the buccaneers of the West Indies, whose predatory activites were patronised by the governors of the English-held islands, were little concerned whether war or peace existed in Europe. Sir Henry Morgan, a bloodthirsty buccaneer from Port Royal, carried out a series of devastating attacks on the Spanish settlements, culminating in the sack of Panama in 1670. The French buccaneers fought the Dutch in the Antilles during the war of 1672–8. Nevertheless by the middle of the 1670s both the Dutch and French West India companies had failed. By this time too most of the Spanish possessions in the West Indies had become frightened and enfeebled in consequence of the perpetual raids by buccaneers and by the inability of the Spanish fleet to protect them any longer. In 1670 an Anglo-Spanish agreement recognised all the English claims in the West Indies, including the sovereignty of Jamaica in return for a promise that the buccaneers would henceforward be suppressed. A similar agreement was reached between the English and the Dutch in 1673. And by the truce of Ratisbon the French also promised to put an end to hostilities beyond the line. The reason for this was partly that Louis xiv hoped in any case shortly to acquire advantages throughout the whole of the Spanish empire when a French Bourbon prince obtained his inheritance in Madrid. But the French did not keep their promises and in 1697 seized Cartagena from the Spaniards, the excuse being that France and Spain were again at war all over the world. In the treaty of Ryswick (1697) the Spanish government accepted French sovereignty over St Dominigue, as previously it had recognised the English claim to Jamaica. This treaty more or less marked the end of buccaneering; and though much smuggling continued in defiance of European law, the West Indies became in the eighteenth century subject to ordinary codes of warfare between nations.

The West Indies became highly profitable to Europeans because African slaves were imported to work on the plantations which yielded valuable exports of sugar and tobacco. Here again peace rather than war was conducive to the expansion of commerce and the prosperity of the islands; in fact the development of these European colonies was generally thought to be more promising as sources of wealth than the colonies being set up in North America. In the West Indies the Dutch lost ground, as they had done earlier in Brazil and later West Africa. But the Dutch built up their colonies in the East Indies which continued to flourish until the twentieth century. The English expanded their hold on North America, which had begun in the reign of Queen Elizabeth 1 with the colonisation of Virginia (there were thirteen colonies with a population of 350,000 by the beginning of the eighteenth century) as well as in India and the West Indies, while the French too established a firm position in the West Indies as well as in Canada and along the Mississippi and also in part of west Africa such as Senegal, and at Pondicherry in India. Most of these colonies were sparsely populated and owed more to individual effort than to the state-sponsored trading companies.

Thus the English and French, with their growing populations, were showing considerable colonial enterprise by the end of the century both by exploitation and by settlement, while the Spaniards were able to maintain their hold on part of their empire – particularly in South and Central America, but the Dutch discovered that their naval resources were being overstretched, just as the Portuguese had done at an earlier stage. Yet one should beware of exaggerating the decline of the Dutch. For example, in the decade beginning in 1711 more ships were employed by the Dutch in their East Indian trade than ever before and their entrepot business remained extremely valuable right up to the middle of the eighteenth century. But differences in the size of populations evidently counted for much. It can hardly be doubted that the Dutch themselves recognised the increasing aggressiveness and enterprise of the English before the century ended. In general the expansion of Europe was one of the most extraordinary achievements of seventeenth-century civilisation. It was motivated by a search for economic gain, but it was not till towards the end of the century that it began to yield conspicuous profits.

In what may be called the more advanced countries the amount and effectiveness of government intervention in economic affairs diminished towards the end of the century. The apprenticeship laws were relaxed and merchants often traded more successfully if they were not restricted by the regulations of monopolistic companies. As Dr Coleman points out, whereas 'Sweden, Denmark and Brandenburg all apparently possessed companies for trade in Africa, India or the West Indies, sporadically active at this period' in fact 'they were largely enterprises by Dutch merchants seeking to operate outside the ambits of the Dutch East and West Indian companies.' Much of the internal commerce of Europe, it must also be remembered, was carried out more or less independently by merchants, for example that between England and France, Russia or Turkey; it was only outside Europe – in India, Africa and the Far East, where the pursuit of trade with the natives always demanded both a factory and a fort – that the monopolistic joint-stock or regulated companies, to which merchants paid fees, were essential to provide the necessary capital equipment and staff.

France was the exception among the more advanced countries in the extent to which the government concerned itself directly with trade and commerce. This was a deliberate policy, conceived by Richelieu and extended and pursued by Colbert, sometimes misleadingly called Colbertism, for it was in fact merely what economic historians used to call 'mercantilism' – an idea of national economic policy which, up till recently, was curiously contemporary. Colbert was a hard-working, ambitious and capable organiser who devoted himself first to the service of Mazarin and then to that of Louis xiv. His aims were far-reaching. 'He watches over everything which might be advantageous to the king,' reported a Venetian envoy to France, 'his purpose is to make the whole country superior to every other in wealth, abundance, merchandise, rich in commerce and the production of all sorts of goods.'

A French economic historian wrote of Colbert that 'he loved the people and wanted the prosperity of France'. Another French historian, Professor Goubert, remarks sourly that where his ideas were not banal, they were stupid. Yet an American historian, of whom Professor Goubert approves, claimed that he was 'the real author and instrument of the glory of Louis xiv'. Possibly it was so, but he was as unscrupulous in his methods as he was dedicated to feathering a nest for his own family. 'Trade is the basis of finance, and finance is the sinew of war,' he informed his son. He therefore purposed so to stimulate the economic life of the country that it would yield all the taxes needed to finance his master's battles. That did not mean that he approved of everything his master did. For example, he thought that the move to Versailles was an extravagance and it is doubtful whether, had he lived long enough, he would have favoured the severe treatment of the French Protestants. His aim was to create or recreate industries in France and to cut down the importation of luxury goods. He engaged foreign experts from Italy,

Holland, Sweden and the Spanish Netherlands to help with the textile industries, with ship-building, with glass-making, porcelain manufacture and many other industries. To sustain new industries he provided subsidies – though not upon an excessive scale – and introduced high tariffs. Some industries were administered directly by the government (such as the Gobelins tapestries and the manufacture of arms). Others were subject to state inspection and state regulation.

In the same way Colbert directly promoted companies engaged in foreign commerce; apart from the big companies that traded to the East and West Indies, in the north of Europe and the Levant, other companies were started to do business in Senegal, Guinea and Acadia. But although Colbert also established a first-class navy (he became secretary of state for the navy in 1669) he was unable always to provide the necessary protection for merchantmen against piracy, privateering, buccaneering, or the assaults of the Dutch during the war of 1672–8. Indeed none of the big French companies really surmounted their buffeting during that war, while the East India company, the most promising of them, received further setbacks during the later wars that lasted from 1688 to 1715. Only the French colonies in North America, the West Indian plantations, and the Indian factories were to endure satisfactorily into the eighteenth century, and that was owing mainly to individual rather than state enterprise.

In fact the rigid monopolistic control by the state, which has been called Colbertism, was a failure in almost every economic sphere. After Colbert died it was increasingly recognised, as it was also in England, that minute interferences with trade were stultifying. But Colbert's hard work created the French navy, the French arsenals, improved roads and canals necessary for transport, reduced internal customs barriers, and ensured the collection of taxes needed for wars. It appears that after 1676 or 1679 the frequent, if scattered, peasant revolts against taxation, which occurred so often earlier in the century, subsided. That may have been because the taxation system, at any rate, as between those who were directly taxable was fairer than before or it may have been because the intendants (or provincial governors) were better organised and could call upon military support to enforce obedience by ruthless repression. Colbert's work did not, for the most part, outlive him. If the needs of war inspired him, the facts of war destroyed him. The system of commercial monopolies, artificially created industries, and heavy taxation all resulted in waste and discontent. The prosperity of peace time evaporated. By the end of Louis xiv's reign France, according to Fénelon, had become no more than '*un grand hôpital désolé et sans provision*'.

Colbert understood that the basis of sound war finance was a prospering economy. He was able for a time to reduce the rate of interest, to cut down the number of offices sold by the king, and to increase the yield from taxation. But only England and the United Netherlands were able to build up a really healthy financial structure, and even that was not achieved in Great Britain until the reign of William and Mary. The Bank of Amsterdam was founded as early as 1609; the Bank of England did not come into existence until 1694. It is true that the two banks were not strictly comparable, since the Bank of England was at once allowed to issue notes as well as provide credit for the government, whereas the Bank of Amsterdam, modelled on the Bank of Venice, was essentially a bank of deposit and for transfer payments, but it did in fact later start lending money, for example, to the East India Company. By the time the last war against Louis XIV was being fought both countries had evolved a satisfactory system of state borrowing and of funding the national debts and were therefore able to pay larger subsidies to allied states for the supply of soldiers and arms. Louis XIV found it necessary to consult the doctors of the Church about interest rates. Merchants were not admired or consulted in France, as they were in England and the Netherlands; absolute monarchy, it has been said, was 'only superficially compatible with commercial enterprise'. It was war finance, as much as anything, that in the end defeated the French monarchy in spite of the large population of the kingdom, its rich natural resources, its trained armies. If by the eighteenth century intelligent men everywhere were beginning to realise that the economic interests of states were not fundamentally hostile, it had been the ability of the maritime powers to mobilise their resources for war that explains to a large extent their political success at the end of the epoch. And as far as Great Britain was concerned, it was the rapid commercial and financial progress that helped to create the first British empire, to lay the foundation for industrial expansion, and to justify the view that British preponderance in Europe followed that of the preponderance of France, as that of France had succeeded that of Spain.

Thus economics and war went hand in hand. And if it is true to say, as Professor Nef has said, that in the seventeenth century 'every effort was made to let war interfere as little as possible with economic life', in fact a study of its general history suggests that the effort was not very successful and that war in the long run was rarely conducive to economic progress; only those countries which had been able to create a sound economic and financial system were able to sustain the trials and tribulations that wars brought; others were ruined by them. In the next chapter we shall consider the nature of the long wars both in central and northern Europe which continued almost without remission until Louis XIV died.

CHAPTER 15

EUROPE 1688–1715:
'I HAVE BEEN TOO FOND OF WAR'

Armies were becoming not only larger and more expensive but also more professional. The standing army had become a common institution in the second half of the century. The Spaniards, it has been contended, were the first to maintain such an army in Europe, but soon every German state had its own little army and the larger ones let out their soldiers on hire. For aspiring princes recognised, as did the great elector of Brandenburg, the founder of the Prussian state, that a standing army and a well-filled war chest spelt power. Gone were the days when any nobleman could lead his retainers into battle or raise his own regiments or even command his own warship. Members of the aristocracy or the upper gentry who wanted to serve in the army might even be expected to learn their trade as volunteers. And, as it was no longer so expensive to provide the necessary military equipment – the cavalry, for example, were not so heavily armoured as before – younger sons of the nobility grasped the opportunity to follow a career that was profitable as well as honourable. The big mercenary armies also required a larger administrative organisation in which there were openings for educated clerks. In England the position of secretary of state at war became important; under the first duke of Marlborough he was a key figure instead of a mere secretary to the commander-in-chief.

The general increase in the size of armies is often attributed to the ambition of Louis XIV; but it has also been traced to a military revolution that followed the methods of King Gustav Adolf employed by him with such scintillation in the 'Thirty Years War'. Undoubtedly all armies were growing bigger as well as better organised. France was able to produce big armies because of her population. But other countries with sizable populations which were militaristically inclined also recruited substantial forces, notably Turkey and Russia. The Ottoman army that moved upon Vienna in 1683 was, as we have seen, at least one hundred thousand strong; Pyëtr I of Russia was eventually to recruit an army of two hundred thousand men. These figures compare with armies of five thousand to thirty thousand that had fought at the beginning of the period, and then even the latter figure had been exceptional. But it was no wonder that when the French army was said to consist of four hundred and fifty thousand men Louis XIV was able to terrify Europe.

Soldiers were not especially well paid (the private was actually worse off under Marlborough than he had been under Cromwell) but they had hopes of plunder and pillage and were usually kept in service throughout the whole year. But these larger armies could not so easily live off the country where they were fighting. Proper arrangements had to be made for a commissariat and a train. Indeed it was often the cumbrousness of the supply arrangements that prevented warfare from being more mobile. The general who was best at arranging ordnance depots and supervising his commissariat always enjoyed an advantage. And if he could do this satisfactorily before the normal campaigning season began in the spring, he might achieve complete surprise.

The invention of the bayonet about 1688 and the replacement of the firelock by the flintlock meant that the infantry took a more effective part in war. When the infantry had consisted of pikemen and musketeers fighting in mass formation, as did the Spanish tercios, battles in the open were generally won by the manoeuvrable cavalry even when the horses only moved at a smart trot. But the heavy armour worn by the cavalrymen had made them rather slow moving and it always took time to draw up a whole army in order of battle. So if the weaker side wished to avoid a clash, it could usually manage to do so. Thus in the first half of the century there were relatively few decisive battles – Rocroi, Breitenfeld, Dunbar perhaps. The Swedish combination of firepower and shock employed in linear formation, it has been argued, stimulated the seeking of decision by battle. Certainly by the end of the period Zenta, Narva, Blenheim, Ramillies, Almanza and Poltava were all decisive battles. For by then firepower and the bayonet had given the infantry a larger and less static role, in which they were supported by cannon, while cavalry charges became faster. Napoleon I said 'It is with artillery that war is made.' Gustav Adolf had been one of the first generals to demonstrate the value of artillery and carefully sited cannon were to be of the first importance during the War of the Spanish Succession.

But at the same time siege warfare still influenced military thinking. In war defence frequently reaches a stage where stalemate is imposed until it is broken by new weapons. The attraction of siege warfare was that it was not very costly in lives or in the use of cavalry – the most expensive arm. It was carried out according to regular rules which gentlemen could master and apply. It made war a game of chess, teachable on paper, that could be thought out and calculated in advance. Louis XIV once remarked that he liked big sieges better than battles and Vauban, the ablest exponent of siege warfare, thought they were much to be preferred on all grounds. Thus the engineers of the time were extremely valuable, being able to reduce the assaults on citadels and fortified lines to a fine art. None the less no fortifications were impregnable – Vauban admitted as much – and a clever general could bamboozle his enemy by drawing away forces from some vital point so that he could penetrate a fortified line. Contemporaries admired this gift in Marlborough as much as anything else.

Napoleon said that in his day it was by fire not by shock that wars were won. But firepower, though increasing, had not then become so overwhelmingly significant. It was in fact as a rule by shock, following the attainment of tactical surprise, that victories were gained. Marlborough and Prince Eugen, the Austrian commander, both laid stress on the value of surprise, though pitched battles were usually costly. Indeed they became more costly as time went on (in the English civil wars, for example, battle casualties were low). But in the last resort it was neither the invention of new weapons nor the application of new tactics that was the crucial factor in winning wars: it was the wealth and capable finance of the two maritime powers, England and the United Netherlands, that enabled them to go on fighting the French until they were worn out. Yet in contemplating such broad considerations one should not overlook individual genius. To quote Napoleon again: 'What genius does must be the best of all rules.' The century produced some great generals – Gustav Adolf, Cromwell, Turenne, Charles of Lorraine, Villars, Marlborough, Eugen, Karl XII of Sweden. These men made their own rules. And where sides were evenly matched or even sometimes (as at Narva) where they were not, genius could triumph.

At the beginning of the war that opened in 1688 – a war that has been variously described as the Nine Years War or the first phase of a second Hundred Years War between France and England, or even as the first world war, the French monarchy reckoned to possess several advantages. To start with, it could fight on inner lines against its combination of enemies and could dispatch offensive expeditions to assault parts of Italy, Spain or the Netherlands, while standing upon the defensive along the Rhine. Secondly, it had a large and trained army and although some of the best French marshals had passed away, in men like the ducs de Luxembourg and Vendôme and Marshals Catinat, Villars and Boufflers it had skilful and experienced commanders. The French army and navy were feared and respected throughout Europe. The forcible conversion of the Huguenots, the bombardment of Genoa by a French fleet in 1684, a naval demonstration against Cadiz in 1686, the seizure of Avignon in 1688, together with the invasion of the palatinate and the occupation of part of the electorate of Cologne, all amounted to an impressive record of intimidation. It was capped in the early spring of 1689 by the devastation of the palatinate ordered by the French war minister, Louvois, to promote the defence of the Rhineland. The famous and beautiful city of Heidelberg was set on fire, the bridge destroyed and the castle mined, although some portraits of the electoral family were saved out of deference to Louis xiv's sister-in-law, as it was thought that such an act of courtesy would please her 'when she became a little detached from the desolation of her native land'. An act of terror like that was by no means unusual during the century and was indeed frequent during the 'Thirty Years War' and since, but it certainly aroused the Germans against the French. Finally, on the whole, it was the aim of the French to remain on the defensive in the hope that their enemies would be lulled into making peace or would fall out among themselves. In fact as late as 1689 Louis had hoped to evade a general war, since Willem of Orange was occupied with England and Ireland, the emperor with the Turks, and the Germans with internal divisions.

But the terroristic methods did not work. On the contrary, most of the French king's former allies deserted him. The pope was exacerbated. Not only the empire, England, the United Netherlands and the elector of Bavaria were committed against him, but by 1690 the duke of Savoy and the king of Spain had joined the coalition. The French were forced back on their own resources. They possessed an army of some three hundred thousand men and a navy of over two hundred ships of the line. In the campaign of 1690 they achieved three triumphs: the Anglo-Dutch army under the veteran prince of Waldeck was defeated at the battle of Fleurus in the Spanish Netherlands, Marshal Catinat defeated the duke of Savoy near Pinerolo, and the English fleet was beaten at sea off Beachy Head on 10 July. On the other hand, on the same day Willem of Orange crushed King James ii at the battle of the Boyne in Ireland and thus completed the 'Glorious Revolution' which gave him the thrones of England, Scotland and Ireland.

The war continued with swaying fortunes for both sides. In 1691 Louvois, a ruthless but capable administrator, died, while the French minister of marine, Seignelay, had died in the previous year. But the allies lacked unity of command or brilliant generalship. Willem of Orange tried hard, but Waldeck was too old, Charles of Lorraine was dead, and the genius of Marlborough (who served with Waldeck in the campaign of 1689) was not yet recognised. In 1691 the fortress of Mons fell to the French and in the following year they took Namur. The siege warfare in the Spanish Netherlands was momentarily interrupted by the drawn battle of Steenkerk. At the same time the English and Dutch reaffirmed their command of the sea by overwhelming the French at the battle of La Hogue. In 1693 the French won another victory on land at Neerwinden, but the decision of Willem III to despatch an English fleet to the Mediterranean and to keep it there during the winter of 1694-5 meant that France was now threatened on two sides, for not only were her northern parts bombarded from the sea but the French forces in Catalonia and Italy were menaced. But, on the whole, the French armies were successful in northern Italy and in 1696 by the treaty of Turin the duke of Savoy withdrew from the war on favourable terms.

It may be said of this war that for the first time in European history command of the sea proved vital. After the battle of La Hogue the French fleet did not again put to sea and plans for invading England were abandoned or frustrated. French commerce was attacked, the French navy confined to port, the French expeditionary forces menaced. The French were cut off from supplies of war materials from the Scandinavian countries and were in fact subjected to a partial blockade. On top of that a bad harvest had caused a famine in France in 1692-3. It was these hard facts as much as the ding-dong campaigns in the Low Countries that brought about peace negotiations which opened as early as 1693. As usually happened on such occasions, the various allies had conflicting interests and intrigued against one another. Louis XIV, for his part, had in mind the coming extinction of the Habsburg line in Spain and was anxious to be ready for that eventuality.

By the treaty of Ryswick (1697) Willem III was recognised as king of England and the Dutch were allowed to garrison a line of fortresses in the Spanish Netherlands and obtained some commercial advantages. Barcelona, occupied by French troops early in 1697, was returned to the Spanish empire as was also Luxemburg. The French kept Strasbourg and Alsace, but returned Lorraine to its duke and yielded some of the territories severed from the empire by the 'acts of reunion'. If the emperor therefore gained little in the west, at least he had warded off the French menace, had united Germany against Louis XIV, and been able to consolidate his gains from the Turks in the east. While Louis XIV had been seeking peace, the Turkish army had been annihilated, and, as we have seen, at the treaty of Carlowitz Austria-Hungary was created. Though none of these treaties were to be permanent and the war between the allied powers and France was to be renewed in another four years in consequence of the death of the king of Spain, in fact the ending of the century was a meaningful moment in the history of Europe. The terror of France was broken. The Habsburg empire was strengthened. The command of the sea by the English and Dutch contributed to the expansion of Europe in the new world.

While the French fought with the Germans, Spaniards, Dutch and English in western Europe and the Austrians still contended with the Turks in the east, two young princes prepared to fight each other in the north. For much of the century Russia had remained outside Europe. Mikhail Romanov (1613–45) and Aleksey the Gentle (1645–76) had been chiefly engaged in strengthening the position of their dynasty in Muscovy, though Aleksey had won Smolensk and Kiev from the Poles. They had done this with so much success that by the end of the century women, children and idiots were able to reign from the Kremlin with impunity. But after a period of violence and confusion in 1689 Pyëtr I had overthrown his half-sister Sof'ya and attained personal power at the age of seventeen. It is true that he was then nominally joint tsar with his brother Ivan, who was a cretinous and half-blind epileptic, but by 1696 Ivan had died and Pyëtr became the autocratic ruler of Russia. It is not exact to say that the westernisation of Russia began with Pyëtr, for his father Aleksey had welcomed western actors and musicians and employed westerners as advisers and soldiers – though Muscovites were forbidden to travel abroad without permission on penalty of death, but Pyëtr deliberately determined to learn about western ways for himself, having picked up the idea in the foreign quarter of Moscow.

Like Louis XIV, the Tsar Pyëtr disliked his capital city, was determined to control the old nobility or boyars, and to suppress the streltsy, who had been responsible for violence and revolution. In time Pyëtr was to abandon the Kremlin and build a new capital at St Petersburg, now known as Leningrad. Pyëtr was an extraordinary character, a mixture of cunning and violence. He was licentious and blasphemous. Eventually he married a wife as cunning as he was. He loved using his hands; he adored shipbuilding and when he died his palace was found to be full of snuff-boxes he himself had made. He presided over the orgies or symposia of a group known as the Drunken Synod. He could drink all the rest under the table and resume his work the following morning without a sign of a hangover. He was always half a barbarian, using torture to attain his ends. He really epitomised his own people. For children used to say 'My mother whips me and I whip the top.' Pyëtr was a splendid organiser and, after suppressing the boyars and the streltsy, he built up an army and a navy and imported many western experts to help him modernise his country.

Karl XII of Sweden, who was ten years younger than the Tsar Pyëtr and was to be his greatest enemy, was a very different character, though quite as tough. Pyëtr was seven-foot tall, Karl over six foot (Willem of Orange and Napoleon I were both five foot six: height has little to do with genius). Karl was a dedicated man, excellently educated, cultured enough to read Cicero and Racine, a mathematician and engineer, but, above all, a soldier and lover of war, like many of his ancestors. He did not drink and he never married. He had control over an empire stretching from the Arctic to the North Sea. But though he had inherited a martial tradition, the population of Sweden was only some three millions, compared with the larger populations of Russia and Poland.

With the rise of Pyëtr 'Veliki' (Peter the Great) it looked as if the opportunity for the neighbours and foes of Sweden, the empire of the north, had come. The Russians concluded a treaty at Constantinople with the Turks in 1700. The Turks, weakened by their long war with the Austrians and the Poles, had surrendered the fortress of Azov at the mouth of the river Don to Pyëtr and so for a time the frontier wars of Russians and Turks were halted. Meanwhile in the same year that Karl xii had ascended the throne of Sweden, August the Strong, elector of Saxony had been elected king of Poland in succession to John Sobieski. Louis xiv had tried to secure the election of a French prince, but August was a skilful man, who declared himself a Roman Catholic at the appropriate moment. An expansive ruler, said to have over three hundred illegitimate children, he was induced to join with Pyëtr the Great and Frederik iv of Denmark (who had also come to his throne in 1699) in an assault on the youthful king of Sweden. The main architect of the coalition was a handsome Livonian named Patkul. But the foxes reckoned without their victim. Karl xii led his troops swiftly against Copenhagen and by the treaty of Travendal knocked the king of Denmark out of the war. In the winter of the same year Karl xii with a tiny army surprised the Russians at the battle of Narva, a fortress to the south-west of Lake Ladoga. In 1701 the Swedes recovered Riga in Livonia from the Saxons and then turned their full attention against King August of Poland. For five years Karl xii fought abortive campaigns against the Poles. This gave Pyëtr the Great the opportunity to recover from his defeat, to organise an army and a navy, and make ready to avenge Narva. But the youthful Karl xii was by now recognised by other powers in Europe, the French as well as their foes, as another Lion of the North. And he was courted eagerly by them when Louis xiv renewed his war against the Grand Alliance, a war which became known as that of the Spanish Succession.

The causes of the War of the Spanish Succession and the events that led up to it are complicated. But basically the facts were simple: when King Carlos ii of Spain died without an heir both the French Bourbons and the Austrian Habsburgs could put forward plausible claims to succeed to the vast empire by heredity. Both Louis xiv and the Emperor Leopold were grandsons of Felipe iii of Spain and both had been married to daughters of Felipe iv of Spain. It is true that various renunciations had been made, but undoubtedly they were persuasive claims. Louis xiv realised that he was unlikely to be allowed to acquire the entire inheritance for his family without war and was prepared to negotiate with the emperor to divide the inheritance. Willem of Orange, representing the interests of the two maritime powers, hoped to act as an honest broker and effect a compromise which would prevent a renewal of the war which had been ended by the treaty of Ryswick. Also neither England nor the United Netherlands wanted the French monarchy to obtain control over the Spanish Netherlands which would have meant a threat to their security from the strongest army in Europe. And the merchants of the two countries were not keen to see their French competitors acquire commercial advantages in the many parts of Italy that belonged to the Spanish empire.

It thus came about that France and the maritime powers signed two partition treaties, appendages, as it were, to the treaty of Ryswick, whereby arrangements were reached for the future disposal of the Spanish empire which would prevent trouble and possibly avert war. But to neither of these treaties would the emperor give his approval and the second of them, which provided for the division of the empire between Bourbon and Habsburg claimants, was particularly offensive to the pride of Spain itself. The dying Carlos ii was under tremendous pressure, but he was determined that the empire built up by his ancestors should not be destroyed. Therefore in October 1700 he signed a will leaving the whole of his inheritance to Philippe of Anjou, a younger grandson of Louis xiv, in the hope that his heir, with the aid of France, would be capable of holding the Spanish empire together intact. It was understood that the thrones of Spain and France would be kept separate. But French military resources and French administrative expertise would sustain the Spanish king.

Louis xiv hesitated for a time over whether he would accept the will, when Carlos ii died on 1 November. He was bound by the second partition treaty. Certainly the emperor had never accepted it and was unlikely to relinquish his claims without war. But would the maritime powers force the emperor's hand? That was not at all probable; the most they might do would be to exert moral pressure. So Louis plumped for the will, swearing that the thrones of France and Spain would never be joined. If war with the emperor was coming anyway, he though it wiser to fight for the whole inheritance than merely a small part of it. Nobody wanted war. The maritime powers reluctantly recognised Philippe of Anjou as king of Spain and so did other European governments. But soon the steps taken by the French monarchy as a consequence of this decision provoked anxiety and fear among his former enemies. In the first place, Louis xiv carefully preserved the right of Philippe to succeed to the French throne. Secondly, French troops ejected Dutch garrisons from a line of fortresses in the Spanish Netherlands which they had been permitted to occupy for security reasons since the treaty of Ryswick. That action also frightened the English who did not want to see French armed forces facing them in the Channel ports. Assuming that war with the emperor at any rate must follow, French generals and admirals and officials hastened to take control in Spain and Louis xiv prepared to rule the Spanish empire, on behalf of his grandson, who was still a boy, from Versailles: the Pyrenees, it was incautiously observed, were no more. Gradually public opinion was aroused against France both in Great Britain and the United Netherlands. On 7 September the maritime powers signed a defensive and offensive treaty with the emperor which provided for a partition of the Spanish empire and promised war if the Crowns of Spain and France were not kept apart and if the Archduke Karl (younger son of the Emperor Leopold) did not receive compensation for his claims by being given both the Spanish Netherlands and the Spanish possessions in Italy. For it was thought that the Austrians would not be dangerous neighbours nor successful trading rivals in the Mediterranean. Thus initially the War of the Spanish Succession was fought in order to enforce the break-up of the Spanish empire.

That meant there was to be a different alignment from that which had existed in the previous war. Then Louis xiv had to struggle alone against much of the rest of Europe. Now Spain was his ally: so, for the time being, was Portugal. In Italy he enlisted the alliance of the duke of Savoy, the father-in-law of Philippe of Anjou, in return for honours and subsidies, and he also persuaded the rulers of two important states in Germany to join his side, the electors of Bavaria and Cologne, both members of the Wittelsbach family, long rivals of the Habsburgs. Louis xiv hoped with the aid of his large trained army and his new allies to benefit from holding strategic inner lines as well as control over the Iberian peninsula, much of Italy, and the Spanish Netherlands. With an army of a quarter of a million or more men and two navies, he had high hopes of dividing and defeating his enemies.

But if on paper he appeared strong, in fact it soon developed that his position was much weaker than at the outset of the previous war. In the first place, he had too wide an area to defend not only in Europe but also overseas in Asia and the Americas. The Anglo-Dutch navies were self-assured and could assault France, Spain or Italy at a dozen different points. It also happened that the members of the Grand Alliance had two generals of genius at their disposal: John, duke of Marlborough, who was appointed commander-in-chief by Queen Anne (Anne had succeeded King William iii who died in March 1702) soon after the conclusion of the Grand Alliance and Prince Eugen of Savoy, the hero of the Turkish wars, who had at one time been in the service of the king of France but had resented the treatment there of himself and his mother, a niece of Cardinal Mazarin. The emperor immediately dispatched Eugen over the Alps to Italy where he faced French troops in the neighbourhood of Milan. In the summer of 1702 Marlborough arrived in Holland and took command of the Anglo-Dutch armies, which were in due course reinforced by many subsidised mercenaries including Germans and Danes. In fact the huge financial resources of London and Amsterdam were another factor with which the French king had to contend until the end of his reign.

The main struggle of the war took place, as it had in the other wars in which the French were involved in the second half of the century, upon the plains of Flanders. Gradually the allies fought their way through the line of fortresses that barred the route into France. But the war extended also into Germany, Italy and Spain and across the Atlantic. The emperor was distracted by renewed revolution in Hungary, while Louis XIV had to cope with a Protestant rising in the Cevennes. The fact that the Bavarians were fighting alongside the French was a fresh complication. In 1702 the Bavarians seized the fortress of Ulm upon the Danube and in the following year the elector unsuccessfully attempted to link up with the duc de Vendôme in the Tyrol. In 1704 he was joined by a French army under the command of Marshal Tallard. Sensing that the threat to Vienna from the west was the greatest danger that faced the coalition, the duke of Marlborough led his army from Flanders to the Danube and together with Prince Eugen inflicted a defeat on the Franco-Bavarian forces at the battle of Blenheim (13 August 1704). That was one of the most decisive battles of European history. For the first time since Louis XIV became king a French army was outmanœuvred and demoralised. Next year Marlborough, who had returned to the Low Countries, broke through the French lines and in 1706 the battle of Ramillies, in which he again won an overwhelming victory over the French, led to the conquest of almost the whole of the Spanish Netherlands by the allies. In that same year Eugen relieved Turin (the capital of the duke of Savoy who had again changed sides) and cleared the French out of northern Italy.

At sea also the allies were successful. In 1702 a Spanish treasure fleet was destroyed in Vigo Bay and naval operations compelled Portugal to abandon her alliance with France, thus giving her enemies a sure foothold in the Iberian peninsula. In 1704, in the same month as the battle of Blenheim, a British garrison occupied Gibraltar and Admiral Rooke defeated the French at the battle of Malaga. Only in Spain itself was the alliance less successful. But even here the city of Barcelona was captured in 1705 and by 1706 Philippe of Anjou was temporarily driven from Spain and allied forces entered Madrid, though later they were obliged to withdraw.

After five years of fighting on many fronts, of many defeats on land and sea, Louis XIV was forced to realise that he must seek peace. But in the meantime the allies had extended their war aims. When the Portuguese changed sides in 1703 they had insisted that the emperor's son, the Archduke Karl should, in the event of victory, become the king of Spain. They were afraid that if a French prince ruled in Madrid, Portugal would once more be forced to become a part of the Spanish empire. The maritime powers therefore agreed, somewhat thoughtlessly, to the formula 'no peace without Spain' which meant in effect that they were committing themselves to handing over the whole of the Spanish possessions, once the French were beaten, to the Austrian Habsburgs. Thus when Louis XIV himself revived the idea of partition as the price of peace in 1707 he met with a cool reception.

At that stage in the war both the French king and the Grand Alliance were extremely concerned lest Karl XII of Sweden, having conquered Poland, should elect to interfere in the affairs of western Europe. For five years he had been fighting August of Saxony: Warsaw had twice changed hands; and Karl had produced a rival claimant to the throne of Poland in the cultured Stanislas Leszczynski. Though August had Russian auxiliaries to help him and had fought adroitly, in the end Karl XII marched across Silesia into Saxony and compelled his virtually unconditional surrender. By the treaty of Altranstädt Karl obliged August to abandon the Polish throne and give up his alliance with the Russians. The question then arose where would the fighting king of Sweden strike next?

Karl XII had a number of grievances against the emperor, for example over the treatment of his fellow Lutherans in Silesia, and for that reason a fear existed that he might be tempted on to the French side or be persuaded to offer mediation on his own terms. On behalf of the allies he received in April 1707 a ceremonial visit from the duke of Marlborough at Altranstädt. Marlborough was now fifty-seven, still a handsome man, tolerant and statesmanlike, with the laurels of Blenheim and Ramillies still fresh on his brow. Karl was but twenty-five, a prince of incomprehensible humours, tireless, stern and even vindictive. Marlborough with the bland courtesy for which he was famous told Karl he was eager to learn more of the art of war from him and reassured him about the intentions of the emperor. He was able to report that Karl was unlikely to intervene in the west and was determined to complete his conquests by now turning again against the Russians.

In fact the allies had overestimated the capabilities of the Swedish

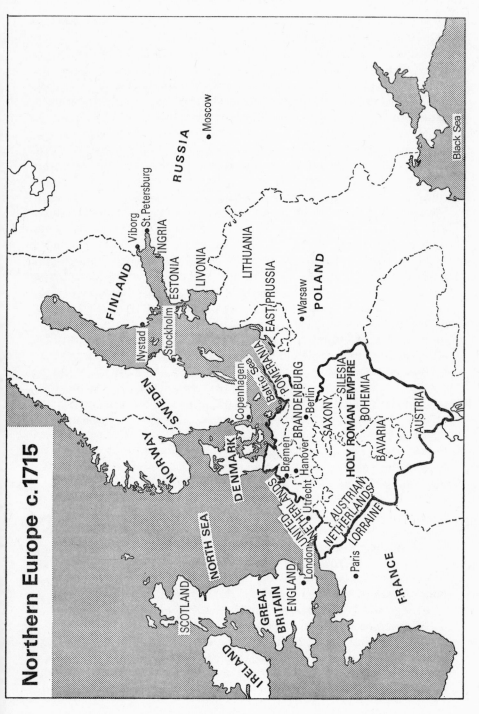

Northern Europe c.1715

P

king and not yet realised the potential of the tsar. For while Karl XII had been struggling in Poland, Pyëtr the Great had been building up his resources for war. He organised the manufacture of bayonets and flintlocks for his army, taught the cavalry to charge with the sword and hired Dutchmen to plan the production of cannon. During the years 1701–4 he reconquered Ingria and retook Narva. Not only was his new capital of St Petersburg being completed but he established an important naval base in the island of Cronstadt nearby. Thus when Karl XII marched across the Vistula to attack him he was fully prepared. As at other stages in Russian history, good use was made of the vast wide open spaces. Pyëtr retreated and scorched the land. A winter of intense cold was his ally. Cut off from his bases, Karl turned south towards the Ukraine in search of food and allies. In October a Swedish force bringing munitions and supplies from Livonia was defeated at the battle of Lesnaya and in the following spring Karl himself, wounded and rendered helpless by a shot fired by a Cossack patrol, was routed at the battle of Poltava in the Ukraine. There the Russians had at least forty-five thousand men and seventy-five modern guns against some twenty thousand Swedes, who, though hungry and dispirited, fought gallantly but were overwhelmed. In 1710 Pyëtr captured Viborg, north-west of St Petersburg, and cleared the Swedes from Karelia. Thus all the Baltic provinces fell into Russian hands. Meanwhile Karl XII had become an honourable prisoner of the Turks at Bender north of Odessa on the Dniester. While he was there he persuaded the Turks to attack the Russians and in July 1711 a Russian army was surrounded and obliged to capitulate at the so-called battle of the Pruth. A peace treaty, which was at once concluded, compelled the Russians to return Azov to the Turks. The intransigence of the Russians and the intrigues of the Swedes then caused the Russo-Turkish war to be resumed, but peace was finally concluded in July 1713. Then Pyëtr the Great was able to resume his war against the Swedes. He defeated them both at sea and on land, conquered Finland, and eventually invaded Sweden itself. Peace was not made until August 1721 when the treaty of Nystad confirmed Russia in the possession of Finland and all the provinces in the eastern Baltic as well as giving her a large indemnity. By then Karl XII, 'the Madman of the North', was dead, mysteriously killed in his trenches, and Pyëtr the Great was acclaimed the Emperor of All the Russias.

Though the Holy Roman Emperor had been relieved of his fears of Swedish intervention, the year 1707 had seen setbacks for the coalition that was fighting Louis XIV. The allies quarrelled among themselves, for example, over the disposal of the Spanish Netherlands which had been occupied by Marlborough's army; the duke of Berwick, Marlborough's nephew (he was an illegitimate son of King James II of England by

Marlborough's sister Arabella), fighting on the French side, had won a great victory over the allies at the battle of Almanza in Spain in April; this had its repercussions on an elaborate scheme to assault France from the south by besieging the naval base of Toulon by sea and land, which ended in complete failure. In 1708 however Marlborough won another victory at Oudenarde, which opened the way for the invasion of France from the south after the successful siege of the frontier fortress of Lille at the end of the year.

The French position was now really desperate. A terrible winter in 1708–9 had ruined the crops; famine and even starvation swept the peasantry. The royal finances were in disorder and the armies were tired and exhausted. Louis xiv's marshals and ministers advised him to make peace. But though the allies too were weary of war, they were not yet prepared to grant terms short of the complete surrender of the whole Spanish empire. Indeed a 'Barrier Treaty' concluded between the maritime powers in 1709, tied the Dutch even more firmly to supporting extreme Austrian demands. Louis xiv, rather than face the humiliation of helping to hand over Spain to the Austrians, determined to fight on and in September 1709 his ablest, if most boastful, general, Marshal Villars with a young and ragged army withstood the allied assault at 'the murdering battle' of Malplaquet. Nor were the allies able to shake off the French hold on Castile, which remained loyal to Felipe v.

Thus stalemate induced peace, though it took three more years to negotiate the treaties. A number of personal events played their part. The Emperor Leopold had died in 1705 and been succeeded by his elder son, Josef. But in 1711 Josef died and the Archduke Karl, the allies' candidate for the throne of Spain, was elected Holy Roman Emperor. The maritime powers no more wished to recreate the empire of Karl v in Europe than they had wanted to accept the predominance of France. Louis xiv's inept son, the dauphin was also dead, and two out of his three most promising sons did not long survive him. However in Louis (the future Louis xv) the baby son of the duke of Burgundy, Louis xiv had a great-grandson as heir to the throne of France. If Philippe of Anjou was recognised as Felipe v of Spain, it was therefore still possible for the thrones of France and Spain to be kept apart. And indeed since for the last century or more no love had been lost between France and Spain, the balance of power in Europe need not in fact be altered. Thus it was finally worked out and agreed by all concerned that while the Habsburgs might acquire the Spanish Netherlands and also the Italian possessions of the Spanish Crown, Felipe v should keep the throne of Madrid and most of the Spanish overseas empire except for Gibraltar and Minorca which went to Great Britain and gave her the mastery of the Mediterranean.

By the terms of the Utrecht settlement of 1713 the Dutch received their promised barrier of fortresses, though it was not as extensive as they would have wished and the barrier system was never effectively to provide the security that geography denied them. They also obtained a number of trading advantages from France and Spain. Great Britain, however, was the main beneficiary on the trading and colonial side. From France she received the island of St Kitts in the West Indies, Newfoundland, Acadia and Hudson's Bay, though Canada remained French. From the Spaniards she received the right to supply slaves to South America for thirty years and also to send an annual consignment of general merchandise there. These concessions (embraced under the name of the Asiento) did not, however, prove as profitable as had been hoped. The French received back the fortresses that they had lost during the last stages of the war at Lille and elsewhere and were allowed to retain Alsace including Strasbourg. The duke of Savoy was awarded the throne of Sicily with the title of king and allowed to retain Nice. The elector of Brandenburg was recognised as king in Prussia. The king of Portugal was given full recognition of his rights in Brazil and the Amazon basin. The elector of Bavaria, who had fought for the French, recovered his hereditary lands.

So after a century or more of war the mighty empire of Karl v and Felipe ii had finally been split up in Europe. The Austrian Habsburgs had extended their ramshackle empire into modern Belgium and modern Italy, had repulsed the Turks as well as the French, and consolidated their hold on Hungary. The security of the United Netherlands had been achieved for the time being, while Great Britain (England and Scotland had been united in 1707) made enormous strides in commerce and at sea and had laid the foundations of a wide-flung overseas empire. Germany and Italy remained geographical expressions, 'vague anarchic regions of uncertain destiny', as a French historian has written; yet in the north the kingdom of Prussia had increased its territories and was a basis for further expansion under Friedrich the Great into a larger Germany, while the duke of Savoy by diplomatic adroitness had opened a road that led eventually to a united and independent kingdom of Italy. In the north the sun of Sweden was beginning to set after the death of Karl xii, while the brilliant light of Pyëtr the Great blazed across the eastern Baltic, presaging a new great power.

What should one say of France, the most populous and most cultured kingdom in Europe which had fought so hard to extend its sway to the Pyrenees, the Alps and the Rhine under Henri iv, Richelieu, Mazarin and Louis xiv? Large territorial gains had been acquired; the map of France was more impressive than at the beginning of the century, though little or nothing had been won by all the blood and treasure expended in this last War of the Spanish Succession. Sainte-Beuve thought that Louis xiv's reign had gone on too long. Still Metz, Toul and Verdun, Artois, Alsace and Franche-Comté, Roussillon and Cerdagne, Strasbourg and other fortresses were now all French; Lorraine might also have been obtained with more forethought and wiser diplomacy. But in general the northern and eastern frontiers of France had been strengthened and consolidated. The cost had been stupendous. One by one, the allies of France had deserted her, England and Sweden, Savoy and Portugal, Poland and Turkey. None of the reforms aimed at by Sully or Colbert became permanent except for a few public works. The Habsburgs were to outlast the Bourbons. Even French historians who have justified the wars of Louis xiv as having been defensive and necessary and the seizure of the Free City of Strasbourg, for example, as entirely legitimate, have written of the financial and moral bankruptcy of France at the end of the reign. The nobility may have been rendered innocuous in the gambling rooms of Versailles and the peasantry may later have recovered from the heavy burden of taxes imposed on them for the payment of armies, hiding their wealth, as best they could, from the prying eyes of the collectors, but the decay of traditional institutions and the undermining of Christian teaching had paved the way for revolution. 'At the death of Louis xiv,' Professor Guérard has written, 'France was ruined' and he had destroyed the identity of king and kingdom. The palace of Versailles and the artists who adorned it and the literature that came from it or entertained its society are perhaps the true monument of the reign, but wars had exhausted France.

Yet Louis xiv had been a highly conscientious and hard-working monarch who had striven ceaselessly for the magnificence and glory and security of his country; he was not a genius but his successors, Louis xv and Louis xvi, proved to be worse kings. In the summer of 1715 when he was in his seventy-seventh year it was known that Le Roi Soleil was dying. He was moved back from his palace of Marly to Versailles to carry out his last duties on earth. His constitution must have been remarkably robust for him to have lived so long, for he had always overeaten grossly. Gangrene, which gradually spread from his legs to his body – signifying no doubt some kind of septicaemia – heralded the end of his life, as it had that of Felipe ii of Spain over a hundred years earlier.

On 26 August 1715 Louis sent for the five-year-old dauphin and said to the uncomprehending infant: 'Do not imitate the taste I have had for buildings nor my delight in war. Try, on the contrary, to keep the peace with your neighbours. Do your duty to God; recognise the obligations that you have towards your subjects: follow always the wisest counsels; try to relieve your peoples, which I have been unhappy enough not to be able to do.' According to a different account he said: 'I have loved war too much. Do not imitate me in that nor in my great expenditure.' On 28 August he talked to his wife, known to history as Madame de Maintenon, whom he loved dearly, and told her that he hoped to see her again soon in another world. Three days later she returned to Saint-Cyr where she kept a school. Louis xiv's last known words are believed to have come from the Psalms. 'Make haste, O God, to deliver me; make haste to help me, O Lord.' He died like a stoic. 'The king's courage is beyond description,' wrote his sister-in-law, 'He gives his orders as if he were going on a journey.' He received all the last administrations of the Church and expired at eight in the morning of Sunday, 1 September 1715. It could be written of him as his epitaph what the Austrian Metternich was later to say of the great Napoleon, another master of France, that he had thought more of himself than he had done of Europe.

CHAPTER 16

WHAT EUROPE WAS

What was Europe? In the second chapter of this book it was assumed that it covered an area stretching roughly from the Iberian peninsula to the river Don and from the Baltic sea to the Mediterranean. But it is difficult to be precise about its geographical confines: it certainly meant a different area to the classical geographers from what it was in the seventeenth century; and its constituents in the seventeenth century were unlike what they are today. In the opinion of Sir Ernest Barker, the English historian of political ideas, Europe could not be described either as 'a fixed quantity' nor as 'a determinate area'. Europe, said the French essayist, Paul Valéry, in an often quoted sentence, 'is only a peninsula of Asia.' Though it is the smallest of the continents, other writers have claimed persuasively that neither Russia nor Great Britain should be counted as parts of Europe. As we have noted already the duc de Sully, writing in the first half of the century about a 'grand design' for a peaceable Europe, excluded Muscovy from it on the ground that it was Asiatic and dangerous. A modern historian of Swiss origin. Professor René Albrecht-Carré, writing as recently as 1966 in a book entitled *The Unity of Europe*, observes that 'Russia lies athwart the great Eurasian land mass of which Europe proper is but a promontory', and later he defines Europe as an area between the Atlantic and a line running from Odessa to Riga. Equally Professor Friedrich Heer, the Austrian historian of ideas, has asserted that 'England does not belong to Europe'. The majority of historians have therefore argued that we cannot or should not define Europe by its geography any more than we can do by its races or by its languages. For its races are inextricably mixed and although its main languages, Romance, Germanic, and Slavonic predominate, they are distinct.

The geographers might perhaps not agree with the historians; but since we have been looking at Europe from the point of view of the history of civilisation, it is right for us to admit the premise that 'Europe is an idea'. What, however, was that idea? On this it can be said that among analytical historians there have been three principal lines of thought: these may be called traditional, radical, and modified. The traditional view was simply and clearly expressed by H. A. L. Fisher. Fisher was a British historian who had studied Europe closely and had written both about the Holy Roman Empire and about Napoleon I. He had served as a minister in Lloyd George's cabinet, where he met all the European statesmen of his time, and after he had left politics to become the head of an Oxford college he devoted the last years of his life to writing a popular history of Europe which was widely read. To him the idea of Europe was plain enough. He agreed that during the history of mankind the interpenetration of east and west had been complex and subtle and that 'to disentangle European elements was a forlorn enterprise'; but, he added, 'nevertheless the broad fact remains. There is a European civilisation. We know a European when we meet one.' The origins of Europe were also certain: 'We Europeans are the children of Hellas'. The cradle of Europe was 'the brilliant city life of the eastern Aegean'. Though race was never a unifying factor, Christianity was. Moreover the classical influences were always decisive upon European culture, while Europe's peculiar contribution to the world was 'the gifts of science'.

Fisher was writing in the 1920s, that is to say in the twilight of European predominance. The war of 1939–45 began as a purely European contest. Hitler hoped to impress his will on Europe by the force of his arms and to achieve his aims in the east he had first to neutralise England and France in the west. But the war of 1939 was not and could not be confined to Europe. By the time it ended the United States of America and the Union of Socialist Soviet Republics were acknowledged to be the great powers in the universe, with China and India, each possessing teeming populations, waiting, as it were, in the wings, to claim their leading parts in the world theatre later on. Thus most historians who have been expressing opinions about Europe since 1945 have been looking back on an epoch which they believed had very obviously ended. Yet that did not necessarily alter their conception of the historic Europe. There are still historians writing today – Professor Albrecht-Carré is one – who accept Fisher's point of view. The seeds of Europe were Greek. Its roots – to vary the metaphor – lay in the Mediterranean at the time of the Roman empire. Europe is therefore Greek in its theoretical ideas, Roman in its practical concepts of government, and Christian in its religious outlook. The barbarians were absorbed and the Mohammedans steadily pushed back from Europe as we understand it. The ideal of European unity was realised from the time of the coronation of Charlemagne at Rome on Christmas Day, 800. The papacy sought after a united Christian Europe and the Holy Roman Empire was its secular counterpart. Though papacy and empire both had declined in authority by the turn of the seventeenth century they had imprinted a European pattern. European congresses to settle the fate of the world began in that century and endured until the twentieth. Thus in the realm of international law as well as of religion and culture, as they were inherited by future generations, was embedded a clearly evolved European idea.

A celebrated French historian of an earlier generation, Albert Sorel, put it even more succinctly, but added patriotically that we owe it all to France.

There is [he wrote] a European atmosphere. The spirit which animates the state and which animates European society, its form of government as well as its thought, comes from Greece by way of Rome, and from Rome by way of France. It is the classical spirit as it is customary to call it: abstract thought for principle, pure logic for method.

To sum up the traditional idea of Europe: Europe owes its political existence to the Roman empire and its spiritual unity to the Roman Catholic Church. For its intellectual achievement it is indebted to the classical world. The Middle Ages fashioned the invading barbarians into a Christian pattern and Europe emerged as a coherent whole under Charlemagne. The Latin language carried the teachings of Greek culture across the deluge of barbarism. Thus European civilisation was compounded of the Latin language, the classical inheritance, and the Christian religion.

A radical criticism of this idea of Europe had been cogently expressed in England by Professor Geoffrey Barraclough and also in Germany and elsewhere. Professor Barraclough, an Oxford historian by origin, writing fewer than twenty years after H. A. L. Fisher's *History of Europe* appeared, was impressed by the war of 1939–45 that had intervened since then and by the emergence of the great powers in the east. He had witnessed the humiliation of France in 1940 and the break-up of the British empire since. The Europe of the 'thirties – the Europe that men like Fisher believed might have endured indefinitely – lay shattered. Moreover it was divided into two parts by the Iron Curtain. Professor Barraclough argues that the Roman empire had been centred upon the Mediterranean and was southern in its spirit. Its culture, its social and economic life, even its political complexion differed as fundamentally from that of northern Europe as did the Mediterranean weather. The Roman empire had comprised parts of Asia and Africa as well as of Europe. It did not include the whole of the British Isles, Scandinavia, or parts of Germany. The Middle Ages were neither Roman nor classical in spirit. It is doubtful if medieval Latin was ever a genuinely universal language. Neither the papacy nor the Holy Roman Empire was ever generally accepted; indeed at times there were rival popes and rival emperors. Even Dante's defence of the empire was really a plea for a united Italy in opposition to the papacy. In fact it was the Byzantine empire with its capital in Constantinople and not Roman Catholic Europe with its capital in Rome that was the true heir to the Roman empire. After the fall of Constantinople in 1453 Russia became the heir of Byzantium and 'the linear descendant of the Roman Empire'. Thus western Europe possessed no monopoly of the Christian tradition. European cultural unity was not established in the Middle Ages. Neither Scandinavia nor Russia was directly infused with Roman elements. Neither the Europe of antiquity nor of the so-called Middle Ages can therefore be described as a historical unity. 'The history of Europe,' says Professor Barraclough tersely, 'is not a sequence of happenings but a series of problems.' One can, no doubt, say the same about life.

The third historical interpretation is what I have called the modified theory about Europe. The theory is that there existed not so much a specifically European civilisation as what has been called, for example by Arnold Toynbee, a 'western civilisation' or 'western society' which is associated closely with the Romance-speaking and Mediterranean lands. According to this view, Great Britain and Russia have always been unique: they have constituted borderlands. Great Britain was less Romanised than other parts of western Europe which looked to the popes and emperors as their leaders. Indeed it has been argued that no fewer than three civilisations have all made their impact on geographical Europe during the years that stretched between the fall of the Roman empire and the end of the first world war in 1918: these were first 'western Europe' or 'the West'; secondly, the eastern, Byzantine or Greek empire; and, thirdly, the Arab-Moslem world which made its impress upon, and left valuable elements of its culture in the Iberian peninsula, in southern Italy and in eastern Europe. Each of these civilisations came to an end in 1918. The West had been compelled to call in the aid of the United States of America to preserve its civilisation from the ravages of the Germans and in consequence itself became Americanised. The Austro-Hungarian empire, the residuary legatee of the Byzantine empire, collapsed forever. The Turks, who had sided with the Germans, were finally beaten back from Europe and so 'the Sick Man of Europe' at last met his death. It has also been argued – at the other end of the scale – that 'the making of Europe' took a remarkably long time, lasting from 476 to 1453 – a thousand years – yet already by the sixteenth century Europe was split into two parts by the triumph of Martin Luther. Then Calvinism created a new culture and a new economic outlook in the western world. Therefore if a united Europe ever existed at all, it was only for an extraordinarily short space of time.

What is usually called European civilisation is in fact a misnomer for 'the West'.

Let us retrace our footsteps a little and reconsider the arguments in support of these different theories about the European idea. In the first place, it seems to be fairly generally agreed that the cradle of Europe was the eastern Mediterranean. The legend, as described by classical authors, is that Europa was a princess, the daughter of a king of Phoenicia (Phoenicia was a kingdom in the Middle East), who was raped by the father of the gods, Zeus or Jupiter, and carried off by him to the island of Crete. Since the celebrated archaeological discoveries by Sir Arthur Evans have shown that an advanced so-called Minoan civilisation flourished in Crete even before the classical age began and since the name of Europe has also been associated with Thrace, it is reasonable to believe that the history of Europe stems from Crete and from Greece. The Greeks in fact began the colonisation of Europe in Sicily. Subsequently the Romans inherited the magnificent culture of Greece. Gradually Roman government spread across the face of Europe and elsewhere from Italy. 'The Greeks,' said Gonzalgue de Reynold in his book *Qu'est-ce que l'Europe?*, written in 1948, 'colonised Europe; the Romans conquered it.' In his view, the Romans discovered Gaul and Germany, the Iberian peninsula, and Great Britain. The Roman achievement was to take hold of the Mediterranean civilisation which became both Christian and universal. Although it is perfectly true that the Mediterranean life preceded the European, nevertheless Roman culture and Roman practices moved north, while north Africa and Asia became largely Arabic and Mahommedan.

What of the Middle Ages? it has been pointed out that if we say that Europe took a thousand years in the making and did not come into being as a civilisation until the fifteenth or sixteenth centuries, then the Middle Ages is a misnomer: they did not in fact exist. On the other hand, all historical civilisations have been slowly built up, have reached an apogee, and then enter into a period of decline or stagnation or 'fossilisation'. In fact the name of Europe was known and used even during the earliest part of the so-called Mediterranean period of civilisation. By the time of Charlemagne the idea of Europe was well established. We can admit too that neither the empire created by Charlemagne nor the papacy built up by Augustine was always the reality that its makers hoped that it would be. Between the idea and the reality falls the shadow, especially for students of modern history. No doubt when we look at Europe from the standpoint of the second half of the twentieth century it is less easy for us to feel certain about its cultural reality than it was, say, for historians in the second half of the nineteenth century. For in our own lifetime we have seen new civilisations in the making in China, India, Latin America and other great powers dominating the world, such as the United States of America and the Soviet Union. Europe has shrunk, but that is not to say that it never existed. Men who lived before us understood that they were Europeans; they knew, as Fisher said, what a European was. Men like Gladstone and Cavour, Briand and Churchill thought of themselves as Europeans. It is true that we owe some of our early science and mathematics to the Arabs (though not much) and that the Crusaders brought back knowledge of various sorts from the Middle East. Nevertheless the Mahommedans were driven back during the making of Europe; in the century that we have been considering the Moriscoes were expelled from Spain and the Turks were beaten back from the gates of Vienna. Our scientific and philosophical ideas do not owe a great deal to the east. Up till the later half of the seventeenth century or perhaps the beginning of the eighteenth the Christian religion in various forms covered virtually the whole of Europe, having been expelled from the land of its birth, and men like Leibniz, who were anxious to foster the European idea, also aimed to reconcile the different brands of Christianity. Again, we no longer live in a primarily Christian society, and historians therefore regard Europe in a rather different way than in the days when most of them, even those like Fisher himself or, say, Ranke, who were not Christians, yet recognised its basically Christian character.

Arnold Toynbee, although he himself has employed the phrase 'a Western civilisation' recognised that Europe might be 'an intelligible field of study'. Assuredly the idea of Europe is more valid than that of 'the West' which has become a popular journalistic phrase only since the last war and since Russian political influence has become effective throughout almost the whole of eastern Europe. But even those nations that dwell behind what western Europeans call the Iron Curtain have reason to appreciate – even if they do not approve – the contribution that the Roman Church and the culture of Europe has played in shaping their own histories. Professor Halecki, who himself was a Pole by birth and in 1950 examined extensively the limits and divisions of European history, has written that:

Europe is a community of all the nations which, in the favourable conditions of a continent small but full of variety, accepted and developed the heritage of Greco-Roman civilisation, transformed and elevated by Christianity, thus giving to the free peoples outside the ancient empire access to the permanent values of the past.

It is perfectly true that today we must give full weight to the plea that if our concern is with what is called contemporary history Europe has ceased to be an intelligible field of study; the historians of tomorrow must aim to study the whole of the universe – and one wishes them joy in their task. That is the price that we pay for the invention of the jet-propelled aeroplane, the rocket gun, and the satellite in orbit. But at best such a study is a tall order: and as Hugh Trevor-Roper has said, the reason why we have not studied, say, the history of black Africa in the past is that black Africa had no history: there is only the history of the Europeans in Africa – the rest is darkness: 'and darkness is not a subject for history'. History is not, and never has been, an exact science. It is understandable that historians writing today feel doubtful about the ideal picture of Europe that was painted by their predecessors. Efforts to create a 'united Europe' since the last world war have had an extremely limited measure of success: and even French attempts to achieve a 'third force' between the giants of the United States of America and the Soviet Union have not carried conviction. Europe has, it seems shrunk for ever; yet it did indeed play a major part three hundred years ago.

If then we can reasonably believe in Europe as a historical idea, should we include within it the so-called borderlands of Great Britain and Russia? Professor Heer's argument is that England has never been a part of Europe, but has always been a counter-weight to Europe. Its inhabitants still talk about 'going to the Continent' for a holiday when they can afford it or are allowed to take it. Its statesmen used to speak of creating a balance of power 'in Europe'. Since the invention of the idea of the balance of power in the Europe of the fifteenth and sixteenth centuries, English statesmen have always been among its most enthusiastic exponents and it can be claimed, as it has been by Heer, that England fought in turn against Felipe II of Spain, Louis XIV of France, Napoleon I, the Emperor Wilhelm II of Germany, and finally against Hitler in order to sustain this balance of power on the European mainland. It is also no doubt true that Great Britain did not become an important power until the Atlantic ocean was opened up by explorers: that so long as the Mediterranean sea remained the heart of civilisation, England was no more than an outlying island. Still England was in fact a part – and by no means a negligible part – of the Roman empire; in the early Middle Ages it was so closely linked with France as to be at one time subject to French or Norman kings and at another, under the Angevins, the masters of France. An Englishman became pope. The English educated classes came to speak the French language. By the sixteenth century English aristocrats were travelling on 'grand tours' throughout Europe to complete their education. By the end of the seventeenth century the exchange of philosophical and scientific ideas between England and the continental mainland was frequent and potent. The work of Newton and Locke was as familiar abroad as the writings of Descartes and Leibniz were in England. Even Bacon and Harvey were well known in Paris and Amsterdam.

Of Russia it is less easy to feel certain that it was then European. As we have seen, even historians who incline to include Russia in Europe often attempt to impose some geographical line at which they say European Russia ended. The Russian social system and economic organisation differed markedly from that of much of Europe (except Poland) at the time when the Romanovs came to the throne. It is generally accepted that it was not until Pyëtr the Great visited western Europe at the end of the century that there was a conscious attempt by Russia's rulers to draw upon European ideas and discoveries. There was no real interchange of ideas. Unlike Sweden and Denmark, Russia made no attempt to intervene in Germany at the time of the 'Thirty Years War' or to take part in the crusade against the Turks. As Professor Halecki has written:

Like Turkey, Russia had started not as an eastern European but as an extra-European state outside the 'Christian republic' of a vanishing past. If Muscovite Russia became part of the modern state system, it was not so much because of a rather slow and superficial cultural Europeanisation as because, in contradistinction to the declining Ottoman empire, it became militarily so strong that all of Europe had to reckon with it.

But that was not until 1709. Meanwhile Russian civilisation was 'in the making'. And maybe its great age is not to be found in the Europe of the past when it suffered defeat in the Crimean war and defeat and then revolution in the war of 1914–18 but in the Pacific civilisation which is growing before our eyes.

Leaving aside the position of Russia still in the making, one may accept that it is possible to think of Europe as a valid idea in the early modern age. Even those who have questioned the traditional concept of Europe in the so-called Middle Ages agree that there was a recognisable striving towards European unity in the seventeenth century. 'The history of European unity in modern times,' says Geoffrey Barraclough in his striking Vogelenzang lecture of 1963, 'is very different from its history in the middle ages.' Whereas medieval thinkers had looked back to the notion of recreating the unity of antiquity, the thinkers of the seventeenth century started from the hard fact of the existence of independent sovereign states. 'This new realisation of the need for European integration was essentially a thing of the seventeenth century,' observes Barraclough. The terrible disunity exemplified by the 'Thirty Years War' made a deep impression upon men. This was reflected in the increased emphasis laid on the concept of the balance of power. As we have noted, that concept originated in Italy but Francis Bacon, for example, spoke of it in relation to the wars of the Emperor Karl v, François i of France and Henry viii of England in the first half of the sixteenth century. The central fact about seventeenth-century European political history was the contest between the Bourbons and Habsburgs. When the century dawned Spain was a mighty power and the rulers of France were to devote their skills to undermining the strength of the Habsburgs. By the second half of the century France had in fact replaced Spain as the dominant European power and the Habsburgs of Austria were for a long time licking their wounds after the 'Thirty Years War'. Yet in the later part of the century we have seen how Willem of Orange gradually built up a coalition in alliance with the Habsburgs to stem the progress of Louis xiv's France and so obtain a balance of power in Europe that would ensure security and peace.

Not only did the idea of a European coalition aimed at preserving a balance of power slowly evolve during the century, but also European congresses or conferences began to meet with the intention of settling territorial problems by international agreement. In the opinion of Ernest Nys, as expressed in his great book on international law, the peace of Westphalia in 1648 gave the first shape to an international society. All the European governments, he says, except those of England and Poland, were represented at the peace congress. Equally when congresses met to discuss the treaties of the Pyrenees (1659) and of Utrecht (1713) they included not merely the affairs of Europe on their agenda but also European interests in the New World. At these peace congresses the idea of Europe as a whole was clearly envisaged – its common concerns as well as the dangers of wars between states; diplomatic documents spoke of the security, the liberty, and the peace of Europe. Both at Nijmegen and Utrecht many states were represented and such matters as the customs of war, maritime laws, questions of contraband and blockade, the freedom of the seas and the rules of neutrality were examined not only by practical statesmen and diplomatists but also by the lawyers and political theorists of the time.

Whatever view we may take about the authenticity of Sully's 'Grand Design', it certainly put forward a specific and ingenious plan for uniting Europe. A peace movement was in this century started by English Quakers and was to be written about at the beginning of the century in Emeric Crucé's *Nouveau Cynée* and at the end of the century by the Abbé Saint Pierre. In such writings Professor Barraclough has pointed out, men were seeking after some kind of federal order, which contrasted with the medieval concept of empire: 'the seventeenth century conceived of Europe as a republic, *une république chrétienne*.' The

223

European community, it was thought, should be based upon a permanent and genuine balance of power. Thus both the theorists and the practical men were thinking – if in imprecise terms – of the Concert of Europe that evolved finally in the nineteenth century.

But though there were men and women – the Quakers and the Quietists in particular – who were shocked by the horrors of war, though idealists imagined the possibilities of a real peace movement, and though European congresses met and searched for general rules and even permanent stability, the fact remains that any historian of this period is bound to accept that war was an essential and irradicable part of the European way of life. Thus when men like Grotius and Puffendorf spoke of international law, what they were primarily considering was how warfare could be made a little more humane and tolerable. Grotius believed that an unwritten code of natural law existed which had been established by the consent of all nations and which could be or should be recognised in time of war: for, he wrote, 'during a war it is necessary constantly to have peace in view'. Among those who thought it was right to set up and to teach a law of nations or *droit de gens* were Jean Bodin, Richard Zouch, a professor of Roman law at the university of Oxford, whose book on the *jus gentium* was published in 1650, and the French foreign minister, the marquis de Torcy. Samuel Puffendorf, who wrote his book on the subject in 1672, was realistic in his approach. He thought that international law consisted partly of natural laws dictated by reason and partly of customs common among civilised nations. But he wanted these to be extended far beyond usages merely mitigating the horrors of what were claimed to be 'just wars'.

If therefore we may say that in the seventeenth century we can detect first the realisation in action of the concept of a balance of power; secondly, a movement towards a concert of Europe to settle problems of general concern; thirdly, the beginnings of peace movements; and lastly the evolution of the idea of international law among civilised nations governing at least the usages of war on land and sea – then it is surely fair to say that here was a clear recognition of the idea of Europe as a whole and even a striving towards a united Europe.

History is not an exact science. We look back on the past from some point in the present and we ourselves are an essential part of the landscape we paint. It can be said that writing today some of us Europeans are guiltily conscious that the history of Europe as once we knew it has now come to an end and that makes us either cynical or romantic about our past. Others of us believe that many European values are still worth preserving and regard it as a tragedy that the movement towards a united Europe that was born after the last world war has made slower progress than we hoped it might do. But it is too easy to pick out things that seem terribly important to us or necessary to sustain our point of view about the political present and to neglect the basic facts that were really significant to people in the past. For example, what probably mattered more to the ordinary man who lived three hundred years ago was the weather and how it impinged on his harvests and his health. And his main concern about the interminable wars that were waged by his masters was whether or not they were going to surge over the area in which he happened to live. If one gauges history in that kind of way, it can safely be said that the miseries caused by the 'Thirty Years War' (real enough, even if they were subsequently exaggerated in statistical terms), the unruly passions released by the civil wars in the middle of the century, and the devastation deliberately carried out by generals like Wallenstein, Cromwell, Turenne and Marlborough in the name of strategy were more meaningful than anything else that happened. Against these harsh realities the ideals of international law expressed by Grotius or Puffendorf might have appeared remote. Yet looking at the century in the light of the evolution of a European civilisation, one can reasonably picture it as a constructive age in which administrative, cultural and scientific progress was recorded. In the final chapter of this book an attempt will be made to assess the achievement of the century.

CHAPTER 17

SUMMARY AND CONCLUSION:
THE UNENDING QUEST

If we accept that Europe is an intelligible field of study in mankind's past, is it possible to select periods of historic time that may equally be called intelligible? In this book we have considered the years between the death of Felipe II of Spain in 1598 and the death of Louis XIV of France in 1715. But clearly neither the reigns of kings nor calendar centuries necessarily correspond with significant phases of historical development. It can in fact be convincingly argued that the middle of the seventeenth century is a more plausible and defensible dividing point to choose in sketching the history of European civilisation. For then it can be said, for example, that the era of Spanish splendour had ended, the last big war to be influenced by Christian divisions had been fought to a standstill, an age of science had come to rack Christendom, and the exuberant Baroque movement was cooling down into a new classical epoch. Moreover the revolutions of the middle of the century, which some modern historians claim to have reflected a 'general crisis' in Europe, can be likened to a shattering storm that cleared the air between one age and another.

But history, except possibly as it manifests itself in the unchanging lives of ordinary men and women who labour in fields and factories upon a prescribed pattern, is rarely static. Though analogies drawn from human beings about the birth and death of civilisations may be misleading and the phrase 'an age of transition' is the stock-in-trade of unthinking writers, any century or long period of time that one selects to examine is likely to offer a meaningful character of its own, to exemplify changes in one direction, growth in another, decline in a third. In fact the attraction of seventeenth-century history is that one can detect genuine transformations or contrasts between its beginning and its end not merely in politics and religion but also in the sciences and the arts. And one may speculate about, though scarcely prove to universal satisfaction, how these different aspects of history were inter-connected.

We have suggested earlier in the book that politically the first half of the century was still dominated by the Spanish empire that had been created by the Emperor Karl v and Felipe ii. Though historians writing in the light of their after-knowledge of events, can see that this empire was already beginning to disintegrate, that was not a fact that was readily grasped by contemporaries. Oliver Cromwell in the 1650s as much as Queen Elizabeth i of England in the 1560s, was impressed by the majesty of Spain and by the mountain of gold it was believed to possess. Cardinal Richelieu, as much as Henry iv, regarded the Spanish Habsburgs as the most dangerous enemies of the French Bourbons. The United Netherlands was not yet assured of its independence of the Spanish empire: Italy was still largely a Spanish dominion, feared by Rome; adventurers from Protestant lands met resistance from Spanish fleets, Spanish soldiers and Spanish colonists almost everywhere in the New World. Spanish customs still influenced polite society; Spanish clothes were imitated, Spanish literature read. Rubens and Velazquez, two of the outstanding painters of the first half of the century, were both the subjects of Spain. Though Spanish shipments of gold from the New World had been reduced by the 1630s and Spanish royal finances were in a constant tangle, it was not until the Spaniards were defeated at the battle of Rocroi in 1643, or perhaps until the Spanish government was obliged to surrender Cerdaña and Rosellón to France at the treaty of the Pyrenees in 1659 or until, after long and costly wars, the Spaniards were in 1668 compelled to recognise the independence of the Portuguese (as twenty years before they had at last acquiesced in the independence of the Dutch) that Europe as a whole could perceive that the Spanish predominance was clearly ended. By then 'Spain had sustained a remarkable creative effort which added immeasurably to the common stock of European civilisation' (Elliott).

To the age of Spanish preponderance in Europe succeeded that of France. Historians today can trace its coming from the reign of Henri iv. France rejoiced then, as it does still, in many natural advantages. It was a more compact country than Spain, it was more fertile, its people were more industrious. Its population may have been three times that of the Spanish mainland. It drew its wealth from its own territory not from a far-flung empire. But it needed the genius of three statesmen, Henry iv, Richelieu and Mazarin, to develop its resources, to secure internal peace and order, and to create an army and navy capable of supporting its diplomatic aims. To his predecessors the young Louis xiv, who assumed personal power in 1661, owed his unique opportunity. From Mazarin he inherited able ministers and soldiers. The opposition to the Crown had been crushed in the wars of the fronde and Spain had been defeated and humiliated. Thus Louis xiv was able to fashion a golden age for his court and for French society. The artistic achievement of men like Molière and Racine, La Fontaine, Lully and Watteau, to whom he lent his patronage, reverberated throughout Europe. The court of Versailles was a magnet to men of genius as the courts of Rome and Madrid had been before. As late as the eighteenth century German princes were building their palaces in imitation of Versailles. But though throughout Europe men admired and emulated French culture, they feared French political ambitions. Just as the English, the Dutch, the Portuguese and the French themselves had entered into alliances to destroy the Spanish empire, so after the vastness of Louis xiv's aims in pursuit of glory were realised, other European powers hesitantly, but, in the end, deliberately banded together to oppose them. During the eighteenth century France was to pay for the interminable wars fought by her 'Sun King', who had thus exhausted his kingdom, and the Bourbons and their aristocracy were alike to perish in the holocaust of the French revolution. But we may remind ourselves that we should not speak too facilely about the rise and fall of kingdoms, since France was to attain yet another period of political and cultural glory under the imperium of Napoleon i.

Leadership in resistance to the French monarchy passed towards the end of the century from the Habsburgs to what are usually called the maritime powers, that is to say the United Netherlands and Great Britain. So long as Willem of Orange lived the Dutch were the senior partners. But in the reign of Queen Anne, although the British were obliged to acquiesce in the Dutch demands for a strategic barrier, the influence of the English government became paramount. That was not only because of the abilities of the duke of Marlborough and the importance of the British navy but also because of the large financial resources at the disposal of the court of St James's since the successful foundation of the Bank of England had meant it could become the principal paymaster of mercenary armies. When Queen Anne's government decided to withdraw from the war, both the Dutch republic and the Habsburg empire had in the end to come to terms with France as well. Historians are not agreed about the exact date when the golden age of the United Netherlands reached its end, but plainly by 1715 England was beginning to outstrip her Dutch allies as an imperial power.

The third shift in political strength took place in northern Europe. Here at the outset of the century Denmark had wielded the greatest influence and had controlled the Baltic sea, while Poland was also a considerable power. But the victories gained by the Vasa kings of Sweden, notably by Gustav Adolf, Karl x, Karl xi and Karl xii had converted the Baltic almost into a Swedish lake. Yet the victory of the Tsar Pyëtr at the battle of Poltava in 1709 was a decisive event, foreshadowing the time when Russia was to become the major power in northern Europe. Poland was crushed between Sweden and Russia never to recover and later to disappear. But during the seventeenth century under the new dynasty of the Romanovs Russia was still in the making : it had not 'entered' Europe.

So far as internal politics were concerned, the century witnessed the rise of absolutism. This was neither universal nor complete. It could be argued, for example, that in Great Britain and the United Netherlands the tendency was the other way. In the 1620s English parliamentarians boasted : 'We are the last monarchy in Christendom to retain our original rights and constitutions.' But after the defeat of the Whigs in the 1680s the authority of the monarchy in Great Britain had waxed : both Charles II and James II admired the autocracy of Louis XIV and would certainly have liked to imitate it, only they were nervous of their parliaments and feared a renewal of civil war. The invasion of Willem of Orange in 1688 proved that it was impossible for a monarch to govern against the wishes of the classes represented in parliament and although the authority of the monarchy remained substantial throughout the eighteenth century, it was never an absolutism of the kind that existed in France, Germany or the Scandinavian kingdoms. Nor did Willem of Orange himself at any time – in spite of the admiration he commanded after his resistance to Louis XIV and his conquest of England – exercise anything like absolute control in the United Netherlands. Elsewhere, however, absolutism developed apace. Modern historians are now inclined to take the view that the strengthening of central governments in this way was essential for the preservation of internal peace. The revolutions of the mid-century had disclosed the anarchic tendencies in kingdoms where governments possessed neither a police force nor a large standing army nor mass means of communication that could arouse national loyalty. Political philosophers like Spinoza and Hobbes were impressed with the evidence that society could not hold together unless the absolute power of the government was generally accepted. In France, Spain, Sweden, Denmark, Poland and Russia the dynasties carried on a prolonged contest with their nobility or great ruling families. They invoked against them the support of the bourgeoisie or middle classes not as voices in parliaments but as efficient and ruthless administrators. By the end of the century monarchy was almost everywhere buttressed by bureaucracies and standing armies.

The monarchs were also fortified by their control over the Church. Since the Reformation the doctrine of *cujus regio lius religio* had prevailed. In England and to a large extent in France the Church became independent of the papacy. In Spain the Church and monarchy worked hand in hand. Churchmen continued to take a central part in government: in England Archbishop Laud, in France Cardinal Richelieu, in Spain Cardinal Portocarrero. Rulers and ambitious princes no longer thought, as they had done in the Middle Ages, of invoking the sanction of the papacy in support of war or rebellion. The popes in the first half of the century carried little weight. The 'Thirty Years War' is sometimes described as the last of the religious wars in Europe: in a sense it was so because it was concerned with the rivalries of Protestants and Catholics in Germany. But its close analysis shows that political aspects and motives were significant, if not dominant, and it was its international setting that gave it longevity and ferocity. As during the civil wars in England, religious and secular considerations were inextricably mixed. But from then on Europe conclusively entered into an age of purely secular wars (except perhaps for the crusade against the Turks where, as in the medieval crusades, motives again were confused). Moreover religious certainties were being gradually undermined. The undermining stemmed not merely from the rapid development of science. The Reformation itself had first created dissent and dissidence. In the Protestant countries, notably in England and the United Netherlands, many varieties of Christianity had arisen and been practised. The old quarrel between the doctrinaires of free will and determinism acquired a new ardour among Puritans and Arminians in England, between Remonstrants and Contra-Remonstrants in Holland, between Jansenists and Jesuits in France and the Spanish Netherlands. These divisions were too deep and bitter to be healed or even suppressed by the action of governments or Churches. It is true that religious persecutions can succeed: they did so largely among the Moriscoes of Spain and the Huguenots of France and, for a time, among the Protestants of Bohemia and Hungary. But when the aristocracy itself began to experience doubts about the doctrines of the Churches, then doubt spread more widely. It may be questioned whether either Charles II of England or Louis XIV of France were intensely religious men: at best they were superstitious. The era of the *politiques* had arrived. Philosophers like Hobbes and Spinoza, though repudiated as atheists, had an insidious effect on educated opinion in many parts of Europe. Descartes had introduced the idea of God as the great clockmaker rather than the God of Love. Largely because the ruling classes were aware of the controversies over the Christian faith and because the universe – and Europe itself – had been proved to be smaller places than they were thought to be before, from the second half of the century onwards a movement towards wider freedom of thought and deliberate religious toleration grew apace.

Here indeed we are confronted with one of the fundamental para-doxes of the century, a century that was full of them. How were men expected to combine a deferential attitude to authority, as expressed in the idea of absolute monarchy and the supremacy of the Church, with the freedom of thought advocated and practised not merely by philosophers and scientists but also sought by English nonconformists, French Calvinists or Spanish Quietists? Louis xiv, observes Professor Goubert severely, 'isolated in Versailles by his pride, by an intriguing woman, some priests and courtiers, ignored or wanted to ignore that his time had become one of reason, science and liberty.' As we have seen, the French classical spirit, which infected much of Europe in the last half of the century, was itself a compromise, a compromise between the romantic enthusiasm of the High Baroque ideals and the measured rules of balance and correctitude laid down by the academies. It was also necessary for Frenchmen to find a compromise between the Christian and monarchical tradition embodied in the majesty of the Sun King and the humanist rationalism taught by Descartes and his followers. Had not Descartes written: 'We should never accept a thing as true unless we know it clearly and evidently to be such'? The philosophers, playwrights, and poets increasingly began to doubt, as Descartes himself had once doubted. It is true that in his case doubt led to certainty. But with others that was not so. Men as different as Milton and Molière found difficulty in embracing all the traditional doctrines of the Christian Church. Oliver Cromwell, who himself perforce used autocratic means to sustain order in revolutionary England, believed passionately in the right of the individual Christian to follow his own bent wherever it led him. The flight of Huguenots from France shocked Protestant Europe: it rallied too to the appeal of the Protestants of Savoy, Bohemia and Hungary for their religious freedom. The teaching of men like Spinoza, Locke and Leibniz penetrated the European intellectual world. Men still accepted that they must obey the commands of governments in order to sustain internal peace: even in revolutionary England there were many believers in the virtues of absolute loyalty to the throne even to the extent of 'passive obedience' to what they thought was wrong – but their minds were more and more groping towards mental freedom. Hence the steady growth of toleration and freedom of thought in Europe towards the end of the century. Once the classical ideal degenerated into a mere habit, remarked Paul Hazard, 'once again the mind of Europe set out on the unending quest for truth and freedom'.

The century saw the rise of the bourgeoisie and of bureaucracy. That is not to say that a rising gentry and merchant class cannot be traced much farther back into European history. Nor were kings above using clerks or upstarts as their ministers from the very earliest times. But certainly one gains the impression that what may inexactly be called 'middle classes' – merchants, industrialists, financiers, professional men, independent farmers – were becoming more numerous and active, at any rate in advanced countries. The old nobility was repressed and restrained by monarchies, often deprived of its traditional political privileges, even if its economic and ornamental position was left more or less untouched. The purchase of offices of course also created new nobilities and corruption infected the new bureaucracies as much as the old aristocracies. Moreover generalisations about the rise of these new classes are not of universal application. Some countries – Spain, for instance – had virtually no middle class; in others – the Russia of Pyëtr the Great and his mother, for example, the destruction of the power of the old nobility came later. In England contests ranged between the nobility represented in the House of Lords and the gentry classes in the House of Commons right into the eighteenth century.

What of the vast mass of the people who did not belong to the privileged or successful classes? Marxist historians have made much of the peasant revolts in France and the appearance of the political group known as the Levellers in England in the middle of the century. But it seems pretty well established that the unrest of the French peasants – chiefly owing to the burden of taxation, which was an outstanding grievance everywhere – was fomented by upper classes discontented with the French government, while it has been proved that the Levellers were neither democrats nor communists but represented the interests of a kind of rising lower-middle class. In fact, though rumblings might occasionally be heard, the life of the peasants was static. In Sweden, an advanced society, Mr Stewart Oakley has recently written: 'most peasants still used wooden ploughs and harrows; lived in simple wooden cabins without chimneys or glass and furnished sparsely as in the fifteenth century and made all their own clothes.' Most people were, on the whole, inarticulate because they were too poor to worry over politics: their lives were totally absorbed in the interminable struggle for existence.

Such statistical evidence as we have tends to suggest that in some countries at least the standard of living was raised a little towards the end of the period, even if money wages did not alter much. Plagues became fewer, famines less frequent, and life a little more tolerable as time went on. If the total size of the European population did not materially increase during the century, at any rate it did not fall except perhaps in a few peripheral areas. Industry, apart from cloth manufacture, was of relatively small importance in Europe as compared with agriculture on which the essential needs of life depended – food, drink and clothing. If it is true that an 'industrial revolution' took place, it occurred during the first half of the century and then only limited areas of Europe. Industrial advance was slow in Great Britain, in the United

Netherlands, in the Spanish Netherlands, in Sweden and in France. Both in Spain and Italy industry declined, while the efforts of Colbert to create state industries in France had only a small and limited degree of success. Textile industries of one kind or another existed in most parts of Europe, but it was not a factory industry, being based on a 'putting-out' system even if that system may be called capitalistic. Apart from textiles, most manufacturing industry was of a luxury character and served, it seems only the upper classes. War was probably the most effective stimulant of industry, for the manufacture of arms required iron, copper and lead.

Of commerce, on the other hand, it can be said with some measure of assurance that it was a century of progress. The late Professor Richard Tawney, who devoted so much of his life to the study of the economic history of the sixteenth and seventeenth centuries, was of the opinion that something approaching a commercial revolution was taking place at that time. The Dutch and the English – and to a lesser extent the French and the Swedes – following in the footsteps of the Portuguese and Spaniards – opened up markets outside Europe. They bought and they sold, they imported and exported, they paid for goods in bullion if they would make useful re-exports. They imported pepper and spices – which were not luxuries, as they were necessary for the preservation of food – sugar and tobacco, coffee and tea, the raw materials needed for ship-building, and certain sorts of new and attractive textiles from different parts of the world and thereby they must have stimulated trade and raised civilised standards. International trade certainly increased. Yet neither in industry nor in commerce do such figures as we possess suggest there was any sensational advance. It was not until the eighteenth century that improvements in finance and business methods paved the way for a European economic revolution.

There was, however, considerable pressure for the liberation of business and trade. In the advanced countries it was recognised that state intervention contributed little to economic progress. In England during the civil wars – when revolutionary circumstances aided a larger expression of opinion – those who wrote about such matters pleaded for the freeing of commerce and industry from medieval restrictions. In agriculture the case for permitting enclosures either to promote a more efficient use of arable land or to allow conversion from arable into pasture was largely proved and accepted well before the end of the century, though the process of conversion was a slow one. In industry the apprenticeship laws were relaxed. In commerce monopolies tended to be confined to those areas where it was necessary to provide protection for merchants. The idea that peace was better than war for trade was recognised by the majority of those who were concerned in it.

Yet if writers tended to advocate less interference by the government in economic affairs, in politics the case for absolutism was being strengthened. In earlier times a balance struck between the powers of monarchial governments, the privileges of the nobility and the claims of the Church created at least for the upper classes an area of individual freedom and social responsibility. But many thinking men came to dread the idea of political anarchy. In large parts of Europe it was felt that the need was for a firm hand to reduce the fissiparous tendencies of regional authorities and even of parliaments. The advocates of law and order as the supreme necessity came to believe that only a strong central government could guarantee internal peace. If an adequate police force did not exist, then the monarch with his standing army at his orders was more likely to secure that than anybody else. Only perhaps in the United Netherlands, an extremely advanced kind of European society, were the anarchical tendencies of confederation tolerated for most of the century. Elsewhere the trend of governments towards absolutism was in fact approved by many political thinkers. Monarchs, aided by increasingly competent bureaucracies, were also becoming more conscious of their responsibilities and thus were evolving in the direction of more genuinely enlightened absolutism. At least historians incline to believe this. The dying words of Louis xiv were a signpost.

But the greatest achievements of the century – there can be no question – were neither economic nor political: they related, above all, to the arts and sciences. These were what made Europe lead the world; they were what makes us call it a golden century. On first reflection it might be said that the early part of the century was that of the highest cultural achievement, the era of Rubens, Velazquez, Caravaggio, Carracci, Bernini, Shakespeare, Cervantes, Corneille, while the second part of the century was the noblest epoch of science and philosophy, of Descartes, Spinoza, Leibniz, Locke, Huygens, Newton. But yet when we come to think about it more closely, we realise that such a generalisation would be far too facile. For the first part of the century was also the age of Gilbert and Harvey and Bacon in England, of mathematicians and pioneer astronomers including Kepler and Galileo, while the second part of the century also witnessed the supreme genius of Milton, Bunyan and Dryden, of Racine, Molière and La Fontaine, of the later Vermeer and the earlier Watteau. If the second half of the century was a period of rapid advance in mathematics and physics, the earlier half had seen the dawn of modern astronomy and anatomy. If High Baroque spread across Europe and manifested itself in paintings, buildings and the decorative arts, the later part produced superb examples of a new classical style in Stockholm as well as Versailles, in Germany as well as in England.

In fact it is impossible, as H. A. L. Fisher said, to detect any precise pattern of development in the history of European civilisation. One can, it is true, observe and describe certain obvious trends and tendencies, contrasts and comparisons in cultural prowess as the century advanced. But to place this in a setting of political and economic life is less easy. One is inclined to think that what artists needed above all was patronage and prosperity, not the stimulus of any particular master or milieu. In our own time we have seen how in England, where parliamentary democracy prevails, artists like T. S. Eliot, William Walton, Yehudi Menuhin, and Margot Fonteyn found the patronage they needed, while equally in the Soviet Union we have seen Pasternak, Shostakovich, Rostropovich and Ulanova emergent and appreciated. The writer who produced masterpieces in a garret is an exception to the general rule: possibly Bunyan, Rousseau, and James Joyce were exceptional men of genius who overcame earlier hardships without much patronage. But broadly in the seventeenth century patronage was essential and was to be found, as it is still to be found, more usually in the prospering cities and countries, in the Spain of the three Felipes, in the United Netherlands at the height of their economic success, in the England of Charles I and Charles II, and of Queen Anne, in the France of Richelieu, Mazarin, and Louis XIV. Shakespeare could write for James I and Molière for the Sun King. But the splendour of the arts diminished with the decline of Dutch prosperity, of Spanish affluence, and Italian wealth at the end of the century, while in England poetry and prose flourished even more vigorously as commercial and financial progress was attained.

For the scientists and philosophers, however, what was needed during the century was not so much patronage as a sense of freedom from restraint, the ability that Descartes enjoyed of being able to think in a warm room. As we have observed, nearly all the most valuable work in these fields was done in the Protestant countries, particularly in those Protestant countries where the movement towards intellectual toleration was gaining ground. It is hard for us in the twentieth century to measure the revolution that these philosophers and scientists were achieving. What the Church resented was not so much the discovery of mechanism as the way in which the world worked as the fact that men like Bacon or Descartes were breaking completely – or almost completely – with the traditional medieval, Aristotelian framework of thought. It can be argued that all that was happening was a reversion to a more Platonic approach. But in fact what had evolved was an entirely new outlook, and however good Christians scientists like Descartes or Leibniz or Newton may have been, the leaders of the Churches were, on the whole, conservative, and such thinkers realised themselves that they must be careful about what they said and that to pursue their thoughts in safety they required the protection of a tolerant government and an enlightened society. The advance of science and philosophy, in the face of clerical and conservative resistance is indeed the supreme fact in later seventeenth-century history.

To repeat what was said at the opening of this book. For the mass of mankind it is right that we should look at history in material terms, that we should ask the questions whether social and economic progress was taking place in the past, whether the productivity of agriculture and industry was improving, whether international trade was raising standards of living, whether populations were increasing and if so, whether medicine and public charity were contributing to the welfare of the community at large. People, it is often said and tediously enough, must always be given what they need or what they think they want and not what the ruling classes happen to believe is good for them. Otherwise they are being exploited; indeed some would say that all history is the tale of the exploitation of the poor by the rich or of the unsuccessful by the influential. If we look at the history of Europe in that kind of way, it would be difficult to assert with conviction that mankind as a whole was better off when Louis XIV died than it was when Felipe II of Spain expired in the Escurial. In some countries maybe the standard of social welfare improved; in others that is extremely doubtful. But if we are thinking in terms of what we understand by civilisation, that is of the highest achievements of the human spirit, then surely it cannot be questioned that the period of which we have been writing was a golden century. All who value the arts and sciences can look back with pride to the great men of that time, to paintings and sculptures, to buildings and gardens, to music and literature, to philosophical and scientific works that still exist today and are rightly admired. Those who love the past can gaze at Versailles or Amsterdam, Antwerp or London, Rome or Vienna not to examine the uniformity wrought by the all-pervading influence of American mass culture but to detect the distinguished monuments of a golden age. For that age was indeed, if not the apogee, certainly a high point of civilisation in which all Europeans have reason to glory.

BIBLIOGRAPHY

In dealing with so vast a subject over so long a period it is impossible to produce a comprehensive list of books for further reading: to do so would require a detailed work of scholarship. Nor would the author himself pretend to have read more than a portion of the multitude of books bearing on his subject or all the articles that appear in dozens of learned journals in different languages. I have concentrated mainly on books published in Great Britain, France and the United States of America, although I have also examined books in languages I can read such as Spanish and German. If the following notes on authorities seem unduly orientated in particular directions, it is, I suggest, understandable in an English author.

General

The latest and most complete bibliography is edited by John Roach, *A Bibliography of Modern History* (Cambridge, 1968), based on the *New Cambridge Modern History*.

An asterisk is placed against books containing bibliographies. The *Historische Zeitschrift Sonderheft 1 and 2* (1962–5) contains lists of books in different European languages and lists are also given in the *Annual Bulletin of Historical Literature*, published by the Historical Association in London. Godfrey Davies, Bourgeois and André, Sanchez Alonso, and Dahlmann-Waitz are the standard bibliographies in English, French, Spanish and German respectively up to their dates of publication.

Three American books cover this period: Carl J. Friedrich, *The Age of Baroque**; F. L. Nussbaum, *The Triumph of Science and Reason**; and J. B. Wolf, *The Emergence of the Great Powers**. In French there is H. Hauser, *La Prépondérance Espagnole 1559–1660** and A. de Saint-Léger and Philippe Sagnac, *La Prépondérance Française sous Louis xiv 1661–1715**; R. Mousnier, *Les xvie et xviie Siècles*, vol. iv in Maurice Crouzet, *Histoire Generale des Civilisations**, expounds the view that the

237

seventeenth century was one of 'general crisis'. In German there are the *Propyläen Weltgeschichte*: vol. 7 (1964) ed. Golo Mann and August Nitischke includes chapters by V. L. Tapié and Ivan Roots. In English besides David Ogg, *Europe in the 17th Century** and G. N. Clark, *The Seventeenth Century*, the *New Cambridge Modern History* will eventually cover the ground comprehensively by subjects. Trevor Aston (ed.) *Crisis in Europe 1560–1660* (1965) contains many stimulating contributions from the 'Past and Present' school.

H. Trevor-Roper (ed.) *The Age of Expansion, 1559–1660* was published since this book went to press.

Political History

For *France* the volumes in E. Lavisse, *Histoire de France* are still a first-class introduction: Jean H. Mariéjol, *Henri* IV *et Louis* XIII is an admirable book in this series. V. L. Tapié, *La France de Louis* XIII *et de Richelieu* is authoritative; C. V. Wedgwood, *Richelieu and the French Monarchy* is a good short book in English; see also D. P. O'Connell, *Richelieu* (1968). For the reign of Louis XIV see for an apologia L. André, *Louis* XIV *et l'Europe* and for a book reflecting the work of the 'Annales' school, Pierre Goubert, *Louis* XIV *et Vingt Millions de Français* (1966). Earlier books on the reign of Louis XIV are summarised by J. B. Wolf in an article in the *Journal of Modern History* XXXVI (1964). Wolf's own biography of Louis XIV appeared in 1968.

For the *United Netherlands* Pieter Geyl, *The Netherlands in the Seventeenth Century* is the standard authority; see also B. H. A. Vlekke, *Evolution of the Dutch Nation* and C. R. Boxer, *The Dutch Seaborne Empire 1600–1800* (1965), and J. Huizinga, *Dutch Civilization in the 17th Century and Other Essays* (1968). For the *Spanish Netherlands* Henri Pirenne, *Histoire de Belgique*.

For *Spain* John Elliott, *Imperial Spain 1596–1716* and various books by J. V. Vives. A bibliographical article on 'L'Espagne aux XVIe and XVIIe Siècles' appeared in the *Revue Historique* CCXX (1958). J. Lynch, *Spain under the Habsburgs* (1964) and J. H. Parry, *The Spanish Seaborne Empire* (1966) are other recent books in English. For the Popes see L. Pastor's comprehensive work. J. P. Trevelyan wrote *A Short History of Italy* (1956). For *Germany* J. Janssen, *Die Geschichte des deutsches Volkes* and for *Austria*, A. Huber, *Geschichte Ossterreichs*. Stewart Oakley, *History of Sweden* is a recent summary; there is also C. Hallendorff and A. Schuck, *History of Sweden*. M. Roberts, *Gustavus Adolphus, A History of Sweden 1611–1632* is masterly: this is supplemented by his *Essays in Swedish History* (1967) and *The Early Vasas* (1968). R. M. Hatton, *Charles* XII *of Sweden* is definitive. For *Norway* see K. Larsen, *History of*

Norway, for *Denmark* Palle Lauring, *A History of the Kingdom of Denmark* (1960); for *Russia* books by Sir Bernard Pares (ed. 1955), V. O. Klyuchevsky and M. N. Pokrovsky (Marxist). B. H. Sumner, *Peter the Great and the Emergence of Russia* is a useful summary in English. The best recent book on Peter the Great is in German by R. Wittram; in Russian there is Vasili Klyuchevsky's book. For *Poland* see O. Halecki, *A History of Poland* and the *Cambridge History of Poland to 1696* (1950).

Social and Economic

The *Cambridge Economic History of Europe* when published will cover the whole ground and there are or will be valuable chapters in *The New Cambridge Modern History.* D. V. Glass and D. E. C. Eversley (eds.) *Population in History* (1965) summarises some recent work on this subject. For French social history see Emile Magne, *La Vie Quotidienne de Temps de Louis* XIII, Georges Mongredien, *La Vie Quotidienne sous Louis Quatorze,* and J. Lough, *Introduction to 17th Century France.* For the economic history see C. W. Cole, *Colbert and a Century of French Mercantilism,* H. Pigeonneau, *Histoire du Commerce dela France,* vol. II and E. Levasseur, *Histoire de Classes Ouvrières avant 1789,* vol. II. For the United Netherlands see *inter alia* E. Baasch, *Holländische Wirtschaftgeschichte* (1927) and V. Barbour *Capitalism in Amsterdam* (1950). For social history see Paul Zumthor, *Daily Life in Rembrandt's Holland* (1961). For Spain various books by E. J. Hamilton which have lately been subjected to criticism, and by J. V. Vives. An article by C. M. Cipolla, 'The Decline of Italy', *Economic History Review,* 2nd series, V (1952) summarises the facts in an up-to-date manner. Charles Wilson, *England's Apprenticeship* (1965) is the best recent summary of English social and economic history. Peter Laslett, *The World We Have Lost* (1965) introduces recent work on sociological and demographical history; for France see the work of the 'Annales' school outlined in Goubert, e. g. books on civilisation by Mandrou. For women in society see G. Reynier, *Le Femme au* XVIIe *Siècle* (1929) and P. W. Bomli, *La Femme dans l'Espagne du Siécle d'Or* (1950). For prices and wages see books by W. H. Beveridge (Britain), M. J. Elsas (Germany), H. Hauser (France), N. W. Posthumous (United Netherlands) and A. F. Pribram (Austria).

The Arts

For invaluable summaries about painting, sculpture, and architecture the English Pelican series is excellent, particularly the books by Sir Anthony Blunt on France 1500–1700, Rudolf Wittkower on Italy, and J. Rosenberg, S. Silve, and E. H. ter Kuile on the United Netherlands. V. L. Tapié, *Baroque et Classicisme* (1957) and *La Baroque* (1961) are useful introductions; see also R. A. Weifort, *Le Style Louis* XIV (1941). Manfred F. Bukofzer, *Music in the Baroque Era* is the standard work on music. For literature see H. J. Grierson, *The First Half of the Seventeenth Century*, Olive Elton, *The Augustan Ages*, A. Adam, *Histoire de la Litterature Française au* XVIIe *Siècle*, D. Mornet, *Histoire de la Litterature Française Classique*, Martin Turnell, *The Classical Moment*, H. A. Hatzfeld, *Literature through Art*, Gerald Brenan, *The Literature of the Spanish People*, E. Rose, *A History of German Literature* and Basil Willey, *The Seventeenth Century Background*.

Philosophy and Science

Bertrand Russell, *A History of Western Philosophy* is lively and entertaining, W. Windelband, *History of Philosophy* is solid and sound. See also S. V. Keeling on Descartes, Bertrand Russell on Leibniz, Stuart Hampshire on Spinoza, Keith C. Brown (ed.) *Hobbes Studies* (1965) for a collection of essays on this highly controversial figure and Maurice Cranston's biography of Locke. For political philosophy see W. A. Dunning, *A History of Political Theories from Luther to Montesquieu* and H. Sée, *Les Idées Politiques en France au* XVIIe *Siècle*. For religion and morals see P. Benicheu, *Morales du Grand Siècle*, A. W. Harrison, *The Beginnings of Arminianism*, W. H. Greenleaf, *Order, Empiricism and Politics*, Michael Walzer, *The Revolution of the Saints*. For science see A. E. Bell, *Christian Huygens and the Development of Science in the 17th Century*, H. Butterfield, *Origins of Modern Science 1300–1800*, M. Ornstein, *The Role of Scientific Societies in the 17th Century*, A. Wolf, *A History of Science, Technology and Philosophy in the Sixteenth and Seventeenth Centuries*, A. R. Hall, *From Galileo to Newton* and G. N. Clark, *Science and Social Welfare in the Age of Newton*.

Here are some further bibliographical notes listed under chapters:

CHAPTER I

For Theophile de Viau see W. D. Howarth, *Life and Letters in 17th Century France* (1965). For the death of Felipe II, Martin Hume, *Philip* II (1906). The quotation of Sir William Temple is taken from his *Observations upon the United Provinces of the Netherlands* (ed. G. N. Clark, 1937) p. 44.

CHAPTER 2

Population is a highly debatable subject for there are no exact statistics, only estimates. E. J. Hobsbaum in *Crisis in Europe*, pp. 7–8 criticises Sir

George Clark's conclusions in chapter II of his *Seventeenth Century*. Some recent views e.g. of Beloch and Cipolla are given in Glass and Eversley, *op. cit. supra*. Goubert thinks the population of France ranged around nineteen million. The figure for Muscovy was a guess by the late B. H. Sumner. The quotation by H. Heaton is from his *Economic History of Europe*, p. 429. For Spanish sheep see Julius Klein, *The Mesta*. The quotation by Sir Edward Coke is in Menna Prestwich, *Cranfield*, (1966). For Mr V. G. Kiernan's views on nationalism see 'State and Nation in Western Europe' in *Past and Present* No. 31 (1965). For the inflation of honours see *inter alia*, Lawrence Stone, *The Crisis of the Aristocracy* (1965).

CHAPTER 4

The quotation from Rudolf Wittkower is in his *Art and Architecture in Italy 1660–1750* (1958) and of Emile Cammaerts from his book on Rubens. The references to Baroque are in Tapié and Friedrich. For Richelieu and the theatre see L. Batiffol, *Richelieu and Corneille* (1936). For Rembrandt Christopher White, *Rembrandt and his World* (1964) is particularly stimulating; see also J. Rosenberg, *Rembrandt his Life and Work* (1964). For Velazquez Carl Justi, *Velazquez und sein Jahrhundert*. The quotations from Sir Herbert Grierson are from his *Cross Currents in English Literature of the 17th Century*.

CHAPTER 5

The quotation by V. L. Tapié is from his *La France de Louis* XIII *et de Richelieu*. For the Great Chain of Being see the book of that title by A. O. Lovejoy. For the sale of offices see K. W. Swart, *Sale of Offices in the 17th Century* and R. Mousnier, *La Venalité des Offices sous Henri* IV *et Louis* XIII. Professor Nef's views are in his *Industry and Commerce in France and England 1540–1640*. For mercantilism see the book by E. F. Heckscher: his views are not generally accepted. The quotation by Charles Normand is from his book *Le Bourgeoisie Française 1604–1661*. For studies of social life see the writings of Goubert and the 'Annales' school in France and of Peter Laslett and his team in England.

CHAPTER 6

For the heliocentric theory see D. Stimson, *Gradual Acceptance of the Copernican Theory of the Universe*. Sir Geoffrey Keynes has recently published a large *Life of William Harvey* (1966). For Huygens see Bell and for Descartes K. Jaspers. There is no good biography of Grotius: W. S. M. Knight has written of him in English: *The Life and Works of*

Grotius (1925). For a recent book on Vincent de Paul see Mary Purcell, *The World of Monsieur Vincent* (1963). For the Arminians see A. W. Harrison. Ogg summarises the rise of 'Jansenism'.

CHAPTER 7

A brief recent summary of '*The Thirty Years War*' *and the Conflict for European Hegemony 1600–1660* is by S. H. Steinberg (1966) with a short up-to-date bibliography. The standard books are by C. V. Wedgwood and G. Pagès. See also Von Srbik, *Wallenstein's Ende* (1952) Fritz Dickmann, *Das Westfälische Friede* (1965) and Theodore K. Rabb (ed.), *The Thirty Years War : Problems of Motive Extent and Effect* (1964).

CHAPTER 8

The revolutions are summarised in R. B. Merriman, *Six Contemporaneous Revolutions* (1938) and their interpretation is discussed in *Crisis in Europe*. For Catalonia see John Elliott, *The Revolt of the Catalans* (1963). For England Ivan Roots, *The Great Rebellion 1642–1660* (1966) contains an up-to-date bibliography. For the Frondes see E. H. Kossmann, *La Fronde* (1954). Professor Charles Wilson's argument is in *Bijdragen en Mededelingen van het Historisch Genootschap gevistigd te Utrecht*, vol. 77 (1963). For the peasant revolts in France see Boris Porchnev, *Les Soulèvements Populaires en France 1613–1648* (1963): this has been criticised by R. Mousnier: the present position is summarised by Menna Prestwich in a review in the *English Historical Review* (July 1966) pp. 565 *seq.*

CHAPTER 9

I understand that Bertrand Russell's views on Leibniz are not accepted by all other philosophers. Stuart Hampshire's book on Spinoza was first published in 1951. For Pierre Bayle see H. Robinson, *Bayle the Sceptic* (1931). For some radical views on Hobbes and Locke see C. B. Macpherson, *The Political Theory of Possessive Individualism* (1962). For Vauban and Fénelon see *inter alia* Arthur Tilley, *The Decline of the Age of Louis* XIV. Dr Greenleaf's book is *Order, Empiricism and Politics*.

CHAPTER 10

For Ancients and Moderns see R. F. Jones's book of that title (1961). For the academies see M. Ornstein, *op. cit. supra* and the article by A. R. Hall in the *New Cambridge Modern History* vol. v. Michael Walzer's book is *The Revolution of the Saints* (1966). For the Huguenots see E.

Haase, *Einführung in die Literatur des Refuge* (1959) and W. Scoville *The persecution of the Huguenots and French economic development 1680–1720* (1960). I am also indebted to a lecture given by Hugh Trevor-Roper to the English Historical Association which is to be published shortly. H. F. Stewart's book is *The Holiness of Pascal*. For Fénelon see the biography by A. Cheruel (1934) and for the Cambridge Platonists the book of that title by F. J. Powicke (1926).

CHAPTER II

The quotations at the beginning of the chapter are from Louis xiv's so-called memoirs (ed. Jean Lognon). A recent book on Queen Kristina of Sweden is by Sven Stolpe (1961). The quotation from Professor Kossman is from the *New Cambridge Modern History*, chap. xii.

CHAPTER 12

For a recent account of the siege of Vienna and its setting see John Stoye, *The Siege of Vienna* (1964).

CHAPTER 13

I have borrowed the title of this chapter from Mr Martin Turnell. For Versailles see Pierre Nolhac, *La Création de Versailles* and *Versailles Residence de Louis* xiv (1925). The quotation from Lytton Strachey is in his *Landmarks in French Literature*.

CHAPTER 14

The quotation by Sir George Clark is from his *War and Society in the Seventeenth Century* (1958), that by E. J. Hamilton is from his *War and Prices in Spain 1651–1800* (1947). Sir George Clark's views may be contrasted with those of J. U. Nef in his *Western Civilisation since the Renaissance* (1950). The quotation by Marc Bloch is from his *Caractères originaux de l'histoire rurale française*. The quotation from Dr Coleman is in the *New Cambridge Modern History* v, p. 37. The American historian of whom Professor Goubert approves is C. W. Cole. Colbertism, like 'mercantilism', is a highly controversial subject and the literature is large.

CHAPTER 15

For armies see Sir George Clark's *War and Society* and Michael Roberts, *The Military Revolution 1560–1660* (1956). The quotation by Professor

Albert Guérard is from his book on France in the University of Michigan *History of the Modern World*. The account of the death of Louis xiv derives from Lavisse and Saint-Simon (ed. Boislisle).

CHAPTER 16

Books here referred to include Ernest Nys, *Le Droit International*, O. Halecki, *The Limits and Divisions of European History*, G. Barraclough, *History in a Changing World* and *European Unity in Thought and Action*, Friedrich Heer, *The Intellectual History of Europe*, René Albrecht-Carré, *The Unity of Europe: an Historical Survey*, H. A. L. Fisher, *A History of Europe*, Arnold Toynbee, *Study of History*. Gonzalgue de Reynold, *Qu'est-ce que c'est l'Europe?* and Hugh Trevor-Roper, *The Rise of Christian Europe*.

CHAPTER 17

The late Professor Tawney's views about the growing importance of commerce were expounded to me by him in the nineteen-thirties. They can be seen in his last book *Business and Politics under James* i (1958), chap. ii. The quotation by Paul Hazard is from his *La Crise de la conscience européen*.

Note: The dates of books that have gone into several editions or been published in different languages are not given.

INDEX

Academia del Cimento, 133
Academie royale des sciences, 133, 134
Acadia, 212
Addison, Joseph, 12, 183
Agriculture, 14, 68–69, 189 *seq.*, 232
Alba, duque d', 2, 7
Albrecht, archduke of Austria, 7, 11, 32
Albrecht-Carré, René, 215, 216
Aleksey, Tsar of Russia, 148, 149, 203
Alexander VII, Pope, 182
Algiers, 161
Almanza, battle of, 199, 211
Alps, the, 212
Alsace, 97, 153, 165, 170, 212, 213
Althusius, Johannes, 126, 137
Altona, congress of, 172
Altranstädt, 208
Amazon basin, 212
America, central, 2, 194
America, north, 194
America, south, 2, 194
Amsterdam, 7, 13, 16, 39, 49, 54, 65, 114, 115, 137, 207, 222, 236; town hall, 12, 56
Ana (Anne) of Austria, Queen, 3, 24, 41, 112, 113
Anabaptists, 80
Andalusia, 102, 106
Andrusovo, treaty of, 149
Anne, Queen of England, 206, 235
Antwerp, 7, 13, 43, 190, 236
Aquinas, St Thomas, 73, 75, 81, 141
Arabs, 218, 220
Aragon, 2, 23, 104, 107
Arbitristas, 30
Architecture, 12, 56
Arcos, duque de, 107
Aristotle, 77, 124, 140
Armada, the Spanish, 2, 8, 31

Armies, 17–18, 29, 30, 188, 198, 199
Arminians, 143, 230
Arminius, 80
Arnauld, Antoine, 81, 121
Artillery, 29
Artois, 2, 213
Asiento, the, 212
Astronomy, 73 *seq.*
Athens, 169
Atlantic ocean, 215, 221
Aubignac, Abbé d', 47
Aubigny, Agrippa d', 52
Augsburg, league of, 173
Augsburg, treaty of, 5, 20, 78
August the Strong, Elector of Saxony and King of Poland, 204, 208
Austria, 5, 10, 26, 152, 160, 167, 169, 173; population of, 14
Austria-Hungary, 24, 100, 169, 202, 218
Avignon, 170, 201
Azov, 149, 204, 210

Bach, Johann Sebastian, 185
Bacon, Francis, 52, 75, 124, 132, 140, 222, 223, 234; quoted, 8, 75–76, 77
Balearic islands, 2
Ballet, 47
Baltic sea, 9, 64, 65, 67, 92, 212, 215, 228
Bank of Amsterdam, 197
Bank of England, 190
Bank of Venice, 197
Barbon, Nicholas, quoted, 67
Barcelona, 23, 104, 105
Barker, Sir Ernest, 215
Baroque, 45 *seq.*, 175, 177, 231, 234
Barraclough, Geoffrey, 217, 218, 222, 223
Barrier treaty, 211, 212
Barwälde, treaty of, 94, 95

245

Bavaria, 95, 201, 206, 207 *seq.*, 212
Bayle, Pierre, 12, 124, 137, 138
Beachy Head, battle of, 201
Beaujoyeulx, 184
Behn, Aphra, 179
Belfort gap, 96
Belgium, see Netherlands, Spanish
Belgrade, 165
Bender, 210
Benserade, Isaac de, 184
Bernard of Saxe-Weimar, 96, 97, 101
Bernini, Giovanni Lorenzo, 13, 44, 46, 176, 182, 234
Berwick, duke of, 210
Besançon, 165
Biron, Marshal, 34, 35
Blenheim, battle of, 199, 207
Bloch, Marc, quoted, 189
Blunt, Sir Anthony, quoted, 176
Bodin, Jean, 27, 125, 126, 144, 224
Bohemia, 5, 10, 21, 82, 83, 85 *seq.*, 100, 101, 160, 230, 231
Boileau, Nicolas, 178, 180, 181, 183, 184
Bologna, 46
Bordeaux, 113
Borelli, Alfonso, 134, 135
Borromini, Francesco, 46, 182
Bossuet, bishop, 130, 171, 172, 179, 180, 182
Boufflers, Marshal, 200
Bourbons, the, 27, 35, 40, 85, 116, 119, 146, 147, 150, 204, 205, 213, 227
Bourgeoisie, see Middle classes
Boxer, C. R., quoted, 157
Boyle, Robert, 11, 132, 133, 135, 136, 140
Boyne, battle of the, 201
Brabant, 153
Braganza, House of, 106
Brahé, Tycho, 12, 73
Braithwaite, Richard, 56
Brandenburg, 24, 28, 40, 88, 92 *seq.*, 100, 133, 148, 149, 158, 167, 172, 174, 212
Brazil, 2, 106, 107, 194, 212
Breda, 97
Breda, treaty of, 151
Breisach, 97, 157, 165
Breitenfeld, battles of, 94, 97, 199
Briand, Aristide, 220
Broussel, Pierre, 113
Browne, Sir Thomas, 77
Bruegel, Jan, 13, 49

Bruno, Giordano, 12, 74, 137
Brussels, 3, 7, 43
Bruyère, Jean de la, 179
Buckingham, George Villiers, first duke of, 39, 43
Buda, 163
Budapest, 169
Bukofzer, Manfred F., quoted, 184
Bull, John, 43
Bunyan, John, 183, 234, 235
Burgundy, duchy of, 2, 6
Burgundy, duc de, 175, 179, 211
Buckhardt, Jakob, quoted, 46
Burton, Robert, 52
Butler, Samuel, 183
Butterfield, Herbert, quoted, 132, 134, 139
Buxtehude, Dietrich, 185
Byzantine empire, 218

Cadiz, 8, 105, 201
Calderon, Pedro, 11, 48
California, 2
Calixtus, Georg, 144
Calvin, John, 13, 78 *seq.*, 138, 140
Calvinists, 5, 20, 39, 40, 47, 79, 109, 138, 144, 163, 230
Cambridge, 51
Cambridge Platonists, 143–144
Cammaerts, Emile, quoted, 49
Canada, 194, 212
Canary islands, 2
Capitalism, 191
Carinthia, 160
Carlos II, King of Spain, 108, 152, 153, 204, 205
Carlowitz, treaty of, 169, 202
Caravaggio, Michelangelo de, 45, 50, 51, 55, 185, 234
Carracci, Annibale, 45, 185, 234
Cartesianism, 139
Casale, 166, 170
Cassini, Domenico, 133, 138
Castile, 2, 23, 103, 104, 107, 118
Catalonia, 2, 23, 102, 103 *seq.*, 117, 118, 202
Catholic league, the, 85, 87, 89, 94
Catinat, marshal, 200, 201
Cavalry, 29, 199
Cavour, Camillo, 220
Cecil, Robert, earl of Salisbury, 8

Cecil, William, Lord Burghley, 8
Cerdaña (Cerdagne), 2, 104, 213, 227
Cervantes, Miguel, 3, 11, 12, 48, 51, 53, 55, 183, 234
Ceuta, 2
Cevennes, 207
Ceylon, 9, 192
Chambers of reunion, 165
Chambre de Saint-Louis, 112–113
Champlain, Samuel, 34
Charlemagne, Emperor, 206, 219
Charles I, King of England, 11, 12, 39, 43, 79, 89, 109 seq., 114, 116, 129, 235
Charles II, King of England, 5, 22, 26, 61, 62, 107, 116, 137, 155, 156, 166, 167, 182, 192, 229, 236
Charles of Lorraine, 168 seq.
Chartres, 4
Child, Sir Josiah, 62
China, 9, 220
Chotin, battle of, 163
Church of England, 8, 143
Churchill, Sir Winston, 220
Civil wars, 102 seq.
Classicism, French, 175 seq.
Clagny, 180
Clarendon, 1st earl of, 61
Claris, Pau, canon of Urgell, 105
Clark, Sir George, quoted, 165, 187
Clark, Sir Kenneth, quoted, 51
Claude, Lorraine, 12, 176
Clement VIII, Pope, 4, 6, 12
Clergy, 17
Cleve, 35, 40
Cloth industry, 8, 15, 61, 62, 63, 190, 191, 232, 233
Coal, 62, 64
Coen, Jan Pieterzoon, 192
Coffee, 66
Colbert, Jean Baptiste, 61, 133, 152, 153, 170, 176, 177, 180, 186, 190, 195 seq., 213
Cologne, 173, 174, 206
Colonization, 64, 65
Commerce, 64 seq., 189, 192, 233
Compiègne, 96
Concini, Concino, 40
Condé, 'great' Prince de, 97, 113
Condé, Princesse de, 35
Congreve, William, 183
Constantinople, 218

Constantinople, treaty of, 204
Conti, Prince, 113
Contra-Remonstrants, 39, 80, 230
Conversos, 33, 60
Copenhagen, 9, 27
Copernicus, 12, 73, 74
Corbie, 96
Corinth, 169
Corneille, Pierre, 12, 47, 53, 55, 56, 176, 178, 179, 183, 184, 234
Cortez, Hernando, 2
Cortona, Pietro da, 46, 182, 185
Couperin, François, 185
Cossacks, 149, 163
Cotton, Sir Robert, 52
Counter-Reformation, 5, 138
Court, Pieter de la, quoted, 67
Courtrai, 168
Covent garden, 47
Coypel, Antoine, 177
Crete, 149, 150, 161, 169, 219
Cromwell, Oliver, 27, 60, 61, 107, 108, 119, 129, 142, 146, 150, 151, 192, 199, 225, 226, 231
Cronstadt, 210
Crucê, Emeric, 223
Crusaders, 220
Cuba, 2
Cuyp, Aelbert, 181

Dante, Alighieri, 218
Day of dupes, 92
Defoe, Daniel, 182
De la Fosse, Charles, 177
Denmark, 9, 10, 21, 25, 26, 30, 36, 38, 64, 89, 90, 93, 148, 149, 151, 172, 222, 228, 229
D'Entragues, Henriette, 34
Deputation (Diputacío), 104
De Ruyter, admiral Michel Adriaan-zoon, 156
Descartes, René, 11, 12, 76 seq., 120, 121, 133, 135, 136, 137, 138, 139, 140, 176, 182, 186, 222, 230, 231, 234, 235
D'Estrées, Gabrielle, 34
De Witt, Johan, 150, 155
D'Hémery, Particelli, 112, 114
Dijk, Anton van, 12, 43
Dimitri, the false, 36
Dixmude, 168
Domenichino, Zampieri, 46

Dominicans, 13
Don, river, 204, 215
Donauwörth, 40
Don Juan of Austria, 7, 105, 108
Donne, John, 51, 53, 78, 186
Don Quixote, 3, 12, 47, 56
Dort, synod of, 40
Dover, treaty of, 155, 158
Downing, Sir George, 61
Dragonnades, 171
Drake, Sir Francis, 2, 73
Dryden, John, 11, 183, 185, 234
Dunkirk, 151, 156
Dutch see Netherlands, United

East India companies, 65, 192, 193, 197
Elbe river, 94
Electoral College, 85, 87
Elizabeth I, Queen of England, 2, 6, 8, 9, 20, 31, 58, 70, 79, 109, 110, 227
Elizabeth, 'Queen of Bohemia', 39, 86
Elliott, John, quoted, 69, 227
England, 2, 8, 31, 32, 47, 60, 62, 102, 108, 131, 137, 149, 150, 151, 159, 166, 197, 201, 206 *seq.*, 212, 213, 221, 232, 233, 234, 235; agriculture, 15; art, 47; commerce, 64–65; gentry, 18; industry 15, 62, 19; literature, 183, population, 14
Escurial, the, 2, 4
Essex, 2nd earl of, 8, 31, 58
Estonia, 36
Esztergom, 168
Etherege, Sir George, 183
Eugen, Prince of Savoy, 169, 200, 206, 207
Europa, 219
Europe, concept of, 215 *seq.*, 226, 236
Evangelical union, the, 40

Far East, 65, 192, 195
Fayette, Madame de la, 179, 180
Fazel Ahmed, 150, 161
Fedor, Tsar, 10
Fehrbellin, battle of, 157
Feiling, Sir Keith, quoted, 155
Felipe II, King of Spain, 1, 2 *seq.*, 7, 8, 30, 84, 103, 212, 213, 221, 226, 227, 235
Felipe III, King of Spain, 11, 20, 30, 31, 32, 33, 41, 47, 48, 84, 103, 104, 204

Felipe IV, King of Spain, 11, 20, 21, 41, 43, 48, 96, 105, 107, 108, 147, 152, 204
Fénelon, Archbishop François, 142, 172, 176, 179, 180, 196
Ferdinand, the Cardinal-Infante, 96, 97, 104
Ferdinand II, Emperor, 24, 40, 82, 84 *seq.*, 96
Ferdinand III, Emperor, 93, 95, 96, 97
Ferrol, 8
Filmer, Sir Robert, 126, 127, 130
Finland, 9, 191, 210
Fisher, H. A. L., 216, 217, 220, 235
Flanders, 6, 165, 168
Fishing, 16, 65
Fleurus, battle of, 201
Florence, 26
Florio, John, 52
Fontaine, Jean de la, 179, 228, 234
Fontenelle, Bernard le Bovier de, 134, 179
Fouquet, Nicolas, 176
Fox, George, 142
France, 4, 6, 8, 23, 26, 27, 28, 30, 33 *seq.*, 41, 42, 57, 64, 92, 102, 142, 146 *seq.*, 165 *seq.*, 191, 196, 197, 201 *seq.*, 212, 221, 227, 229, 233; agriculture, 68–69; art, 44; commerce, 65; 187; industry, 195 *seq.*, 233; peasantry, 18, 30, 69, 70, 213, 232; population, 14; taxes, 18, 30, 33–34, 213
Franche-Comté, 2, 96, 153, 155, 165, 213
Frankfort-on-Main, 94
Frankfort-on-Oder, 94
Franquero, Don Pedro, 32
Frederick V, Elector Palatine, 39, 86 *seq.*, 95, 110
Frederik III, King of Denmark, 149
Frederik IV, King of Denmark, 204
Frederik Hendrik, Prince of Orange, 50, 97
Freiburg, 157, 165
Frescobaldi, Girolano, 54
Friederich Wilhelm, the Great Elector of Brandenburg, 100, 148, 198
Friederich the Great, 212
Friesland, 15
Frondes, the, 103, 112 *seq.*, 131
Fürstenburg, Cardinal, 166

Gabelle, 33, 70

Gabor, Bethlen, 87
Gabrieli, Giovanni, 53
Galigai, Leonora, 40
Galen, 75
Galilei, Galileo, 12, 52, 73, 74, 75, 133, 137, 140, 234
Gassendi, Pierre, 123
Geer, Lodewyck, 63, 66
Genoa, 64
Gentry, 17, 18
Georg Wilhelm, Elector of Brandenburg, 93
Germany, 5, 6, 10, 41, 84 seq., 138, 156, 157, 160 seq., 182, 201, 207, 212, 229; art, 182; music, 185; population, 14
Geulincx, Arnold, 77, 120
Geyl, Pieter, quoted, 23, 115, 182
Gibraltar, 207, 211
Gilbert, William, 73, 75, 76, 135, 234
Gilds, 64, 66
Gladstone, William, 220
Glanville, Joseph, 132
Gobelins, 177
Godunov, Boris, Tsar, 10, 36
Gomarus, 80
Reynold, Gonzalgue de, quoted, 219
Goubert, Pierre, quoted, 195, 230
Gramont, Scipion de, 70
Grand Alliance, the, 174, 206, 208
Grand Remonstrance, the, 111
Great Britain, 212, 215
Great Chain of Being, 58, 125
Greece, 169
Greenleaf, W., quoted, 130
Greenwich, Queen's house at, 47
Gresham college, 133
Grisons, the, 35, 85
Groningen, 6
Grotius, Hugo, 12, 41, 80, 126, 128, 130, 137, 138, 144, 224, 225
Guinea, 2
Guise, Henri de, 4, 58
Gustav Adolf, King of Sweden, 11, 18, 27, 36, 37, 38, 59, 63, 89 seq., 148, 152, 198, 199, 228
Guyon, Madame Jeanne-Marie, 142

Haase, Erich, 138
Habsburgs, 2, 3, 4, 6, 10, 20, 23, 24, 27, 40, 42, 85, 90, 92, 94, 97, 119, 146, 147, 148, 150, 167, 169, 202, 205, 212, 213, 227

Hague, the, 12, 115, 166, 169
Hainault, 153, 168
Halecki, Oskar, quoted, 220, 222
Hall, A. R., 140
Halley, Edmond, 136
Hals, Franz, 4, 6, 49, 50, 55
Hamburg, 59
Hamilton, E. J., quoted, 188
Hampshire, Stuart, 122
Handel, G. F., 185
Hartlib, Samuel, 136
Harvey, William, 11, 75, 76, 234
Hazard, Paul, quoted, 231
Heer, Friederich, quoted, 215, 221
Heidelberg, 201
Hein, Piet, 193
Henri III, King of France, 4, 58
Henri IV, King of France, 4 seq., 21, 24, 33 seq., 40, 53, 57, 59, 64, 71, 85, 89, 114, 212, 227
Henriette Marie, Queen, 89, 151
Herbert, lord of Cherbury, 78, 124
Herrick, Robert, 11, 52
Hitler, Adolf, 216, 221
Hobbema, Meyndert, 181
Hobbes, Thomas, 120, 121, 123 seq., 132, 133, 137, 140, 229, 230
Hohenzollerns, 24
Holland, 7, 15, 23, 39, 114, 156, 181, 188, 191, 207
Hollar, Wenceslaus, 12
Holstein-Gottorp, 172
Holy Catholic league, 4
Holy league, the, 4, 40, 169
Holy Roman Empire, 5, 24, 86 seq., 131, 150, 166 seq., 216 seq.
Hondschoote, 190
Hooft, Pieter Corneliszoon, 52
Hoogh, Pieter de, 50
Hooke, Robert, 132, 136
Hooker, Richard, 126
Hudson's Bay, 212
Huguenots, 13, 30, 33, 39, 59, 79, 91, 138, 143, 144, 171 seq., 190, 195, 200, 230, 231
Humfrey, Pelham, 184
Hungary, 5, 10, 100, 101, 148, 150, 160, 161 seq., 207, 212, 230, 231
Huygens, Christian, 12, 77, 132, 133, 135, 136, 138, 139, 234
Huygens, Constantyn, 50

Ibrahim, Sultan, 149
Ijssel river, 7
Index, the, 43
India, 9, 192, 195, 220
Industry, 15 seq., 66, 188, 189, 232
Inertia, law of, 74
Infantry, 29, 199
'Inflation of honours', 17, 58
Ingria, 38, 210
Innocent XI, Pope, 143, 167, 170
Inquisition, the Spanish, 6, 13, 31, 43, 75
Ireland, 22, 31, 32, 109, 201; population, 14
Iron, 62, 63, 64
Isabella, Princess, 11, 44, 96
Italy, 2, 6, 10, 23, 28, 63, 84, 85, 93, 182, 202, 206, 207, 212; art, 182; industry, 15, 63, 190; music, 182 seq.; population, 14
Ivan the Terrible, Tsar, 10, 36

Jamaica, 193
James I, King of England, 17, 20, 27, 31, 36, 39, 47, 59, 66, 70, 71, 79, 86, 89, 109, 110, 235
James II, King of England, 22, 131, 144, 151, 155, 158, 173, 201, 210, 229
Janissaries, 149, 165
Jansen, Cornelius, 81
'Jansenists', 81, 82, 140, 141, 142, 178, 230
Jesuits, 5, 8, 13, 20, 45, 80-81, 82, 85, 88, 129, 139, 141, 142, 230
Jews, 13, 33, 60, 138
John Casimir, King of Poland, 149
Johan III, King of Sweden, 9
João IV, King of Portugal, 106
Jones, Inigo, 46, 47
Jonson, Ben, 11, 51, 53
John Sobieski, King of Poland, 163, 168
Jordaens, Jacob, 181
Josef I, Emperor, 211
Joseph, Father, 93, 97
Jülich, 35, 40

Kara Mustafa, 163, 168
Kardas, treaty of, 149
Karelia, 38, 210
Karl V, Emperor, 3, 212, 225, 227
Karl VI, Emperor, 206, 208, 211
Karl IX, King of Sweden, 9, 36, 37, 58

Karl X, King of Sweden, 148, 149, 160, 228
Karl XI, King of Sweden, 21, 158, 228
Karl XII, King of Sweden, 21, 26, 203-204, 208 seq., 228
Kepler, Johann, 12, 73, 74, 75, 135, 234
Kiernan, V. G., quoted, 27
Kiev, 203
King, Gregory, 136
Kirkholm, battle of, 36
Kiuprili, Mohammed, 149-150
Knäred, treaty of, 30, 38
Kneller, Sir Godfrey, 183
Knox, John, 126
Kossmann, E. H., quoted, 157
Kristian IV, King of Denmark, 9, 27, 41, 92
Kristina, Queen of Sweden, 18, 95, 148, 182

La Bruyère, Jean de, 124, 180
Ladislaus IV, King of Poland, 149
Laffemas, Bathelemy, 59
La Hogue, battle of, 202
Lairesse, Gerard de, 181
Languedoc, 24
Largillière, Nicolas, 177
La Rochefoucauld, duc de la, 52, 124, 176, 179, 180
La Rochelle, 89, 91
Lastman, Peter, 50
La Tour, Georges, 55
Laud, Archbishop William, 230
Lavisse, Ernest, 138
Le Brun, Charles, 177, 180, 181, 184
Le Cid, 12, 55
Leeuwenhoek, Anthony de, 12, 137
Leibniz, Gottfried Wilhelm, 11, 12, 120, 121 seq., 132, 133, 135, 139, 140, 144, 182, 220, 222, 231, 234, 235
Leiden, university of, 80
Lely, Sir Peter, 183
Lemercier, Jacques, 176
Le Nain, Louis, 55
Le Nôtre, André, 180
Leopold I, Emperor, 24, 147-148, 155, 160 seq., 201, 202, 206, 207, 211
Lerma, duque de, 30, 32, 33, 103, 118
Lesnaya, battle of, 210
Le Tellier, Michel, 153
Letter of Majesty, 86, 88

Le Vau, Louis, 175, 176, 180
Lille, 155, 211, 212
Lionne, Hugues de, 153
Lisbon, 105
Leviathan, the, 127
L'Isola, Franz Paul, 161
Livonia, 36, 149, 204, 210
Loans, 71, 112, 119, 197
Locke, John, 11, 12, 121, 123, 124, 127 *seq.*, 138, 139, 144, 222, 231, 234
London, 8, 11, 13, 115, 207, 236
Lorraine, 156, 157, 202, 213
Louis XIII, King of France, 3, 24, 35, 41, 47, 89, 91, 96, 97, 114, 180
Louis XIV, King of France, 3, 21, 24, 25, 122, 130, 133, 143, 146 *seq.*, 166, 168, 169, 170 *seq.*, 175 *seq.*, 195, 200, 201 *seq.*, 212 *seq.*, 226, 227, 230, 234, 235, 236
Louis XV, King of France, 211, 213
Louis XVI, King of France, 213
Louvois, François Michel Le Tellier, Marquis de, 61, 133, 171, 201
Louvre, the, 176, 177
Lully, Jean-Baptiste, 43, 184, 228
Luther, Martin, 78 *seq.*, 218
Lutherans, 5, 40, 82, 138, 148
Lützen, battle of, 95
Luxembourg, duc de, 200
Luxembourg palace, 11, 43, 56
Luxemburg, 166, 169 *seq.*, 202

Mabillon, Abbé, 135
Machiavelli, Niccolò, 26, 126, 129
Madrid, 1, 11, 12, 13, 27, 32, 208
Maes, Nicolas, 181
Magdeburg, 94, 174
Maintenon, Madame de, 142, 171, 179, 214
Malaga, battle of, 207
Malebranche, Nicolas, abbé, 120
Malherbe, François de, 179
Malplaquet, battle of, 211
Mander, Karel van, 49
Mannerism, 44, 45, 175
Mansart, François, 176
Mansart, Jules Hardouin, 180, 181
Mansfeld, count, 87
Mantua, 53
Mantua, dukes of, 11, 91, 166
Margarita of Savoy, Princess, 106

Mariana, Juan de, 125
Marie de Médicis, Queen, 11, 21, 34, 35, 40, 43, 53, 91, 177
Marino, Giovanni Battista, 51
Marlborough, duke of, 198, 199, 200, 206 *seq.*, 225
Marly, palace of, 213
Marvell, Andrew, 183
Mary I, Queen of England, 8
Masaniello, 107–108, 117
Massa, Prince, 108
Mathematics, 75
Matthias, Emperor, 87
Maurits, Prince of Orange, 7, 32, 39, 40, 58, 84, 89
Maximilian I, Emperor, 5
Maximilian II, Emperor, 40
Maximilian, duke of Bavaria, 40, 82, 85 *seq.*, 100
Mazarin, Cardinal Jules, 23, 46, 97, 112 *seq.*, 131, 146, 151, 176, 195, 207, 212, 227, 235; quoted, 72
Mazarinades, 112, 116
Medici, Cardinal Leopold, 133
Medina-Sidonia, duque de, 106
Mediterranean, 202, 211, 215, 219
Mehmed III, Sultan, 6
Mehmed IV, Sultan, 149
Mercantilism, 66 *seq.*
Merchants, 110
Mercoeur, duc de, 4
Mesta, the, 60
Metz, 97, 165, 213
Meuse, 7, 156
Mexico, 2
Middle classes, 17, 18, 33, 59, 61, 114, 147, 231
Mignard, Pierre, 177
Middlesex, earl of, 59
Mikhail I, Tsar, 38, 203
Minorca, 211
Milan, 2, 59, 63, 207
Milton, John, 11, 53, 78, 128, 139, 183, 186, 231, 234
Mobility, social, 27
Mohammedans, 33, 145
Moldavia, 165
Molière (J. B. Poquelin), 176, 178–179, 182, 183, 228, 231, 234, 235
Molina, Luis, 81, 141
Molinos, Miguel, 142

Monads, 122, 123
Monarchy, 19–22, 57, 58, 59, 125 seq., 234
Monck, General George, 112
Mons, 201
Montchrétien, Antoine de, quoted, 67
Montecucculi, Raimondo, general, 150
Monteverdi, Claudio, 53, 184
Moravia, 5, 82
Moriscoes, 33, 48, 103, 220, 230
Moscow, 27
Motteville, Madame de, 179
Mountjoy, lord, 31
Moscow, 36
Mozambique, 2
Mun, Thomas, quoted, 67
Münster, treaty of, 100
Murad IV, Sultan, 149
Murillo, Bartolomé Esteban, 11, 48
Muscovy see Russia
Music, 43, 44, 53 seq.

Namur, 201
Nantes, edict of, 24, 171, 173
Naples, 2, 48, 102, 103, 107, 108, 117, 118
Napoleon I, Emperor, quoted, 199, 200; 221
Narva, 210
Narva, battle of, 199, 200, 204
Navies, 152–153
Neerwinden, battle of, 202
Nef, J. U., quoted, 62, 63, 197
Netherlands, the Spanish, 2, 7, 8, 84, 85, 137, 153, 155, 168, 188, 201, 202, 205, 206, 210, 232, 233; industry, 190
Netherlands, United, 2, 4, 6, 7, 22, 23, 26, 28, 31, 32, 39, 47, 55, 60, 61, 64, 68, 80, 84, 89 seq., 100, 103, 105, 107, 114 seq., 133, 149, 150, 151, 152 seq., 166, 167, 172, 173, 174, 194, 201, 205 seq., 221, 233, 234, 235; agriculture, 15, 69, 190; art, 49 seq.; church, 40; commerce, 64 seq.; industry, 16, 61, 65; population, 14
Newfoundland, 212
Newton, Sir Isaac, 11, 12, 74, 77, 122, 123, 124, 133, 135, 136, 139, 140, 222, 234, 235
New York, 151
Nijmegen, treaty of, 156, 157, 158, 161, 165, 166, 167, 223

Nobility, 17, 18, 21, 25, 41, 57, 58, 114, 117, 232
Nördlingen, battle of, 96
Normand, Charles, quoted, 69
Norway, 63, 191
Nuremberg, 95
Nys, Ernest, 223
Nystad, treaty of, 210

Odessa, 215
Offices, sale of, 71, 232
Ogg, David, quoted, 114, 191
Oldenbarnevelt, Johan van, 39, 40, 58, 80
Oliva, count, 32
Oliva, treaty of, 149
Olivares, Gaspar de Guzmán, conde-duque de, 23, 48, 55, 91, 97, 103, 104, 105, 106, 108, 116, 118
Opera, 53
Opitz, Martin, 51
Oran, 2
Orleans, Philip, duc d', 113
Orthodox Christian Church, 10
Ostend, 32
Ottoman empire, 149, 150, 163, 169, 198
Oudenarde, battle of, 211
Overijssel, 15
Oxenstierna, Axel, 37, 59, 95, 96, 148
Oxford, 51, 133

Padua, 75
Painting, 12, 43, 55, 177 seq.
Palais Royale, 56, 176
Palatinate, the, 88
Panza, Sancho, 52
Papacy, 217, 229, 230
Paris, 3, 4, 27, 41, 113, 115
Parliaments, 20–21, 41, 60, 103 seq.
Parker, Henry, 125
Partition treaties, 161
Pascal, Blaise, 13, 77, 81, 137, 140, 141, 142, 176
Patronage, 43
Paul, St Vincent de, 81, 82
Paulet, Charles, 33
Paulette, 33, 41, 60, 112
Peasants, 16–17, 18, 25, 69, 112, 114, 117, 196
Pelagians, 81
Pepys, Samuel, 133

Peri, Jacopo, 53
Peru, 2
Petty, Sir William, 136
Philippe of Anjou, King of Spain, 205 seq.
Philippines, 2, 174
Philippsburg, 97, 157
Physics, 74, 75
Pietism, 142
Pinerolo, 201
Pizzaro, Francisco, 2
Plagues, 70, 72, 163, 187, 232
Pohlan, Christopher, 191
Poland, 9, 10, 16, 25, 26, 30, 36, 38, 41, 89, 148, 149, 160, 163, 167 seq., 213, 228, 229
Police, 131
Poltava, battle of, 199, 210, 228
Pomerania, 92, 93, 94, 100, 148
Poor, the, 18
Pope, Alexander, 11, 183
Population of Europe, 14, 69, 187, 189, 232
Port Royal, 81
Portocarrero, Luis Fernández, Cardinal, 230
Portugal, 2, 23, 102, 103, 105 seq., 115, 117, 147, 151, 152, 189, 206, 207, 208, 212, 213
Poussin, Nicolas, 12, 44, 48, 51, 53, 176, 181, 186
Prague, 12, 86, 95
Prestwich, Mrs Menna, quoted, 117
Prices, 62, 63, 64, 69, 70, 102, 116, 187
Professional classes, 59, 60, 61, 110
Protestant union, 85, 88
Prussia, 24, 148, 212
Ptolemy, 74, 75
Puffendorf, Samuel, 120, 128, 129, 130, 131, 137, 224, 225
Purcell, Henry, 184
Puritans, 8, 41, 79, 109, 140, 230
Pyëtr (Peter) the Great, 16, 22, 63, 182, 191, 198, 203, 204, 210, 212, 228, 232
Pyrenees, 212
Pyrenees, treaty of, 147, 223

Quakers, 80, 142, 224
Quebec, 34
Quinault, Philippe, 184
Quietism, 142, 144, 224, 230

Racine, Jean, 81, 175, 178, 183, 184, 203, 228, 234
Rakoczy, Prince George II, 160
Ralegh, Sir Walter, 52
Ramillies, battle of, 199, 207
Ranke, Leopold von, 220
Rationalism, 143
Ratisbon, diet of, 6, 93, 169, 170, 173
Ratisbon, truce of, 193
Ravaillac, François, 35
Régale, the, 170
Regensburg see Ratisbon
Rembrandt van Rijn, 13, 48, 49, 50, 51, 55, 181, 185
Remonstrants, 39, 40, 80, 230
Reni, Guido, 45, 46
Restitution, edict of, 90, 93
Reunion, acts of, 165 seq., 202
Revolutions, 102 seq.
Rhine river, 7, 174, 212
Ribera, Jusepe de, 48
Richelieu, Armand Jean de Plessis, Cardinal, 23, 27, 41, 42, 46, 47, 55, 57, 67, 89 seq., 97, 106, 114, 159, 195, 212, 227, 230, 235
Riebeeck, Jan van, 192
Riga, 204, 215
Rigaud Y Ros, Hyacinthe, 177
Roberts, Michael, quoted, 68, 91, 92
Rochester, Lord, 183
Rocroi, battle of, 97, 199
Rococo, 185
Roemer, Olaus, 134, 138
Rohan, duc de, 57
Roman empire, 216 seq.
Romanovs, 27, 36, 222, 229
Romanov, Nikita, 10
Rome, 6, 43 seq., 182, 236
Rosa, Salvator, 13, 45, 46, 48
Rosellón (Roussillon), 2, 104, 105, 213, 227
Rousseau, Jean Jacques, 170, 235
Rowen, H. H., quoted, 25
Royal Observatory, Greenwich, 134
Royal Society, 132, 133
Rubens, Peter Paul, 11, 12, 13, 41, 43, 48–49, 54, 55, 177, 185, 234
Rudolf II, Emperor, 5, 6, 7, 12, 40
Rurik, House of, 10
Ruisdael, Jacob van, 181
Russell, Bertrand, quoted, 12, 73, 78, 123

Russia, 9, 10, 16, 21, 26, 30, 36, 64, 149, 163, 203, 210, 215, 218 *seq.*, 221, 222, 229, 232; agriculture, 14–15, 69; population, 14
Ryswick, treaty of, 193, 202, 205, 206

St Augustine, 219
St Cyran, Abbé de, 81
St Dominigue, 193
St Gothard, battle of, 150, 160, 163
St Kitts, 212
St Petersburg, 203, 210
St Peter's cathedral, Rome, 13
Saint-Cyr, 214
Saint Pierre, Abbé, 223
Savoy, dukes of, 34, 35, 174, 201, 212
Saxony, 86, 88, 92, 94, 204, 208
Scarlatti, Domenico, 185
Scarron, Paul, 179
Schütz, Heinrich, 54
Science, 13, 73 *seq.*, 234, 235
Scotland, 109, 212; population, 14
Scudèry, Madame de, 179, 182
Seafaring, 15
Sévigné, Madame de, 179; quoted, 157, 180
Seville, 48
Seignelay, Charles Colbert, marquis de, 201
Shaftesbury, earl of, 61
Shakespeare, William, 11, 13, 51, 56, 183, 234, 235; quoted, 58
Sicily, 2, 102, 107, 212
Sidney, Algernon, 129
Sigismund III, King of Poland, 9, 30, 36, 38, 41
Silesia, 5, 82, 160, 208
Silk manufacture, 16, 34, 64, 65, 66
Silver, 3, 70
Simon, Richard, 135
Smith, Adam, 60
Smith, John, 143
Smith, Sir Thomas, 126
Smolensk, 203
Sobieski, King John of Poland, 26
Sorbonne, 176
Sorel, Albert, quoted, 217
Spain, 2 *seq.*, 8, 11, 22, 23, 28, 30, 31, 35, 60, 66, 84 *seq.*, 100, 102 *seq.*, 147, 153 *seq.*, 167 *seq.*, 193, 206 *seq.*, 212, 227, 229, 235; agriculture, 14–15; art, 49,

182–183; classes, 19, 232; economy, 30, 32, 187 *seq.*; industry, 15, 63; taxation, 31
Spanish succession, war of the, 26, 204 *seq.*
Sparre, Eric, 58
Spengler, Oswald, 11
Spinola, General Ambrogio de, 32, 58, 90
Spinoza, Benedict de, 11, 120, 121, *seq.*, 137, 138, 229, 230, 231, 234
Sprat, Thomas, 132
Stanislas Leszczynski, 208
Starhemberg, count Rüdiger von, 168
Steele, Sir Richard, 183
Steen, Jan, 55
Steenkerk, battle of, 202
Stewart, H. F. quoted, 141
Staffini, Agostino, 185
Stockholm, 234
Stolbova, treaty of, 38
Stoye, John, quoted, 169
Strachey, Lytton, quoted, 177
Stuarts, the, 27
Stubbe, Dr Henry, 140
Strasbourg, 165, 166, 170, 202, 212, 213
Styria, 160
Suarez, Francisco, 125
Sully, Maximilien de Béthune, duc de, 31, 34, 59, 138, 213; 223; quoted, 67
Swanenburgh, Jacob van, 50
Sweden, 9, 11, 12, 17, 19, 25, 28, 30, 36 *seq.*, 63, 92 *seq.*, 100, 137, 147, 148, 149, 151, 160, 165, 166, 167, 172, 189, 191, 204, 212, 213, 222, 229, 232, 233; agriculture, 69; architecture, 182; industry, 191; taxes, 18
Sweenlinck, Jan Pieterzoon, 43, 54
Swift, Jonathan, 183
Switzerland, 26, 103, 118, 172

Tailles, 18, 33, 70, 117, 190
Tangier, 2
Tapestries, 34, 62
Tapié, V. quoted, 51
Tassoni, 12, 51
Tawney, R. H., 138, 233
Taxation, 18, 71, 110 *aeq.*, 189, 196, 197
Tea, 66
Telescopes, 73, 75
Temple, Sir William, quoted, 1
Tenison, Thomas, Archbishop, 144

Theatres, 47, 183

Theology, 77 *seq.*, 139

'Thirty Years War,' the, 30, 40, 75, 82, 83, 84 *seq.*, 100, 101, 102, 116, 119, 138, 143, 144, 185, 201, 222, 225, 230

Thokoly, Imre, 163, 167

Thou, Jacques Auguste de, 52

Tillotson, John, Archbishop, 144

Tilly, count, 87, 88, 90, 93, 101

Tintoretto, Jacopo, 48

Toleration, 13, 143

Tortensson, Lerab, 97

Toul, 97, 165, 213

Toulon, 211

Tournai, 165

Towns, 59

Toynbee, Arnold, 218, 220

Trade unionism, 191

Transylvania, 148, 160, 165

Trent, council of, 5, 44, 45, 74, 81

Trevor-Roper, Hugh, 117–118, 138, 221

Trianon, 180

Tripoli, 161

Tübingen, university of, 75

Tunis, 161

Turenne, Henri de la Tour d'Auvergne, marshal, 97, 113, 156, 225

Turin, 207

Turin, treaty of, 202

Turkey, 5, 10, 26, 38, 148, 152, 160, 161 *seq.*, 201, 202, 203, 204, 212, 213, 218, 230

Turnell, Martin, quoted, 178

Tuscany, 2

Ucedo, duque de, 103

Ukraine, 103, 149, 163, 165, 210

Union of Arms, 103

United States of America, 216, 218, 221

Uppsala, 9

Urban VIII, Pope, 45, 46, 89, 91, 97

Utrecht, treaty of, 212, 213

Utrecht, union of, 2, 22

Valencia, 33, 104, 107

Valéry, Paul, quoted, 215

Valladolid, 32

Val Telline, 85

Vanbrugh, Sir John, 183

Vanini, Lucilio, 12

Vasas, 24, 27

Vasconcellos, Miguel de, 106

Vasvar, truce of, 152, 160, 161

Vauban, Sebastien, 130, 180, 200

Vega, Lope de, 11, 47

Velasquez, Diego, 3, 11, 12, 13, 43, 48, 185, 234

Velde, Willem van de, 181

Vendôme, duc de, 200, 207

Venice, 10, 26, 43, 54, 59, 63, 85, 118, 161, 169, 181

Verdun, 97, 165, 213

Vermeer, Jan van Veldt, 50, 234

Vervins, treaty of, 2, 4, 7, 35

Versailles, palace of, 3–4, 12, 44, 175 *seq.*, 213, 234, 236

Viau, Théophile de, 1, 13

Viborg, 210

Vienna, 5, 145, 161 *seq.*, 166, 168 *seq.*, 236

Vigo bay, 207

Villars, Claude Louis Hector, marshal, 200, 211

Vistula river, 210

Voltaire, François-Marie Arouet de, quoted, 11, 123

Vondel, Joost van den 13, 51

Wages, 62, 63, 64, 70

Waldeck, Prince de, 201

Wallachia, 165

Wallenstein, Albrecht, general 90, 92, 95, 101, 225

Waller, Edmund, 183

Walzen, Michael, quoted, 138

Warfare, 18, 25, 29–30, 198 *seq.*, 233

Warsaw, 208

Waterhouse, Ellis, quoted, 50

Watteau, Antoine, 177, 228, 234

Weber, Max, 138

Wedgwood, C. V. quoted, 96

West Indies, 2, 23, 65, 193, 194, 195, 212

West Indies companies, 65, 192

Western Europe, 218 *seq.*

Westphalia, treaty of, 223

Whichcote, Benjamin, 143

Whitehall, 12, 47

White Hill, battle of, 88

Wilenski, R. H., quoted, 181

Wilhelm II, Emperor of Germany, 221

Wilkins, bishop John, 132

Willem I, Prince 'the Silent', 7

Willem II, Prince of Orange, 103, 114, 115, 116

Willem III, Prince of Orange and King of England, 27, 61, 131, 156 *seq.*, 166, 168, 173, 174, 201, 202, 204, 223, 229

Wilson, Charles, quoted, 117

Windelband, W., quoted, 123

Wines, 65, 66

Witch burning, 13

Wittelsbachs, 206

Wittkower, Rudolf, quoted, 46, 182

Women, 72

Wool, 65

Wren, Sir Christopher, 13

Wycherley, William, 183

Zealand, 7, 15, 94, 156

Zemsky sobor, 10

Zenta, battle of, 169, 199

Zouch, Richard, 224

Zurbarán, Francisco de, 11